Thunder in the Heartland

Ohio's counties

Thunder in the Heartland

*A Chronicle of Outstanding
Weather Events in Ohio*

Thomas W. Schmidlin and
Jeanne Appelhans Schmidlin

THE KENT STATE UNIVERSITY PRESS

Kent, Ohio, and London, England

© 1996 by The Kent State University Press, Kent, Ohio 44242

Library of Congress Catalog Card Number 96-5626

ISBN 0-87338-549-7

Manufactured in the United States of America

03 02 01 00 99 98 97 96 5 4 3 2 1

Library of Congress Cataloging-in-Publication Data

Schmidlin, Thomas W., 1954–
    Thunder in the heartland : a chronicle of outstanding weather
events in Ohio / Thomas W. Schmidlin and Jeanne Appelhans Schmidlin.
      p. cm.
    Includes bibliographical references and index.
    ISBN 0-87338-549-7 (cloth : alk. paper) ∞
    1. Ohio—Climate—History.   2. Storms—Ohio—History.
  I. Schmidlin, Jeanne Appelhans, 1956–   . II. Title.
  QC984.03S36   1996   96-5626
  551.69773—dc20   CIP

British Library Cataloging-in-Publication data are available.

To our daughters

EMILY APPELHANS SCHMIDLIN *&* KATHERINE LEE SCHMIDLIN

Emily and Kate relish the rain, anxiously await the snow, and stand in awe of rainbows. They do not like lightning and hope the tornado sirens remain silent.

We hope they will weather all of life's storms.

Contents

Preface

OUTSTANDING WEATHER EVENTS over the past thirty years dominate the memory of Ohioans. Among these events are the Palm Sunday Tornadoes of 1965, the July Fourth Storms of 1969, the 1974 Xenia Tornado, the Blizzard of 1978, the drought and heat in the summer of 1988, and the record cold of January 1994.

Older residents remember the March 1913 floods, the Great Lakes Hurricane of November 1913, the Blizzard of 1918, the 1924 Lorain Tornado, the 110-degree heat in the summers of 1934 and 1936, the Ohio River floods in 1937, and the Thanksgiving Blizzard of 1950.

Ohio's earliest residents had their own weather legends—the severe cold and snow at Marietta in 1818, the Big Frost of June 1859, the hard winter of 1855–56, the Cold New Year's of 1864, the floods of February 1884, and the epic cold wave of February 1899, when unofficial thermometers showed -44 degrees in the Muskingum Valley.

This book is about the significant weather events of the past two hundred years in Ohio. In addition to providing the first complete chronicle of these events as a reference work, we hope the information in this book will form a proper historical context in which to place future storms and unusual weather. In our lifetimes we will experience a variety of weather. It may be reassuring to know that unusual weather events, even those of great severity, have been experienced by our grandparents, our great-grandparents, and other earlier residents of Ohio.

The more than two hundred weather events described and documented here were unusual in their severity, unseasonal timing, widespread impact, or damage or injuries. They include heavy snowfalls, unseasonal snows, ice storms, extreme cold, summer frosts, extreme heat, drought, floods, windstorms, tornadoes, hailstorms, and lightning.

The extent of each weather event is described in text and sometimes illustrated with a map. The magnitude of each event is also detailed—

how much snow fell, the height of a river during a flood, the temperature range during a heat wave, and so on. In some cases, the meteorological setting of the weather event is described.

We also describe the impacts of these outstanding weather events on Ohioans. The occurrence of injuries and deaths are noted, along with the extent of disruption—to work, school, business, communication, and transportation—in the daily pace of life. These elements associated with day-to-day life changed dramatically as Ohio evolved from a rural frontier state in the early nineteenth century to an industrial / agricultural leader in the mid–twentieth century. The manner in which Ohioans reacted to and were affected by severe weather changed over two hundred years. We have attempted to describe these changes, providing a historical record and perhaps giving insight into society's adaptability to changing climate in the future.

Primary sources for the meteorological information are the official government documents—the daily weather maps and the monthly publications—giving daily temperatures, rainfall, snowfall, and winds at weather stations in Ohio: *Climatological Data-Ohio, Local Climatological Data, Storm Data,* and *National Weather Summary.* Early chronicles of outstanding weather events, especially those of Alexander (1924) and Mindling (1944), were also consulted.

The impacts of severe weather events on society are not as well documented in official publications, which is one reason we embarked on this book. Newspaper accounts of storms and other unusual weather events provide information on society's reactions to the events from the perspective of the writers and editors and thus were used extensively to document the impacts of outstanding weather on Ohioans. Sources for our information are provided in the bibliography.

Not every storm could be included in this book. In fact, dozens of "storm" events occur each year in Ohio, numbering in the thousands over the past two centuries. They are the windstorms, small tornadoes, heavy snows, ice storms, minor floods, and periods of heat and cold that are a common feature of our climate. They cause stress, inconvenience, minor damage, and perhaps a few injuries to those exposed to the hazard through carelessness or bad luck. But we stress that these events are normal. They should be expected every few months or years and are not outstanding in the broad perspective of two centuries of Ohio weather. Thus, from thousands of storms, we selected more than two hundred that may be considered outstanding in their meteorological importance or impact on Ohio.

But take heart! Most days in Ohio are not stormy. We awake to good weather most mornings. Skies are sunny for much of the year, especially in summer and early autumn. Winds are usually light and temperatures are mostly pleasant. Outdoor activities are comfortable on most days.

It is not a popular position, but we consider good weather to also include those days with rain or snow. These wet days fill Lake Erie and our many streams, lakes, and reservoirs. They water our gardens, farms, and forests. And they provide opportunities for family table games, reading a book by a fireplace, and for lovers' walks under an umbrella. Yes, this book is about the outstanding and sometimes tragic weather events of the past, but we write with the realization that our ancestors found Ohio weather allowed them to grow crops that would feed their families and later the world, enabled them to provide water transport on rivers, canals, and Lake Erie, and led to a prosperous industrial-agricultural society of more than ten million residents.

This book was several years in the making, and many persons have assisted us in the research and writing. Our primary source for information on the impacts of weather was the archives library of the Ohio Historical Society in Columbus. This library is a treasure of early Ohio newspapers and other documents. The staff was very helpful during the nearly three hundred hours we spent there. We also used the libraries of Kent State University, University of Toledo, Toledo-Lucas County, the Ohio State University, Western Reserve Historical Society, and the Stark County Public Library. In obtaining local information, the staff at the following libraries were helpful: Bryan Public Library, Conneaut Carnegie Library, Jerome Library of Bowling Green State University, Public Library of Cincinnati and Hamilton County, Wauseon Public Library, Montgomery County Library, and the Bossard Library of Gallia County.

Staff members at county historical societies assisted us in gathering information on their regions. These include Sarah Sessions, Montgomery County; Carol Carey, Fayette County; Lisa Hess, Ross County; and Joan Baxter, Greene County.

We appreciate the prompt and helpful responses to questions posed to the staff at the National Weather Service offices in Ohio. Grant Goodge and William Angel of the National Climatic Data Center provided information not available in Ohio. We also thank Jacquelyn Youse Whetro for the information she provided.

At the beginning of the project weather historian David Ludlum graciously loaned us his files on Ohio weather.

A faculty sabbatical from Kent State University for Tom during the spring of 1993 allowed this work to proceed. We are grateful for assistance in this project from the Department of Geography at Kent State University.

CHAPTER ONE

Climate of Ohio

THE CLIMATE OF a place is determined by its location on earth with respect to latitude, elevation, prevailing air currents, and proximity to oceans or large lakes. Ohio is in the middle latitudes, at low elevations, in the eastern interior of North America, and south of the Great Lakes. This location in the Heartland of North America gives Ohio a climate with four distinct seasons, large seasonal temperature ranges, frequent precipitation, and the wide variety of weather so typical of the middle latitudes.

Severe and extreme weather of various sorts are also typical of the Heartland. Temperatures in Ohio have ranged from 113 degrees to nearly -40 degrees. Frosts have blackened corn in July and shirtsleeve weather has prevailed at Christmas. Blizzards have isolated communities for days and flood waters have surged twenty feet deep through the main streets of Ohio's cities. Some of the most powerful tornadoes in the nation have killed entire Ohio families and blown neighborhoods of homes into splinters and bricks. Drought has withered crops, hail the size of baseballs has punched through roofs of homes, and winds have blown lake freighters through bridges, trains off tracks, and homes onto sleeping occupants.

Temperature follows a seasonal cycle controlled by changes in the amount of solar radiation and movement of air masses across the Heartland. Winter arrives in late November or early December as days shorten, the sun is low in the sky, and polar air masses become colder and frequently penetrate as far south as Ohio. In a typical winter, the jet stream fluctuates north and south across the region, bringing alternately mild and cold air. Average daytime January temperatures are near 32 degrees in northern Ohio and 40 degrees in the south (fig. 1). Overnight lows drop to about 15 degrees in the north and 20 degrees in southern Ohio. Storm centers originating to the west and south of Ohio bring rain or snow, but snow covers usually last only a few days before milder air arrives.

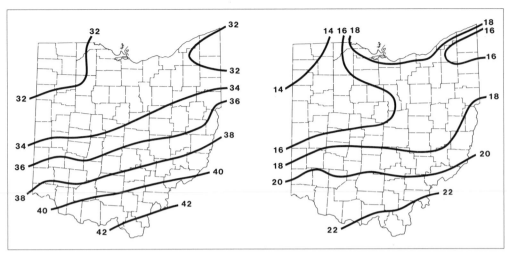

Fig. 1. Average daily high *(left)* and low *(right)* temperature (in degrees Fahrenheit) in January.

Winter releases Ohio gradually in March as days lengthen and the jet stream, marking the boundary between warm and cold air, retreats north-ward to its summer position over Hudson Bay. Spring is a time of wide variety, as temperatures swing from near 80 degrees to far below freezing and back, often within a week. The clash of spring air masses breeds large storms bringing heavy rains, snow, strong winds, or tornadoes. Average daytime temperatures rise above 60 degrees in April but are cooled along the North Coast of Ohio by the cold waters of Lake Erie (fig. 2).

Long days and a dominance of warm tropical air masses bring summer weather to Ohio by late May, continuing into September. Summer weather patterns are quieter than during the colder seasons. Changes in tempera-tures are smaller during summer and, although severe weather may come with summer thunderstorms, winds and storm systems are generally weaker in summer. Average high temperatures in July range from near 80 degrees along the North Coast to above 88 degrees in extreme southern Ohio (fig. 3). Summer nights typically cool into the upper 50s to middle 60s.

The shorter days of autumn begin the transition toward winter. The transition is a pleasant one though, with mild days, cool nights, abundant October sunshine, and the changing colors of forests and fields.

Precipitation is rather evenly distributed across Ohio and through the seasons. The state does not have distinct dry or wet seasons, although the greatest average rainfall comes in summer and winters are drier. The per-ception may be the opposite, however, because there are actually more days of precipitation in winter and, with cooler temperatures and snow, the landscape is wet in winter.

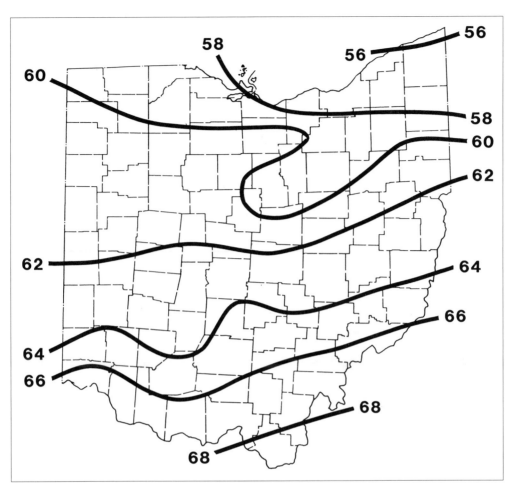

Fig. 2. Average daily high temperature (in degrees Fahrenheit) in April.

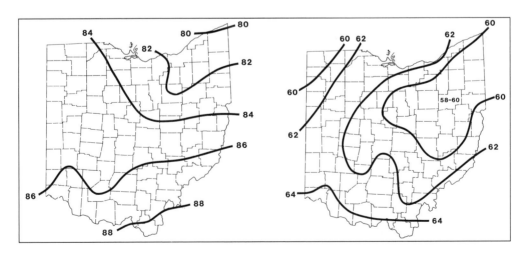

Fig. 3. Average daily high *(left)* and low *(right)* temperature (in degrees Fahrenheit) in July.

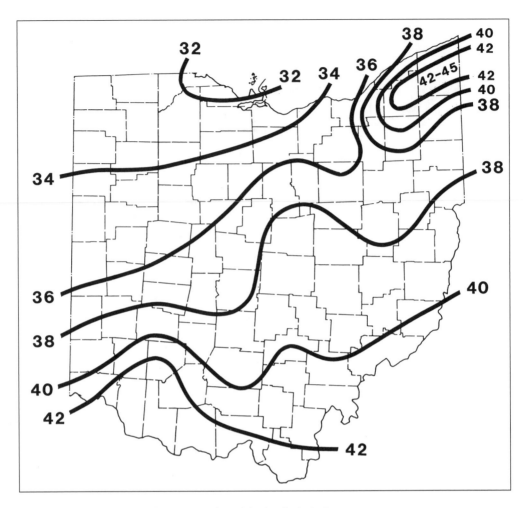

Fig. 4. Average annual precipitation (in inches).

Northwestern Ohio, with a low elevation and greater distance from the Atlantic and Gulf of Mexico moisture, is the driest location in the state (fig. 4). Average annual precipitation there is thirty-two to thirty-four inches. Precipitation increases to the south and east, reaching more than forty-two inches in extreme southern Ohio and in the northeastern snowbelt, where moisture from Lake Erie increases the autumn and winter precipitation.

Average annual snowfall is 25 to 50 inches over most of Ohio, with a general increase toward the colder northern counties (fig. 5). Higher elevations in northeastern Ohio from eastern Cuyahoga County through Lake, Geauga, and Ashtabula Counties, receive an average of 80 to 100 inches of snowfall. This is the Lake Erie snowbelt, where cold winter winds from Lake Erie and Lake Huron become moist and unstable, producing extensive winter cloud cover and frequent deep snowfall. Chardon

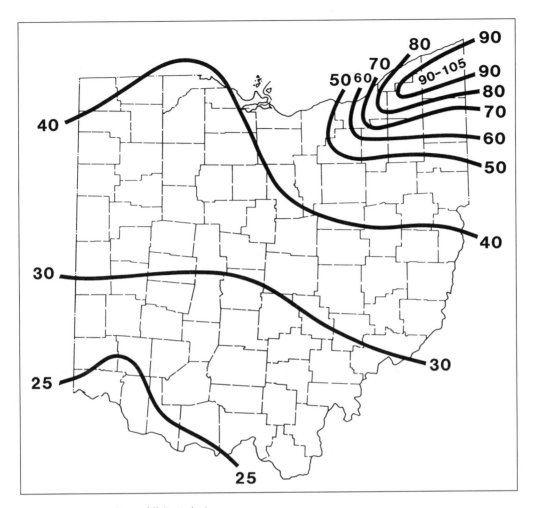

Fig. 5. Average annual snowfall (in inches).

is the snowiest weather station in Ohio, with an average of 106 inches (Schmidlin 1989a), but other locations along the ridges facing the lakeshore have similar snowfall.

In the late 1970s cold winters and a thirty-year cooling trend in global temperatures raised fears of a coming ice age. Warming global temperatures during the late 1980s and the 1990s turned the discussion to "greenhouse warming" and how we might reverse it or adapt to the change. Climate is always changing. Most of Ohio was covered hundreds of feet deep in a glacial ice sheet eighteen thousand years ago, the last of several to have covered portions of Ohio over the past million years. The repeated appearance and demise of continental ice sheets attest to the wide natural fluctuations in climate. Humans may change the climate through deforestation, agriculture, industry, or chemical releases, but we can be assured that climate will change naturally with or without our influence.

CHAPTER TWO

Snow and Ice Storms

Storms bringing snow to Ohio have their origins in the Canadian prairies as the Alberta Clipper, in the southern Plains, or in the Gulf of Mexico. Deep snow also arrives in eastern Ohio from Atlantic coastal storms. The amount on snow that falls in Ohio from a low pressure storm system depends on the path of the storm, the amount of moisture drawn into the system from the Gulf of Mexico or the Atlantic, and the intensity of the storm.

Low pressure centers that track directly across Ohio or to the south and east are most likely to deliver heavy snow. A track west or north of Ohio often brings just rain, even in midwinter. Storms that originate in the warm waters of the Gulf of Mexico can incorporate huge amounts of tropical moisture and are closely watched by forecasters. Very heavy snow may result if the storm intensifies as it moves toward Ohio and if cold air is poised over the region. The heaviest snow from a storm falls in a band less than one hundred miles wide, so it is common for about one-half of Ohio to be affected by each major snowstorm.

Snowfall of six inches or more in a day is usually considered a "heavy snow" in Ohio. This depth is expected once or twice a year in northern Ohio and once every two or three years in extreme southern Ohio (Miller and Weaver 1971). Ohio's greatest snowfalls have occurred in the eastern counties, where strong storms moving along the Appalachians provide plenty of moisture from the Atlantic. Twenty to thirty inches of snow has fallen during these storms.

Lake-effect snow is a feature of the northeastern Ohio snowbelt. Cold winter winds become moist and unstable over Lake Erie and localized snow squalls deposit frequent snowfall in portions of Ashtabula, Lake, Geauga, and Cuyahoga Counties. Snow amounts are generally a few inches, but persistent heavy snow squalls can give more than twenty inches of snow in one day. Lake-effect snow falls in smaller amounts inland through north-central and northeastern Ohio as far south as Mansfield, New Philadelphia, and Steubenville.

Snowfalls in early autumn or late spring result from the proper, but rare, combination of very cold air and a storm system producing precipitation. For Ohio, this usually means arctic high pressure to our north with temperatures within a few degrees of freezing and low pressure south of Ohio producing a large area of rain. The northern or western edge of this rain area changes to snow where temperatures are near freezing, and a band of unseasonable snow blankets a portion of Ohio.

Freezing rain was often called "sleet" early in the twentieth century, but the term is now used for rain that freezes into small ice pellets *before* reaching the ground, whereas the "freezing rain" that creates the ice storm freezes *after* striking surfaces. Both types of precipitation occur when air warmer than 32 degrees Fahrenheit overlies surface air that is colder than freezing. Average surface air temperatures are 30 degrees during freezing rain (Bilello 1971), but this type of precipitation can occur at temperatures as low as 15 degrees.

Weather conditions that produce freezing rain in Ohio generally occur in bands twenty-five to one hundred miles wide, oriented west to east as a low pressure system and warm front approach from the south or southwest. Warm clouds and rain flow northward a few thousand feet above the surface with a layer of colder, subfreezing air trapped below. These weather systems move eastward at thirty to fifty miles an hour, so freezing rain typically lasts only an hour or two. However, persistence of conditions producing freezing rain may give more than six hours of ice accumulation.

Ice storms can generally be forecast several hours in advance, but a slight change in temperature at the surface or in the lower atmosphere can move the location of the storm more than one hundred miles. Therefore, forecasting of the location and amount of ice accumulation are not precise.

3 February 1818
Deep Snow for Marietta Pioneers

Pioneer Marietta weather observer Dr. Sam Hildreth reported that a severe snowstorm began very early on 3 February 1818 and continued through the day (Ludlum 1966). An undrifted depth of twenty-six inches was measured at Marietta. Although daily snow observations are not available for other locations in 1818, depths also reached twenty inches this month at Hudson in the Western Reserve. Cold air following this snowstorm pushed temperatures below -20 degrees in eastern Ohio. Hildreth, writing in the 9 May 1832 issue of *New England Farmer,* noted that the deep snow of 1818 protected trunks of peach trees so that, although the upper portions were killed by the cold, "fresh vigorous shoots were thrown up, producing fruit in one or two years."

This deep snow and cold weather in the upper Ohio Valley created the most wintry spell of weather that could be remembered. The residents had not experienced "such extreme conditions at any time since the country was first settled in 1788" (Ludlum 1966).

15 January 1863
Cincinnati's Great Snowstorm

"The city was quiet, except when now and then a sleigh, with bells and robes, would dash along." Such was the view of Cincinnati given by the *Cincinnati Enquirer* on 16 January 1863, the day after their greatest snowfall.

The Great Snowstorm began as rain on 14 January 1863. As colder air filtered into the Ohio Valley, rain changed to snow during the evening and continued all through Thursday, 15 January. The official snowfall was recorded as twenty inches in twenty-four hours (Alexander 1924, 322, 328). However, the *Cincinnati Enquirer* reported twenty-seven to thirty inches had fallen by midnight on the fifteenth. Even at twenty inches, this stands yet as the greatest twenty-four-hour snowfall in Cincinnati's history.

This was a heavy, wet snow that exceeded the capacity of many roofs. Residents spent Thursday afternoon shoveling the accumulating snow from their houses. Pedestrians trudging in the knee-deep snow had to watch for snow tossed from roofs above. Several large-span roofs collapsed under the load. The roof of the Palace Garden on Vine Street collapsed with a tremendous crash. Fortunately, none of the Union soldiers stationed there were injured. A 60-by-156-foot iron roof over a coal house attached to the Gas Works also gave way. Just before midnight, the iron roof collapsed on Mosely's roof and iron bridge "manufactory" near Stone and Third. Throughout the city awnings were early victims of the deep snow. Traffic was slow or impossible. Streetcars could not make progress, even with four horses attached. Business was slow in the downtown, and "trade everywhere was dull."

In spite of the Great Snowstorm, January 1863 was a mild month at Cincinnati. Temperatures averaged about five degrees warmer than normal and the lowest for the month was only 11 degrees.

31 January 1878
Cleveland Snowburst

One of the most intense snowfalls recorded in Ohio fell at Cleveland on Thursday, 31 January 1878. It had been a mild winter. "'Old Probabilities' has been tardy and hesitating this winter in the matter of snow," the *Cleveland Plain Dealer* reported. However, the 31 January 1878 edition noted that "the Snow King set out early on Thursday morning and was in the highest glee."

According to the *Plain Dealer*, "From eight o'clock until eleven in the forenoon, the fall of snow in this section was unprecedented in the same three hours. It came down in a perfect sheet with scarcely a breath of wind to change its course, and in that time not less than twenty inches of the white mantle covered the brown earth." Hyde (1905) called this the most remarkable snowstorm in Cleveland up to 1895. He reported that 22 inches fell between 4:00 A.M. and 9:00 P.M., of which 18 inches fell in the eight hours from 8:00 A.M. to 4:00 P.M. Hyde reported that when the snow was most intense, 4 inches fell in just twenty minutes. The 22 inches of snow melted to produce 1.98 inches of water, according to Hyde (1905), so the snowfall was about average in density.

The discrepancy between the extraordinary *Cleveland Plain Dealer* report of 20 inches in three hours and the later report by Hyde of 18 inches in eight hours may have resulted from exaggeration in the newspaper or from different points of measurement within Cleveland. Hyde's statement of 4 inches in twenty minutes certainly attests to the great intensity of snowfall.

Nearly all train traffic was halted through Cleveland Thursday as rails were "obstructed to a degree never before known here." Streetcars were forced to "put on their snow plows and add largely to their horse power" to move through the deep snow. Most Cleveland streetcar lines were abandoned by late morning. Pedestrians were few and their paths were soon covered from sight. Store clerks stood idly over their counters without customers, and the Cleveland river front produce markets were quiet.

Reports from train passengers arriving in Cleveland showed the snow was one to two feet deep over a wide area extending south to Columbus and Cincinnati and west to Indianapolis. Trains were stalled, arriving many hours late after adding locomotives to gain mileage through the snow in Ohio.

21 May 1883
Record Late Snow in the West

May snow has fallen several times in Ohio history, usually an inch or two during the first week of the month. The event of 21 May 1883 stands out as an exceptionally late, heavy snow in western Ohio, one that has not been matched in more than 110 years.

A drizzling rain on Monday morning, 21 May, turned to snow at 9:00 A.M., and the air was filled with large, damp flakes all day. The *Sidney*

Journal (Shelby County) reported that "though it thawed, it lay six inches deep on Tuesday morning." Considering that much of the snow melted as it fell, a total snowfall of fifteen to twenty inches was estimated for Sidney. Snow depths of ten inches were measured on the north side of buildings at Houston in Shelby County. For some places, this 21 May storm was the deepest of the winter!

Trees were in leaf, and the weight of snow caused branches to droop to sidewalks; limbs came crashing down, and some trees split in two. Residents of western counties shook snow off their trees to save them from damage, but the woods were full of broken limbs and fallen trees. Orchards suffered as trees split under the weight of the snow. At Lockington, between Sidney and Piqua, there was almost "enough snow to sleigh ride if ground had been frozen." Three inches accumulated at Hamilton, and crops were damaged in Butler County. The heavy snow was limited to western Ohio and eastern Indiana. Little snow fell at Cincinnati, Columbus, or Cleveland.

The deep snow was the capping event of a cold, backward month of May. The *Butler County Democrat* reported, "The severe snow storm Monday sent fear and consternation to each heart. In the memory of the oldest inhabitants a snow storm has never taken place in this vicinity as late as May 21st." The *Sidney Journal* raised the specter of 1816, the "year without a summer," in noting that 1883 was so far similar to the spring of 1816, when summer brought frosts and snow. As it turned out, summer 1883 was cool in Ohio, but not of record-breaking proportions.

12 February 1894
A "Dakota" Blizzard

A weak winter storm had passed over the Great Lakes on 9 February, with a cold front trailing southwestward to Texas. In a pattern familiar to meteorologists, another low pressure storm center formed along the front in Texas and strengthened as it moved to Louisiana and curved northeast toward Ohio. By the time it crossed the Ohio River on Monday, 12 February 1894, this was a major winter storm.

Rain and freezing rain fell south of the storm track in southern Ohio, but heavy snow accompanied by high winds slammed into northern counties at dawn. With seven inches of snow and winds of sixty miles an hour it struck with the "fury of a Dakota blizzard" according to the *Toledo Blade*. "Pedestrians could hardly make their way . . . and snow cut exposed faces like fine sand," the *Toledo Blade* reported. Temperatures remained near 20 degrees all day in the north. Weather Bureau forecaster Hanner remarked, "I've been waiting for a storm like this for years" as he clocked the wind from his office atop the Toledo Post Office building.

Deep drifts blocked rural roads by late morning across northern Ohio, and streetcar service was halted in cities. Retail stores, though mostly open, were empty of customers. The *Toledo Blade* reported store clerks were taking it easy and "watching the clock with renewed interest." A few stores closed at noon to allow employees to get home by supper. There were similar circumstances in Findlay, Defiance, Tiffin, Bowling Green, and east to Cleveland.

It was not the custom to close city schools for bad weather in the late nineteenth century. Teachers were expected to be present and pupils, if possible, made their way to the schoolhouses. Lessons were taught to those who showed up. Toledo superintendent Harvey Compton estimated that less than 10 percent of the students were present Monday during the Blizzard of 1894.

Trains kept moving but were many hours late. The *Columbus Evening Dispatch* reported a train from Toledo to Columbus had three hundred men with shovels who, at each drift, would get out and shovel the snow aside for the train to pass. Ice-choked lake waters were driven up the Maumee River into Toledo by the northeastern gales. Water rose over the wharves between Adams and Oak Streets and flooded riverfront basements.

The storm abated Monday night, and a cold wave swept Ohio as the cleanup proceeded. The Tuesday, 13 February 1894 *Toledo Blade* reported, "Snow shovels are in great demand today as well as strong-armed individuals who know how to use them." Downtown streets were cleaned by noon, hemmed in by great banks of snow at the curbs. Streetcars began running as tracks were cleared and switches freed from ice. Urban life returned to normal across northern Ohio Tuesday evening, but rural highways remained blocked by drifts for several days.

28 February–1 March 1900
Toledo's Deepest Snowfall

Toledo's greatest snowstorm began during the midnight darkness on Wednesday morning, 28 February 1900. Heavy snow had blanketed the states to the west, and Chicago and St. Louis were buried in wind-blown snow.

The snow accumulated quickly through the day of 28 February in Toledo. Seven inches were on the ground at 7:00 A.M., eleven inches by noon, and eighteen inches had accumulated by 7:00 P.M. The snow finally ended at noon on 1 March with twenty-two inches on the ground. This is the most snowfall in one storm in Toledo history and the deepest snow cover measured at Toledo since official records started in 1884.

Temperatures were near 20 degrees and winds were light early on 28 February, but increasing winds caused some drifting later in the day. By afternoon the city was completely snowbound. A major concern was the risk of fire. Toledo's fire department doubled horse teams to pull heavy fire-fighting equipment through snow-clogged roads. Light fire-fighting equipment was put on runners, but Fire Chief Wall warned that fire fighting would be difficult and that "if a fire should break out in the business district the result would be appalling."

Mayor Samuel Jones met with the street commissioner and they concluded, "This was an emergency to be met, and that expense should not be considered." Thus, one hundred extra men were employed on 1 March to clear snow from streets. The snow was removed later that night and dumped into the river. Streetcar tracks and sidewalks were cleared first and snow was piled six to ten feet deep between the tracks and curbs. Two hundred men were hired by the Traction company to shovel snow from routes. Many more men applied for the work, but shovels were not available.

Most Toledo businesses shut down on 1 March, including the Ford glass plant. A few roofs collapsed from the weight of snow. Residents and business owners began shoveling snow off the heavy-laden roofs, sometimes burying unwary pedestrians on the sidewalk below! Shoe stores were besieged by customers who bought out the entire stock of overshoes and rubber boots.

Mail was light because trains from the west and east were delayed by the storms. However, the *Toledo Blade* reported on 1 March that, upholding the best of traditions, "all mail was delivered yesterday, notwithstanding the blinding blizzard, and some carriers in outlying districts suffered severely. The situation was worse this morning, but all carriers started out, no routes were abandoned, and deliveries were made as fast as possible."

The snowfall was much lighter south of Bowling Green but was deep to the east. In Cleveland there was heavy freezing rain and sleet along with thirteen inches of snow, which brought down trolley and telephone lines.

The chaos and short-tempers that often accompany modern snowstorms seemed not to prevail at the turn of the century. The *Toledo Blade* reported on the 28 February front page: "Downtown streets, to-day, are deserted except by those compelled to be out on business, and all public work and outside building operations are at a standstill. Otherwise the city moves serenely, and the people in general seem to be enjoying the snow."

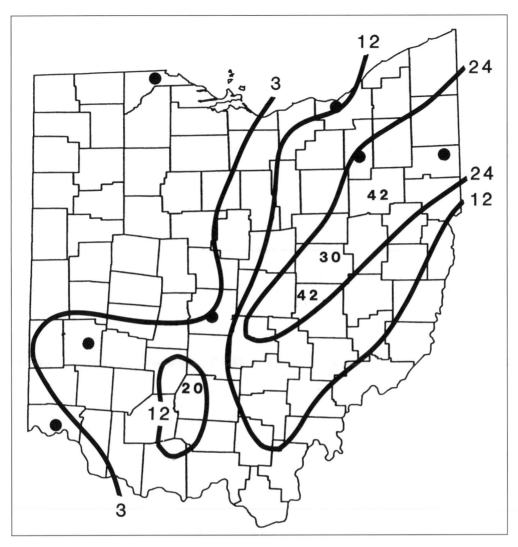

Fig. 6. Snowfall (in inches) during 19–21 April 1901. A total of 42 inches was reported at Gratiot, west of Zanesville, and 35 inches was measured at Warren and several other sites. These totals rival those of November 1950 as the greatest recorded in Ohio.

19–21 April 1901
Deepest Snowfall Known in Eastern Ohio

Any snowfall in late April is notable, but the snow depths from the storm of 19–21 April 1901 were among the greatest ever recorded, and the weight of the snow, greater than ever seen before, or since, caused hundreds of buildings to collapse. A nearly complete disruption of business, rail travel, and communication occurred for two to three days in the eastern half of Ohio.

The storm that caused the unusual spring weather formed in western Texas on Tuesday, 16 April. It moved slowly eastward to Louisiana by the eighteenth and was connected by a cold front to another low over central Canada. The cold front bisected Ohio, so temperatures were in the 60s over eastern Ohio Thursday morning but had cooled to the 30s behind the front in western counties.

By Thursday evening, the Gulf low moved into Georgia and the cold front crossed Ohio into Pennsylvania, pulling cool air across all of Ohio. Moisture was flowing northward and heavy rain was falling through the Appalachians. Heavy, wet snow began to fall in eastern Ohio by Thursday evening. For some communities, this was the beginning of fifty hours of continuous snowfall.

The storm center moved northward to the Carolinas on Saturday and stalled over Virginia on Sunday, 21 April. Its slow movement caused a prolonged period of precipitation over West Virginia, Pennsylvania, and eastern Ohio. Newspapers were full of news of impending record floods on the Ohio River.

In Ohio, the big news was snow. East of a Sandusky-Cincinnati line, precipitation continued from Thursday evening to Sunday morning. Temperatures hovered near the freezing point, so some areas had periods of rain that reduced the snow depths. Where snow continued uninterrupted, depths reached twenty-five to thirty-five inches, with drifts much higher from strong winds on Saturday.

Snowfalls of more than twenty inches were reported in a band between Fairfield County and Ashtabula County (fig. 6). At Gratiot, ten miles west of Zanesville, snow fell for fifty-six hours and a total of forty-two inches was reported. Snowfall at Warren was thirty-five inches, including thirty inches on 20 April alone. Observers at Lancaster and Coshocton measured thirty inches and undrifted snow was twenty-five to forty-five inches deep at Wooster. Drifts of ten feet were common.

The *Canton Repository* quoted weather observer C. F. Stokey, "I do not remember of such a snow fall at one time since the winter of 1855–'56." The density of the snow at Canton was twice that of ordinary snow, and the city was snowbound. Milk delivery was blocked on Saturday, tree limbs snapped, and telephone and telegraph lines were down. Many workmen were busy throwing snow from building roofs to prevent their collapse.

The situation reported from Canton was typical throughout central and eastern Ohio. Roofs collapsed under the weight of snow at Akron, Zanesville, Salem, and many other communities. At Niles, where about thirty-five inches of snow fell, the roofs of four mills of American Sheet Steel collapsed on Saturday. In Coshocton County, cattle and sheep were killed as sheds collapsed under thirty inches of wet snow.

The deep spring snows of 31 March and 4 April 1987 in eastern Ohio and throughout the Appalachians were similar to this 1901 storm. However, the depths in 1987 were not as great as in 1901, and heavy rain did not precede or follow the heavy spring snows of 1987. The weight of snow experienced in the April 1901 storm is estimated to have been about thirty pounds per square foot in level accumulations and may have exceeded seventy pounds per square foot in drifts on roofs. These values were far in excess of the snow loads buildings were designed to withstand and even exceeded roof strength required by modern building codes (Schmidlin, Edgell, and Delaney 1992).

14–16 February 1909
Telephones and Trolleys Succumb to Ice

Freezing rain followed by heavy snow hampered communication, electric service, and travel across northern Ohio from Sunday, 14 February until Tuesday, 16 February 1909. Up to an inch of ice accumulated on wires, causing a widespread failure of electricity, telegraph, and telephones.

Electric trolley and rail service was halted until Wednesday, although steam trains continued running. When the first interurban car left Findlay for Toledo Tuesday evening, a line car preceded it to clear tracks but was derailed by ice near North Baltimore, injuring an employee. The next attempt, this time successful, was made Wednesday morning. Restoration of electric service was delayed until danger of more fallen wires had passed late in the week. Electric service was restored to Findlay by the evening of 18 February, and travel was possible again across most of northern Ohio.

January 1910
An Old-Fashioned Winter

"There is every probability that those who have been longing for an old-fashioned winter with lots of snow are going to have their wishes more than gratified in the next few weeks." This forecast in the 3 January 1910 *Toledo Blade* proved uncannily true as cold weather and several snowstorms made January 1910 a real winter month in Ohio.

December 1909 had been a very cold month, and temperatures fell to near zero in the first days of 1910. The first snowstorm of the year struck central and southern Ohio on 6 January. Twelve inches of snow and 15-degree temperatures stopped streetcars and delayed trains in Columbus. Hundreds of men and scores of horse teams were hired to clear snow from downtown streets, according to the *Columbus Evening Dispatch*. The city asked residents to push snow from the sidewalks into the gutters, where it was loaded into big wagons and moved to snow dumps.

Cold temperatures created the best ice in years on Maumee Bay, and the *Toledo Blade* reported, "Ice yachtsmen are simply in their glory." Ice at Toledo's Riverside Park was the best in five years by 9 January, and twenty-five hundred skaters on Sunday night made up a "good natured crowd of young and old."

A foot of wet snow in the north on 13 January slowed trains, interurbans, and streetcars again. Winds of more than forty miles an hour caused great drifting on the fourteenth and closed businesses and schools. Two interurbans on the Lakeshore line stalled at Genoa in Ottawa County on the thirteenth. Bobsleds from nearby farms were enlisted to carry the forty-two passengers fourteen miles to Toledo by the next morning.

Any among the unemployed or homeless of Toledo asking for food or money after the snowstorm were sent out to shovel for the city, the Rail-Light, coal companies, or residents. The city paid two dollars a day and hot soup meals for shoveling. Downtown streets were cleared first by the shovelers and then the snowbound residential streets were attacked. The Humane Society warned truckmen of the coal companies not to over-work horses in the deep snow. Mail was late, and the usual two daily deliveries were not made. With streetcars mired in deep snow at Toledo, bobsleds and horse teams charged ten cents for a ride downtown. The *Toledo Blade* reported "men and women alike availing themselves of the old-fashioned means of transportation."

Cold weather in January 1910 also meant an abundant ice crop. Ice prices in the summer of 1910 at Toledo were set at six dollars a ton delivered to homes compared to eight dollars a ton in 1909. Toledo ice dealers generally cut ice in Zuke, Lakeland, or Whitmore Lakes in southern Michigan, but in mild winters they went as far as Lake George in Frankfort, Michigan. This winter ice could be cut closer to home and in large quantities.

Rain on snow had caused flooding across central Ohio on 14 January, and warmer weather caused high water for the next week. Cold weather and snow returned by 22 January, ending the threat of major flooding. Snowfall in Columbus was 24.3 inches for the month, the greatest January total up to 1910 since records began in 1885 (Alexander 1924).

17–18 February 1910
Statewide Snow

Heavy snow fell over a wide area of the eastern United States during mid-February 1910. Snow began in Ohio late on Wednesday 16 February and continued for two days. Most of Ohio measured ten to twenty inches by Friday, and winds of forty miles an hour piled the snow into drifts ten feet deep. The *Columbus Evening Dispatch* called this the "heaviest snowstorm in the history of the state."

This claim is substantiated by the number of snowfall records established. Single-storm records of 11 inches at Cincinnati and 15.3 inches at Columbus stood until the 1970s (Ludlum 1971). This storm also contributed to making February 1910 the snowiest month on record up to that date in Dayton (31.6 inches), Cleveland (30.5 inches), and Columbus (29.2 inches). These records generally stood until the 1970s. In addition, the winter of 1909–10 was the snowiest known to that time in Cleveland (80.9 inches), Columbus (67.8 inches), Sandusky (65.1 inches), and Cincinnati (40.4 inches) (Ludlum 1971).

Among the greater snow depths for the storm of 17–18 February were 25 inches at Urbana and 20 to 22 inches in Canton, Marion, Knox County, and Holmes County (Mindling 1944). The *Cincinnati Enquirer* reported 18 inches at Bellefontaine, and the *Columbus Evening Dispatch* told of 18 inches at Troy. A record depth of 18 inches was measured at Dayton on 17 February.

In spite of the records, previous storms were recalled, perhaps with enhanced dimensions. The *Columbus Evening Dispatch* noted, "Still the old gray-whiskers say 'Winters ain't what they used to be when I was a boy,'" perhaps remembering the cold of 1856 or Cold New Year's of 1864.

Transportation was crippled throughout Ohio. Streetcar sweepers attempted to keep the tracks free of snow but often could not keep up with the accumulation. Railcars mounted with plows kept city lines open, but the Columbus Railway and Light Company hired two hundred men to shovel snow from suburban tracks. Interurban traffic was stuck in rural drifts and those that made it through the storm were many hours behind schedule. Trains were running more than twelve hours late and many were abandoned after becoming mired in drifts. Schools were closed in most counties and mail delivery canceled in some locations. Members of the Ohio General Assembly usually left Columbus for home Thursday evenings but were snowed in on 17 February 1910. As the *Columbus Evening Dispatch* reported, "The state will get an unexpected half day's work out of them to-morrow."

Dozens of buildings collapsed under the weight of snow in central and southern Ohio. Most buildings that succumbed to the snow load were old or poorly constructed, including service garages, livery stables, sheds, and barns. Among the larger buildings to collapse was the auditorium on Sixth Street in Zanesville. It was a 150-by-190-foot building that sat one thousand people and was used for polo and skating. In Columbus, the Old Columbus Auditorium on Goodale Street collapsed Friday afternoon.

The building was totally destroyed but, fortunately, there were no injuries in any of the structures that fell under the weight of snow.

21 February 1912
Toledo Snowstorm

Transportation came nearly to a standstill on Wednesday, 21 February 1912 in Toledo's worst snowstorm since the record twenty-two inches in 1900. Snowfall began just after midnight and eleven inches had accumulated by early afternoon. Winds measured to forty-eight miles an hour whipped the snow into huge drifts and covered paths as soon as they could be cleared. Temperatures were near twenty degrees during the snowfall. Not until the Blizzard of 1918 would a snowstorm so disrupt the pace of life in northwestern Ohio.

Streetcar traffic was stopped on most lines Wednesday morning, requiring a walk to work for thousands of Toledoans. With the failure of public transportation, auto taxis were in great demand, as were carriages pulled by horses. The *Toledo Blade* noted, "Livery and auto companies report the largest single day business in their history." Absenteeism was 50 percent at many factories. Attendance at Toledo schools was light Wednesday morning, so afternoon school sessions were canceled. The city put to work anyone willing to shovel. Snow was scooped from streets and dumped into the Maumee River.

The Rail-Light put out a call at 3:00 A.M. for 250 men with shovels. A full crew, including 100 of the city's homeless, turned out and worked until noon, when the Rail-Light finally gave up and closed most lines. Telephone and telegraph companies sent sleighs out to bring in their employees so communication was not interrupted. Interurbans ran several hours late, and many were mired with a load of passengers in eight-foot drifts between northwestern Ohio communities. The *Toledo Blade* reported interurban motormen were forced to back up and repeatedly make runs to force their way through drifts.

Railroads were hampered by frozen switches and deep drifts in rural areas. At some locations, a "snow melting device" with burning oil was used to keep rail switches open. Three hundred men shoveled the tracks and rail yards at the Union Depot in Toledo. The *Toledo Blade* related that "within the round house young engineers told their tales of war against an irresistible, merciless enemy, while old gray beards smiled and dropped the old, old hints about the winters 'we used to have.'"

Downtown department stores sent clerks home early in the afternoon. The clerks, however, found no streetcars running and sought other means of transport. At the Lion Store, 300 employees emerged and found the company's delivery wagons available for their ride home.

Six women crowded into the seat with the driver and another twelve or more jammed into the enclosed rear portion of each wagon and were delivered one by one to the safety of homes. The scene was repeated at Lasalle and Koch Company, where 150 clerks were conveyed home. Several clerks at the Tiedtke store rode four miles to their country homes with a milkman.

Although the snowstorm was a large and costly disruption, the *Toledo Blade* reported that "in reality, a majority of Toledoans appeared to enjoy the novelty of the situation. Soon after 7 o'clock hundreds were plowing their way on foot through the drifts that filled the thoroughfares. Everybody had a pleasant word for his neighbor. In fact, the shouting and 'kidding' of the pedestrians, as they fought their way to the business center or to the outlying shop districts, were like that of a bunch of boys and girls just turned out of school."

The storm may also have contributed to making Sandusky County "wet" again, after it was voted "dry" in 1909. A bitterly contested local county option election on 21 February resulted in the wet vote after rural residents, with most of the dry votes, could not get to the polls through the snowstorm.

Elsewhere in Ohio, heavy snow fell in the west, but snow changed to rain in central counties. The *Dayton Journal* reported business and traffic was slowed by deep snow and fifty teams of horse-drawn wagons at work clearing Dayton streets. As the storm passed Columbus, a record low barometric pressure of 28.87 inches "was coincident with Colonel Roosevelt's address" in the city. Theodore Roosevelt, seeking a third term as president, came in third on the 1912 Ohio ballots, behind Woodrow Wilson and William Taft.

9–11 November 1913
Great Lakes Hurricane

The immense storm that ravaged the Great Lakes during 7–13 November 1913 has been called the "Great Lakes Hurricane," the "Ultimate Storm," and the "Big Blow." In Ohio, it was a storm unmatched for early winter severity and rivals even the great January blizzards of 1918 and 1978 for wind speeds, snow depths, disruption, and damage in eastern Ohio.

Ohio was buffeted from Sunday, 9 November to Tuesday, 11 November. It was one of the greatest winter storms in Cleveland's history and established snowfall records at Cleveland that remain unmatched. Government meteorologist William Alexander (1913) wrote that the storm had a "well-nigh paralyzing effect" coming so early in the season and "combining as it did the chief features of the windstorm, the snowstorm, the ice storm, and the cold wave."

The storm of November 1913 remains today as the most damaging for the Great Lakes shipping industry. Nineteen commercial lake boats were total losses, twelve of them lost with their entire crews (Catton 1985, Martin 1992). Another twenty lake boats were driven onto the rocks and later salvaged. Twenty of the freighters lost or stranded were owned in Cleveland and many of the crew were Ohioans. These were large boats—among them the *Charles S. Price,* a 524-foot, 6,300-ton steel freighter loaded with coal from Cleveland that sank with 28 men in Lake Huron. The toll of sailors was officially 235 (Martin 1992), but crew lists were incomplete and up to 300 may have perished. Most losses were on Lake Huron, although a lightship sank with 6 men in eastern Lake Erie.

Rain, snow, and temperatures in the mid-30s prevailed over northern Ohio early on Sunday, 9 November. Temperatures fell through the day and freezing rain was followed by a wet snow. The intensity of the storm increased during the afternoon with heavy snow, winds of forty to sixty miles an hour, and temperatures in the 20s. According to the *Cleveland Plain Dealer,* "Cleveland was virtually a city in splendid isolation at midnight. Snowed under, cut off from all telegraph and telephone communication with the outside world, streetcar service held up in a maze of wrecked poles and miles of swirling wires, not a glimmer of light in scores of its thoroughfares and in hundreds of homes, with the blizzard still raging furiously and continuing its work of devastation and demolition, the situation was without parallel for the time of the year."

Freezing rain and wet snow coated telegraph, telephone, and electric wires Sunday morning, and many lines, poles, and trees were toppled when winds increased to more than forty miles an hour during the afternoon (fig. 7). A one-minute wind average of seventy-nine miles an hour was recorded in Cleveland at 4:40 P.M. on Sunday. This led to almost complete loss of communication in Cleveland and eastern Ohio and blocked streets for traffic. Wind also wrecked signs and awnings and broke many windows in downtown Cleveland. Pedestrians had to dodge fallen electric lines. An eighteen-year-old man died when he touched a fallen wire, and a horse was electrocuted when a live wire fell across its back. Communication in Cleveland and Youngstown was out until late Tuesday.

Precipitation fell for fifty hours, although snow was heaviest from Sunday afternoon until Monday evening. Total storm snowfall at Cleveland was 22.2 inches. A record 17.4 inches fell in twenty-four hours, ending at 7:00 P.M. on Monday, 10 November, exceeding the previous twenty-four-hour snowfall record of 13 inches on 9 February 1896. (Hyde [1905] reported a 22-inch snowfall in seventeen hours at Cleveland on 31 January 1878). Winds were generally from the west or northwest during the storm and averaged forty-nine miles an hour for sixteen hours beginning at 2:00

Fig. 7. A trolley stranded by tangled utility lines along Superior Avenue in Cleveland after the blizzard of 9 November 1913. (Photograph courtesy of the Western Reserve Historical Society)

P.M. Sunday, 9 November. Barometric pressure at Cleveland reached a minimum of 29.07 inches (sea level) Sunday morning (Alexander 1913).

Snowfall during the storm was 10 to 20 inches in eastern Ohio and decreased to less than 6 inches in the west (fig. 8). Cincinnati had only an inch. The greatest amounts of 22 to 25 inches fell in portions of Cuyahoga, Medina, Portage, Summit, Guernsey, Coshocton, and Noble Counties. The *Youngstown Vindicator* reported it to be "the worst blizzard ever known in this vicinity during the same season of the year," rivaling "the great record-breaker of April 19, 1901."

Shortages of milk and food caused concern as dairies were unable to get milk in from farms and meat and vegetables were stranded on trains or trucks. The *Cleveland Plain Dealer* reported fifty-eight hundred cattle, hogs, and sheep in railcars stalled around the city. Men on horses rode to dairy farms east of Cleveland and instructed farmers to bring milk on sleds to Euclid Creek, where trucks would meet them and transfer milk to the city dairies. Cleveland dairies announced that delivery of milk was impossible but parents with children could come to the dairy and get milk. Milk arriving at the train station in Hudson to be transported to Cleveland was "confiscated" by the station master to feed children on

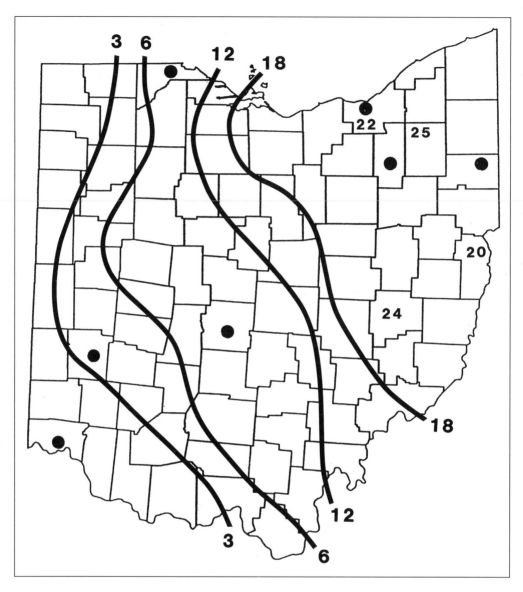

Fig. 8. Snowfall (in inches) during the Great Lakes Hurricane of 9–11 November 1913. High winds and bitter temperatures accompanied the deep snow.

eight trains stalled there, according to the *Youngstown Vindicator*. Special efforts were also made to get milk to children in hospitals.

Some buildings collapsed under the weight of snow. In Cleveland, a man was killed in the collapse of a shed and the roof collapsed on the Co-operative Store Company at Central Avenue S.E. and East Sixty-seventh Street. A ten-thousand-square-foot garage at Herman Schroeder Cartage Company on East Fourteenth Street in Cleveland collapsed early Tuesday, burying forty horses and twenty wagons. Rescuers retrieved horses from the debris, but some were badly injured. The Gunn and Pettit greenhouse collapsed in Salem and at Coshocton, where snow was two feet deep, the Standard Garage collapsed onto twenty-five cars.

West gales caused the western end of Lake Erie to fall six feet Sunday and boats were left sitting on the mud of Maumee Bay. Although no large boats were lost on Lake Erie, several were damaged. The steamer *G. J. Grammer* struck a breakwall trying to enter Lorain harbor Monday and was beached one hundred feet from the bank. At Sandusky, the steamer *Col. Woodward* was torn from her moorings and smashed against the East End Waterworks crib. Hurricane force winds in the Cleveland harbor caused the steamer *State of Ohio* to break her lines at the East Ninth Street pier. She was swept into the opposite pier, smashing a fleet of anchored motorboats (Martin 1992). Thirteen barges of the Pittsburgh Steam Company broke from moorings at Cleveland and were blown across the harbor onto the beach.

Business was at a standstill across eastern Ohio Monday and Tuesday, 10–11 November. Employees could not get to stores and there were few customers either. Only shoe stores were busy with people seeking boots and overshoes. All Cleveland hotels were filled with stranded travelers. The White Company automobile plant employed twenty-three hundred men in Cleveland, but only eight hundred made it to the factory Monday. Mills and factories in Youngstown and Warren were on uncertain schedules as trolley lines were shut down and most workers could not get to work.

A huge effort was required to clear deep snow, wires, poles, and trees from streets. Cleveland director of public service, W. J. Springhorn, advertised in the *Cleveland Plain Dealer,* "The street cleaning department needs several hundred extra men to clean snow from the streets today." The city was using fifty teams of horses and three hundred men to clear snow off streetcar intersections and catch basins. City prisoners were put to the task of clearing streets in Akron. Transportation began to recover Tuesday in Cleveland, but many rural roads remained blocked by deep drifts. Streetcars were running again and some trains began arriving at Cleveland.

Concern was high for a fire disaster in Cleveland. Telephone service was disrupted, streets were nearly impassible, and hydrants were buried in snow. The number of horses on fire engines was increased from three to five, and the fire chief asked Boy Scout troops to clear snow from around fire hydrants. Fortunately, no large fires broke out, but an explosion at the Standard Oil Plant on East Twenty-third Street demonstrated the difficulty in responding to emergencies. Six ambulances attempted to reach a man injured in the blast. All auto ambulances became stuck in snow and a one-horse ambulance could not pull through the debris-littered streets. A second horse was hooked up and the double team succeeded in reaching the victim. The horses were reported to be exhausted upon reaching St. Alexis Hospital.

The storm created new interest in a "wireless station" for Youngstown. The *Youngstown Vindicator* reported city council passed an ordinance "under suspension of the rules" Monday night allowing the John Brenner Jewelry Company to construct and maintain laterals over West Federal Street for a wireless station on top of the Wick block. The jewelry company would use the wireless station to get correct time from Washington, but it could also be used for communication in emergencies.

Temperatures rose to the 50s on Thursday, and sunshine brightened the attitude and eased the cleanup efforts of Ohioans. Cleveland schools reopened Thursday, communication was restored, food shortages alleviated, and trains were on schedule. Snow melted gradually and was easily absorbed into the unfrozen soils. The *Cleveland Plain Dealer* reported pedestrians were "forced to indulge in a new cold weather sport"—dodging cornices of melting ice falling off buildings.

The winter storm of 9–11 November 1913 stands as one of the most severe in Ohio history. The *Toledo Blade* quoted ninety-eight-year-old John Williams of Sandusky: "Whenever some old-timer tries to tell you that the old-fashioned winter was worse than the sample we've just had, put him down as an imaginative chap."

24 October 1917
An Early Southeastern Snow

An unprecedented autumn snowfall paralyzed southeastern counties early on Wednesday, 24 October 1917. A belt about fifty miles wide from Licking and Perry Counties eastward into West Virginia (centered along the present Interstate 70) received six to ten inches of wet snow.

The *Cambridge Daily Jeffersonian* reported, "The entire Cambridge district was almost totally paralyzed this morning by the heavy blanket of snow which fell during the night." Business was at a standstill Wednesday morning as electric power was out and streets were difficult to travel. The slush in roads was reported to provide "fine breeding for pneumonia." Communication was disrupted when the weight of snow brought down telephone and telegraph lines. Some poorly constructed buildings collapsed under the weight, and trees that had not lost their leaves fell from the burden of clinging snow.

The damage and disruption reported from Cambridge was repeated throughout the hills of southeastern Ohio. The snow was reported very destructive to trees and wires at Zanesville, Caldwell, and Barnesville. This cold period contributed to making October 1917 the coldest in at least thirty-five years in Ohio, and the year 1917 was the coldest in Ohio since records began in 1883 (Karl et al. 1983).

12 January 1918
Severe Statewide Blizzard

It is rare for a true blizzard to affect all of Ohio. When this occurs, the state is paralyzed for several days and the storm remains in residents' memories for decades. The Blizzard of 1918 belongs to this elite group of Ohio storms.

This storm was compared to the New Year's Blizzard of 1864 and was not matched in Ohio until the blizzard of January 1978. Meteorologist William Alexander (1918) wrote of the blizzard, "Nothing like it has occurred in this state within the memory of the oldest inhabitants, and certainly all available records have been searched in vain for anything closely comparable to it."

The Blizzard of 1918, like the 1978 blizzard of more recent memory, came during a winter of bitter cold and deep snows in the Heartland. The winter of 1917–18 was referred to as an "old-fashioned winter" for the way it resembled the winters of the nineteenth century (Brooks 1918a, 1918b). It now ranks as the fourth coldest winter since 1883 in Ohio.

The Blizzard of 1918 also resembled the Blizzard of 1978 in the track of the storm and its passage across Ohio from south to north. The low pressure moved out of the coastal sections of Texas late on 10 January and tracked northward into southwestern Ohio late on 11 January. At the same time, arctic high pressure was building southward with extremely cold air from Canada. The Texas low strengthened rapidly as it crossed Ohio, and gale-force winds pulled the arctic air across the region in its wake.

Because winds circulate counterclockwise around these storms, the bitter arctic gales swept into Ohio from the southwest as the storm passed northward through the state. The cold wave entered Cincinnati at 7:00 P.M. on Friday, 11 January, reached Columbus at 10:00 P.M., Toledo at midnight, and moved through Cleveland and Akron about 2:00 A.M. on 12 January.

Prior to the arrival of the cold air, temperatures were near freezing but fell by 40 to 50 degrees in a few hours. As the blizzard arrived in Cincinnati, temperatures fell from 30 to -16 degrees overnight. Unofficial readings of -21 degrees were noted that morning in the Queen City. At Toledo, temperatures plummeted from 28 to -15 degrees in eight hours, and in Cleveland the thermometer fell from 34 to -8 degrees Saturday morning. Winds averaged thirty to fifty miles an hour all day on Saturday, 12 January. Average wind speed for the day was forty-eight miles an hour at Toledo, with gusts of fifty-eight to sixty-three miles an hour for fifteen hours. These winds, combined with deep snow and afternoon temperatures of -10 to -20 degrees, made this the coldest day in memory.

On Saturday, with temperatures near -15 degrees and winds of sixty miles an hour, the wind chill across western Ohio was near -80 degrees. Alexander (1918) wrote, "It is scarcely possible to portray adequately the real penetrating character of the bitter, biting winds that blew with gale force all day, causing great suffering and even death to man and beast, . . . rarely if ever has there been in this state a combination into which all the weather elements entered with such force and persistency as during . . . January 12, 1918." Snowfall during the blizzard was difficult to measure due to the extensive blowing and drifting. New snowfall was reported at ten to fifteen inches across most of western and northern Ohio, but drifts of ten to fifteen feet covered houses, vehicles, and trains.

The impacts of the blizzard were widespread. Several persons died— some freezing to death outside, some dead from cold in their home, others dead of heart attacks after exertion in the storm. One man died when he lost his way in the storm and walked into the path of a train. Twelve people were hospitalized for frostbite in Lima, and two thousand were treated for frostbite in Toledo.

Most churches in the state did not hold services Sunday morning, but many opened their doors to the poor and others who did not have coal for home heat. Persons trapped in downtown Toledo Saturday night found refuge for the night in theaters. On Sunday night, Toledo school superintendent William Guitteau asked that all downtown theaters flash on their screens that schools were closed on Monday.

Transportation and retail trades were severely affected. Train traffic was halted statewide, as were most urban streetcars. Many troops on their way home from the war were stranded a few agonizing miles from their destinations. A train on the Detroit, Toledo, and Ironton Railroad stalled in drifts four miles from Washington Court House, and passengers were brought to town in sleds to prevent their freezing in the -20 degree cold. Cattle froze in railcars.

Stores and factories closed early Saturday, grocers refused to make deliveries, and most mail delivery was stopped by the blizzard. No milk was delivered in Toledo on Sunday. By 13 January, the Ohio River was frozen at Gallipolis for the first time in eleven years, and at Cairo, Illinois, people walked across the Ohio for the first time in history (Day 1918). Ice on the Maumee River was twenty inches thick at the end of January.

Coal supplies were scarce in Ohio and through much of the eastern United States. The stoppages of rail traffic halted coal deliveries while the extreme cold created record demands for coal. Businesses, including bars, retail stores, and barber shops, were closed for ten Mondays beginning 21 January to save fuel supplies. In the Cleveland area, the Armour and Swift meat packing plants closed due to lack of coal, and half of Cincinnati's schools were closed by 16 January due to the coal shortage.

On the positive side, Cincinnati police reported only nineteen arrests over the weekend, compared to the usual one hundred. The *Cincinnati Enquirer* reported, "Not in 50 years, it is said, have the police records shown a smaller number of arrests for a Saturday and Sunday period."

The cold eased somewhat as temperatures rose above zero on Sunday and into the teens Monday, but more deep snow arrived on 14 and 15 January, with eight inches generally across Ohio to continue the "old-fashioned" winter of 1917–18. It was not until 1976–77 and 1977–78 that Ohioans experienced colder winters than 1917–18 and a blizzard comparable to the Blizzard of 1918.

30 March 1928
Northwest Encased in Ice

The ice storm of 30 March 1928 was one of the most destructive ever experienced in Ohio. The center of a spring storm passed through southern Ohio overnight on 29–30 March, and rain fell throughout the state. Temperatures fell below freezing in the north, and rain began freezing on all surfaces. The longest duration of freezing rain and greatest ice accumulation, one-half to one and a half inches, was in the northwest. Findlay, Bowling Green, Tiffin, Fostoria, Fremont, and Toledo were most affected, but smaller towns were isolated for a full day.

Damage to trees, poles, and wires was extensive through a fifteen-county area as the weight of ice and stress of strong winds exceeded the strength of materials. Falling branches also caused many wires to fall. Electric power and telephone and telegraph communications were cut, in many cases for several days. It was said that Findlay had not been so isolated from the outside world since the Flood of 1913. Poles and trees littered streets, schools were closed, and lights were out.

Secondary roads and many primary highways were blocked by thousands of fallen trees. The task of clearing the debris from city streets exceeded the capability of Findlay crews, so Boy Scouts were asked to meet at the fire station Monday morning to spend the day clearing limbs. They were asked to wear work clothes, not their Scout uniforms, and to bring their axes.

All schools in the affected area were closed on Friday, and some remained closed the following Monday, as power, communication, and traffic were restored. Findlay city schools were closed for the entire next week and did not reopen until 10 April. Rural Hancock County schools reopened sooner than city schools because they did not have electricity in 1928 and therefore were "not discommoded by lack of power."

Ice began melting Saturday afternoon, allowing line crews to begin restoring electricity, phone, and telegraph service. The damage to utilities was appalling and expensive. By Tuesday, 3 April the Ohio Bell Telephone Company estimated 20,000 miles of their phone lines were down and more than 10,000 poles were broken. Ohio Bell had twelve hundred linemen at work restoring service but were awaiting delivery of poles and wire. The Postal Telegraph Company had 300 poles down east of Defiance. Initial estimates of repair costs were $750,000 for Ohio Bell and $250,000 to $500,000 for Western Union Telegraph Company. Lima Telephone and Telegraph sustained large losses and brought linemen in from out of town to assist in repairs. The New York Central Railroad had 217 telegraph poles down and 5,410 breaks in telegraph wires along their 293 miles of track in the affected region.

Orchards sustained damage from broken limbs and trees. Many neighborhoods lost a substantial number of their largest shade trees, and nearly every tree on the campus of Findlay College was damaged. Losses were great at poultry hatcheries when loss of electricity caused the heaters to fail and the cold killed eggs and chicks. The tower of WSPD radio in Toledo fell under the barrage of ice and wind. Interurban cars were stopped or far behind schedule, buses were late, hotels and restaurants were crowded, and candles and coal oil were in demand.

16 November 1932
Deepest November Snow in the Northwest

The deepest November snowstorm on record in northwestern Ohio came on Wednesday, 16 November 1932. Snow depths of 10 to 15 inches covered the northwestern counties, exceeding the depths in the 9–11 November 1913 storm. The nearest November rival to this snowstorm was in 1966, when snow reached 12 to 15 inches in Van Wert, Mercer, and Auglaize Counties on 2 November.

Heavy snow began falling overnight and was 6 to 9 inches deep at dawn. By noon, depths reached 11.5 inches at Toledo and 12 inches in Van Wert. Temperatures were just below freezing as the snow fell, so it was heavy and wet, packing solidly on the streets. Deep, wet snow collapsed a 24-by-200-foot shed at the Lorber Lumber Company in Van Wert. A brick garage owned by William March in McClure collapsed and wrecked twelve cars inside.

Hundreds of men were at work clearing streets in Depression-era Toledo. The *Toledo Blade* reported, "The snowfall was expected to be a boon to the unemployed" as scores of men with shovels started out early to find work shoveling snow from sidewalks. Street Commissioner William DeBree employed two shifts of 250 men each to shovel snow from main streets and clear storm sewer inlets. The men were provided to the city by city relief agencies and paid a week's worth of groceries for their labor. A city bulldozer and four road scrapers were at work, and seventy trucks, all the city owned plus those regularly hired, carried snow from streets to the Maumee River.

25 December 1935
Christmas Blizzard

The Christmas season of 1935 had been the best of recent years in Ohio. Depression economies had improved, money was available for shopping, and wintry weather prevailed. Factories closed for the holiday at noon on 24 December and many gave Christmas bonus checks. Business was great at stores on Christmas Eve, so extras were hired to handle the shopping rush. Hundreds of carolers were out in neighborhoods on Christmas Eve. The *Dayton Journal* proclaimed, "Ushered in by a cold, snow-blanketed Christmas Eve, today marks the climax of what has been one of the most brilliant yuletide seasons in the recent history of Dayton."

The weather became even more wintry on Christmas Day as a sharp cold wave and brief blizzard swept across Ohio from the southwest. The cold air entered Cincinnati and Dayton about noon, reached Columbus at 2:00 p.m., Toledo at 3:30 p.m., and Cleveland at 6:00 p.m. Similar to the brief blizzard on 24 February 1990, temperatures dropped twenty degrees in an hour, winds gusted to more than thirty miles an hour, and blinding snow drifted onto highways. William Alexander, Ohio director of the Weather Bureau wrote, "Blizzards are not very common in Ohio and that of the 25th was a forceful reminder of the historic January 12, 1918."

Temperatures dropped below zero by late afternoon. The low of -4 degrees in downtown Columbus Christmas evening was the coldest Christmas reading since the Weather Bureau was established there in 1878. The Christmas 1935 cold record at Columbus, like other places in Ohio, was not exceeded until Christmas 1983, when the low was -12 at Columbus and -10 to -20 degrees elsewhere.

This was the first white Christmas since 1929 for much of Ohio. Snowfall was difficult to measure during the brief blizzard but was estimated at three to five inches in most areas and at more than twelve inches in the Lake Erie snowbelt. Drifts were much deeper, of course, and many rural roads were blocked. This seemed to be a small inconvenience on the holiday as commercial traffic was stopped anyway and few workers had to report to jobs. Children found the storm provided opportunities for "coasting" with sleds on the hills and roads, although Dayton police chief Rudoph Wurstner warned parents not to let children hitch rides from cars while coasting. The *Dayton Journal* on 26 December summarized the mood: "Daytonians in general stayed close to the fireside yesterday as the storm swirled fiercely and the mercury sank lower and lower."

19–26 January 1936
Bitter Snows

A long period of extreme cold and snow tormented Ohio and most of the United States from mid-January into February 1936. February 1936 remains the coldest month on record in the northern Great Plains, with lows of -60 degrees in North Dakota (Diaz 1979). In Ohio, deep snowfalls, strong winds, and subzero cold combined during 19–26 January to bring the pace of life in Ohio nearly to a halt. The *Columbus Dispatch* reported fifty-three persons dead in Ohio from the severe winter weather by 27 January.

A snowstorm swept across southern and eastern Ohio on Sunday, 19 January, with ten to twelve inches of snow in most communities. Pomeroy registered fifteen inches and the fourteen-inch fall at Marietta was the deepest since 1898. Strong winds piled drifts of ten to fifteen feet, closing roads, schools, and coal mines. Streets in Steubenville were impassable for thirty-six hours.

A second snowstorm and cold wave hit Ohio on Wednesday, 22 January just as the state began to recover from the weekend storm. Snowfall of three to six inches, combined with winds of thirty-five miles an hour and rapidly falling temperatures, nearly shut the state down again Wednesday afternoon. The *Columbus Dispatch* called it a "blinding blizzard" as temperatures fell from 31 degrees at dawn to 17 degrees at noon. In northwestern counties, temperatures fell to 4 degrees by Wednesday afternoon and to -10 by evening. As thermometers fell to -56 degrees in northern Minnesota, papers proclaimed, "The rawest cold since the turn of the century came howling down from the Canadian Northwest today."

Schools had started the day with ordinary winter weather, but rapidly deteriorating conditions turned the day into a school superintendent's nightmare. Some schools stopped classes early and sent students home, but in many cases it was too late. Drifts, blowing snow, and near-zero cold clogged roads and made travel difficult and dangerous. The result was that, in cases in which superintendents wisely chose safe haven over sending buses into the storm, some students were stranded in schools. Other students, already on buses, were stranded on the highways and sought shelter for the night in farmhouses. Fifty students in Elida, Allen County, spent the night with residents in town and were bused home Thursday morning. At the Staunton School near Troy, three hundred students slept in the school while fourteen teachers watched over them. Plows were working toward the school by Thursday morning.

Forty students were rescued from a bus at Rock Hill, another twenty at Centerville, and sixty students were taken from two buses near Fairpoint. Forty students on a stranded bus in Belmont County were rescued by farmers in horse-drawn bobsleds. Fourteen Brown County students suffered from exposure after they walked a mile from their stranded bus to a farmhouse. Another twenty students suffered exposure after making their way to a farmhouse near Waverly. The last stranded schoolchildren were rescued near Neptune in Mercer County Thursday afternoon. Overall, the *Lima News* estimated that six hundred Ohio schoolchildren spent Wednesday night away from home in the safe care of teachers or helpful strangers.

In another dramatic rescue, five Works Progress Administration (WPA) workers and five horse teams were stranded for twenty-eight hours while building roads near Newark. They were trapped in deep drifts by noon Wednesday and burned logs to keep warm in temperatures that fell to -16 degrees overnight. A rescue team of forty WPA men began digging toward the trapped workers on Thursday with shovels and plows. After four miles of clearing drifts, the trapped men were freed without major hardship.

Rural schools and roads were still closed by extreme cold and deep drifts across Ohio on Thursday and Friday. Bitter cold following the snowstorm created additional hardship and brought some of the coldest weather in thirty-seven years. Moderation allowed most roads to reopen by Sunday, 26 January, but another cold wave closed schools and kept temperatures below zero on the twenty-seventh.

13–14 February 1940
Southeastern Snowstorm

A storm that became a blizzard along the Atlantic Coast buried southern and eastern Ohio with eight to sixteen inches of snow in mid-February 1940. High winds blew the snow into drifts that clogged and shut many roads. Snow began in Cincinnati on Tuesday afternoon, 13 February and totaled seven inches by Wednesday morning. Tuesday evening rush-hour traffic was snarled and several roads were closed, including the Gilbert Avenue hill. Lunken Airport shut down for a time Tuesday afternoon.

Columbus Airport also closed Tuesday afternoon as five inches of wind-blown snow accumulated. City crews dumped snow from Columbus streets into the "Snow Hole" on Chestnut between High and Front Streets. Three to five inches of snow at Cleveland slowed traffic but caused no major disruptions. No snow fell in Toledo or Lima.

Southeastern and east-central Ohio were hardest hit, with more than 10 inches of snow from Chillicothe through Zanesville to Marietta and up the Ohio Valley past East Liverpool. Cambridge and Steubenville, where 13.5 inches fell, were isolated. Sixteen inches fell at Martins Ferry in Belmont County, where 20-foot drifts were reported. Some rural roads were closed for several days, keeping schoolchildren home and thousands of coal miners out of the mines. Temperatures fell to near zero after the storm on 15 February.

A tragedy unfolded on Lake Erie as the storm ended Wednesday afternoon. George Edam, a Put-in-Bay physician, was returning from calling on patients on Middle Bass Island when his car went through the ice of Lake Erie into thirty feet of water. Dr. Edam, his wife, and two small children drowned in the accident.

12–28 December 1944
Lake-Effect Siege

December 1944 brought extraordinary snowfalls to the Lake Erie snow-belt of extreme northeastern Ohio. The siege began on Tuesday, 12 December as about twelve inches of heavy wet snow and six-foot drifts forced the closing of most Ashtabula County roads. Jefferson schools dismissed classes at noon Tuesday and did not reopen the rest of the week, according to the *Jefferson Gazette*. A Jefferson school bus became stuck early Tuesday afternoon while taking children home. Local farmers delivered the children to their homes by bobsleds, and the bus was still stranded in the drift two days later.

Ashtabula County roads remained closed for most of the week by snowfall and drifting. Those that were open were cleared only enough to allow one lane of traffic to pass. By 15 December the winter storm was being called the worst in at least twenty-five years for Ashtabula County. Jefferson postmaster John Jones kept local weather records and was quoted in the *Jefferson Gazette* as saying snows this week rivaled the big snows of 1917–18. Milk trucks could not travel from Ashtabula County, so Cleveland faced a milk shortage by 15 December.

Plows had operated continuously in Ashtabula County from late Monday, 11 December to Friday, 15 December, and they were wearing out. At one time on Wednesday, only one of eight county snowplows was on the road. The others all sat in the repair shops. At noon on Thursday, six of sixteen state plows in the county were also in the shop.

Schools and main highways in Ashtabula County reopened by Monday, 18 December, but, with more snow over the weekend, secondary roads remained blocked. Conneaut Township roads and schools remained closed the week of 18 December. More snow fell on 20–21 December, and secondary roads were again closed across most of Ashtabula County. Christmas dawned with sleet falling. This turned to snow by afternoon with about five inches overnight.

3 January 1947
Northwest Crippled by Ice

One of the worst ice storms in years began in northwestern Ohio on Thursday, 2 January 1947 and continued into Friday, 3 January. Ice one and a half inches thick on Toledo Edison electric wires was the "heaviest old-timers among servicemen could recall," according to the *Toledo Blade*. Miles of electric and telephone lines were down, some falling under the weight of ice and others ripped by falling trees. Toledo Edison had three hundred linemen working to restore power but could not keep up with the destruction.

Most schools were closed in northwestern Ohio on Friday. Appeals were made for parents to keep children inside away from downed power lines. The *Toledo Blade* reported that the greatest handicap caused by lost electricity was in houses with "thermostatically controlled furnaces." Buses and streetcars were operating in Toledo and were jammed with those not wanting to drive on the icy roads. Toledo Municipal Airport was open, but no planes landed or departed. Cinders were spread on runways to provide traction.

Thousands of trees were down in the neighborhoods and city parks of Toledo. It was observed that oak trees stood up best and were rarely felled by the ice. Fallen trees and branches blocked many side streets. Sixty Toledo sanitation workers were assigned to clearing trees and branches from streets.

29 January 1947
Ice Returns to the Northwest

The second severe ice storm of the month in northwestern Ohio, worse than the first, came on Wednesday, 29 January 1947. Telephone and electric utility workers called this the worst ice storm in their experience, and at Bryan it was called the worst in twenty-three years.

A large swath of ice was laid down by the storm from Iowa through northern Illinois and Indiana, into Wisconsin, southern Michigan, and northwestern Ohio. While it was raining and 30 degrees all day at Toledo, temperatures reached over 70 degrees in southern Ohio and a tornado raged through Springfield Thursday morning. Accumulated ice in northwestern counties once again toppled thousands of trees and miles of electric and telephone lines and made driving or walking treacherous. New poles just set by the telephone company after the ice storm of 3 January were broken off between Wauseon and Napoleon.

Schools closed Thursday and Friday in Toledo and many rural districts. Streetcars and trackless trolleys could not get traction on icy roads and rails, and trains were blocked by fallen poles and trees. Put-in-Bay was isolated for two days after ice and strong winds downed trees and lines, cutting all services for the island community.

1 January 1948
New Year's Ice Storm

A strong low pressure storm center drifted slowly from Arkansas to Indiana on Thursday, 1 January 1948 and spread a variety of severe weather across Ohio and other states. More than twenty people were killed by tornadoes in southern states, and at least twenty-four died in the snow and ice storm in the northern states. Ohio was at the middle of the stormy mix.

The *Columbus Dispatch* observed: "Nature staged one of its wildest orgies in the Buckeye State, throwing almost everything in the way of weather tricks." A tornado unroofed homes and flattened barns in Clermont County. Rain and hail lashed Columbus amid 55-degree temperatures. Fog on New Year's Eve closed airports in Toledo and Cleveland. The *Cleveland Plain Dealer* reported that "two blankets of fog, one from the sky and the other from the bottle, made a mixture that the police whoopee squad eyed with apprehension."

It was in northwestern Ohio where freezing rain and northeast gales caused the greatest damage. Toledo had a potpourri of fog, freezing rain, snow, hail, thunder, and lightning on New Year's Day. Ice accumulated to a thickness of 1 inch north of Tiffin and Paulding, and damage to trees and wires was severe in Toledo, Bowling Green, Defiance, Napoleon, Bryan, and Put-in-Bay. Destruction was accelerated by northeast winds gusting to more than fifty miles an hour, toppling ice-laden branches and wires. Temperatures at Toledo ranged from 27 to 33 degrees on New Year's Day, with 1.3 inches of freezing rain.

Northeast gales accompanying this storm drove Lake Erie waters and ice against the western shores. Six homes were pushed off their foundations by wind-driven ice at Reno Beach, and Route 2 was submerged by the rising lake. Lake Erie at Toledo reached 574.8 feet above sea level at 6:00 P.M. This was 6.2 feet above low-water datum and exceeded the previous record for high water set on 26 May 1929. This New Year's 1948 record held until a level 4 inches higher was reached in March 1952. (The present record is 576.7 feet on 14 April 1980.)

Recovery was slow from the ice damage, especially in rural areas. Toledo Edison reported five hundred electric poles snapped by ice. Ohio Bell reported three hundred telephone poles down, the worst in more than twenty years according to the *Toledo Blade*. Toledo Municipal Airport remained closed through Saturday, 3 January by ice on the runways. Roads were mostly open by Saturday, although rural routes were icy. Electric power and telephone service was restored to most communities by the weekend. In Toledo, where an estimated eighty thousand trees were damaged, officials asked for help in completing the cleanup and offered wages of $1.18 an hour for laborers.

24 January 1948
Snow Blankets Ohio

Heavy snow from this Atlantic coastal storm began falling across Ohio during the morning of Saturday, 24 January 1948. Northwestern Ohio was at the margin of the storm and received only two to four inches, but snowfall was generally six to ten inches in southern and central Ohio. Eastern counties, closer to the storm center, had the heaviest amounts, with as much as nineteen inches at Youngstown. This was the deepest snowfall since April 1901 at Youngstown, but it was to be exceeded less than three years later in the Thanksgiving Blizzard of 1950.

Strong northeast winds and temperatures near 10 degrees added to the disruption and discomfort. Drifts of three feet were common, and some as great as ten feet blocked roads and rails. Several people collapsed and died while shoveling snow, some died from exposure or car accidents, and others died in house fires started by overheated furnaces or wood stoves.

Overall disruption was lessened by the fact that the storm occurred on Saturday, when schools were closed and fewer persons were required to travel to work. Cold temperatures resulted in light, dry snow, which was easily removed by plows. Ashing trucks and slag trucks, spreading cheap, noncorrosive material to aid traction, worked along with plows all day Sunday, so most roads were in good condition by Monday morning.

Subzero temperatures prevailed for the last week of January in the wake of the snowstorm. New Lexington weather observer Roy Cotterman recorded -26 degrees on 28 January, and lows of -24 degrees were measured at Cambridge and Jackson. An unofficial thermometer hanging outside a grocery store at Cannelville in Muskingum County was variously reported to have shown -35 or -38 degrees, and residents proudly claimed their community was the "icebox of southeastern Ohio," according to the *Cleveland Plain Dealer*. Claims of extraordinary temperatures ten degrees or more below official values are common in cold waves. They may represent a truly cold site but often result from a thermometer exposed in the open that cools well below the true air temperature. A properly exposed thermometer is shielded on all sides to prevent loss of radiated heat to the night sky.

Subzero cold and thick ice closed locks and stopped traffic on the Ohio River on 24 January 1948. It was the first stoppage since 1940, and at least two hundred barges were trapped in the ice or seeking shelter in river ports. Many of the barges hauled coal, and their delay threatened Ohio steel production. Some movement of river ice and barges resumed on 30 January.

A natural-gas shortage developed in the days following the snowstorm. The *Findlay Republican Courier* reported that Ohio Fuel Gas Company, which served half of the state, asked residents to turn off gas hot-water heaters, leave empty rooms unheated, and postpone Monday clothes washings. A total cutoff of gas to industrial users was announced on 24 January. Gas-heated schools, churches, theaters, and "drinking establishments" were asked to close in Columbus. Seven Columbus branch libraries closed on 27 January to save gas; only libraries heated with fuel oil or coal remained open. East Ohio Gas shut off gas to industrial users in Youngstown and Warren, forcing the layoff of eighty-five hundred workers. Some restrictions were relaxed by the thirtieth, but the *Youngstown Vindicator* reported that on that date thirty thousand Ohio workers were idle due to the gas curtailments.

23–27 November 1950
The Great Thanksgiving Storm

The Thanksgiving snowstorm of 1950 was the deepest in Ohio's history and is generally credited with providing the Ohio record for a twenty-four-hour snowfall: 20.7 inches at Youngstown and, the Ohio record snowstorm, 36.3 inches in three days at Steubenville (Ludlum 1982, 289). Virtually all of Ohio had more than 10 inches during the last week of November, and communities in the eastern half of Ohio measured 20 to 35 inches during that period (fig. 9). Strong winds and record cold temperatures made this one of the most disruptive Ohio snowstorms.

The weather disturbance that caused the Great Thanksgiving Storm formed as a small low on a cold front over the North Carolina mountains

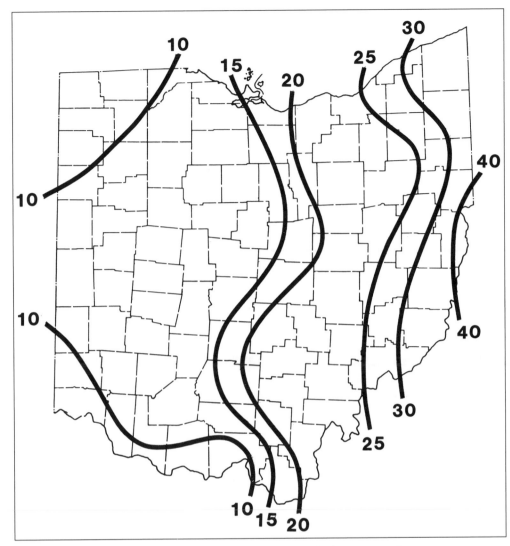

Fig. 9. Snowfall (in inches) during 23–27 November 1950. This was the deepest statewide snowfall in Ohio history.

early on 24 November (Smith 1950). This was nothing unusual, and the low might have been expected to move on up the east coast with little influence in Ohio. However, strong, cold low pressure in the upper atmosphere moved from Wisconsin to the Ohio Valley on 24 November and caused the North Carolina low to strengthen rapidly. In addition, a very strong high pressure area was centered over Maine and eastern Canada and did not move for several days, blocking all weather systems to the west.

The range of extreme conditions was illustrated by the fact that Dayton set a November record for low pressure (29.06 inches) and Caribou, Maine, set a November record for high pressure (30.77 inches)—all within a twenty-four-hour period. The result was a steep pressure gradient, very strong winds, record cold, a blocked weather pattern, and several days of storm conditions from Ohio eastward to the coast.

Weather forecasts on Thanksgiving, 23 November warned of a cold wave approaching from the northwest, but forecasters did not anticipate the explosive development of the eastern storm and its impact on Ohio. Thanksgiving temperatures were in the 40s across Ohio. Rain began during the afternoon in the northwest and changed to snow late on Thanksgiving. Snow started overnight in the eastern counties and became heavier statewide on the twenty-fourth.

The cold wave from the northwestern region of the state spread late on Thursday and reached the southeastern region early Friday morning. By Friday morning the Weather Bureau thermometer at Toledo Municipal Airport registered 3 degrees above zero, the coldest ever recorded so early in winter. At Steubenville, the temperature on Friday dropped from 38 degrees at midnight to 18 at dawn and to 14 by noon. At Marietta, the temperature plunged from 47 degrees Thursday afternoon to a record 13 degrees at 8:00 A.M. Friday.

As the North Carolina low strengthened, it moved into Maryland and central Pennsylvania on 25 November. North gales across Ohio held temperatures down to midwinter levels all weekend. Winds intensified and reached forty to sixty miles an hour on Saturday. The powerful storm center moved westward from Pennsylvania, an unusual path, and was centered over northern Ohio from late on 25 November to 26 November before finally weakening on 27 November.

The worst storm conditions occurred on Saturday, 25 November as near-blizzard conditions prevailed throughout Ohio. The *Toledo Blade* proclaimed, "The worst blizzard in modern times paralyzed northern Ohio today." Snowfall was heaviest east of a Sandusky-Ironton line, where by late Saturday the snow was ten to twenty inches deep. Steubenville reported twenty-two inches on Saturday and drifts were reaching twenty-five feet in the upper Ohio Valley. Businesses were closed, buses had stopped, and rail lines were running two hours late. At Marietta, snow was fifteen inches deep Saturday afternoon and falling heavily.

The classic Ohio State–Michigan football game was scheduled for Saturday afternoon in Columbus, the Big Ten championship and a trip to the Rose Bowl on the line. It will come as no surprise to anyone who lives between the Ohio River and the Straits of Mackinac that, although the state was virtually shut down by the blizzard, many roads closed by drifts, fuel supplies low, and all ordinary aspects of life were put on hold, the athletic directors of the two schools decided the game should proceed as scheduled!

So with a Saturday morning temperature of 5 degrees and winds of forty miles an hour, preparations were made for the "Blizzard Bowl" in Columbus. Players pulled on woolen long underwear, the OSU band poured glycerine into their horn valves to keep them from freezing, and the grounds crew struggled to remove frozen tarps from the field. Of the 82,700 tickets sold, a surprising 50,503 ticket holders actually attended.

The game statistics reflect the playing conditions. Michigan won the game 9–3 on twenty-seven total yards gained and without achieving even one first down! The two teams punted a total of forty-five times in the sixty minutes of play. Many spectators found they could not get far from Columbus after the game. At the Oakland Hotel in Marysville, all one hundred rooms were full Saturday night and another one hundred travelers slept in the lobby. (Michigan went on to beat California 14–6 in the Rose Bowl.)

The storm continued into Sunday, and by the morning of Monday, 27 November snowfall totaled thirty-three inches at Steubenville, thirty inches at Geneva, and twenty-nine inches at Youngstown. Cleveland, Akron, and Canton had twenty to twenty-two inches with drifts over ten feet deep. At Marietta, where weather records extend back to the early 1800s, the *Marietta Daily Times* reported the twenty-seven inches in this storm was the "greatest in any known record here."

Throughout eastern Ohio, roads and rails were blocked, schools, stores, and industries were closed, and communities were isolated. Governor Frank Lausche declared Monday a legal holiday so Ohio banks and courthouses could remain closed. Virtually all businesses and schools were closed again Tuesday, and only a few opened on Wednesday.

Damage from the storm was widespread across Ohio. Wires and trees were blown down by the wind and all travel in the east was at a standstill for five days. Nursery stock of shrubs, evergreens, and fruit trees were destroyed by the weight of snow in Lake County. The weight of twenty to thirty-five inches of snow, with drifts of several feet, was more than many roofs could support. The Jefferson County Courthouse roof collapsed under two feet of heavy snow on 25 November, causing damage estimated at $200,000. A Steubenville parking garage collapsed onto several cars, and a furniture warehouse collapsed in Mingo Junction. The roofs of Wayne's Market and Elston Lumber gave way in Marietta. Merchants shoveled snow from store roofs to prevent additional damage.

Main roads were opened by Tuesday, 28 November, but many side roads remained blocked and schools were closed. Bulldozers were used to reach two pregnant women in Jefferson County and to open a path for an ambulance to deliver them to a hospital. Ohio National Guard troops used Jeeps to transport people to hospitals in southeastern Ohio and to deliver food to homes. A week after the storm started, drifting again closed many roads on 30 November. Steubenville schools finally reopened on 4 December.

Three persons were found dead in snowdrifts in northern Ohio and three died in traffic accidents. The press reported up to seventy persons were killed in Ohio by the storm, mostly from overexertion and heart attacks. The Ohio Highway Patrol rescued fifty motorists from Route 6 west of Sandusky, carrying some on their backs through waist-deep snow. The record snow depths did not last long, however, as temperatures in the 50s and 60s caused melting by 2 December.

31 January 1951
Winter Wonderland

Barely two months after the Great Thanksgiving Storm of 1950, Ohio once again dug out of heavy snow in bitter temperatures. Snow began in southern Ohio early on Wednesday, 31 January and continued into the first day of February. Freezing rain accumulated in eastern and southern Ohio early during the storm and was followed by heavy snow and temperatures of -25 degrees.

Snow depths across Ohio were six to fourteen inches, except in the extreme southeast, where only three inches fell. The impacts of the winter storm were greatest where more than ten inches accumulated in a southwest-northeast belt from Cincinnati through Lancaster to Akron and Cleveland.

Memories of the Great Thanksgiving Storm of November 1950 were fresh in the minds of central Ohioans, and the response to this snowfall reflected an attitude of action and coping with winter storms. The 1 February *Columbus Dispatch* reported, "Remembering the November 26 'big snow,' Mayor James Rhodes called an early morning conference of all city department heads to plan the campaign to maintain some semblance of normal activity in the city." Mayor Rhodes declared a state of emergency, and heavy road equipment was requested from the Ohio National Guard and Lockbourne Air Base. Plows, trucks, and graders were hired from thirty private contractors. Columbus city streets were mostly cleared by 2 February, although rural highways remained blocked by deep snow.

Another lesson learned from the great snow of November 1950 was that milk supplies in large cities dwindle quickly when rural roads are blocked for days by deep drifts. After the 1950 storm, the Central Ohio Milk Producers sent cards to all producers in a fourteen-county area asking them to list equipment they could use or share to get milk into Columbus in the event of another blizzard.

Replies from 637 milk producers showed the availability of 912 tractors, 237 ton-and-a-half trucks, 176 spreaders, 67 plows, 113 sleds, and 1,082 wagons and trailers to haul milk in an emergency. Some of that equipment was used in this storm to get milk from farms onto main roads into Columbus, so, as the *Columbus Dispatch* reported, "Perhaps the 'big snow' in November was a blessing in disguise."

After the storm a *Columbus Dispatch* editorial praised Ohioans: "The way in which local folk generally adjusted to the conditions brought about by the second smothering snowfall, after the first experience, shows again how adaptable the human animal is when faced by a series of abnormal situations."

1–4 March 1954
Late Winter Storms

After a warm February, winter struck Ohio hard during the first four days of March 1954. Heavy snow on Monday, 1 March disrupted travel over nearly the entire state. Another storm with high winds and severe drifting snow on 3 March added to the late winter weather woes (fig. 10).

Snowfall of six to twelve inches was common on 1 March, except in the southwest, where less than two inches fell. Strong winds accompanied the snow and caused drifts that blocked highways and closed schools. Wet snow clung to trees and power lines, many of which toppled in the wind. The *Lancaster Eagle-Gazette* reported that snow was six inches in diameter on wires in Fairfield County.

At Cleveland, where fifteen inches fell on the first day of March, the airport was closed, buses and mail delivery ran late, and hundreds of workers who could not return to suburbs crowded into downtown hotels Monday night. About a dozen Cleveland-area residents died from heart attacks while shoveling snow. The *Cleveland Plain Dealer* reported the overall impact in Cleveland was lessened, however, because emergency plans developed after the November 1950 storm were put in place to maintain order and city services. Continued drifting kept many rural schools closed on 2 March in northern and central Ohio.

A winter storm warning system set up for schools in northwestern Ohio by Don Coleman, then chief of the Weather Bureau in Toledo, was used heavily on 1 March, according to the *Toledo Blade*. Weather Bureau staff, along with the Lucas County sheriff and Ohio Highway Patrol, called the sheriffs in all thirteen counties served by the Toledo Weather Bureau

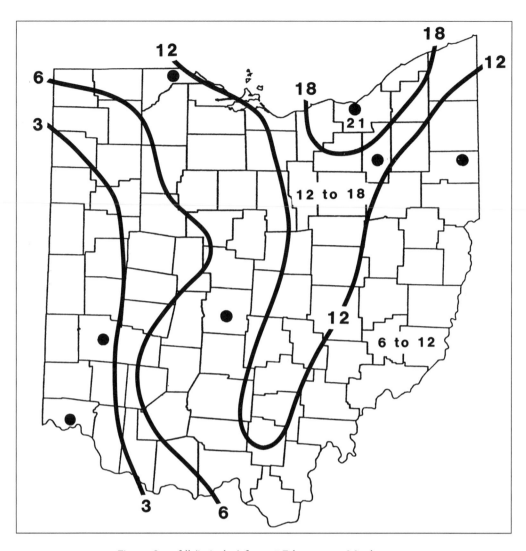

Fig. 10. Snowfall (in inches) from 28 February to 4 March 1954.

office to deliver the weather forecast. County sheriffs then called the county school superintendents to keep them updated on severe winter weather and assist in decisions to close schools and ensure the safety of students and employees.

The second storm hit Wednesday, 3 March and continued into the next day. Less snow came with this storm, generally two to four inches, but winds gusted to more than fifty miles an hour and blew the new and old snow into large drifts. Temperatures fell from near freezing in the morning to the teens during the afternoon as the strong cold front crossed Ohio. Blizzard conditions were reported in northwestern and north-central counties.

Once again, highways were blocked, schools were closed, and businesses closed early to allow employees to travel home. Some schools opened Wednesday morning only to close again at noon as rural highways began to drift shut. Huge traffic jams developed in cities of northern Ohio Wednesday evening as the swirling snow reduced visibility and caused dozens of minor accidents. Route 2 was closed between Port Clinton and Toledo on Wednesday by blowing snow and drifts, according to the *Toledo Blade*. Toledo and Cleveland Airports were closed for a time, and Greyhound buses were running three hours late.

Some rural schools remained closed on Thursday, 4 March, but highway and air traffic was slowly returning to normal across northern and central Ohio. Recovery was delayed in Cleveland and the eastern suburbs by more than twelve inches of lake-effect snow on Thursday and Friday. Suburban roads and schools in the snowbelt remained closed through the week, and traffic did not resume a normal pace until the weekend. Stranded commuters again crowded into Cleveland hotels, where, the *Cleveland Plain Dealer* reported, there was a "carnival atmosphere." Marooned employees of the Cleveland Home and Flower Show in Public Hall slept on 150 cots provided by the Red Cross.

7–8 April 1957
Spring Snow in the North

The deepest April snowstorm since 1901 snarled traffic and closed schools across northern Ohio during 7–8 April 1957. Heavy snow fell in a band across the state north of a Lima-Mansfield-Youngstown line. The greatest totals of twelve to sixteen inches extended from Montpelier eastward through Tiffin, Cleveland, Painesville, and Ashtabula. The snow followed an ice storm in the west on 3–4 April and high winds on 5 April.

Snow began early on Sunday, 7 April and continued into the eighth. Temperatures hovered near freezing during the snowfall, so it clung to trees and wires and was difficult to shovel or plow. Trees were broken and power lines down in Toledo, Cleveland, and other areas where snow accumulated to more than six inches. At least twenty-two thousand customers of Cleveland Electric Illuminating Company were without power during the storm, and one thousand remained in the dark on Wednesday morning. The Monday evening commute in Cleveland took two hours or more. Schools closed Monday and Tuesday through much of the zone of heavy snow. Cleveland Airport was closed by low visibility Sunday afternoon and again Monday evening.

The most celebrated traffic jam developed in Geauga County. Sunday was the last day of the Geauga County Maple Festival at Chardon. The festival, accustomed to fickle spring weather, continued in the snowstorm, with thousands lining Chardon Square to watch the parade. However, as sixty-five thousand people attempted to drive home Sunday afternoon, traffic jams five miles long developed in each direction on Routes 6 and 44 out of Chardon. The traffic was not cleared until 11:00 P.M. and some people chose to spend the night with relatives or in local motels. The *Cleveland Plain Dealer* reported personnel at the state highway garage in Burton claimed Geauga County roads were plowed and passable. They blamed traffic jams in Geauga County west and north from Chardon on road crews in neighboring Lake County, where snow removal did not start until late in the day.

23 February 1962
Southwest Battered by Ice

One of the worst ice storms in memory struck southwestern Ohio late on Friday, 23 February 1962. Ice extended as far north as Delaware and as far east as Newark, but the greatest accumulation was in the triangle made by present-day Interstates 70 and 71 in southwestern Ohio. Northern Hamilton County was without power after trees and lines fell. Water service was interrupted when electric power was lost. Gas service was also cut to large sections where uprooted trees tore out gas lines. Cincinnati Gas and Electric vice president S. M. Hamill called it the worst ice storm in that company's 125-year history, according to the *Cincinnati Enquirer.* About 20 percent of the company's 400,000 customers were without electricity after the storm.

The *Columbus Evening Dispatch* reported that more than one inch of freezing rain fell in Columbus, causing hundreds of trees to fall in that city. Roads were blocked, buildings damaged, and electric and phone service cut in Columbus and rural areas. Similar problems were reported in Dayton and Hamilton.

Although major impacts from the ice storm were felt in the cities of central and southwestern Ohio, it was in Clinton County that the storm had its greatest effects. Ice accumulated at least one and a half inches thick on all exposed surfaces. Clinton County had the most widespread failure of electric and phone service during the storm. Clinton Memorial Hospital was on emergency power for two hours, with only operating rooms, nurses' stations, and stairways receiving electricity. Forty-one poles were down on a three-mile stretch of Route 134 south of Wilmington, and numerous county roads were blocked by fallen trees and poles.

Hundreds of electric utility workers came from around Ohio and surrounding states to erect new poles and install lines in Clinton County.

More than one hundred were staying in Wilmington motels, some doubling-up in rooms, one crew sleeping while the other worked a twelve-hour shift. Linemen had to use sledge hammers to remove ice from poles before they could climb. Some electric lines repaired on Saturday were broken again Sunday as ice thawed and tree limbs came up from under the wires. About 90 percent of electric service was restored in Clinton County four days after the storm, but telephone communication was still sporadic. Some customers were without electric service yet on 2 March, one week after the ice storm.

6–14 December 1962
Record Snowbelt Depths

The nine days of 6 to 14 December 1962 provided the heaviest snowfalls known in the Lake Erie snowbelt of northeastern Ohio. Snowfall during this period exceeded the great lake-effect snows of December 1944. Lake-effect snow squalls are relatively small, and the most intense squalls may not get recorded at an official weather station. Reports of snow depths from police and highway crews, as reported in the press, combined with data from weather stations at Chardon and Geneva, give ample evidence for exceptional snowfalls and depths of more than three feet in the snowbelt during December 1962.

Warm air during the first days of December 1962 gave way to much colder air on 6 December and the development of a statewide snowstorm. Little snow fell in the extreme south, but six to ten inches of snow was common elsewhere across Ohio, closing roads and schools. Northeastern counties caught the brunt of this storm, wet snow and strong winds prevailing on Thursday and Friday, 6 and 7 December. Snowfalls of eight to twelve inches fell at Akron-Canton and Cleveland Airports. The two-day total was twenty-three inches at Chardon and eighteen inches at Hiram.

The heavy lake-effect snow developed with the invasion of colder air on Sunday and Monday, 9 and 10 December. The official weather station two miles south of Geneva recorded twenty-three inches of snow on Sunday and twelve inches on Monday, giving a five-day total of forty-seven inches. Other totals reported in the press for 6–10 December include twenty-six inches at Cleveland Heights and about thirty-six inches at Jefferson. The development and position of snow squalls are very dependent on prevailing winds. Subtle shifts in wind direction and strength from day to day lead to a wide range in snowfalls among snowbelt communities.

Schools were closed for several days throughout the snowbelt. Most Ashtabula County schools were closed from Friday, 7 December through the next week. Residents of the eastern suburbs of Cleveland were warned to clear snow from fire hydrants so fire crews could find them in the event of a fire. Police cruisers were authorized to buy tire chains at retail stores and bill them to City Hall.

A third round of heavy snow hit Lake and Ashtabula Counties 11–13 December. Portions of Ashtabula County had twenty-four inches of new snow overnight on 11 December. Lake-effect snow is usually of low density and settles considerably from its original depth in a day or two. The official snow depth of thirty-four inches at Chardon on 12 December and depths of three to four feet reported in Ashtabula County attest to the extreme snowfalls during this period.

This period of extreme snowfall in the snowbelt established a state record monthly snowfall of 69.5 inches at Chardon and a record depth of 45 inches in northern Ashtabula County on 11 December. The Chardon weather station continues to operate, and the December 1962 monthly snowfall has not been matched. Cleveland Airport established a December record snowfall of 30.3 inches.

12–13 January 1964
Snow Shuts Down Ohio

Roads, airports, schools, and factories were closed on Monday, 13 January 1964 after the heaviest statewide snow since November 1950. Snow began in western counties early on 12 January as a low pressure storm center moved from Kansas to western Kentucky. The storm center tracked through Kentucky on Sunday as a stronger coastal storm developed off the North Carolina coast (Kocin and Uccellini 1990). The coastal storm intensified as it moved north and caused snow to continue through Monday, 13 January in Ohio's eastern counties.

Snowfall was eight to twelve inches across most of Ohio, with lesser amounts in the far northwest. The coastal storm caused the greatest snowfall along the eastern border of Ohio, where about fifteen inches was measured at Youngstown and Steubenville. A steep pressure gradient to the north of the Kentucky storm caused winds from the northeast of more than thirty miles an hour on Sunday evening, closing many roads with deep drifts all across Ohio.

Lima mayor William Nungester declared a state of emergency Monday morning, closing streets for the day to all but emergency traffic. Emergencies were also declared in Findlay, Celina, St. Marys, and Wapakoneta to reduce road traffic and allow plowing operations to progress efficiently. The *Lima News* reported only Interstate 75 was passable in the Lima and Findlay areas. Some rural highways remained closed on Tuesday. Ten-foot drifts in Hardin County thwarted attempts by plows, so bulldozers were called in to open the highways.

Schools were closed in most of Ohio Monday, and many remained shut Tuesday while rural highways were cleared of drifts. Dayton Airport closed to arrivals at noon Sunday, and Monday classes were canceled at the University of Cincinnati by nine inches of wind-blown snow. The Ohio Turnpike remained open, but Gate 5 was closed for a time, forcing three to four hundred travelers to spend Sunday night at a service plaza east of Toledo.

Banks, schools, and department stores were closed at Youngstown and most eastern Ohio communities Monday. The *Youngstown Vindicator* reported steel mills operated normally Sunday night and Monday as night crews worked on overtime until replacements showed up Monday. Many workers could not get to the mills Monday, but steel workers already at the mills kept production going through the day.

Storms and people in need bring out the best in Ohioans. Hundreds of stranded travelers were put up in rural farm homes Sunday night. The 14 January 1964 *Dayton Journal-Herald* praised this virtue of rural society. They related how stranded motorists had to "abandon their cars and struggle through the snow, perhaps keeping in sight a distant lighted window. The windows grew brighter. Doors opened. Hot food and drink were offered. Use of the telephone. And a bed. Outside the snow continued. But the farmhouses were warm and the company congenial and Sunday night passed. It seems country people still know that the stranger in trouble might someday be themselves."

24 February 1965
Rush Hour and Ice

The disruption caused by ice storms depends not only on how much freezing rain falls but also on the timing of the storm. An ice storm overnight or on a weekend, for example, may cause fewer problems than ice during rush hour on a weekday. The southwestern Ohio ice storm of Wednesday, 24 February 1965 was especially disruptive because it began at 7:25 A.M., just as morning traffic was becoming heavy.

Freezing rain continued through the morning from Dayton southward. Dayton police called this storm more paralyzing than the November 1950 snow. Drivers had little control of their vehicles on the iced hills, and police reported at least four hundred accidents in Dayton on Wednesday. In the confusion, many accidents were not reported and estimates ran as high as one thousand accidents in the city. Body shops were booked with repairs for weeks.

School buses started on their runs before the freezing rain began, but many were caught by the ice and could neither proceed to school nor return students home. Many students spent the morning on a bus. Taxi drivers put on tire chains for the first time since the November 1950 snowstorm. Downtown Dayton stores closed by midmorning when it became apparent employees and customers would not be coming.

Hot sand kept runways open at Dayton Airport, but several flights were canceled. Municipal courts were closed as judges and juries could not get downtown. Most factory production workers began their day shift at 7:00 A.M., so they arrived for work before the ice arrived. Salaried factory workers, however, began their day at 8:00 A.M., so were caught in the traffic jams as the ice storm started.

The *Dayton Journal Herald* reported that on Wednesday 337 people were treated at city hospitals for injuries due to ice, most for sprains or contusions in falls or other accidents but about 15 percent for fractures. A Dayton Power and Light lineman died when he fell thirty feet while re-stringing a line near Celina.

This ice storm caused the worst traffic jams in thirty years in Cincinnati. The morning commute to work took some people longer than three hours, and more than two hundred accidents were reported in the Queen City. Five cars attempting to negotiate an incline toward a city parking lot slid into the Ohio River. The drivers jumped to safety before the cars went over the edge.

9 May 1966
Springtime Interrupted in the Northeast

A vast, cold high pressure system covered the eastern two-thirds of the United States during 9–11 May 1966, setting hundreds of cold records and spreading snow across the lower Great Lakes region. Record late snows fell in northeastern Ohio, and the coldest temperatures ever recorded during May occurred in southern valleys. Average temperatures in Ohio this month were the coldest for May since 1925.

Temperatures began falling late on Sunday, 8 May, and overnight rain changed to snow by dawn on 9 May. Occasional snow continued through noon on Tuesday. The *Akron Beacon Journal* observed, "It seemed like a bad dream this morning—in cold black and white." Temperatures hovered near freezing, so grassy surfaces became snow covered while roads were mostly slushy as some of the snow melted as it fell.

Snowfall during 9–10 May totaled 3.2 inches at the Akron-Canton Airport and 5.4 inches at Youngstown Airport, both records for May. One to 2 inches was common westward across Ashland and Mansfield to Bucyrus and Delaware. Only flurries fell in central and western Ohio. The usual snow-belt areas of Geauga and Ashtabula counties received only a trace of snow.

Slush and snow on roadways caused traffic delays and some accidents. One jet flight was canceled at Youngstown Airport due to slush on the runway. Low temperatures of 24 degrees at Youngstown and Akron-Canton Airport on 10 May were the coldest ever so late in the season. The low temperature of 17 degrees at Jackson was the coldest May temperature ever recorded in Ohio, and extensive damage occurred in Ohio's fruit crops.

2–3 November 1966
Early Deep Snow in the West

The heaviest snowfall so early in the season for western Ohio began on 2 November 1966. Snow started to fall just after midnight and continued through the day. All areas west of a Mansfield-Portsmouth line received substantial amounts (fig. 11). The deepest accumulations, 12 to 15 inches, were in the Van Wert, St. Marys, and Lima areas. Celina weather observer Harold Howick measured 15.4 inches. The 14-inch depth at Celina on 3 November was the deepest snow observed anywhere in Ohio for the winter of 1966–67.

Temperatures were near freezing as the snow began, so much of it melted as it touched roads and sidewalks. However, as temperatures fell into the 20s during the day and winds increased to forty to fifty miles an hour on Wednesday evening, the snow accumulated and drifted onto roads. The quick and unexpected accumulation of snow Wednesday afternoon trapped many children in schools. In the Mercer County community of Maria Stein, 150 children of the Marion Local High School spent the night in homes near the school. Nearly 100 children spent the night in Auglaize Local School in Harrod, east of Lima, and were delivered home the next day in Ohio National Guard trucks. A farm home in eastern Auglaize County was shelter for the night to 35 schoolchildren whose bus became stuck in deep drifts. A state highway patrolman who was sent to assist the bus and help the children to shelter spent the night in the farmhouse with them.

School administrators were criticized for not dismissing school early Wednesday while roads were still passable. A front-page commentary in the 5 November issue of the *Celina Daily Standard* asked whether administrators were reluctant to dismiss schools during the storm because of fears over losing state funding if the minimum number of school days was not met. The staff writer continued: "In some cases, this possible loss of state aid has even seemed to outweigh the safety of children who are forced to ride buses on days when it isn't safe to ride buses." School administrators countered that a check of conditions at midday showed just

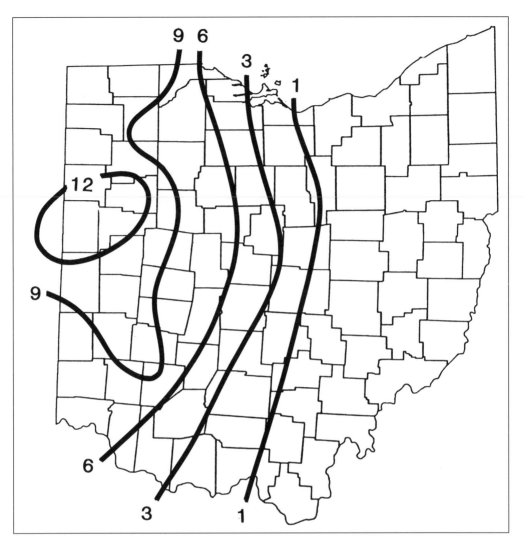

Fig. 11. Snowfall (in inches) during 2–3 November 1966. The snow depth of 14 inches at Celina on 3 November was the deepest recorded anywhere in Ohio for the winter of 1966–67.

slush on roads and the quick freeze-over and road-clogging drifts of the afternoon were not anticipated.

Celina mayor Robert Hecht declared a state of emergency Thursday morning. He asked that schools remain closed, which they did through the end of the week across west-central Ohio. Interstate 75 was closed Wednesday night near Wapakoneta, one thousand motorists were stranded near Piqua, and more than seventeen hundred trucks were stuck in drifts and clogged roads near Van Wert.

Temperatures remained below freezing all day Thursday and drifting continued until Thursday night. Temperatures fell as low as 11 degrees at

Greenville on Friday morning. Another traffic jam involving hundreds of vehicles developed Thursday night on Interstate 70 at the Indiana border. Some roads, including U.S. 30 east of Van Wert, were not cleared of abandoned cars and opened to traffic until Friday. Farm tractors, which are often used in Ohio to extract cars from ditches and drifts, were still hooked to harvesting apparatus and were thus unavailable for usual winter duties.

27 January 1967
Ice Isolates the Northwest

Record warmth in the upper 60s on 24 January 1967 turned into a winter disaster as freezing rain began falling over northwestern Ohio late on 26 January. Ice continued to accumulate into Friday, 27 January west of a Lima-Findlay line and counties on the Indiana border were isolated from outside communication. Winds blew to more than thirty miles an hour as the ice storm ended, causing trees and wires to come crashing down. Hundreds of miles of electric and telephone lines were down in Mercer, Van Wert, and Paulding Counties. Some poles were coated with three inches of ice on their windward sides.

Ice also cut power and disrupted traffic north to Williams County. Streets were littered with broken branches and entire trees. Van Wert police chief Lynn Kennedy asked parents to keep children indoors to avoid hazards of downed wires and falling trees and branches. Schools were closed throughout the region Friday, and the community of Convoy lost its water supply as power failed.

Electric utility crews from around Ohio and other states converged on the region Friday and remained over the weekend, working eighteen-hour shifts to restore electric service. Most electric and phone service was on by Monday, but some rural areas west of Van Wert were still not connected. Amateur radio operators relayed emergency messages from residents and government offices in northwestern Ohio, where other communication failed for two days or more. A week later Van Wert city crews were still working shifts of nine and a half hours clearing limbs and debris from the community.

5 November 1967
Three Feet of Early Snow in Ashtabula County

"A possibility of heavy snow near the lake" was reported in the Friday, 3 November 1967 *Conneaut News-Herald* as the first cold wave of the year swept across Lake Erie. Snow squalls began as forecast the next day, but, to everyone's surprise, the squalls continued through Sunday and into

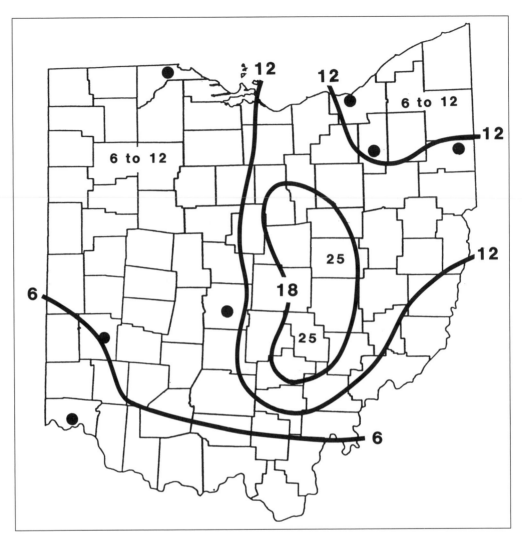

Fig. 12. Snowfall (in inches) during 12–15 January 1968. Weather observers at New Lexington and Coshocton measured 24.7 inches.

Monday morning, dumping twenty-four to thirty inches of wet snow in northern Ashtabula County. A depth of thirty-seven inches of undrifted snow was reported at Conneaut on 6 November, one of the greatest snow depths known in Ohio. Lesser amounts fell in Lake and Geauga Counties, and there was no snow cover at all in southern Ashtabula County.

Drifts three to four feet high blocked Interstate 90 east of Painesville on Sunday. Some rural Ashtabula County roads were also closed for a time Sunday, but all main highways were open Monday morning, a testament to the ability of highway crews to handle deep snow in Ohio's snowbelt. Schools were closed Monday due to unplowed lots and slippery roads, and they remained closed Tuesday after another six inches of snow fell Monday night. The snow collapsed the roof of a storage building in Conneaut but caused no other major structural damage.

Businesses and factories in the area reported near-normal operations Monday and little absenteeism. The *Conneaut News-Herald* reported phone service remained intact and there were only scattered electrical outages. Mail delivery was sporadic in the region Monday, partly because mail trucks did not arrive from Cleveland Monday morning. Sunshine and warmer air returned by Wednesday, melting one of Ohio's deepest snowfalls.

14 January 1968
Two Feet in the Southeastern Hills

The deepest snow since April 1901 fell across portions of east-central and southeastern Ohio on the weekend of 13–14 January 1968. Precipitation began as freezing rain over the southeastern part of the state early on Saturday, 13 January but quickly turned to snow and accumulated fast. Snowfalls of 6 to 8 inches were common across western Ohio, with more than 10 inches in the east. A six-county region from Holmes County south to Hocking County had 20 to 25 inches by Sunday night (fig. 12). Strong winds, cold weather, and light snow continued into Monday.

Official snowfall totals were as great as 24.7 inches at New Lexington and Coshocton, although the *Zanesville Times Recorder* reported 27 inches at New Lexington. Disruption was kept to a minimum by the storm's occurrence on a weekend, but many schools and businesses remained closed Monday due to snowy roads. Zanesville schools had a "snow day" Monday for the first time since November 1950. Zanesville Airport, with only one snowplow, was closed for five days. Thirty guests at the Clear Fork Valley ski resort near Mansfield were snowed in Sunday night. Transportation on major highways was back to normal by Tuesday, but rural schools remained closed through Wednesday.

The great depth of snow caused some buildings to collapse. The *Mansfield News Journal* reported one building collapsed in Mansfield and a store in Mansfield hired a helicopter to blow snow from their roof after it began sagging from the weight of snow. Most collapsed structures were carports, porches, and others not designed for large snow loads. Wires were brought down by fallen trees in Morgan County.

The deep snow of January 1968 did not cause the collapse of as many buildings as the April 1901 storm, which was wetter, heavier, and deeper than the 1968 snowfall. Better construction of buildings may have averted damage from the snow loads in 1968.

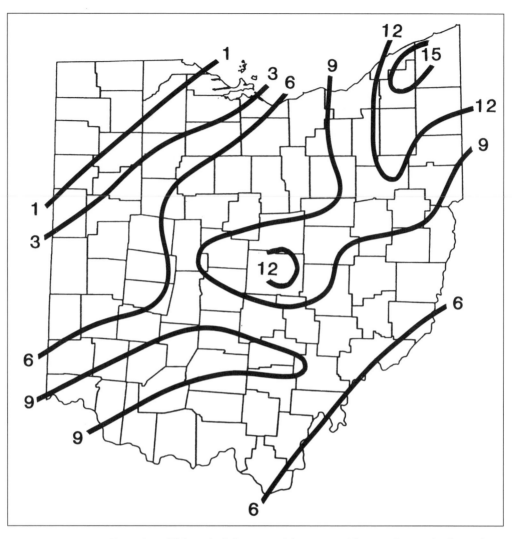

Fig. 13. Snowfall (in inches) during 8–9 February 1971. The 10-inch snow depth at Columbus was the greatest in twenty years.

8–9 February 1971
Heaviest Statewide Snow in Twenty Years

The most significant statewide snowstorm since November 1950, affecting all but northwestern Ohio, struck on 8–9 February 1971, producing strong winds and bitter cold and leaving snowfalls of six to twelve inches. The snow began early on Monday, 8 February and continued into Tuesday morning. Many businesses and schools closed as the magnitude of the storm became apparent early on the eighth, and some remained closed through the ninth. Winds of thirty to forty miles an hour caused the snow to drift across highways, and temperatures of 5 to 15 degrees made outdoor activities hazardous, conditions that prompted blizzard warnings for much of Ohio on Monday.

Snow totals with this storm were greatest in central and northeastern Ohio (fig. 13). Newark and Millersburg had 12 inches, and 11 inches fell at Circleville, Washington Court House, and Youngstown. Snowbelt communities had up to 20 inches. Among the major cities, Cincinnati, Columbus, and Cleveland all received about 9 inches with extensive drifting. Hundreds of abandoned vehicles hampered efforts to remove snow from roads. Fourteen deaths were attributed to the storm, eleven from heart attacks after shoveling snow.

At Columbus, the twenty-four-hour total of 8.9 inches was the greatest since the 11.9 inches recorded on 6 January 1910. On Tuesday morning, the snow stood 10 inches deep in the Capital City, the greatest since November 1950. Most communities in northeastern Ohio had no mail delivery Tuesday, and the airports at Cleveland, Akron-Canton, and Youngstown were closed for several hours.

Rush-hour Monday evening in Cleveland lasted until midnight as accidents and drifts blocked roads. A massive traffic jam on the southbound Interstate 75 hill out of Cincinnati resulted in many Kentucky commuters staying in the city all night. Major interstates were open, but speed limits were reduced to forty miles an hour on the Ohio Turnpike, and Interstate 90 was down to one lane in Ashtabula County. Many secondary roads were closed throughout Ohio on Tuesday. Life returned to normal Wednesday as roads, schools, and businesses opened as usual.

1–2 December 1974
Deep Snow in the North

A record-breaking deep snowfall across northern Ohio on 1–2 December 1974 was one of the most disruptive experienced in Ohio. It began early on the Sunday of Thanksgiving weekend and thwarted thousands of travelers in their attempts to drive or fly home.

Low pressure moving through northern Kentucky on Sunday, 1 December stalled over West Virginia and Pennsylvania on Monday and delivered a long period of heavy snow in Ohio. Depths of fourteen to twenty-four inches extended from Toledo southeastward through Tiffin and Medina to Youngstown (fig. 14).

Temperatures were slightly above freezing during the storm, and warmer locations had less snow and little accumulation. For example, snow depths did not exceed 6 inches at the lakeshore communities of Sandusky and Painesville, where much of the snow melted as it fell. Just inland however, from Tiffin through Medina and Wooster to Akron, Ravenna, and

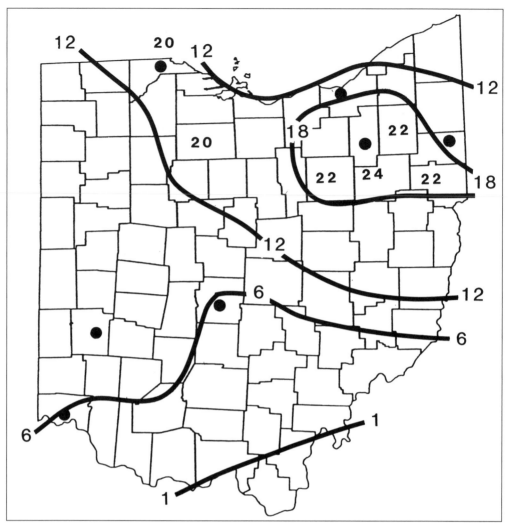

Fig. 14. Snowfall (in inches) during 1–2 December 1974. A total of 24 inches was measured at the Akron-Canton Airport.

Canfield, snowfall was 20 to 24 inches and little melting occurred during the snowfall. Depths exceeded 20 inches and established records at several locations. National Weather Service personnel at Akron-Canton Airport measured 24.3 inches of snowfall Sunday and Monday, with 17.9 inches falling in twenty-four hours. This storm nearly matched the total of 24.6 inches at Akron on 19–26 April 1901, and a depth of 20 inches tied the record set in November 1913.

Nearly all travel was stopped Sunday and Monday in northern Ohio. Deep snow clogged roads, and thousands of stranded cars and trucks prevented plows from clearing highways. State Police tried to shut major roads, including Interstate 75 from Findlay to Toledo, so that tow trucks could remove stuck vehicles and plows could clear the snow away. However, motorists continued to attempt the roads and continued to get stuck. Heavy tow trucks were not available to remove all the large trucks.

Thousands of travelers were put up in churches, schools, fire stations, community halls, bowling alleys, night clubs, roller skating rinks, and homes Sunday night. Motorists who had spent the night stranded in cars along Interstate 75 or Interstate 280 in Toledo were escorted off the expressways Monday morning by police and tow trucks and taken to the Sports Arena, where twenty-five hundred spent the day reading, talking, and waiting to move on, the *Toledo Blade* reported. When the Sports Arena staff ran out of food, additional food arrived from McDonald's restaurants. Six members of a Detroit motorcycle club helped unload supply trucks at the Toledo Sports Arena, and stranded doctors and nurses attended to minor ailments.

Travelers from U.S. 25 and I-75 in Wood County were given shelter, beds, and food at Bowling Green State University, the Wood County Courthouse, and the National Guard Armory. A supermarket delivered peanut butter and jelly to the shelters. Findlay College and churches became temporary homes for those stranded in Hancock County. In the Akron area, the *Akron Beacon Journal* reported one hundred travelers from I-76 spent the night at the Norton Fire Department and fifty motorists and a dog spent the night at the Wadsworth United Methodist Church.

All major airports in northern Ohio were closed for portions of Sunday and Monday. Toledo Airport shut down Sunday afternoon, Akron-Canton Airport was closed Sunday evening, and Cleveland Airport stopped operations at 6:00 A.M. Monday. The major universities of northern Ohio were also closed Monday to remove snow and allow students to return from the Thanksgiving break. Secondary schools were closed for two or three days.

At least a dozen Ohioans died after shoveling the deep, heavy snow. Electric power and phone service were disrupted when heavy snow and strong winds blew down wires and trees. Several buildings collapsed under the weight of snow. Hospitals managed with minimal staffing. Employees could not drive to the hospitals, so those on duty put in long hours at any job needed. Typical was the case at Akron Children's Hospital, where a security guard became the chief cook and the laundry supervisor his assistant.

An editorial in the 3 December 1974 *Akron Beacon Journal* summarized the beauty and peace to be found in the snowstorm. In spite of frustrations to modern life, one "could see magic in tapestries woven in trees, the softness of transformed landscapes and the serenity of a world muzzled by a thick mantle of snow. . . . Strangers who normally lock their doors . . . cheerfully pulled over and opened their car doors to their fellow man. Neighbors pulled on heavy jackets and plunged outside to help free cars from driveways, shovel off buried sidewalks, and to reminisce about other big snows and bad storms and happy times." The paper continued: "We tend to remember the peace that permeates the inconveniences of getting snowed in. We all need times like this from time to time."

28 January 1977
Blizzard of '77

Winter hammered on Ohio during January 1977 like no month ever had. It was the coldest month known in the state in the coldest winter in a century, and natural-gas shortages caused the declaration of a statewide energy emergency. Factories, commerce, and education reeled from closures due to the weather and gas shortages. Much of the nation suffered during this winter. As snowflakes fell in Miami Beach, the national press asked if another ice age was coming.

Severe winter weather in Ohio during January 1977 culminated with a statewide blizzard on Friday, 28 January. True blizzards, with several hours of snow, winds of more than thirty-five miles an hour, and temperatures below 20 degrees, are rare in Ohio. However, January 1977, and January 1978, were notable for their statewide blizzards.

National Weather Service forecasts called for a blizzard warning across Ohio early on 28 January 1977. The cold wave and high winds swept the state at dawn. Temperatures at Toledo fell from 20 to -2 degrees in just ninety minutes and settled to -7 degrees at noon. Columbus thermometers fell from 24 to -3 degrees, and temperatures in Cleveland dropped from 26 to -10 degrees during the day.

The other element of a blizzard, high winds and blowing snow, came with the frigid air Friday morning and continued into Saturday. Only two to four inches of new snow came with the storm, but previous snowfalls had left six to twelve inches of snow over all of Ohio as the blizzard began. Winds of thirty-five to forty-five miles an hour, gusting to sixty, lifted the snow into the air, obscuring visibility and creating huge drifts. These wind speeds combined with midday temperatures of zero to -10 degrees caused wind chills below -50 degrees. The situation was summarized in Saturday's *Cleveland Plain Dealer*: "With factories, schools, and stores closed by the blizzard and natural gas shortages, Greater Clevelanders went home early yesterday to stack the wood and prepare hot drinks for a weekend that could make the rest of this awful winter look like summertime."

It was not an exaggeration. Ohio was shut down by Friday afternoon, and little improvement came until late Saturday. Nearly all schools in Ohio were closed Friday. Most of the state's major airports were closed for several hours Friday and early Saturday. Cleveland Hopkins Airport was shut for nearly twenty-four hours by fifty-mile-an-hour winds and drifts seven feet deep on the runways and landing lights. State roads and secondary highways were closed, and some counties were entirely isolated. Even the Ohio Turnpike was closed for several hours in both directions from Lorain to the Indiana border. Stores, factories, and government offices not already closed by gas shortages were shut down by the blizzard.

Emergencies arose when normal methods of transportation failed entirely during the blizzard. Persons in need of medical attention were put in life-threatening situations. Others were stranded in rural homes without heat, food, or water. Heroic actions performed by the Ohio National Guard, police and fire crews, and hundreds of ordinary citizens saved dozens of lives and gave comfort to hundreds more.

Governor James Rhodes called on the Ohio National Guard with their heavy vehicles and helicopters to rescue stranded persons, provide medical evacuations, and clear roads. Kidney dialysis patients and stroke victims were flown to hospitals in National Guard helicopters. Two National Guard trucks carried ninety-eight schoolchildren home from snowbound Lake County schools. Hundreds of stranded Fayette County residents were airlifted to shelter by National Guard helicopters. These scenes of rescue by the Ohio National Guard would be repeated on an even larger scale just one year later in the Blizzard of '78.

Efforts of rescue and comfort held the death toll to twenty in the blizzard, according to the *Toledo Blade*. In the most dramatic tragedy, five Springfield men died of carbon monoxide in their car stuck along Buckley Road near Fostoria. They were found by snowmobilers Friday evening, the exhaust pipe of their car blocked by a snowdrift.

Even the great high-wire walker Karl Wallenda found the storm frightening. Wallenda, then seventy-two, performed at the Mentor PTA circus on Friday. After his car spun out of control on Route 2 in Lake County, Wallenda was quoted in the *Cleveland Plain Dealer* as saying, "I have never been so nervous on the high wire in my life as I was driving in the blizzard."

Ohio recovered from the blizzard over the weekend, in spite of continued drifting and near-zero temperatures. Airports and interstate highways reopened by Saturday afternoon, and most other roads were cleared Sunday. Businesses, factories, and schools that were not shut by natural-gas shortages reopened on Monday. Only in the snowbelt of Geauga

Fig. 15. A house in Wood County nearly buried after the blizzard of 26 January 1978. (Photograph courtesy of Stephen Chang)

County, where snow was more than two feet deep, did drifted roads keep schools closed another day.

26 January 1978
The Great Blizzard

The worst winter storm in Ohio history struck before dawn on Thursday, 26 January 1978. The Blizzard of '78 continued through Thursday and into Friday. Transportation, business, industry, and schools were closed statewide for two days, with the normal pace of society not returning to the state for five days.

Wednesday evening, 25 January 1978, was relatively quiet in Ohio. Rain and fog were widespread, some freezing rain was falling in the northwest, and temperatures were in the 30s and 40s. Wednesday evening's weather map, however, presented an ominous combination of weather headed for Ohio. A strong winter storm was moving northward from the Gulf of Mexico through Tennessee and Kentucky, bitterly cold air was moving eastward through Iowa and Illinois, and tropical air was flowing north along the Atlantic Coast. Computer models of the National Weather Service forecast a major winter storm over Ohio for Thursday.

The southern storm intensified as it tracked northward, entering Ohio near Portsmouth at midnight and exiting across Lake Erie from Cleveland at 4:00 A.M. Thursday. Records for low atmospheric pressure were already being set Wednesday evening in eastern Tennessee, and more records fell as the storm intensified through Ohio.

Atmospheric pressure of 28.28 inches at Cleveland was the lowest pressure ever recorded in Ohio. This was also the second lowest pressure not associated with a hurricane recorded this century in the forty-eight contiguous states (Blackburn 1978). Other low pressure records included Akron-Canton with 28.33 inches, Youngstown with 28.39 inches, Columbus with 28.46 inches, Toledo with 28.49 inches, and Cincinnati with 28.81 inches (Blackburn 1978). Old pressure records were exceeded by .3 inch or more at most cities.

The rapidly intensifying storm pulled bitter cold air from the west across Ohio on winds of fifty to seventy miles an hour by Thursday morning. These conditions combined with heavy snow and blowing of deep snow already on the ground to cause full blizzard conditions all across Ohio. Blizzard conditions arrived first with the arctic cold front in Cincinnati at 1:00 A.M., reached Dayton an hour later, Columbus and Toledo at about 3:00 A.M., and extended northeast to Akron, Youngstown, and Cleveland by 7:00 A.M. on 26 January.

The arrival of the cold front and blizzard were unmistakable. Temperatures fell thirty degrees in two hours, winds increased to more than 50 miles an hour, and blinding wind-blown snow filled the air. Wind gusts of more than 40 miles an hour continued through most of the day, reaching 69 miles an hour at Dayton and Columbus and 75 at Akron (Blackburn 1978). A wind gust to 82 miles an hour at Cleveland Hopkins Airport was the strongest ever measured in Cleveland. The ore carrier *J. Burton Ayers,* stranded in thick Lake Erie ice off Sandusky, reported sustained winds of 86 miles an hour and gusts to 111 on Thursday morning, according to the *Cleveland Plain Dealer.* Temperatures fell to near zero as the blizzard began and remained near 10 degrees for most of the day. Wind chills were below -50 degrees all day.

Widespread wind damage occurred across Ohio. Thousands of trees and miles of electric and telephone lines were blown down, cutting many important communication links. Countywide electric failures were reported, with a total of about 175,000 homes without power Thursday. About 100,000 homes were still without electricity Friday night, and the effort to restore electric power continued through the weekend. Most home heating failed because electric power was needed even for gas and oil-burning furnaces. Winds also caused structural damage on buildings, blew down barns, broke many windows, and blew down signs. A

Fig. 16. Groceries and other necessities were transported home by sled or snowmobile after the blizzard of 26 January 1978. (Photograph courtesy of the Toledo–Lucas County Public Library)

Fig. 17. Finding your parked car was only half of the problem. It still had to be dug out after the 26 January 1978 blizzard. (Photograph courtesy of the Toledo–Lucas County Public Library)

two-hundred-foot crane was toppled by the wind at the Perry Nuclear Power Plant in Lake County.

Snowfall was difficult to measure during the blizzard due to the strong winds. Official measurements ranged from five to ten inches at most weather stations and up to fifteen inches reported at some sites. The actual depth of new snowfall is of little consequence in a blizzard because the greatest effects of the blizzard are the huge amounts of snow blowing through the air and the drifts of fifteen to twenty-five feet thereby created (fig. 15). Drifts caused roofs to collapse on dozens of buildings.

This blizzard caused the most complete disruption of transportation ever known in Ohio. Maj. Gen. James C. Clem of the Ohio National Guard reported the immobilization of Ohio was comparable to the results of a statewide nuclear attack (Clem 1978). Prolonged blizzard conditions created enormous snowdrifts that stopped highway and rail transportation and isolated thousands of persons. Air travel was stopped for two to three days by low visibility and deep snowdrifts on runways. The almost complete immobilization of Ohio continued through Friday (figs. 16 and 17).

Some highways and airports reopened late Friday or Saturday, but many roads were not passable until Monday, 30 January. State roads remained closed in half of Ohio counties on Saturday. Interstate 75 was closed for three days, and a portion of Interstate 475 near Toledo was closed for six days. Motorists stranded on Interstate 75 near Findlay broke into a truck weigh station for shelter. The entire length of the Ohio Turnpike was closed for the first time in its history. The turnpike was reopened east of Elyria Friday afternoon but remained closed in northwestern Ohio until Saturday. Airports at Cleveland and Toledo reopened Saturday, but schedules were uncertain and delays common. In many communities, a snowplow was parked at each fire station to clear the snow ahead of the fire truck if a fire broke out.

A caravan of nearly seventy semitrailers was stopped Saturday at Van Wert, when state workers plowed a fifteen-foot pile of snow across Route 30 to stop the caravan from proceeding. Highway maintenance crews considered the road impassable, and it was feared the trucks would become stuck in twenty-foot drifts near Delphos. The angry truckers spent the night at the local YMCA, reported the *Cincinnati Enquirer.*

Food supplies were curtailed by closed highways, and shortages of milk, eggs, and bread were reported. State highway patrolmen escorted food trucks from Detroit to Toledo after shortages developed. A Red Cross unit in Springfield bought eighty thousand loaves of bread from a bakery, and National Guard helicopters delivered them to six area cities, where they were given away, two loaves per family. Cargo planes of the U.S. Coast Guard flew thirty tons of government surplus food into Cincinnati for distribution to low-income families. Restaurants that remained open during the blizzard and following days had few customers but stayed busy packing food orders for electric utility workers, stranded factory workers, and police crews.

Ohio schoolchildren are occasionally stranded at school or on buses when highways are blocked by fast-moving winter storms. The early morning arrival of the Blizzard of '78 prevented that from happening in this case. It was obvious in the predawn hours that this was an extraordinary winter storm, and nearly all schools in Ohio were closed Thursday. This timing was fortunate, because a midday arrival of the blizzard would have left thousands of children trapped in schools or on buses. Ohio schools remained closed Friday and did not reopen until Monday or Tuesday of the following week.

Governor James Rhodes activated the Ohio National Guard Thursday morning, opening armories for public shelter and calling the Guard for duty. By 28 January, 5,005 men and women of the Guard were on state active duty. Most could not get to armories until Friday but were then pressed into long hours of duty with heavy equipment clearing roads, assisting electric utility crews in getting to fallen wires, rescuing stranded persons in emergencies, and transporting doctors and nurses to hospitals. They used nearly 800 National Guard vehicles, including four-wheel-drive trucks, ambulances, graders, and bulldozers.

The Ohio National Guard also performed heroic airborne rescues. Forty-five National Guard helicopters flew twenty-seven hundred missions across Ohio and rescued thousands of stranded persons, many in dire medical emergencies. They were assisted by army helicopters from Fort Campbell, Kentucky, and by the Eighty-third U.S. Army Reserve Command at Columbus.

Helicopters worked around the clock for three days on medical evacuations, rescue missions, and resupply. Kidney dialysis patients were flown from their homes to hospitals in Columbus, Chillicothe, and Dayton. National Guard helicopters delivered twenty-five persons to hospitals in Toledo on Saturday. A private helicopter and crew from Dana Corporation also worked long hours delivering fifteen persons to Toledo hospitals. National Guard helicopters were still surveying rural sections of Ohio six days after the blizzard to assure that families were safe.

President Jimmy Carter declared a federal disaster in Ohio Thursday evening and dispatched three hundred federal troops of the Twenty-seventh Engineer Battalion, Eighteenth Airborne Corps, based at Fort Bragg, North Carolina. The federal troops were air-lifted to Toledo Express Airport Sunday morning with arctic gear and sixty pieces of heavy equipment, including front-end loaders, bulldozers, personnel carriers, and fuel tankers, to clear roads and rescue persons in north-western Ohio.

The U.S. Army Corps of Engineers was charged with hiring private contractors to open snow-clogged roads across the state where no other assistance was available. The corps issued 1,662 contracts to clear thirty-one thousand miles of Ohio roads at a cost of $8 million.

Thousands of volunteers with snowmobiles and four-wheel drives responded to pleas from police statewide to deliver medicine and take doctors and nurses to hospitals. In Cincinnati, 150 four-wheel drives showed up to help the Red Cross. Toledo Edison crewmen were carried to inaccessible trouble spots by volunteers on snowmobiles. Ohio radio stations abandoned regular programming to issue storm information and serve as communication links when electricity and telephone communication failed and highway travel was blocked.

The Miami University basketball team was stranded in Vandalia early Thursday morning returning from a game at the University of Toledo. The team slept in the city jail and then walked to the Franklin Nursing Home, where they assisted the 150 residents during the blizzard. The Miami basketball players fed residents, shaved men, mopped floors, and emptied trash, according to the *Portsmouth Times*.

The death toll of fifty-one reported in the January 1978 issue of *Storm Data* made this one of the deadliest winter storms known in Ohio. There were twenty-two deaths among persons walking outdoors leaving their stranded vehicles or homes without heat. Another thirteen people were found dead in stranded automobiles, thirteen died in unheated homes, and two persons were killed in buildings that collapsed under the weight of snow. On the positive side, there were no highway traffic deaths in Ohio for the weekend of 27–29 January, as many highways were closed.

Agricultural losses in Ohio totaled $73 million in dead livestock, lost production, lost crops, and property and equipment damage. More than 90 percent of Ohio's 12 million pounds of daily milk production was dumped Friday when storage and transport was not available. Farmers dumped another $1 million of milk Saturday. Milking machines on modern dairy farms could not be used where electricity had failed. A Pickaway County farmer lost five thousand chickens when blizzard winds blew the roof from the building.

Comparisons to the other great blizzard of this century, on 12 January 1918, show colder temperatures in the 1918 storm, similar snowfall, and perhaps lighter winds than in 1978. But there was less overall disruption of society in 1918 than in the Blizzard of 1978. Modern society may be more vulnerable to severe winter storms, in spite of our advanced technology. We depend heavily on our cars for transportation and on electricity for the ordinary routine of life. Thomas Seliga, head of the Atmospheric Sciences program at Ohio State University in 1978, was quoted in the 28 January 1978 *Portsmouth Times:* "Just 30 years ago I think weather certainly affected us seriously but we were not nearly as socially affected. . . . We were individually able to cope with it because we did not depend on electricity in the home for our heat . . . and we didn't depend on going to the grocery store as we do today."

6–9 April 1982
Winter in April

April has a reputation for severe weather, as winter and summer clash over the Heartland. This was never clearer than during the first ten days of April 1982, when storms swept the entire country and brought severe winter weather to Ohio that was outstanding even for April. This stormy period across the United States was dramatized in a wonderfully illustrated children's book, *The Big Storm,* by Bruce Hiscock (1993).

The first storm dumped sixteen feet of snow in the Sierra Nevada Mountains of California on 31 March, causing an avalanche that killed six persons, and then produced tornadoes in the southern states on 3 April. This storm brought temperatures of 65 to 75 degrees and high winds to Ohio on Saturday, 3 April. The *Columbus Dispatch* reported six persons were injured when a tornado destroyed two mobile homes in Knox County and a Boy Scout died when a tree fell on his tent near Cincinnati. Winds on 4 April blew the roof from a Williams County motel and caused power outages across western Ohio.

The first storm pulled cold air across the central United States and set the stage for a second storm, which was gaining strength over Oklahoma early on 5 April. The second center followed an "Interstate 70 path" from St. Louis through Columbus to Pittsburgh early on Tuesday, 6 April. Severe winter storm conditions enveloped northern Ohio.

Wind-driven snow began late on 5 April and continued through most of 6 April. Accumulations of 6 to 12 inches were typical across far northern Ohio, with 2 to 4 inches in central counties. Cleveland's 11.2 inches was a twenty-four-hour record for April, exceeding the old record of 7.6 inches on 8 April 1957. Strong northeast winds of forty-five to fifty-five miles an hour caused blowing and drifting of snow, which, combined with temperatures near 20 degrees, made 6 April 1982 a day of "winter in April" for northern Ohio.

The *Toledo Blade* reported interstate highways in northwestern Ohio were open but only one lane was cleared in each direction. All other roads were closed by drifting snow in the northwest. Toledo Express Airport and Cleveland Hopkins Airport were each closed for more than twelve hours during the storm. Schools were closed all across northern Ohio, and classes were canceled at Bowling Green State University and the University of Toledo. Hospitals were staffed with the help of volunteers who transported doctors and nurses with four-wheel-drive vehicles.

Northeast gales across Lake Erie created a wind setup in the western basin. Lake waters rose 30 inches in nine hours at Toledo, reaching 575.8 feet above sea level at 11:00 P.M. on 5 April. This lake level was *10 feet* above the level recorded during southwest gales two days earlier and just 9 inches below the record lake level set on 14 April 1980. Roads were flooded in the Point Place neighborhood of Toledo. Coastal communities of Long Beach and Sand Beach in Ottawa County were evacuated when the lake rose and waves began battering homes. Freezing water from breaking waves and spray cased homes in tons of ice. The *Toledo Blade* reported on 10 April that damage in Ottawa County was estimated at $2.3 million, with twelve homes destroyed and four hundred homes and twenty-five businesses damaged.

Bitter cold air poured across Ohio on 7 April in the wake of the snowstorm. Lows of 8 degrees at Toledo and 14 degrees at Columbus established records for the month of April in those cities. The coldest temperatures in the state were 1 degree at Hoytville and 2 degrees at Wauseon in northwestern Ohio. These readings approached the state cold record for April of -1 degree set near Mansfield on 1 April 1964.

Snowfall for the winter of 1981–82 totaled 100.5 inches at Cleveland after the snowstorm of 6 April. This was the snowiest winter in more than a century of weather history at Cleveland, exceeding the previous record of 90.1 inches in the famous winter of 1977–78. (This 1981–82 record was exceeded by a new record, 101.1 inches in the winter of 1995–96.)

27–29 February 1984
Leap Year Political Storm

The Leap Year Storm that became a political storm was forecast well in advance for Ohio. In the 27 February 1984 *Columbus Dispatch* forecasters called for the "winter's worst snowstorm for the next three days." They were right. Significant snows covered all but extreme southern Ohio, and strong winds created near blizzard conditions.

Forecasters recognized the ingredients for an Ohio snowstorm—strong low pressure passing through the Gulf Coast states, a cold trough of low pressure in the middle troposphere (seventeen thousand feet) over the Great Plains, and a jet stream directing the Gulf low toward the northeast. Under these conditions, the Gulf low strengthened into a powerful

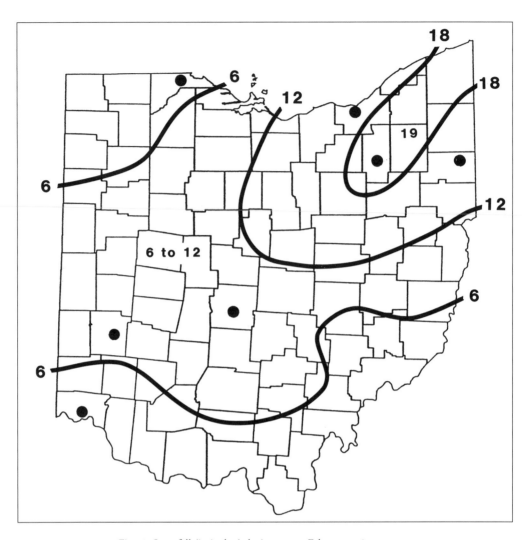

Fig. 18. Snowfall (in inches) during 27–29 February 1984.

winter storm as it moved slowly from Georgia to West Virginia, Pennsylvania, and into northern New York during 27–29 February.

Snow began at Cincinnati near dawn on Monday, 27 February and covered the state by midafternoon. Winds of thirty to fifty miles an hour and temperatures in the 20s created near-blizzard conditions in central and northern Ohio. The storm continued through Monday night and Tuesday, finally ending in the northeastern part of the state on Wednesday.

Snowfall exceeded six inches over most of Ohio, and a band of more than ten inches fell from Dayton and Celina in the west, through Columbus, and into north-central and northeastern Ohio (fig. 18). Fifteen to 20 inches blanketed portions of the northeast. Warmer air over extreme southern counties caused some of the precipitation to fall as rain, so snowfall totals there were only two inches.

The Leap Year Storm of 1984 established several February snow records for the National Weather Service office at Akron-Canton Airport, where the three-day snowfall was 18.3 inches. A twenty-four-hour total of 12.3 inches broke the previous February record of 8.1 inches set in 1976. The maximum depth of 17 inches on 29 February exceeded the 15-inch February record set in 1977.

Although depths were greatest in the northeast, conditions were worst in north-central Ohio. Here the storm of 27–29 February 1984 rivaled the Blizzard of '78 for disruption of transportation and services. Strong winds, 6 to 12 inches of snow, and the open landscape led to deep drifts and impassable roads. Emergencies were declared in Erie, Sandusky, and Ottawa Counties, where all driving was prohibited. Traffic was snarled on the Ohio Turnpike by dozens of accidents and stalled vehicles between Sandusky and Toledo.

A political storm brewed in Cleveland as a result of the winter storm. Mayor George Voinovich had recently laid off many city employees, including snowplow drivers, after voters refused a tax increase in a 7 February election. If city streets were not cleared quickly, the mayor said, it was because the city no longer had the resources to handle a sixteen-inch snowfall. The *Cleveland Plain Dealer* reported that city councilman Dennis Kucinich accused the mayor of not doing enough to clear the deep snow from city streets. Kucinich and councilman Jay Westbrook, both Democrats, claimed that Republican Voinovich hoped that poor snow removal would convince voters that the additional tax revenue was needed and would improve chances of a tax hike in the next election. One suburban commuter, noting the change from clear suburban streets to snow-clogged Cleveland streets, was quoted in the *Cleveland Plain Dealer:* "It happens every time it snows, not just now, when Cleveland professes to be poor."

31 March 1987
Cleveland's Second Greatest Snow

A double punch of spring snowstorms hit Ohio in 1987—the first on 30–31 March and the second on 4 April. The first began in southwestern Ohio on the afternoon of Monday, 30 March as low pressure moved northeast from Georgia through the southern Appalachians. The snow spread across central and northeastern Ohio Monday evening with 4 to 5 inches of wet snow in just a few hours. Lightning and thunder accompanied the snow in some areas.

Heavy snow continued in portions of northeastern Ohio Tuesday morning as the storm center continued northward across central Pennsylvania. By the time the snow ended, a March record 16.5 inches had fallen at Cleveland Hopkins Airport. This was the second heaviest twenty-four-hour snowfall on record at Cleveland, exceeded only by the 17.4 inches that fell during the great storm of 9–11 November 1913.

Snowfall during 30–31 March totaled 6 to 8 inches in a band from Cincinnati and Dayton through north-central Ohio. Nearer to the storm track, 10 inches fell north of the Ohio Turnpike from Lorain east to Youngstown, with 16 to 17 inches in Cuyahoga and Geauga Counties. Schools and offices were closed on Tuesday, 31 March in the region of heaviest snowfall. Wet clinging snow broke tree branches and power lines in southwestern Ohio, causing numerous power failures Monday night. Cleveland Hopkins Airport closed Tuesday morning as the snowfall approached 16 inches. Most schools, businesses, and factories in the Cleveland area, including three Ford factories, were also closed Tuesday.

Cleanup of the snow was hard on city, county, and state snow-removal equipment. The snow cover at Cleveland weighed about 13 pounds per square foot, so an eight-foot plow would have to move 275 tons of snow per mile of roadway. The *Cleveland Plain Dealer* reported that 18 of 78 Cleveland city trucks and half of the 160 city plows were broken by Wednesday from battling the record spring snowfall.

This deep snowfall would have been welcomed a month earlier by skiers, but 75-degree temperatures the previous weekend had ended the winter sports season. Boston Mills Ski Center had phone inquiries all day about skiing, but Ohio ski areas could not open due to the mud below the deep snow.

4 April 1987
Record Snowfall for Columbus and Akron

The second heavy spring snow in five days fell across eastern and central Ohio on Saturday, 4 April 1987. The first snowstorm on 30–31 March laid a blanket of snow six to ten inches deep from the southwestern counties across central Ohio into the northeast, with more than sixteen inches at Cleveland. The track of the second storm on 4 April was about one hundred miles east of the first storm, so the heaviest snow fell in central and eastern Ohio.

Snow began in south-central Ohio on Friday, 3 April as the low pressure storm center causing the snow developed over Georgia. The storm center moved to eastern Virginia by the morning of 4 April and then drifted into West Virginia during the day. Snow moved northward across Ohio and intensified Friday night and through the day Saturday.

Snowfall totals from this storm were reminiscent of the deep April snowfall in 1901. Most of the eastern half of the state, except the lakeshore, received more than 12 inches of snow, and the region from Canton through

Zanesville to Athens was covered with 17 to 20 inches. Two of Ohio's large cities established records for twenty-four-hour snowfall during this storm. Akron-Canton Airport reported 20.6 inches of snow, exceeding the old record of 17.9 inches set on 1 December 1974. A twenty-four-hour snowfall record was also established at Columbus, where 12.3 inches exceeded the previous record of 11.9 inches on 6 January 1910.

Temperatures during the snowfall were between 30 and 34 degrees, and, typical of spring snows, it clung to trees and power lines, which broke under the load. Wind gusts to forty miles an hour added to the burden and caused some drifting. Approximately 154,000 Ohio homes lost electricity Saturday, according to the *Zanesville Times Recorder.*

The weight of the snow exceeded the strength of some roofs. The *Akron Beacon Journal* reported a thirty-by-fifty-foot section of the roof at Mentor Mall in Lake County collapsed Saturday evening. Eastern Ohio's 10 to 20 inches of snow cover on 4 April contained 1.5 to 2.5 inches of water. This melted quickly over the next three days, causing streams to rise, but with unfrozen soil and no heavy rain, major flooding was averted.

19 October 1989
Record Autumn Snowstorm

A deep pool of cold air over the eastern Midwest led to a record early snowfall across western and northern Ohio in 1989. Rain changed to snow early on Thursday, 19 October and accumulated for much of the day. Southwestern and west-central Ohio received 4 to 6 inches (fig. 19). Two to 3 inches fell in the northwestern region and in a band from Mansfield through Akron to Youngstown. The 5 inches measured at Dayton exceeded the 2.8-inch record total for the month of October set in 1925.

Wet snow on 19 October 1989 caused hundreds of trees and large limbs to break, with many landing on power lines. As a result, about 160,000 Ohioans were without electricity Thursday. About 100,000 of these were customers of Cincinnati Gas and Electric, and 15,000 Dayton households still had no power Thursday night. Dayton motels that had electricity were filled and rentals of portable generators, kerosene heaters, and chain saws were brisk. Falling trees and wires also cut power to 10,000 Toledo Edison customers.

Numerous traffic accidents occurred on the slushy roads. The Montgomery County road superintendent said the snow "caught us with our pants down," as they normally got snowplows and trucks ready for snow removal on 26 October. Nevertheless, twenty-two county trucks were quickly outfitted for plowing and spreading salt on overpasses in the

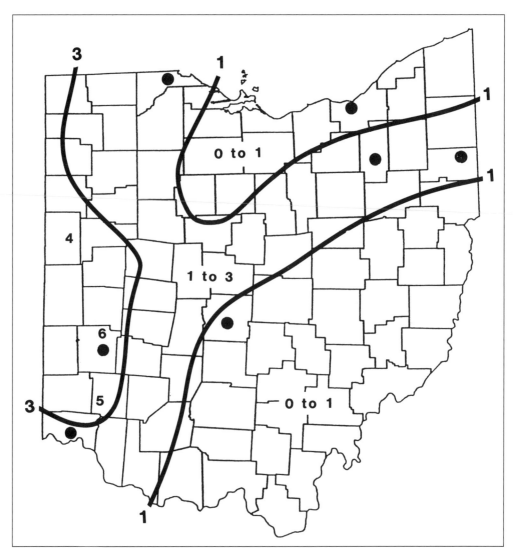

Fig. 19. Snowfall (in inches) during 19–20 October 1989, establishing records for early snowfall in southwestern Ohio.

Dayton area. Gale warnings and eight-foot waves during the October snowstorm disrupted the first day of duck hunting along the Lake Erie shore. One boat capsized and hunters were rescued by the Coast Guard after ninety minutes in the water.

24 February 1990
A Deadly Whiteout

Morning forecasts on Saturday, 24 February 1990 indicated that a change of weather was on the way. Winter storm watches were upgraded to winter storm warnings for the afternoon, but few Ohio residents anticipated the ferocity of the reversal from Friday's 60-degree temperatures.

Light snow, south winds, and temperatures near freezing prevailed through the morning and early afternoon of 24 February. An arctic cold front that forecasters had watched all morning began to sweep into Ohio's western counties early in the afternoon. Fronts are boundaries between air masses, and it often takes many hours for a new air mass to make itself evident after a front passes. This front, however, was as distinct as any could be. Its passage was marked within minutes by a shift in wind direction from south to northwest, a rapid increase in wind to more than fifty miles an hour, and much colder temperatures.

The snow that accompanied the colder air mass behind the front was not heavy—new snowfalls were only two to four inches at most sites. Strong winds kept the snow in the air and, as temperatures dropped to the teens, visibility was poor and roads became icy and difficult to drive. As the deadly combination of cold, wind, and snow became evident, blizzard warnings were issued for northeastern Ohio late in the afternoon.

Scattered power and phone outages were reported as wind blew lines down, but Ohio's interstate highway traffic suffered most under these rapidly changing winter conditions. Motorists struggled in whiteout conditions as the roads iced over and visibility was cut to a few yards. Chain-reaction accidents littered the interstates. The deadliest accident occurred on northbound Interstate 75 near Tipp City, where sixteen cars and two trucks collided and several were consumed in fire. Nine motorists died, six were admitted to hospitals, and more than fifty others were treated for injuries.

13 March 1993
On the Fringe of the "Storm of the Century"

Forecasters watching a storm system over the Gulf of Mexico on Friday, 12 March 1993 correctly predicted a major winter storm for Saturday across the eastern United States. Bitter cold air held tight over the Canadian border states while record warmth covered the south (Forbes, Blackall, and Taylor 1993).

Blizzard warnings were issued from Georgia to New York Saturday morning as the storm center left the Gulf and entered northwestern Florida and southern Georgia. The storm was exiting from the subtropical jet stream and entering a strong polar jet stream at that point and intensified rapidly (Forbes, Blackall, and Taylor 1993).

The storm continued to intensify as it moved across North Carolina to New Jersey by Saturday evening. Low pressure records were established at

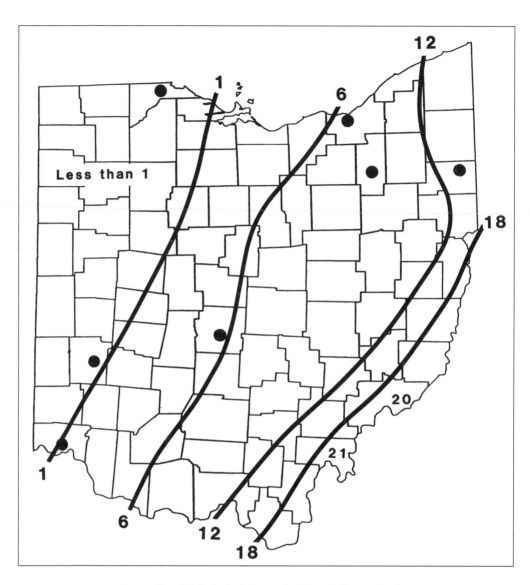

Fig. 20. Snowfall (in inches) during the blizzard of 13–14 March 1993.

several coastal cities along the track, exceeding some previous records set by hurricanes. (The lowest, 28.38 inches at White Plains, New York, did not match the Ohio record low pressure of 28.28 inches set at Cleveland during the blizzard of January 1978.)

Winds of more than eighty miles an hour were measured along the East Coast from Myrtle Beach to Boston, and a foot of snow fell along a wide swath from Alabama to Maine. More than thirty inches of snow fell in the mountains of North Carolina, West Virginia, Maryland, Pennsylvania, and New York. Weather historian David Ludlum (1993) called this a "great atmospheric upheaval" and a "rare superstorm," surpassing all other winter storms of the twentieth century in its extreme dimensions.

Ohio was at the western fringe of this record-setting storm. Blizzard warnings were issued for the eastern two-thirds of Ohio early Saturday morning. The intense storm over the southeastern states caused strong, cold, north winds in Ohio, and moist Atlantic air was pulled across the Appalachians, causing heavy snow in Ohio's eastern counties.

The Ohio River communities from Ironton up through Gallipolis, Marietta, Martins Ferry, and Steubenville received eighteen to twenty-two inches of snow from this storm (fig. 20). Typical of East Coast storms, the heavy snowfall reached only as far as central Ohio. More than six inches fell east of a Lorain-Columbus-Hillsboro line, but less than one inch fell at Toledo, Findlay, Dayton, and Cincinnati. Wind gusts reached forty-five to fifty miles an hour across eastern Ohio and temperatures remained in the teens through the day on Saturday. Deep snow combined with these strong winds and cold temperatures created true blizzard conditions in the eastern two-thirds of Ohio.

Impacts of the blizzard in Ohio were less severe than with previous blizzards because of its occurrence on a Saturday and the location of heaviest snow along the less-populated Ohio River counties of the southeast. Excellent forecasts for blizzard conditions issued by the National Weather Service several hours in advance of the storm also helped minimize the storm's effects.

However, blizzard conditions and deep drifts blocked most roads and closed smaller airports in eastern Ohio. The Ohio Turnpike was closed east of Youngstown and all highway travel into Pennsylvania was blocked. Governor George Voinovich declared a "statewide weather emergency" Saturday, and several counties banned all highway travel. Deep drifts were not cleared from Ohio River towns until Monday.

26 December 1993
Christmas Buried in the Snowbelt

Strong northwest winds and temperatures hovering near 10 degrees created persistent lake-effect snow squalls from the lakeshore in Lorain and Cuyahoga Counties inland across Cleveland and its eastern suburbs to Geauga County and southern Lake County. Snow began Christmas Day 1993 and continued through Sunday, 26 December.

Deep snow is not unusual in Ohio's snowbelt, but the depths in this event were exceptional. More than twenty inches fell in a band from downtown Cleveland east into southern Lake County and most of Geauga County. Snowfall of twenty-four inches was recorded in Mayfield, Pepper

Pike, Mentor, Chardon, and Burton. At Kirtland the new snow was measured at twenty-eight to thirty-three inches, with some reports of forty inches, according to the *Cleveland Plain Dealer*. In Geauga County, the heart of the snowbelt, twenty-four to thirty inches fell in Chester Township and twenty-eight to thirty-six inches fell in Middlefield.

Secondary roads were impassable Sunday, and even some interstates were closed for several hours. Deep drifts and stranded cars forced the closure of Interstate 271 from Bedford Heights north to Interstate 90 at 1:00 P.M. One lane of the three-lane highway was reopened in each direction at 4:30 P.M. Other interstates remained open but were snow covered, and travel was slowed by blowing snow. Routes 6 and 306 through Geauga County were closed Sunday and many Geauga County roads remained blocked Monday morning.

Malls and other stores were nearly empty the day after Christmas, normally a busy shopping day. Impacts of the snow were lessened by its weekend occurrence. Traffic was light Sunday and roads were plowed efficiently. Highways were reopened and life was back to normal in most areas Monday morning, as temperatures fell to zero. Geauga County officials maintained a snow emergency on Monday, allowing the cleanup to proceed.

17 January 1994
A Southern Snowfall

January 1994 was an "old-fashioned" winter month in the upper Ohio Valley, with two exceptionally deep snowfalls followed by record cold on 19 January. Snowfall on Tuesday, 4 January totaled twelve to twenty inches from Marietta to Steubenville, and a state of emergency was declared in four counties. Ohio National Guard troops moved into the river communities to remove snow and assist stranded persons. Strong winds caused power failures to about half of the sixty-two thousand residents of Washington County during the snowstorm.

A greater snowfall arrived on Monday 17 January. This storm left six to ten inches across nearly all of Ohio but, again, the deepest snow was along the Ohio River. Portsmouth received twenty inches of snow, and thirty inches was reported at Lucasville. Twenty-two to twenty-four inches fell in Adams County, with fifteen inches reported in Piketon and Jackson. Snowfall intensities of five inches an hour were measured at Chillicothe.

Highways were closed Monday by deep drifts and abandoned cars in extreme southern Ohio. Nine south-central counties declared snow emergencies Monday morning, banning all but emergency travel and essentially shutting down the region. Temperatures were cold, so the snow did not stick to trees and there was no widespread disruption of phone and electric service. Businesses assisted residents who could not get out in the deep snow. The pharmacy at Kroger's in Portsmouth delivered medicine to customers who were unable to travel, according to the *Portsmouth Daily Times*. Southern Ohio Medical Center employees were picked up and delivered to the hospital in four-wheel-drive trucks and rescue squads.

Major roads were reopened Tuesday, but rural highways of southern Ohio were blocked and families remained snowbound. The effort to clear side roads continued into Wednesday. Schools were scheduled to be closed Monday for Martin Luther King Day and remained shut all week in southeastern counties by the deep snow and temperatures below -25 degrees.

The 216th Engineering Battalion of the Ohio National Guard continued working through the week with eight Humvees, two field ambulances, a grader, and heavy trucks in Scioto County. They assisted in clearing roads but also worked twelve-hour shifts in emergency medical evacuations of snowbound persons.

Snowfall during January 1994 totaled 45.5 inches at Newport and 33.3 inches at Marietta. These were among the heaviest monthly snowfalls ever recorded in Ohio outside of the Lake Erie snowbelt. At the Parkersburg Airport, five miles south of Marietta, snowfall totaled 40 inches during January 1994. This was a record for any month, exceeding the old record of 35 inches in November 1950. The January snowfall was more than had fallen in the entire past two winters combined in southeastern Ohio.

8 February 1994
Hundreds Injured in the Southwest

In a winter that left Cincinnatians weary from extreme cold and snow, an ice storm crippled the region and caused extensive injuries. Freezing rain began early on Tuesday, 8 February 1994 and continued into Tuesday night, when thunderstorms illuminated the ice storm. The *Cincinnati Post* reported that nearly an inch of ice had accumulated in southwestern Ohio, pulling down trees and power lines and causing extensive transportation problems.

Interstate highways were open through the storm, but portions of interstates had to be closed for an hour or more as multiple-vehicle accidents were cleared away. Dozens of side roads were closed by accidents, stalled traffic, or fallen tree limbs. The *Cincinnati Enquirer* reported there were so many emergency calls for accidents and falls that all city fire trucks and ambulances were utilized and fire division scout cars were pressed into service as makeshift ambulances.

About half of the schools in southwestern Ohio were closed Tuesday, and nearly all shut down Wednesday. Cincinnati public schools decided at 4:00 A.M. Tuesday to open schools after receiving a forecast that temperatures would rise above freezing by 7:00 A.M. However, freezing rain continued all day and twenty-two school buses were involved in minor accidents.

This ice storm caused a large number of injuries, primarily from falls on icy sidewalks, steps, and parking lots. *Storm Data* reported 1,568 persons were injured in Ohio, mostly due to falls and sledding accidents. More than 100 persons were admitted to hospitals with serious injuries, most commonly injured backs and fractured hips, elbows, and ankles.

CHAPTER THREE

Cold

Temperatures below freezing are expected in Ohio from November to April. The coldest temperatures of winter come with arctic air masses from northwestern Canada. This bitter air is moderated as it approaches Ohio by the longer days in these latitudes and by the warmer waters of the Great Lakes. Winter air masses pass over one or more of the Great Lakes before they enter Ohio, unless the cold air arrives from the west or southwest. Although Lake Erie freezes over in most winters, the other lakes usually retain extensive open water.

The coldest temperatures occur with a fresh cover of snow, clear skies, and calm winds. These conditions are met a few days after a low pressure storm system has deposited snow across the landscape and arctic high pressure has arrived from the northwest and centered itself over Ohio. Low temperatures under these conditions may vary several degrees within a small area. Rural areas are usually colder than urban sites, and valleys become colder than ridges as the dense cold air settles into the lowest terrain. Thus, a thermometer on a downtown building may show -3 degrees when it is -20 ten miles away on a rural valley farm.

In a typical winter, temperatures will fall below zero on two to five days within a few miles of Lake Erie and along the Ohio River (Schmidlin 1990). The coldest temperature of winter is usually near -5 degrees in these milder regions (fig. 21). The remainder of Ohio, away from Lake Erie and the Ohio River, can expect five to fifteen days of subzero temperatures each winter, and the coldest temperature of winter is usually -8 to -14 degrees in these regions. About one year in ten in Ohio, the temperature will fall into the range of -15 to -25 degrees (fig. 22).

The coldest temperatures on record are -15 to -20 degrees along Lake Erie and the Ohio River and -20 to -30 degrees inland. Ohio's coldest temperatures are not in the north, as one might expect, but in the valleys of central and southern Ohio, where temperatures below -30 degrees have

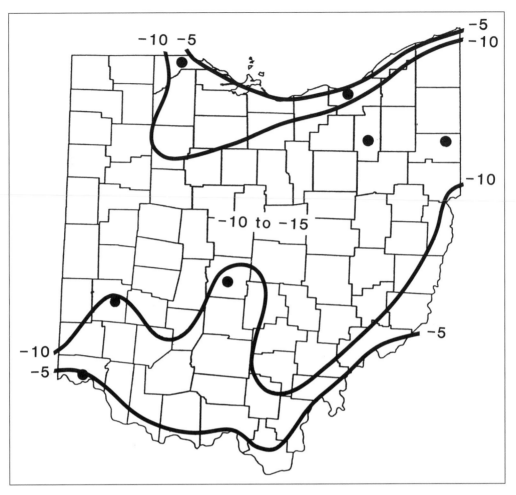

Fig. 21. Extreme minimum temperature (in degrees Fahrenheit) with a 50 percent annual probability of occurrence (from Edgell 1992). This temperature is the median coldest temperature of winter for the period 1961–90.

been recorded. Hilly terrain in these areas promotes the accumulation of extremely cold air in valleys, and the moderating influence of the Great Lakes is less than in the north.

Exceptional cold waves can also develop during the warm season in Ohio if the arctic air mass arriving from the north is uncommonly cold, perhaps by developing for several days over the still snow-covered Canadian arctic and moving southward into Ohio so quickly that it does not have time to warm. Unusual summer cold is promoted by very dry air and ground surfaces. The surface loses heat very rapidly overnight under these conditions and, even if the days are warm, record cold may develop by dawn. Thus, the ideal condition for record summer cold is a northern air mass with dry air settling over a dry surface.

Frost may occur on grass or crops even if the "official" temperature in a shelter five feet above the ground is 36 or 37 degrees. Without any

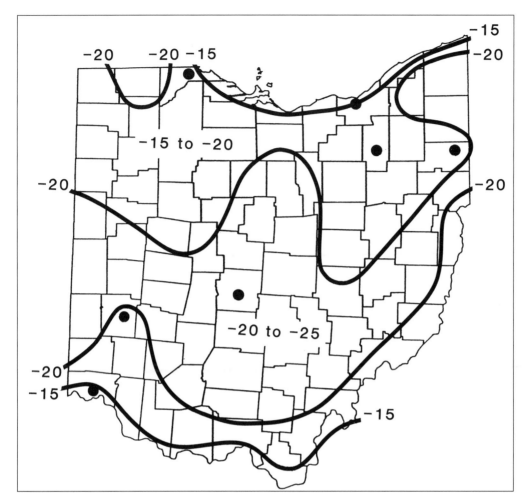

Fig. 22. Extreme minimum temperature (in degrees Fahrenheit) with a 10 percent annual probability of occurrence (from Edgell 1992). This temperature may be expected, on average, every ten years.

covering, these exposed surfaces cool a few degrees below the air temperature. Low spots in the terrain, known as "frost pockets," will be a few degrees cooler than hills on clear, calm nights and may have freezing temperatures when nearby thermometers show temperatures well above freezing.

This chapter describes the outstanding cold events in Ohio and the impacts on society through two hundred years of history.

8 January 1797
Early Cold at Cincinnati

Settlements were established at three sites near present-day Cincinnati in the fall of 1788, just a few months after the first white settlement in Ohio was established at Marietta (Knepper 1989). There were no organized systems of weather recordkeeping in those days, but diaries occasionally gave glimpses of unusual weather events, and some medical doctors and scientists kept detailed weather records.

Dr. Daniel Drake made daily measurements of Cincinnati weather from 1806 to 1813, and measurements were taken by various professors at College Hill beginning in 1814. Unfortunately, much of the data from College Hill from 1814 to 1834 were lost. Complete weather observations started in 1835 in the lower portion of the city by professors at Woodward College (later Woodward High School).

Weather historian David Ludlum (1966, 1968) provided a summary of early winters in the Ohio Valley from the publications of Daniel Drake and others. Ludlum (1966) showed the winters of 1785 to 1791 were generally mild, the winter of 1791–92 was cold, and the winters of 1792 to 1796 were again rather mild.

The winter of 1796–97 was "exceedingly rigorous" in Ohio, according to Ludlum (1966), with arctic cold from early December to the end of January. The Ohio River was frozen for thirty days or more, and mail boats were interrupted by ice for eleven weeks. The diary of Winthrop Sargent indicated a temperature of -18 degrees in Cincinnati on 8 January 1797 (Devereaux 1919), a temperature that was "a record up to then and unsurpassed there until the Great Arctic Outbreak of February 1835" (Ludlum 1966).

1816
Cold Summer

The weather from 1811 to 1817 was uncommonly cold in the eastern United States and culminated in the famous cold summer of 1816 (Alexander 1924, 709). Crop failures were reported in Europe and North America (Appleby 1980). Repeated summer frosts and snow in New England killed most crops and initiated "Ohio Fever" for a westward migration in 1817 (Ludlum 1976).

In Ohio, the summer of 1816 did not reach the legendary status attained in New England, although frequent cold weather prevailed. Data for Cincinnati showed summer 1816 to be 1.5 degrees cooler than normal but not unusual for the early nineteenth century (Alexander 1924, 313). The year 1816 was "remarkably cold and dry" at Cincinnati, with the lowest winter temperature at -8 degrees. The last spring frost at Cincinnati in 1816 was 15 May. This was fairly typical, and frosts occurred as late as 25 May in several years of the 1830s.

10 February 1818
Record Cold at Marietta

A combination of deep snow and extreme cold made the winter of 1817–18 the most severe in Marietta and the upper Ohio Valley since the region was settled in 1788 (Ludlum 1966). Marietta weather observer Dr. Sam Hildreth reported 26 inches of snowfall in a great storm on 3–4 February, and snow was reported 20 inches deep near present-day Akron.

Arctic air followed the storm and dropped temperatures to -20 degrees on 9 February and -22 degrees on 10 February at Marietta (Ludlum 1966). This temperature was not matched at Marietta until -22 degrees was recorded again in February 1899. To the west in the Scioto Valley, Chillicothe reported -21 degrees on 10 February 1818.

8 February 1835
Great Arctic Outbreak

Winter 1834–35 had been mild up to early February, when one of two great arctic outbreaks of the nineteenth century began. The temperature reached -19 degrees on 8 February 1835 at College Hill in Cincinnati, and three readings gave an average of -6 degrees for the day (Ludlum 1968). Alexander (1924) listed an official low of -17 degrees at Cincinnati for this month. Dr. Sam Hildreth's thermometer fell to -15 degrees at Marietta, and all old peach trees in the area were killed. February remained cold through the end of the month to give a monthly average 9 degrees colder than normal at Marietta (Ludlum 1968).

The February 1835 low temperature of -17 to -19 degrees at Cincinnati was not matched until February 1899, and a lower temperature was not officially observed until -20 degrees was recorded at Lunken Airport in January 1963. The present record for Cincinnati is -25 degrees recorded 18 January 1977 at the National Weather Service site at Greater Cincinnati Airport across the river in Kentucky. This is a more rural site than the early Cincinnati weather stations of the nineteenth century and it is possible that a rural site near Cincinnati may have recorded a temperature of -25 degrees or colder in February 1835.

1855–56
Siberian Winter

"This is a Siberian Winter!" proclaimed the *Columbus Daily Ohio State Journal* on 9 January 1856 as temperatures in central Ohio plunged under -20 degrees. Although it is difficult to compare the temperatures of 1856 with twentieth-century cold waves because of differences in thermometers, shelters, and observation practices, extremely cold mornings later in the nineteenth century were often compared to the cold of 1856, thus establishing this winter as a benchmark for cold in Ohio.

Chemist L. Groneweg was a weather observer for the Smithsonian Institution in Germantown, fifteen miles southwest of Dayton. He reported the snow that fell on Christmas 1855 was still on the ground on 3 March 1856, a rare event today in Dayton. Groneweg (1856) wrote that the average temperature for January 1856 was 15.4 degrees, and the average for the three winter months, December to February, was 21.9 degrees at Germantown. This was 8.7 degrees colder than normal and, to make comparisons Ohio pioneers could understand, Groneweg observed this was "nine degrees colder than the winter in Berlin, Prussia, and only five degrees warmer than the winter in Petersburg, capital of Russia."

Persistent cold marked the period from Christmas 1855 until 10 February 1856, but extreme cold, which was to be remembered for three generations, occurred on 9 January and 4 February 1856. On 8 January temperatures were below zero all day and there was a "piercing wind." The *Daily Ohio State Journal* reported temperatures at dawn on Wednesday, 9 January were -17 degrees in Columbus with reliable reports of -20 degrees. The *Daily Ohio State Journal* called this the "coldest night on record in this vicinity, since our remembrance," and a letter to the paper from D. C. Pearson, a weather-watcher near Columbus, called this the "coldest day known in Ohio."

Groneweg (1856) measured a 9 January temperature of -26 degrees on the Smithsonian thermometer at Germantown, and a mean of -14 degrees for the day. Lows of -18 to -27 degrees were reported in Cincinnati. John Lea, quoted in the 11 January 1856 *Daily Ohio State Journal,* claimed 9 January in Cincinnati was colder by 2 degrees than any other day of the past sixteen years. Daily temperature measurements for January 1856 taken by T. G. Wormley at the Esther Institute in Columbus showed a minimum of -24 degrees on the ninth. The mean for the month was 14.6 degrees at the Esther Institute.

Extreme cold returned on Monday, 4 February with temperatures at some sites even colder than in January. Groneweg measured -31.4 degrees at Germantown, and the *Columbus Daily Ohio State Journal* reported -27 degrees at the Xenia railroad depot. Other thermometers at Xenia showed -29 degrees, Springfield reported -21 degrees, and Dayton -21 degrees, although the *Daily Ohio State Journal* acknowledged that "thermometers vary considerably as they are more or less exposed."

Problems caused by the extreme cold included disruption of railroad schedules by engines that would not run and rails that snapped in the cold. Fires became an even greater hazard than usual as it became nearly impossible to deliver water through hoses to fight a fire. A cabinet and chair factory burned in Columbus when temperatures of -16 degrees froze water in the hoses.

5 June 1859
The Big Frost

The remarkable summer frost of June 1859 was referred to as the "Big Frost" well into the twentieth century in Ohio. Temperature data are sparse for this early date, but we can judge the degree of cold by the extent of crop damage.

Initial reports of frost damage were more pessimistic than reality later supported. The *Cleveland Plain Dealer* of 6 June declared, "Sad and sickening are the reports from the country to-day." Wheat, corn, potatoes, and fruit were damaged to some degree throughout northern Ohio and in scattered sections in the south. Fruit, especially the peach crop, was damaged in most sections. Apples the size of hickory nuts were frozen solid in Geauga County. Vegetable gardens were also frozen throughout the state. The frost at Delaware made a "clean sweep of corn and potatoes." Gardens and vineyards escaped damage along the Ohio River at Ripley, but all corn and vegetables were killed a few miles back from the river. Weather observer Dr. Sam Hildreth measured a temperature of 33 degrees at Marietta and reported that a fog in the city held temperatures three to four degrees above that measured on surrounding land. No fruit was damaged in Toledo, but fruit was killed to the west in Washington Township and to the east at Elmore.

A June morning white with frost caused blackened and wilted vegetation and dire predictions of crop failure and ruined vegetation; however, several days of warm sunshine led to optimistic revisions of initial predictions of disaster. The *Wooster Republican* first reported great damage to wheat, corn entirely damaged, and fruit almost wholly destroyed. A week later it reported that enough wheat remained in Wayne County "for home consumption and some to spare, corn is fast recovering and will be a good crop, fair crop of apples."

Wheat was a staple crop of the day, for both home use and cash sales. Initial reports of widespread freezing of wheat created a scare of shortages and "famine prices." In the final analysis however, not more than 20 percent of the Ohio wheat crop was destroyed by frost. The *Wooster Republican* reported that because 20 percent more wheat was sown in 1859 than recent years, an average crop was expected statewide. The 21 July 1859 issue of the *Canfield Republican Sentinel* also reported the wheat crop would be good in Ohio, despite the Big Frost, due to the large acreage planted. The greatest wheat damage occurred north of the National Road (near present Interstate 70) and east of a Columbus-Sandusky line. This region produced about 28 percent of Ohio's 25-million-bushel wheat crop in the 1850s.

Although the Big Frost of 5 June 1859 was not an economic disaster to Ohio, it is clear that widespread damage to a variety of crops occurred. Some farmers lost their entire crops of wheat, corn, potatoes, fruit, or vegetables. It was a significant summer freeze that was carried in the memory of Ohioans for several generations.

1 January 1864
Cold New Year's

An extraordinary weather event's standing as a legend may be judged by the length of time that later events are compared to it. The cold New Year's of 1864 stood the test of time very well—Ohio cold waves were compared to this event well into the twentieth century.

The last week of 1863 had been dreary and dismal, an almost incessant rain falling, in Ohio. The *Columbus Daily Ohio State Journal* reported that the mud in Columbus streets "was fathomless." Temperatures on New Year's Eve were in the 40s with rain. However, a strong northwest wind entered the western counties just before midnight to usher in the coldest New Year's ever known in Ohio. It has been called the "New Year's Blizzard" and was later compared to the blizzard of 12 January 1918 (Alexander 1924, 714).

The temperature at Toledo fell from 42 degrees at 9:00 P.M. on 31 December to -14 degrees at dawn the next day, a fall of 56 degrees in twelve hours, and it remained at -8 degrees at noon on 1 January. The average temperature for New Year's Day was -10 degrees at Cincinnati (Alexander 1924, 328). The coldest reading in Ohio was in the far northwest, where it was -23 degrees in Williams County (Alexander 1924, 714). The "wind blew almost a hurricane." The *Toledo Blade* reported, "This, we believe, is the coldest weather ever experienced on the Maumee."

Trains were late, and the bitter cold interfered with New Year's festivities. "Calling [visiting] was almost entirely out of the question" due to the storm. The loss of many stored apples and potatoes was feared, "as many of the best cellars were entered by the penetrating force of the cold."

25 January 1884
Coldest Morning in a Bitter Month

This was a cold, snowy month through much of the Heartland. Three cold waves swept Ohio and snow was unusually deep in portions of the state. A 20-inch snowstorm hit eastern counties on 8 January, and 22 inches of snow on the ground at Marietta was the deepest there since 1818. The 26 January 1884 *Dayton Daily Journal* reported that the "sleighing season" of six weeks was the longest since 1857–58.

The first cold wave began on 3 January, and on the fifth, Bellefontaine, with -27 degrees, had their coldest morning since New Year's 1864. The cold wave peaked on 6 January when the average minimum temperature among all Ohio stations was -16 degrees. Wauseon was coldest with -25 degrees, and the low of -20 at Findlay was the coldest since 1855. Temperatures of -17 degrees were reported from portions of Toledo, and livestock froze to death in the city. The low of -20, recorded by G. W. Harper in the Cincinnati suburb of Mount Auburn, was the coldest since records began there in 1856.

A remarkable lesson on the urban heat island and exposure of thermometers occurred during the second cold wave on 21 January. A surprising temperature of -31 degrees was recorded by observer William Alwood at Ohio State University, while just three miles away the official Weather Bureau thermometer in downtown Columbus registered only -4 degrees. The *Columbus Daily Ohio State Journal* reported the -31 temperature did "not seem to have been regarded with any very high degree of credulity." However, a thermometer on the farmhouse at the university also registered -31, and -30 degrees was recorded at the chemical lab.

The Weather Bureau thermometers in the city were suspended in a closed box, with an open bottom, high on the side of a building. The warmer temperature on the city thermometers was explained by heat rising from the building and being trapped in the thermometer box. The city was generally warmer than the rural districts due to the city being "continuously covered by smoke."

The most frigid air settled over Ohio during the third cold wave on 25 January, when the average low temperature was -20 degrees among all the stations in Ohio. Lows of -14 to -28 degrees at Dayton, -24 at Norwalk and Piqua, -28 at Urbana, Springfield, and Celina, and -30 at Eaton, Xenia, and Junction (Paulding County) were the coldest known in those towns. The coldest official temperatures on 25 January were recorded in northwestern and west-central Ohio, with -32 degrees at Wauseon and -34 at Sidney. T. C. Mendenhall, director of the Ohio Meteorological Bureau, stated, "It is believed that these temperatures are entirely unprecedented in the history of the state."

The low of -34 degrees on 25 January 1884 at Sidney was a state record at the time and was not exceeded in Ohio until 10 February 1899. The descent to the record at Sidney was described in the Friday, 25 January *Sidney Journal.* They reported that 24 January was a snug winter day, and the light snow made excellent sleighing. Last evening the sky was cloudless. At 10 o'clock the thermometer registered 16 below zero and half an hour later 18 below. The cold kept steadily increasing, and at daylight the four thermometers furnished by the State Weather Bureau to G. S. Harter registered 33 1/2 degrees below zero—the coldest ever recorded in Sidney. Trees, houses and roofs cracked like pistols all night in their contractions. . . . To-day is intensely cold, but the air is perfectly still. The morning of January 25, 1884 stands unparalleled in rigor for this part of Ohio.

9 July 1895
Record July Cold

A cool, dry July 1895 produced several days with temperatures in the upper 30s at Ohio weather stations. Lows of 34 degrees at Norwalk on 4 July and at Auburn (Geauga County) on 9 July established the state cold record for July. That record has not been exceeded, but it was tied on 1 July 1988 by a 34-degree temperature near Caldwell. Several other Ohio weather stations reported temperatures of 35 to 37 degrees during early July 1895. As usual, the temperature was a few degrees cooler at the ground surface than on the official thermometers and frost was reported in low-lying areas. Frost damage to crops was localized, however and was not important statewide.

Because Ohio was in the grip of severe drought during July 1895, the air, soils, and vegetation were dry. This condition promotes rapid heat loss at night and very cool night temperatures. A similar drought situation existed during July 1988 and contributed to record low minimum temperatures in Ohio and the Midwest (Schmidlin 1992).

10 February 1899
Coldest Temperature Known in Ohio

This cold wave was one of the most extensive and severe ever experienced in the eastern United States. Hundreds of all-time records were set and many of these stand today. Perhaps most impressive was the number of state cold records set in this arctic blast, including Ohio with -39 degrees, that have not been eclipsed nearly a century later.

The cold wave began in Ohio on Wednesday, 8 February as a powerful storm moved up the Atlantic coastline. This storm pulled a vast region of intensely cold air out of arctic Canada and across the entire eastern United States. By 11 February, the barometric pressure had risen to 31.42 inches at Swift Current, Saskatchewan, as the cold dome of high pressure moved southward across the Plains.

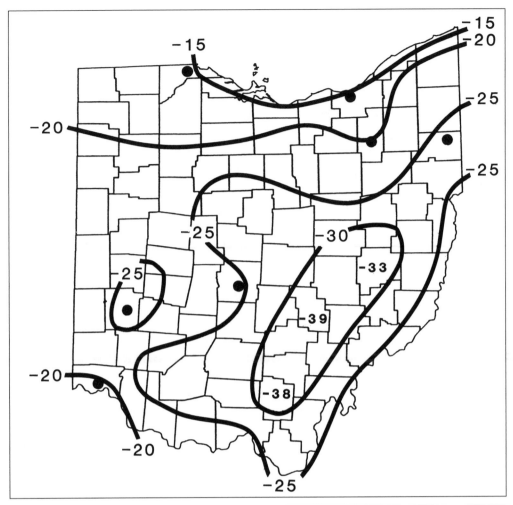

Fig. 23. Low temperatures (in degrees Fahrenheit) on 10 February 1899. A temperature of -39 degrees at Milligan, Perry County, is the coldest ever recorded in Ohio.

Temperatures dropped below zero across Ohio by early afternoon on 8 February, and records began to fall by dawn on 9 February. The coldest air, however, was still centered to the west, where it was -46 degrees at Huron, South Dakota, and -63 degrees at Norway House, Manitoba. In Ohio, early morning readings on 9 February fell to -14 at Cleveland and -12 at Youngstown. Weather Bureau thermometers in downtown Columbus reported -13 degrees, and it was -17 in the suburbs. At the top of the Government Building in Cincinnati it was -16 degrees, but the Cincinnati Observatory reported -26 degrees.

A February cold record that still stands today was established by the Weather Bureau in downtown Toledo with -15 degrees on 9 February. The high temperature was only -2 on 9 February, and unofficial reports showed morning lows of -25 around Toledo. With little snow cover, clear blue ice on the Maumee River was the thickest since 1883. A low of -26 degrees was noted at the Children's Home north of Springfield. Longtime Marietta weather observer Dr. Samuel Hildreth reported that -25 degrees in that city was the coldest he had seen. Up the Muskingum River from Marietta, an unofficial thermometer showed -41 degrees at Clifton on 9 February.

Most of Ohio remained below zero all day on 9 February, an event that would not be seen again in many communities until January 1970. The cold actually intensified during 9 February and into the morning of 10 February as the core of the arctic air moved over the Great Lakes region. Republic, Michigan, cooled to -50 degrees, and White River, Ontario, dropped to -54 degrees.

Bitter cold early on 10 February included -15 degrees at Cleveland, -19 at Akron, -23 at Youngstown, -26 at Alliance, and -27 at the southern tip of Ohio in Ironton. The coldest readings came from the southeastern counties, far from the warming effects of the Great Lakes, in hilly terrain where the coldest air settled into sheltered valleys (fig. 23). Schools closed in Athens when readings of -30 degrees were noted in the city and -36 degrees at other communities along the Hocking River. On the rail line in the Muskingum Valley between Marietta and Zanesville, unofficial temperatures of -32 to -38 degrees were reported. The unofficial thermometer at Caldwell showed -40 degrees, and there were reports of frozen thermometers (mercury freezes at -39 degrees; alcohol is used in official thermometers). Several people reported -42 degrees at Jackson. The *Zanesville Daily Signal* reported that the "cold was frightfully intense."

It was on the morning of 10 February 1899 that the coldest temperature ever officially measured in Ohio occurred. S. B. Eveland was the observer at the small community of Milligan, east of New Lexington in Perry County. The official thermometer at Milligan fell to -39 degrees on 10 February, setting a cold record for Ohio that still stands. Two other official Weather Bureau stations, Jackson and McArthur, almost matched Milligan when they fell to -38 that morning. Prior to February 1899, the Ohio cold record was -34 degrees at Sidney on 25 January 1884. The coldest temperature in Ohio since 1899 was -37 degrees at Milligan in January 1912 and at Logan on 19 January 1994.

The cold wave of 1899 continued into 11 February, although temperatures rose above zero by midday. Effects of the cold wave were widespread, but the state seemed to cope quite well. Frost-bitten ears, noses, and feet were numerous. Natural-gas and water pipes were frozen in many areas. Communication was hampered as telephone and telegraph lines cracked and fell. Trains and electric streetcars ran late. Work stopped in the oil fields around Bowling Green, and gas lines in the city were frozen shut, cutting heat to many residents. Factories and businesses closed in many cities, and East Liverpool potteries were shut down when the clay froze and steam pipes burst.

Dozens of tow boats were frozen in the Ohio River. Boats on the Ohio above Marietta held 7 million bushels of coal when the cold wave trapped them. There was no ice on the Ohio at Cincinnati due to the high stage of water, but steam rose off the water "with such density as to obscure all objects," according to the *Cincinnati Enquirer,* and navigation was suspended to avoid accidents. Wildlife also suffered in the cold. The *Columbus Dispatch* reported flocks of quail were found frozen to death along roads near Chillicothe. Near the core of the coldest air at Zanesville, "the cracking noises of buildings and trees caused by the contraction made the night hideous," according to the *Zanesville Daily Signal.*

Suffering was greatest among the poor. Charitable organizations distributed coal, food, and bed clothes and the mayor's office at Toledo was besieged all day "by half-frozen begging for food." At Cincinnati, where the Weather Bureau thermometer 150 feet above the street showed -17 degrees, the *Cincinnati Enquirer* reported corner stores were crowded with people waiting for streetcars. Only at the noon dinner hour and quitting time were people seen on downtown Cincinnati streets.

Some persistent activities in society, such as religion and advertising, could not be stopped by the cold. Reverend Wharton of Coal Run baptized three of the faithful through a hole cut in the Muskingum River ice in temperatures of -16 degrees late on 10 February. The *Columbus Dispatch* carried an advertisement for the Lazarus department store with a headline, "Cold snaps and snappy bargains, Nature furnishes one, We furnish the other," accompanied by prices for overcoats, gloves, and footwear. Three other elements of society profited—coal dealers, gas dealers, and plumbers. A festive mood prevailed as temperatures rose above zero on Saturday, 11 February. The *Zanesville Daily Courier* reported, "Many people celebrated the return of warmer weather by getting out their sleighs, and all day the merry jingle of bells was heard all over the city."

The degree of cold in southeastern Ohio on 10 February 1899 is unchallenged, as readings of -35 to -40 degrees were common, but some doubt may be cast on the Milligan record. Small changes in the exposure of thermometers can lead to large changes in the temperatures recorded. A note in the observer's record for 28 November 1901 states, "Changed the mounting of max and min thermometers as per instructions." While we cannot know the nature of the improper mounting prior to 1901, the station at Milligan reported very large daily ranges of temperature both before and after 1901. For example, on 30 September 1897 a low of 32 degrees was followed by a high of 92 degrees, and the next day a low of 35 degrees was followed by a high of 93 degrees. On 3 October 1910, a low of

35 and high of 91 were reported, and on 25 February 1914 a low of -23 was followed by a high of 43—a daily range of 66 degrees! However, giving testimony to the quality of the weather station at Milligan, a government form completed on 26 May 1906 showed the station had "standard max and min" thermometers in a cotton region shelter facing north with the floor four feet above the ground. Authorities of the day, such as William Alexander, did not question the integrity of the record at Milligan. It is therefore appropriate that we consider this the coldest official temperature ever measured in Ohio.

4 January 1904
Cold Kills Peach Orchards

The winter of 1903–4 brought an intense, persistent cold that had not been experienced in more than twenty years in Ohio and would not be seen again until the winter of 1976–77. It stands as Ohio's third coldest winter since 1883.

The bitter cold of 1903–4 reached a climax on Monday, 4 January after a snowstorm two days earlier. Temperatures fell below -20 degrees in a broad band across the central portion of Ohio, with the coldest readings -30 at Milligan (Perry County), -28 at Orangeville (Trumbull County), -27 at Cambridge, and -25 at Garrettsville and New Bremen. (Cambridge observer Samuel Mehaffey recorded 70 degrees on 22 January to give a range of 97 degrees in one month!) Lows at Cleveland and Sandusky along Lake Erie were near -5 degrees, but thermometers showed -14 to -17 degrees a few miles inland at Wellington, Vickery, and Rocky Ridge.

Schools reopening from Christmas break on 4 January delayed their start a few hours to allow the buildings to heat up. Much coal was burned in Ohio cities in 1904 and there were no modern pollution controls. Cold still air allowed an accumulation of these pollutants. The *Columbus Dispatch* reported, "There was practically no air stirring, the atmosphere was heavy and the smoke and steam hung down over the streets and wrapped the tall buildings in a heavy veil. One could scarcely see a square ahead of them and the air was so filled with gases and smoke that it was almost as stifling as though a terrible fire was raging throughout the city."

Cold weather in January 1904 is credited with "finishing" peach trees along Lake Erie in Ottawa County, as reported in the March 1905 issue of *Climate and Crops: Ohio Section.* In fact, the causes of extensive killing of peach orchards were complex, including extremely cold temperatures, deeply frozen ground, and the ill health of some orchards due to San Jose scale disease and poor management.

It was inevitable that the unusually cold winter of 1903–4 would invite comparisons with earlier winters. Wauseon weather observer Thomas Mikesell wrote in the January 1904 issue of *Climate and Crops: Ohio Section,* "Much has been said this winter that we are having an 'old fashioned winter' meaning a steady cold one." He listed the winters of 1842–43, 1855–56, 1872–73, and 1880–81 as being consistently cold with snow cover for two or three months.

However, these old fashioned winters, Mikesell wrote, "were never the rule, but the exception, and were as rare as those that were very warm." Later writers would describe winter 1917–18 as old-fashioned. Ohioans today remember the winters of 1976–77 and 1977–78 as old-fashioned, the snow and cold weather lasting for months. These types of winters remain the exception rather than the rule in Ohio, as Mikesell pointed out in 1904.

13 January 1912
Coldest January Temperatures

Winter 1911–12 began slowly, as mild autumn temperatures persisted through December. However, bitter cold air swept into Ohio during the first week of January and the wintry pattern lasted into February. January 1912 was one of the coldest months known to that time, and it stands now as the fourth coldest January in Ohio since 1883, exceeded only by the Januarys of 1918, 1940, and 1977.

From 4 to 16 January was among the coldest periods known in Ohio, rivaling even the cold of February 1899. Several cold waves during this period pushed the average temperature for these thirteen days down to 10 degrees at Cincinnati. The first cold wave on 4 January brought winds of forty-eight miles an hour at Columbus and temperatures falling to zero by midnight. On Sunday, 7 January temperatures barely climbed above zero and coal deliveries were made all day to satisfy demand for home heating.

The cold of 1912 was most intense on the morning of 13 January (fig. 24). Much of Ohio cooled to below -20 degrees, with temperatures as low as -30 in many eastern and southern communities, including New Waterford, Garrettsville, Cambridge, Amesville, Frankfort, and Haydenville. Among official government thermometers, the coldest temperature in Ohio that morning was -37 degrees at Milligan in Perry County. This temperature stands as the coldest January temperature ever recorded in Ohio, although it was matched by -37 at Logan in January 1994. Milligan also holds the all-time cold record for Ohio, -39 degrees, set in February 1899. Two unofficial thermometers showed -40 degrees on 13 January 1912 at Chandlersville (Muskingum County).

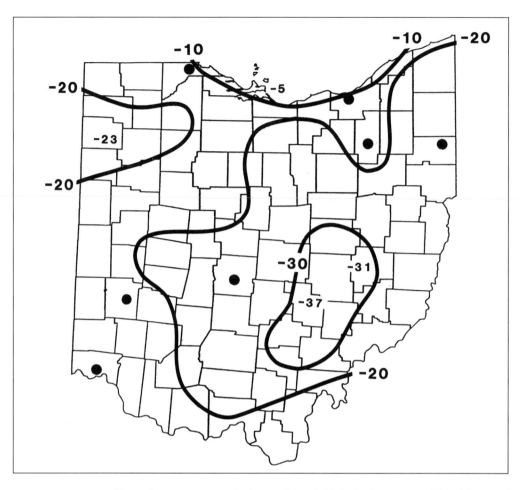

Fig. 24. Low temperatures (in degrees Fahrenheit) during January 1912. The minimum of -37 degrees at Milligan is the coldest ever recorded in Ohio during January, although this was matched at Logan in January 1994.

Large differences in temperature were noted within short distances due to the effects of cities, Lake Erie, or elevation. The Cleveland Weather Bureau thermometer atop the Society Bank Building showed -8 degrees, while farther from the lake in the rural eastern suburb of Gates Mills it was -31 degrees. The Weather Bureau thermometer in downtown Columbus was -5 degrees, while it was -23 degrees three miles away at Ohio State University. Similarly, the low recorded by the Weather Bureau atop the Nicolas Building in downtown Toledo was -3 degrees, but other parts of the city recorded -10 to -18 degrees, and it was -21 in Bowling Green.

Elevation was also important, as lower sites showed colder temperatures than those on hilltops on a clear, calm night. At Hiram, a hilltop station in Portage County, the low was -10 degrees, but three miles away and 255 feet lower at Garrettsville, it was -30 degrees. Two stations at Philo were 268 feet apart in elevation—the higher site was -7 degrees, while the valley site was -27 degrees the same morning (Smith 1912b).

The cold of January 1912 produced widespread effects. Trains were late statewide for several days due to extreme cold and snow. Coal was in short supply in Cleveland by 13 January. The *Columbus Ohio State Journal* reported that hundreds of people without heat were sheltered in Columbus churches. At Springfield, where it was -26 degrees, coal merchants were "reaping a harvest" and gas supplies were short. It was so cold in Summit County that the ice harvest on area lakes was stopped.

The 15 January 1912 *Columbus Ohio State Journal* reported the first auto crossing of frozen Lake Erie from Port Clinton to Put-in-Bay on 14 January. B. Weller of Cincinnati, Ezra Brockford of Put-in-Bay, and F. Gernhard of Port Clinton made the twelve-mile crossing in less than two hours. Their transportation was a Mitchell auto. Large cracks in the ice were bridged with planks, and deep snowbanks were dug out for their passage. The date and success of their return trip was not noted.

1917–18
Old-Fashioned Winter

Winter 1917–18 brought the coldest December and coldest January known in Ohio up to that time, records that stood well into the twentieth century. Persistent cold and frequent snowfall led to comparisons with winters of the mid-nineteenth century, and the description of 1917–18 as an "old-fashioned winter." Reviews of this unusual winter from the national perspective were given by Day (1918) and Brooks (1918a).

Snowstorms struck Ohio during October 1917 to give a chilly preview of the upcoming winter. December averaged 21.4 degrees across Ohio, exceeding the 22-degree average of 1872 to become the coldest December since at least 1854, as reported in the December 1917 issue of *Climatological Data—Ohio Section.*

Some of the coldest December temperatures ever recorded in Ohio occurred in the wake of a snowstorm that blanketed the Ohio Valley on 7 December 1917. Deep snow in southern Ohio promoted development of extremely cold air as arctic high pressure settled over the region on 9–11 December (Brooks 1918a, 1918b). This pattern was seen again recently when an Ohio Valley snowstorm was followed by record cold during 17–20 January 1994. Low temperatures in southern Ohio on 11 December 1917 fell to -23 degrees at Hillsboro, -26 degrees at Waverly, and -27 degrees at McArthur. Residents of Peebles, where it was -31 degrees, awoke to the coldest temperatures in the state that morning. This remains as the coldest temperature recorded during December in Ohio since -32 degrees was measured at Wauseon in December 1884.

The second December cold wave had its origins with some of North America's coldest weather: -71 degrees the day after Christmas, the coldest reading ever taken in the Northwest Territories of Canada. As this air slid south, temperatures along the Ohio River plunged to -24 degrees at Ironton on 30 December and -23 degrees at Batavia on 3 January.

The core of this extraordinary winter came during January 1918, with record cold, record snowfall, and a severe blizzard. In these respects, this month was similar to January 1978. Meteorologist William Alexander, writing in the January 1918 *Climatological Data—Ohio Section,* observed, "The month of January, 1918, has made for itself in Ohio, at least, a very permanent place in the memory of the present generation and will not be forgotten soon, if ever. It is safe to say it satisfied to the last degree the longings of the most fastidious for an 'old-fashioned winter.'"

The statewide average temperature during January 1918 of 14.9 degrees was 3 degrees colder than in cold January 1912. A colder month was not experienced in Ohio until January 1977 (11.9 degrees). The cold spell from 8 to 23 January 1918 "prevailed without interruption and with great severity," according to Alexander, and was the longest and severest cold the state had experienced.

For most weather stations in northern Ohio, the coldest temperature of the month came during the severe blizzard on 12 January. Temperatures fell to -10 to -18 degrees, with winds blowing at forty to sixty miles an hour. Toledo weather observer W. S. Currier noted that 12 January was "a day long to be remembered" as having "more suffering than during any single storm for many years." Temperatures fell below -15 degrees again in central and southern Ohio on 20 January, with the lowest, -28 degrees, recorded at Kenyon College in Gambier and at Summerfield (Noble County).

After one more cold wave in early February, a sharp reversal of weather patterns brought warm air across Ohio during the second week of February and ended the old-fashioned winter of 1917–18. The weather reversal brought storms and cold weather to the western United States, where drought and warmth had prevailed during the Heartland's cold winter. This bitter winter was followed by extreme summer heat in Ohio. August 1918 was the hottest in thirty-one years, temperatures reaching 110 degrees in Athens County and 109 degrees at Wauseon.

Aside from the blizzard of 12 January 1918, the severe winter of 1917–18 had wide impacts on the eastern and central United States. Wartime shortages were exacerbated by the cold. Delivery of coal was hampered by deep snow and record cold, which slowed mine operations and delayed rail and river-barge traffic. The *Toledo Blade* reported more than two hundred schools were closed across Ohio in late November for lack of coal.

Short supplies of coal continued in the severe cold of December. The Lucas County "fuel committee" reported the county needed 105 railcars of coal during the first week of the month, but only 67 cars had arrived. All Ohio cities were short on coal. The greatest suffering was "among the tenement districts of the cities," according to the *Toledo Blade.* There were novel ways of dealing with the fuel shortage—a probate judge in Upper Sandusky sentenced two men to cut eighty-five cords of wood to relieve the fuel shortage at the Wyandot County Infirmary.

Public gatherings were banned in Napoleon schools, churches, pool halls, and lodges as of 10 January, according to the *Napoleon Northwest News,* to preserve fuel and stop the spread of chicken pox and smallpox. With the coal supply short, the Napoleon light and water plant shut down each night, cutting off electricity to the city after 8:30 P.M. Federal fuel administrator Harry Garfield ordered "workless Mondays" to begin 21 January across the eastern United States and to continue through February to save gas and coal. Fuel deliveries during late January were limited to railroads, public utilities, government buildings, ships, and manufacturers of food. Mild weather in February alleviated most of the suffering brought on by this record cold winter.

25 December 1924
Holiday Chill

> "With snow uttering squeaky protests under foot and wheel, a starry sky and a temperature that added zest to a moderate southwest wind, a more ideal Christmas eve was never experienced in Toledo and vicinity."

So began Christmas 1924, as described in the *Toledo Blade,* the coldest Christmas known up to that time in central and northern Ohio. This holiday chill was not generally exceeded in Ohio until the frigid Christmas of 1983.

The *Toledo Blade* warned on 24 December that Santa was delayed by a cold wave gripping the West with temperatures as low as -65 degrees at West Yellowstone, Montana. By Christmas morning the temperatures fell into the range of -10 to -15 degrees in central and northwestern Ohio. Highs reached only about 10 degrees in the north on Christmas afternoon. The *Toledo Blade* reported that "intense suffering was the experience Thursday by all exposed to the extreme cold." Every coal company in Toledo was busy to capacity Christmas Eve filling an "avalanche" of orders from residential customers. There were scores of frozen water pipes, overheated furnaces, and stalled cars.

In spite of the record cold, Ohioans seemed to enjoy the wintry nature of the holiday. "The Christmas spirit glows through the freezing atmosphere," reported the *Columbus Dispatch,* and Toledo was said to have "old-time Christmas weather." Winter sports were available to a degree to which Ohioans were not accustomed. The sports section of the *Toledo Blade* reported:

> The few ski runners the city boasts enjoy a minor thrill as they scoot down the gentle slopes, which Toledoans call, by courtesy, "hills." Owners of bob sleds go in search of hills that will provide a ride. Ice boats have been put in shape for the season. Hockey enthusiasts have laid out rinks on the Maumee near the Maumee River Yacht Club. The first thing we know the blare of horns and tinkle of sleigh bells will be heard along roads long monopolized by automobiles, and a sled full of young folks, deep in straw and blankets, will slide past. The present weather is the first real winter we have had in a long, long time. Zero temperatures and plenty of snow was Toledo's portion of Christmas time in once-upon-a-time days, but of late milder weather has prevailed.

A drama unfolded on the Lake Erie ice late Christmas night. Dr. H. L. Sowash, the only physician on the Erie islands, was gravely ill at Put-in-Bay. A phone call to Pool Hospital at Port Clinton asked Dr. G. M. Riley to come to Put-in-Bay to save Sowash. Two island mail carriers, Lee Miller and Morris Arndt, left South Bass Island on foot and walked five miles in subzero cold across the ice to Catawba Island, guided only by a light on the Catawba dock. There they met Riley at midnight and quickly left for the return trip guiding the doctor to South Bass Island. The mail carriers were experienced in crossing lake ice, but a night trip was a new adventure. The South Bass Lighthouse was "pressed into service for their special benefit." They carried an iron-sheeted boat behind them in case the ice broke and arrived safely at 1:45 A.M.

15 July 1930
Midsummer Frost

In the middle of the driest July and the driest year in Ohio history, a cold wave dropped temperatures to record levels on Tuesday, 15 July. Temperatures in the 90s were pushed eastward by a strong cold front on 13 July and replaced by afternoon temperatures in the chilly 60s on the fourteenth. Lows Tuesday morning dropped into the 40s in Ohio's cities, but rural areas were a few degrees cooler. According to the *Columbus Dispatch,* "A slight frost was reported in some of the outlying districts, but no damage to crops was reported."

Frost damage occurred elsewhere, however. The Ohio section of *Climatological Data* reported that waist-high corn was frozen at Mt. Vernon, where the official low was 35 degrees, just one degree from the July cold record for Ohio. Frost also occurred at Cadiz Junction, Harrison County, where roofs were white with frost and leaves and straw on the ground were frost-covered.

This record 1930 summer cold wave in the midst of a hot, dry July is not as surprising as it may seem. Dry summer conditions promote temperature extremes, both hot and cold. Because the landscape has little water, it has a small capacity to store heat and therefore changes temperature rapidly. A similar condition prevailed in July 1895 and July 1988.

Heat swept back into Ohio and the eastern United States within days of the 1930 summer cold wave. Mt. Vernon rose to 87 degrees the day after the frost and to 104 degrees on 20 July.

23 January 1936
Intense January Cold

The most severe cold in Ohio since 1918 came in the wake of a major snowstorm on 22–23 January 1936. In many places, the cold of Thursday, 23 January 1936 was not matched again until January 1963. This cold wave ushered in a long period of persistent cold in Ohio. Meteorologist William Alexander wrote in the February 1936 issue of *Climatological Data* for Ohio that "the 30 day period ending on February 19 is believed to have been the coldest period of that length of record."

Arctic air swept Ohio during the day on 22 January, with temperatures falling from the 30s at dawn to near -10 degrees by evening. Cooling continued overnight, so that lows on the twenty-third were the coldest since January 1918 or, in some cases, since February 1899. Edgell (1992) called this the ninth greatest Ohio cold wave of the 1900–1988 period.

Low temperatures on 23 January were generally in the range of -15 to -20 degrees across Ohio. The coldest, as usual, came from the valleys of southern Ohio. Here, far from the moderating influence of the Great Lakes, cold air pooled into valleys and official temperatures fell to -27 degrees at Peebles and -30 degrees at McArthur. Ohio's warmest air during this cold wave was along the shore of Lake Erie, where heat from the lake moderated the bitter cold to near -12 degrees. The cold continued into Friday, 24 January with lows of -10 to -20 degrees and noon temperatures near zero. Some moderation on Saturday gave highs near 15 degrees, but another cold wave moved across the state on Sunday, 26 January and lows were below -10 degrees again on Monday. Appropriately, a three-day meeting of the Ice Manufacturers of Ohio and Michigan convened in Toledo on 27 January with the temperature at -5 degrees. Coal mines in southeastern Ohio, closed by deep snowdrifts on 23 January, reopened with a high demand for coal in Ohio. Deliveries, however, were delayed by the bitter cold and by drifts that remained on rural roads for many days.

Daily low temperatures remained below freezing in Ohio from 16 January until 23 February. For much of this time, daily high temperatures were also under the freezing mark. Among the colder stations, Wauseon registered nineteen days of zero-degree weather. A final cold wave on 19 February sent the temperature to -17 degrees at Newark and Peebles. This was followed by rapid warming, and within a week temperatures were over 55 degrees in northern Ohio and near 70 degrees in the south. Ironically, this severe winter was followed by a summer of extreme heat. In July 1936, temperatures rose to 110 degrees at Bowling Green and to 111 at Paulding, giving a temperature range of 141 degrees in Ohio for the year.

12 March 1948
March Cold Wave

A period of wintry weather in an otherwise warm March brought the coldest March temperature known in Ohio up to that time. A snowstorm on Thursday, 11 March brought traffic and most other activity to a halt across Ohio. Snow depths were generally six to twelve inches across the north-central and northeastern regions, with lesser amounts elsewhere. Strong winds drifted many roads shut, and schools were closed across a wide area.

Temperatures began their slide to record lows on Thursday and were below zero in northwestern Ohio by midnight. By dawn on 12 March temperatures dropped below -10 degrees in a broad belt across the north. Lows of -15 degrees, uncommon even in midwinter, were recorded at Van Wert, Findlay, Bucyrus, Mansfield, and Norwalk. The coldest official temperature in Ohio that morning was -20 degrees at a weather station five miles west of Mansfield. This was the coldest March temperature known in Ohio up to 1948, replacing the previous March record of -17 degrees at Wauseon in 1883. The March 1948 record near Mansfield stood for thirty-six years until -21 degrees was recorded at Fredericktown on 9 March 1984.

2–3 February 1951
Cold Wave Follows Snowstorm

Arctic air spread over the entire continental United States early in February 1951 from a near-record high pressure center in northwestern Canada (Miller and Gould 1951). This cold outbreak was unusual in the intensity of the Canadian high, a barometric pressure of 1,065 millibars (31.44 inches) was measured, and the extent of the nation covered by the arctic air mass. No area escaped the cold. Winter storms along the southern edge of the advancing cold air brought ice storms to the southern states and deep snow to Ohio on the last day of January. Temperatures reached state record lows of -60 degrees in Colorado and -50 degrees in New Mexico on the first day of February as the cold air moved into Ohio.

Midday readings were near zero across Ohio on Friday and Saturday, 2–3 February 1951. Lows fell below -10 degrees in most communities and reached -20 in more than a dozen counties. Peebles was the coldest among official weather stations with -29 degrees. Lows fell to -27 degrees at Millersburg, -26 at Newark and New Lexington, and -25 at Waverly. Cleanup was still underway from the 31 January snowstorm in Ohio, and the cold wave brought the usual problems in starting cars, operating trains, and heating poorly constructed buildings.

A more important impact of the severe cold was widespread shortages of natural gas for heating and industry. Most gas providers in Ohio experienced shortages and lowered pressures in supply lines on 2 and 3 February. Schools were closed Friday due to the cold and gas shortages. Ohio Fuel Gas Company declared a "state of emergency" in its sixty-six-county service area on 2 February and cut gas service to most industries. Dayton Power and Light took similar steps in southwestern Ohio. All industry shut down in the Miami Valley and at Columbus, Toledo, and most other Ohio cities over the weekend so that gas could be preserved for home heating. In spite of the drastic conservation measures, hundreds of homes were without gas for a portion of the cold wave.

21 September 1956
Frost Devastates Crops of Northern Ohio

The earliest killing freeze for much of northern Ohio came on the last full day of summer 1956. It was the final blow of a difficult growing season. A cold, wet spring delayed planting by 20 days, and then the end of the growing season was cut short 20 days earlier than usual by the freeze. At just 120 days between frosts, this was the shortest growing season in Akron history.

All of the Midwest and Great Lakes region was swept by early cold. Two inches of September snow fell in northern Michigan and an inch was measured at Erie, Pennsylvania. In Ohio's snowbelt, Chardon had one-half inch of snow on Thursday, 20 September, and flurries or sleet were reported in Akron and elsewhere. Daytime readings were only in the 40s on the twentieth, some 20 degrees colder than usual.

Low temperatures on Friday morning, 21 September dropped to within a few degrees of freezing across northern Ohio. Only the lakeshore was spared a frost. Akron's low of 32 degrees was the earliest freeze on record, beating by five days the previous early freeze on 26 September 1893. Temperatures reached 29 degrees at Wooster, with unofficial reports of 20 degrees in nearby valleys. A weather station five miles west of Mansfield recorded 24 degrees, and the *Cleveland Plain Dealer* reported the same temperature in Salem.

Damage to crops and gardens was widespread across northern Ohio. Northwestern Ohio's $2 million tomato crop was destroyed in the freeze, according to the *Cleveland Plain Dealer*. All of Wayne County's major crops were damaged, with early estimates of half the corn crop destroyed. Oats, hay, and wheat were also frozen.

10 December 1958
Early Winter Cold

Winter set in hard and early in 1958, with snowstorms over Thanksgiving weekend and subzero cold during early December. Snowfall on Friday, 28 November totaled six inches or more in the north and, by Saturday, six to twelve inches of snow covered the whole state. The nine-inch snowfall in suburban Cincinnati was the heaviest in many years. The *Akron Beacon Journal* reported big crowds of Christmas shoppers Thanksgiving weekend, in spite of the heavy snow, strong winds, and temperatures in the teens.

Arctic air settled over Ohio during the first half of December, dropping temperatures to early winter records on several days. The greatest cold came on Wednesday, 10 December, with lows below -10 degrees across most of Ohio. Among the coldest temperatures were -20 degrees at a weather station six miles west of Mansfield, -19 at Millport in Columbiana County, and -16 at Urbana and London. Several weather stations, including Akron-Canton, where it was -11 degrees, reported their coldest temperatures on record for so early in the winter season. Milder temperatures prevailed near unfrozen Lake Erie, where it was 5 degrees at Put-in-Bay and 3 degrees at Geneva, and in extreme southern Ohio, where the earlier snow had melted and lows fell to only 3 degrees at Portsmouth and Cincinnati.

The cold weather led to an unusual period of early winter snow cover. Except in the extreme south, where warmer days melted the Thanksgiving weekend accumulation, snow was six inches deep across Ohio through much of December. Cold northwest winds caused lake-effect snow in northeastern Ohio, so the landscapes of Lake, Geauga, and Ashtabula Counties had snow depths of twenty to twenty-six inches by 10 December.

24 January 1963
Record Cold in Northern Cities

One of the greatest cold waves of the twentieth century in Ohio (Edgell 1992) came in the bitter month of January 1963. This was the coldest January between 1940 and 1970 and the coldest winter up to that date since 1917–18 in Ohio (Karl et al. 1983).

January 1963 was a cold month nationally. Temperatures fell below zero in every continental state except Louisiana (3 degrees) and Florida (7 degrees). All-time state cold records were set in Kentucky (-34 degrees), Texas (-24 degrees), and Arizona (-37 degrees).

Several cold waves gave persistently cold weather across Ohio during January 1963, but the last cold wave was the most intense. It entered Ohio on 20 January and peaked during the last week of the month. During this period, lows fell to -15 degrees at all weather stations in Ohio and chilled below -20 across a wide swath (fig. 25). In an appropriate political event during the cold, Governor James Rhodes and House Speaker Roger Cloud cut ribbons on 21 January to open Valley High Ski Resort near Bellefontaine.

Three National Weather Service offices in Ohio established all-time record lows on Thursday, 24 January 1963. Temperatures of -17 degrees at Toledo, -19 at Cleveland, and -21 at Akron-Canton were the coldest since the National Weather Service began records in the 1870s and eclipsed old records set in the nineteenth century. (Toledo's 1963 record was exceeded by -20 degrees in January 1984, Cleveland reached -20 degrees in January 1994, and Akron-Canton recorded -25 degrees in January 1994.)

As is usual in Ohio cold waves, the lowest readings were noted in the east and southeast, where cold air settled into valleys far from the warming effects of Lake Erie. Lows of -24 degrees came from Cambridge and Waverly, -26 at New Lexington and Tom Jenkins Dam, and -27 at Athens. The coldest temperature in Ohio, -31 degrees, was recorded 28 January at Jackson. Jackson and Lone Rock, Wisconsin, were, outside of Alaska, the coldest locations in the United States that morning. The -31 at Jackson in January 1963 was the coldest temperature in Ohio between December 1917 and January 1994.

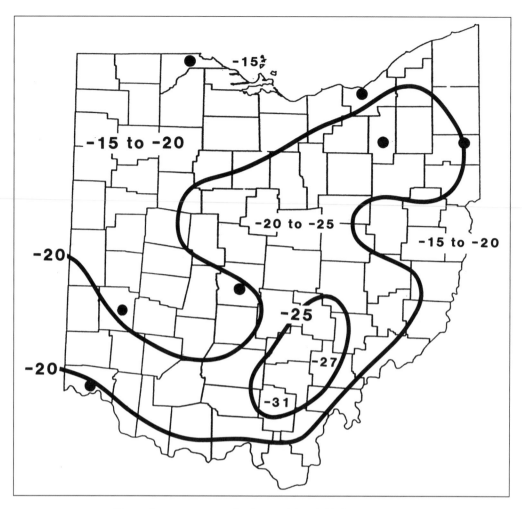

Fig. 25. Low temperatures (in degrees Fahrenheit) during 23–25 January 1963.

Rural roads were closed by drifted snow in many counties. Salt was ineffective at such cold temperatures, so fine stone was spread in some areas. The *Athens Messenger* called area streets "as slippery as a Communist's promise" in this Cold War cold wave, just three months after the Cuban Missile Crisis. The Cleveland office of the American Automobile Association received three hundred calls for assistance in seven hours. They refused to handle routine calls for assistance, instead taking only emergencies, defined as doctors whose cars would not start or cars stalled in intersections.

Cleveland police had the opportunity to try their new "snow ordinance," which allowed cars parked on the street during a snow emergency to be towed. Mayor Ralph Locher called the first snow emergency at 11:00 P.M. on 22 January. Within twelve hours, police had ticketed 190 cars along major roads. Fifty of those cars were towed away by 14 city and 7 private tow trucks. Owners faced a five-dollar fine for parking on the street during a snow emergency and a five-dollar tow fee. Snowplows made good progress on the unobstructed streets, so the mayor declared the snow ordinance a success. Residents whose cars were ticketed and towed complained that the snow emergency was declared while they slept, leaving them no opportunity to move their cars.

Cold prevailed across much of the Northern Hemisphere during January 1963. Central Italy was snowbound, one hundred were dead from the cold in Britain, and snow fell at Istanbul. A four-day blizzard paralyzed portions of Japan, and the port of Inchon, Korea, was frozen for the first time in fifty years. In contrast to the Ohio cold wave, Miami had a record 87 degrees on 27 January and temperatures were above freezing in Nome, Alaska.

1 April 1964
Subzero in April

A covering of fresh snow and an arctic air mass were the right combination for a record low temperature on April Fool's Day 1964. Two to four inches of snow fell across northern Ohio during the last days of March, and as skies cleared on 31 March, temperatures fell to winterlike readings the next morning.

A minimum temperature of -1 degree at an official weather station on Millsboro Road five miles west of Mansfield was the only subzero temperature ever recorded in Ohio during April. The *Mansfield News Journal* headlined, "Zero in April a Poor Joke." Among other cold temperatures were 1 degree at Charles Mill Dam, 2 degrees at Danville, and 4 degrees at Dorset, Senecaville Lake, and Chippewa Lake. Mansfield Airport recorded a low of 11 degrees, as did Toledo, and records were established at Cleveland and Akron-Canton with 10 degrees.

10 May 1966
Coldest May Temperature

One of the coldest air masses ever experienced during May spread across the central and eastern United States during 9–11 May 1966. Rare May snow accompanied this cold outbreak in northeastern Ohio. Freezing temperatures reached into the southern states, and temperatures fell below zero on Mt. Washington, New Hampshire.

Cold air poured into Ohio on Monday, 9 May. Daytime temperatures were only in the 30s and 40s, and up to five inches of snow fell in

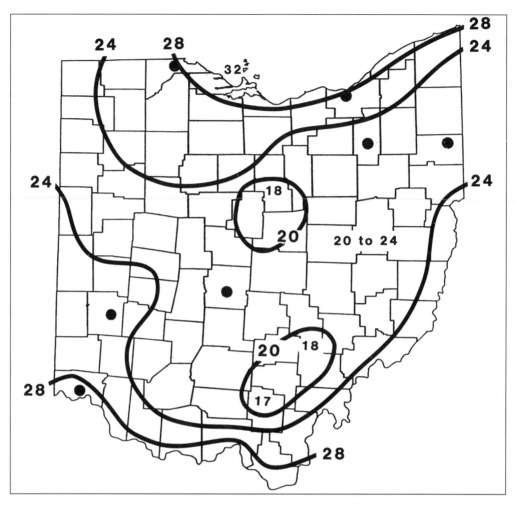

Fig. 26. Low temperatures (in degrees Fahrenheit) during the severe freeze on 10 May 1966. Jackson recorded 17 degrees, the coldest May temperature known in Ohio.

northeastern Ohio. By Tuesday morning, 10 May, temperatures were the coldest ever known during May in many Ohio communities. Lows fell below freezing everywhere except along the shore of Lake Erie, where the water kept temperatures just above freezing (fig. 26). The influence of the lake was evident in Ashtabula County, where it was 33 degrees at Ashtabula and 21 degrees at Dorset, thirteen miles inland. May frosts are common in Ohio, but temperatures on 10 May 1966 fell far below freezing to values not expected after mid-April. Most areas cooled below 28 degrees, and many communities fell into the low 20s.

The coldest temperatures were in the valleys of north-central and southeastern Ohio. Minimum temperatures fell to 19 degrees at Athens and Charles Mill Dam east of Mansfield, and to 18 degrees at Tom Jenkins Dam north of Athens, and near Lexington. The press reported the 18-

degree low at Lexington was the coldest in the United States on 10 May, but the coldest temperature in Ohio was actually 17 degrees at Jackson. This is the coldest temperature ever recorded during May in Ohio, surpassing the previous record of 19 degrees at Millport on 10 May 1947.

8 January 1970
Subzero Day

Persistent cold weather from mid-December 1969 to late January 1970 was reminiscent of the cold winter of 1962–63 in Ohio. Although extreme minimum temperatures in January 1970 did not reach the record lows of 1963, sustained cold gave a state average temperature of 20.4 degrees for January 1970. This was slightly colder than 1963 and made this the coldest month in Ohio since January 1940.

The cold of 1970 culminated in a rare subzero afternoon on Thursday, 8 January. For many communities, including Columbus and Dayton, this was the first day of the twentieth century that temperatures failed to rise above zero. Temperatures dropped below zero late on 7 January and remained below zero in some areas until noon on 9 January. Cleveland had forty-three consecutive hours below zero, breaking the twentieth-century record of forty-one hours during 8–10 February 1934. This 1970 record was exceeded by fifty-six hours below zero in Cleveland in January 1994. Perhaps the greatest tragedy related to this cold wave occurred in Marietta late on 9 January, when a nursing-home fire killed twenty-one persons. Fire fighters were hampered by strong winds, blowing snow, and 6-degree cold.

11 June 1972
Coldest June Temperature

June 1972 was a calamitous month in American weather history. Flash floods swept Rapid City, South Dakota, on 9 June, killing 237 people, and Hurricane Agnes caused flooding that killed 105 in Pennsylvania and New York on 22 June (Ludlum 1982). Wind and rain from Hurricane Agnes affected northeastern Ohio on 23 June, but the major weather event in Ohio was more benign—a widespread freeze on 11 June.

June freezes are rare in Ohio and are usually isolated in the colder valleys of the northeastern region or central hills near Mansfield. The cold wave of Sunday, 11 June, however, brought freezing temperatures to more than one-third of Ohio (fig. 27). For many stations, including Toledo Airport, this was the first June freeze and the coldest June temperature on record.

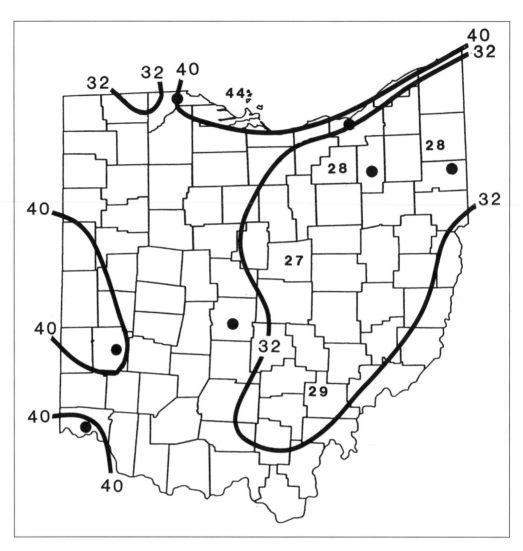

Fig. 27. Low temperatures (in degrees Fahrenheit) on 11 June 1972. Danville recorded 27 degrees, the coldest recorded during June in Ohio. This is the latest freeze known for many Ohio stations.

The low temperature of 27 degrees at a weather station two miles west of Danville established an Ohio cold record for June, eclipsing the previous state record of 28 degrees at Dover on 4 June 1929. The 1929 record was tied, with lows of 28 degrees on 11 June 1972 at Warren, Chippewa Lake, and Millport.

The warming effects of large cities and Lake Erie were evident. Differences between low temperatures at downtown weather stations and rural airports were striking at Toledo (43/32 degrees), Columbus (47/35 degrees), and Akron (41/32 degrees). Heat from Lake Erie gave a low of just

47 degrees at Painesville, but the temperature fell to 31 degrees ten miles inland near Geneva. Put-in-Bay, on South Bass Island, remained at 44 degrees, while it cooled to 33 degrees nearby at Norwalk.

Effects of the freeze on vegetable and field crops were widespread in eastern Ohio. Prices on the Cleveland vegetable markets soared Monday after farmers lost tomatoes, sweet corn, peppers, beans, squash, and beets. Field corn one to two feet high was frozen in low-lying areas where the coldest air settled overnight.

1976–77
Coldest Month in Bitter Winter

The two winters of 1976–77 and 1977–78 were extraordinarily cold in Ohio and throughout the central United States (Wagner 1977, Boyce 1978, Diaz and Quayle 1980, Konrad and Colucci 1989). Average temperatures of 21 degrees in Ohio during both winters were the coldest in recorded history. In addition, temperatures fell below -20 degrees on several days, and heavy snows, including blizzards, created widespread hardship in Ohio during these two outstanding winters. The winter of 1976–77 was slightly colder than winter 1977–78 in Ohio, although 1977–78 was colder at some sites. If wind speed and cold are considered together, winter 1976–77 was more severe than 1977–78 in Ohio (Dare 1981).

Average temperatures during December 1976 were about 7 degrees colder than normal. Highs failed to rise above freezing on about half the days in December and fell below zero on five to ten days in the north and one to three days in the far south. A seven-week period of consistently cold weather that would give the coldest January known in Ohio and contribute to making this the coldest winter in history began on 21 December 1976. December 1976 was a dry month, so, in spite of the cold, snowfall, at five to twelve inches, was near normal. The snowbelt received a little more than usual for December, thirty-eight inches at Chardon.

January 1977 was the coldest month in Ohio since such records began in 1883. The statewide average temperature during January 1977 was 11.9 degrees, nearly 17 degrees colder than normal (figs. 28 and 29). At the coldest sites in northern Ohio, average temperatures during January 1977 were near 8 degrees. These bitter winter temperatures are typical of January in Duluth, Minnesota, and Bismarck, North Dakota, and were far colder than any winter in the experience of most Ohioans. Temperatures remained below freezing throughout January in the northern half of Ohio, and low temperatures fell below zero on fifteen to twenty days during the month. Kalkstein and Valimont (1987) reported that when temperature and wind were considered together in a "weather stress index," winter

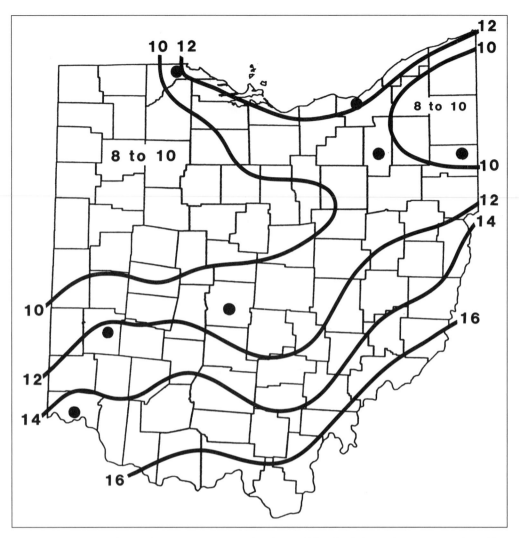

Fig. 28. Average temperatures (in degrees Fahrenheit) during January 1977, the coldest month known in Ohio. Normal January temperatures range from 25 degrees in the north to 32 degrees in the south.

weather severity during January 1977 was greater in Ohio than anywhere in the United States.

The impact of cold weather during January 1977 was intensified by snowfall double the average and a blizzard at the end of January. Frequent snowfall and temperatures that remained below freezing preserved a snow cover through the entire month in central and northern counties. Ground was bare on New Year's in southern Ohio, but snowfall on 5 January was the start of a snow cover that would last until the middle of February. Several weeks with continuous snow cover is a rare event in

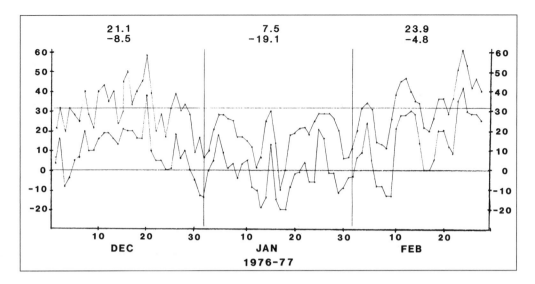

Fig. 29. Daily maximum temperature (upper line) and minimum temperature (lower line) at Kenton, Ohio, during the winter of 1976–77 (temperatures in degrees Fahrenheit). Horizontal reference lines are marked at 32 degrees and zero degrees. Vertical lines mark the dates 1 January and 1 February. This was the coldest winter and coldest January in Ohio history. Numbers above the graph show the average temperature *(top)* for the month at Kenton and the departure *(bottom)* from the 1941–70 average.

Ohio's climate. It would, however, be repeated the next winter with an even longer snow season.

Extreme cold during the winter of 1976–77 peaked on Monday, 17 January, with lows of -15 to -25 degrees. Among the coldest sites were Danville, Milford, and Cincinnati-Fernbank with -25 degrees, and Sidney, Jackson, and Eaton at -24 degrees. Strong winds that accompanied the record cold produced wind chills of -65 degrees and caused snow to drift onto highways. Temperatures dropped to an all-time record -25 degrees at Greater Cincinnati Airport on 18 January 1977, and the *Cincinnati Enquirer* reported thousands of cars did not start, some water pipes were frozen, and furnaces malfunctioned.

Cold weather continued into the first half of February 1977, with temperatures falling under -20 degrees at several stations during 6–8 February. Average February temperatures, however, were only 4 degrees colder than normal, and highs peaked in the 60s by the end of the month, bringing an end to this extraordinary winter. February snowfall was light, but the heavy January snows and continued cold weather during early February brought snow depths of thirty to thirty-five inches in the snowbelt and ten to twenty inches elsewhere across the state during the second week of February. Snow melted from the Ohio landscape during the middle of February and bare ground was visible for the first time in six to eight weeks.

1977–78
Coldest February and Second Consecutive Bitter Winter

Winter 1977–78 was the second consecutive winter of record cold in Ohio. Average temperatures near 21 degrees rivaled 1976–77 as the coldest winter in Ohio history. In contrast to the winter of 1976–77, when January was a record cold month, February was the coldest month of winter 1977–78 (Dickson 1978). With a statewide average temperature of 16 degrees, February 1978 was the coldest February known in Ohio.

In addition to steady cold, the Blizzard of '78 and other heavy snows created widespread hardship in Ohio. Winter snowfall totals of forty to sixty inches in southern Ohio and sixty to eighty inches in the north were twice the average (fig. 30). Snow covered the ground for seventy-five to one hundred days, far more than average in Ohio's climate (fig. 31), and depths reached eighteen to twenty-four inches all across Ohio by the end of January 1978.

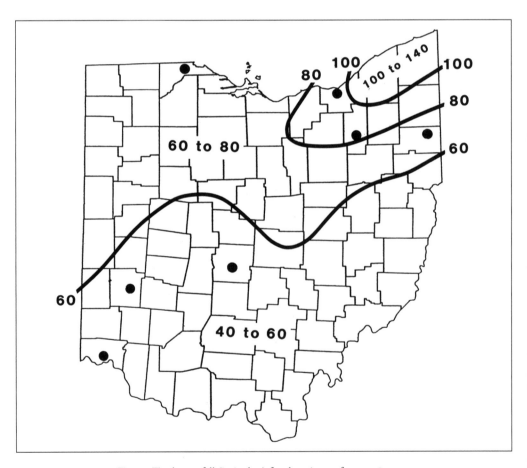

Fig. 30. Total snowfall (in inches) for the winter of 1977–78.

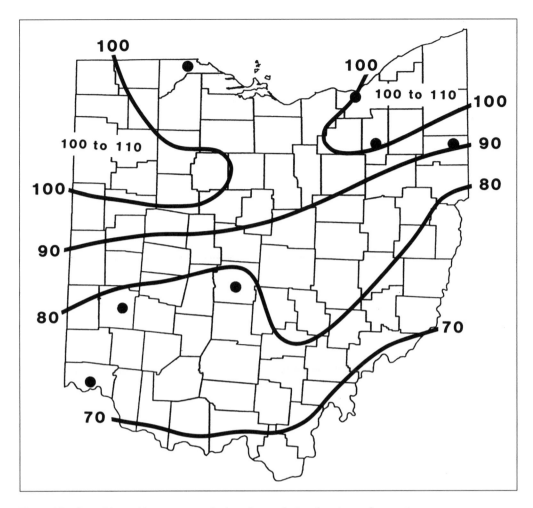

Fig. 31. Number of days with snow cover 1 inch or deeper during the winter of 1977–78.

December 1977 was about three degrees colder than average, not un-usual in Ohio's climate, and extreme cold was lacking during the month. Snowfall was well above normal during December 1977 in northern Ohio. Near-blizzard conditions and ten inches of snow closed roads and schools in northwestern Ohio on Monday, 5 December, and many schools re-mained closed Tuesday. Wind-blown snow snarled traffic in the greater Cleveland area on 6 December and again on 8–9 December. Six to eight inches fell in the city during both storms, but twenty to thirty inches covered the eastern suburbs.

January 1978 was an extremely cold month in Ohio, but it did not match the record cold of January 1977. Temperatures were ten degrees colder than normal, although steady cold, rather than extreme cold, was the rule in January. A series of snowstorms culminating in the Blizzard of

'78 on 26 January provided record snowfall amounts and caused widespread disruption to schools, transportation, industry, and business in Ohio.

Snow totals of twenty-five to forty inches across Ohio during January 1978 equaled the normal snowfall for an entire winter. In the Lake Erie snowbelt, fifty-seven inches of snow fell at Chardon, twice the January average. The heavy snowfall and consistent cold created a snowpack that covered the entire state by 9 January and persisted until the middle of March.

February 1978 was the coldest February since comparative records began in 1883. The statewide average temperature of 16 degrees was about 14 degrees colder than normal, and temperatures remained below freezing in the north until the final days of the month. Subzero temperatures were recorded on ten to twenty days in the north, with lows of -22 degrees at Fredericktown on 15 February and -20 degrees at Chardon and Dorset on 4 February. Southern Ohio had only one or two days below zero in February, but the cold was persistent in the south, too. The unusual weather patterns across the United States this month are described by Dickson (1978).

February 1978 marked a sharp change in the storm track and brought none of the severe snowstorms that characterized January 1978 in Ohio. The result was an extremely dry month, with less than one-half inch of precipitation at most sites. Caldwell recorded no measurable precipitation at all in February 1978. What little moisture fell came as light snow, giving totals five to ten inches, about normal for February. Although there were no major snowstorms, snow cover was retained across the entire state during February and into the first two weeks of March. In the snowbelt at Chardon, the ground was covered with snow from 26 December until 20 March.

Prolonged cold weather and snow covers of the winters in the late 1970s became the norm for Ohioans and the standard against which subsequent winters were compared. When "normal" winters returned in the 1980s, the perception among some was "winters aren't what they used to be," the phrase repeated by every generation that remembers the "real" winters of years past.

10 January 1982
Coldest Football Game in NFL History

Forecasts for Sunday, 10 January 1982 called for afternoon temperatures near zero and a biting wind, but the *Cincinnati Enquirer* proclaimed, "Arctic Chill Can't Cool City's Fever for Bengals."

As the Cincinnati Bengals lined up against the San Diego Chargers for the AFC championship game at Riverfront Stadium on Sunday, temperatures at kick-off were reported to be -9 degrees. The high for the day at Cincinnati Lunken Airport was just -1 degree, and the wind chill of -59 degrees at half-time created the coldest conditions ever encountered during an NFL game. (The famous cold game between the Packers and Cowboys in Green Bay on 31 December 1967 was later reported to have a wind chill of -48 degrees.)

More than forty-six thousand fans were in the stands to watch the Bengals beat San Diego 27–7, although pregame and half-time shows were canceled at the Stadium. NBC television cameras were heated by propane blankets, but five cameras were out of commission at one time with frozen lenses. Players sat on heated benches and wore gloves, long underwear, and two pairs of socks to protect themselves from the extreme chill. Only one frost-bitten ear was reported among the players. Fans kept warm under layers of clothing and blankets, and fans of the Chargers noted it was 70 degrees in San Diego as the game began. (The Bengals lost to San Francisco in the Super Bowl two weeks later.)

Effects of the cold wave were felt far beyond Riverfront Stadium. Sunday, 10 January 1982 was one of the coldest days in Ohio history, with high temperatures ranging from only zero to -5 degrees in most communities. The high of -3 degrees at Toledo was the coldest maximum temperature in that city's history (these records for daytime cold were later exceeded on the Cold Saturday of 20 January 1985).

Temperatures moderated some during the following week, but record cold returned the next weekend, 16–17 January. Low temperatures on Sunday, 17 January were the coldest of the month. Deer Creek Lake was the coldest weather station in Ohio with -30 degrees, but other cold readings included -25 at Wilmington and -24 at Eaton and Jackson. A low of -22 degrees at Akron-Canton established an all-time record that was short-lived. New cold records were set at Akron-Canton with -24 degrees in 1985 and -25 in 1994.

29 August 1982
Record Low August Temperatures

The most severe August freeze known in Ohio came Sunday morning, 29 August 1982. Uncommonly cold air had spread across the Great Lakes and northeastern United States on Saturday. Temperatures fell to 26 degrees at Cadillac, Michigan, and three inches of snow covered Vermont's Killington Mountain Saturday night. Clearing skies Saturday night assured records would fall by Sunday morning. Lows dropped into the 30s across northern and eastern Ohio and were the coldest August temperatures ever recorded at many Ohio weather stations (fig. 32). Warm Lake

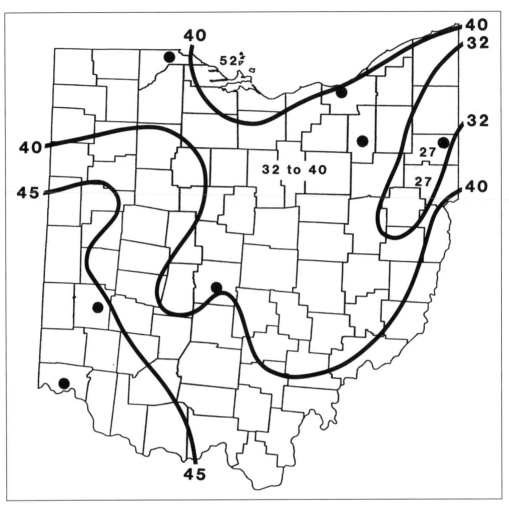

Fig. 32. Low temperatures (in degrees Fahrenheit) on 29 August 1982. Minimums of 27 degrees at Canfield and Millport are the coldest ever recorded during August in Ohio.

Erie waters moderated temperatures along the shore, where Put-in-Bay was the warmest in the state with a mild 52 degrees.

The most extraordinary temperatures were reported along Ohio's eastern border, where lows of 27 degrees were recorded in Canfield and at Millport along Route 644 in Columbiana County. These were the coldest August temperatures ever recorded in Ohio, exceeding the previous state record of 30 degrees at Tom Jenkins Dam on 29 August 1965. Official temperatures also fell to freezing at the Youngstown Airport and to 30 degrees at Dorset and Warren.

Tender garden vegetables were killed by the freeze in valleys of eastern Ohio. Field crops were frozen in some areas, but widespread damage was not noted. Hilltops and cities were generally warmer and escaped the freeze.

25 December 1983
Coldest Christmas

Ohio's coldest Christmas came just one year after the warmest Christmas. This record cold wave affected all of the continental United States except the southwestern deserts. Temperatures dropped to 8 degrees on the Gulf Coast at Mobile, Alabama, to 19 degrees at Daytona Beach and 34 degrees at Miami Beach. Temperatures remained below freezing all day along the Gulf Coast. Some meteorologists called this the "Great Freeze of '83" and the worst cold weather event of the century in the United States (Mogil, Stern, and Hagan 1984).

The cold wave was born on 15 December as a high pressure ridge developed at the 500 millibar pressure level (eighteen thousand feet) over Alaska (Mogil, Stern, and Hagan 1984). Air flowing from the northwest came through Alaska into western Canada and the northern Plains, a common feature of winter. However, this upper air ridge remained in place for many days and allowed a bitterly cold air mass to develop in the snow-covered arctic darkness of Alaska.

The arctic high pressure intensified rapidly and spread into the central United States on 22 and 23 December. Snow covered 74 percent of North America in December, the greatest in eighteen years of data. The result of the intense arctic air mass and extensive snow cover was the Great Freeze of '83. All-time December cold records were set in cities across twenty-nine states from Washington to North Dakota and Florida.

Subzero weather moved into Ohio on Thursday evening, 22 December in advance of the massive southward movement of arctic air. Indications of the cold to come were a temperature of -52 degrees at Butte, Montana, and a new contiguous U.S. record high barometric pressure of 31.42 inches at Miles City, Montana. Temperatures Christmas morning were -10 to -15 degrees in southern Ohio and near Lake Erie (fig. 33). Elsewhere in northern and western Ohio temperatures fell to -15 to -20 degrees. The lowest temperatures in the state were -30 at Eaton and -26 at Springfield. These exceeded readings during the cold Christmas in 1924.

At Toledo, the temperature fell to zero at 8:30 P.M. on 22 December. After a low of -9 degrees on the twenty-third, the temperature struggled to only 1 degree that afternoon, fell to zero again at 6:00 P.M., and did not rise above zero until the twenty-sixth. The noon temperature at Toledo on 24 December was an exceptional -11 degrees. Toledo's low of -15 the same day tied the December cold record set in 1872, and the Christmas morning low of -13 broke the previous Christmas record of -12 set in 1980.

Temperatures at the Akron-Canton Airport were below zero for fifty-four hours from 4:00 A.M. on 24 December to 10:00 A.M. on the twenty-sixth. Cleveland temperatures were below zero after 2:00 A.M. on 24

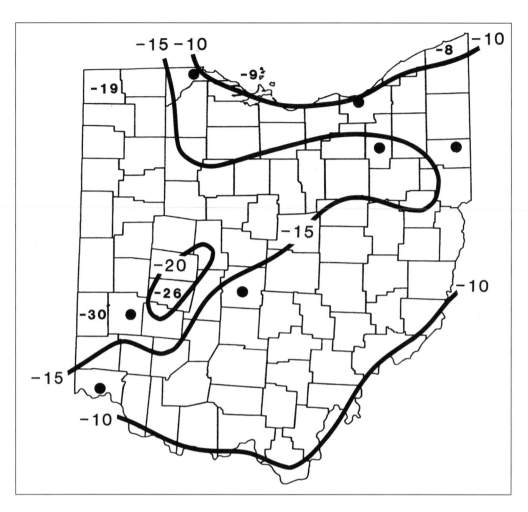

Fig. 33. Low temperatures (in degrees Fahrenheit) on 25 December 1983, Ohio's coldest Christmas.

December and peaked at only 1 degree on Christmas and 26 December. Lows were -10 degrees both days. Strong winds and noon temperatures of -7 on 24 December and -3 on Christmas gave midday wind chills of -50 degrees. In spite of the record cold, suburban shopping malls were busy with Christmas Eve shoppers.

The bitter cold was accompanied by lake-effect blizzards in the snowbelt on 24 and 25 December. Interstate 90 through Ashtabula County was closed both days by high winds and eight-foot drifts. Five hundred stranded motorists spent Christmas in Ashtabula County motels, where the American Red Cross provided cots and even a few Christmas gifts. One Geneva motel offered free space in its banquet rooms after all rooms were filled.

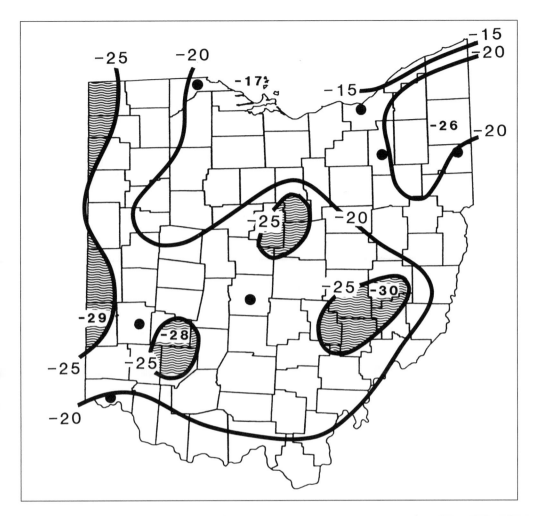

Fig. 34. Low temperatures (in degrees Fahrenheit) on 21 January 1984. A temperature of -20 degrees at Toledo remains as the coldest ever recorded there.

21 January 1984
Toledo's Coldest Morning

"Siberian Express" became a household term during the 1980s as weather forecasters and the media described winter cold waves that swept into the United States from the Arctic. Although some felt this term was over-used, more severe cold waves occurred in Ohio during the 1980s than any other decade of the twentieth century (Edgell 1992).

Winter 1983–84 was especially bitter, with the coldest Christmas known in Ohio and a March cold wave that established a new state cold record of -21 degrees for the month. During January, one of the coldest air masses of the century moved into Ohio on 20 January after two weeks of sub-freezing weather. In the West, a remote weather station at Middle Sinks,

Utah, registered -65 degrees on 18 January 1984. As the coldest air spread into Ohio on the twentieth, it was -40 degrees in northern Wisconsin and snow was falling in Pensacola, Florida. This cold wave came on the thirtieth anniversary of the coldest temperature recorded in the forty-eight contiguous states, -70 degrees at Rogers Pass, Montana, on 20 January 1954.

The coldest air settled over Ohio on Saturday morning, 21 January (fig. 34). The National Weather Service at Toledo recorded -20 degrees at 7:30 A.M., the coldest temperature at Toledo since records began in 1871. This exceeded the previous record of -17 at Toledo set in 1963, 1972, and 1982.

Among the coldest readings were -26 degrees at Warren and New Lexington, -28 at Xenia, -29 at Eaton, and -30 at Senecaville Lake. The low at Senecaville Lake was just the second reading of -30 in Ohio in twenty-one years. Temperatures remained below zero for most of 21 January and moderated slowly on the twenty-second. Saturday noon temperatures were -10 degrees in Toledo and -7 degrees in Columbus. Ice crystals fell from a clear sky across Ohio on Saturday morning, a feature of extremely cold air that is common in arctic climates.

9 March 1984
Coldest March Temperature

Bitter cold arctic air settled over Ohio on Friday, 9 March 1984 in the wake of a snowstorm. Low temperatures fell below zero over the fresh snow cover, except in the extreme south and along Lake Erie (fig. 35). A weather station four miles south of Fredericktown in Knox County recorded -21 degrees. This is the coldest temperature recorded in Ohio during March, exceeding the old record of -20 degrees measured near Mansfield in 1948 and again at Dorset in 1980.

The *Mt. Vernon News* reported temperatures were near zero in town but told of an unofficial -22 degrees on Howard-Danville Road. Among the extremely cold temperatures at government weather stations on 9 March 1984 were -18 degrees at Danville and Charles Mill Dam, -17 at Irwin, and -15 at Ashland and Oberlin.

20 January 1985
Coldest Daytime Known

Ohioans became accustomed to cold waves during the 1980s, but the cold wave of 20–21 January 1985 exceeded all previous records for intense cold and wind. Daytime temperatures of -10 to -20 degrees and winds of twenty to thirty miles an hour gave the coldest day experienced since European settlement of Ohio.

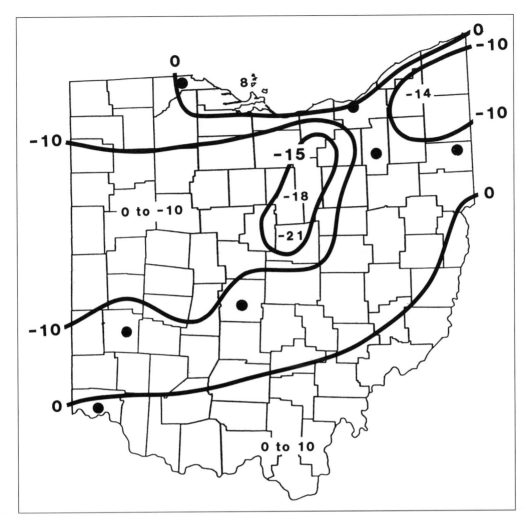

Fig. 35. Low temperatures (in degrees Fahrenheit) on 9 March 1984. The minimum of -21 degrees at Fredericktown is the lowest ever recorded during March in Ohio.

The large atmospheric circulation feature called the Arctic Vortex, which contains the coldest air of the Northern Hemisphere, made an unusual move southward and was centered over the eastern Great Lakes region on 20 January. It provided Ohio and the surrounding region with the coldest temperatures in North America. The Sunday, 20 January morning low of -24 degrees at Dayton was the coldest temperature since -28 was recorded in February 1899. Thermometers at Akron-Canton Airport fell to -24 degrees at midnight Sunday night, breaking the all-time record of -22 set on 17 January 1982. Lows also fell to -24 degrees at Wilmington, Canfield, Lancaster, and Sidney, to -26 at Greenville and Urbana, to -27 at Xenia, and to -30 at Eaton. Only the lakeshore in Lake and Ashtabula Counties remained above -15 degrees (fig. 36).

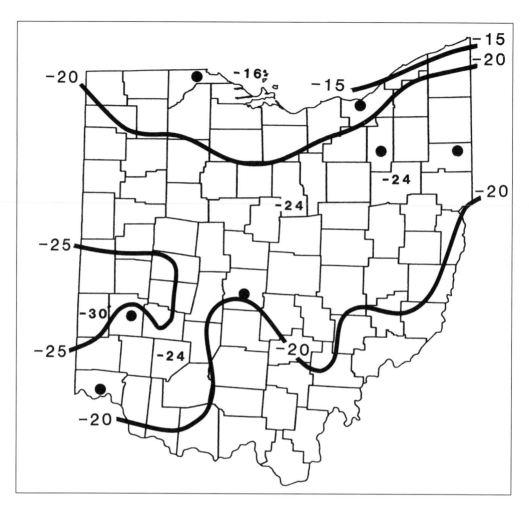

Fig. 36. Low temperatures (in degrees Fahrenheit) on 21 January 1985.

The core of the coldest air spread across Ohio during the day on 20 January, preventing much warming and keeping temperatures at the coldest daytime readings ever known in Ohio. The *noon* temperature at Dayton Airport was an extraordinarily frigid -19 degrees. Elsewhere across the state, noon temperatures on 20 January were -15 degrees at Columbus and Cincinnati, -14 at Akron, and -11 at Toledo and Cleveland. These temperatures are beyond any previous experience in Ohio. Temperatures remained below zero at Columbus for forty-two hours, ending at 2:00 P.M. on 21 January.

Although these temperatures and others across Ohio were sufficient to make this one of the great cold waves in history, the high winds that accompanied the cold established 20 January 1985 as Ohio's coldest day. Average wind speed for the day was eighteen to twenty-two miles an hour across Ohio and gusts exceeded thirty miles an hour. The wind chill, measuring the cooling rate of exposed skin, reached -72 degrees Sunday afternoon in Columbus and -80 degrees Sunday evening at Akron. Wind chills of -50 to -70 degrees persisted for more than twelve hours across much of Ohio.

Such wind chills had not been experienced across Ohio since the Blizzard of 1918, and it is doubtful that such a long period of extreme wind chill occurred even in that storm. Winds were stronger during the Blizzard of 1978, but temperatures were warmer than on 20 January 1985.

1 July 1988
Coldest July Temperature

An extraordinary cold wave enveloped the upper Midwest and Appalachians from 29 June to 2 July in the midst of the hot, dry summer of 1988. Strong, cold low pressure in the upper atmosphere over Hudson Bay pulled polar high pressure into the Heartland. Winds at seventeen thousand feet were from the north at seventy-five miles an hour, with temperatures of -13 degrees at that height (Schmidlin 1992), far colder than normal for summer. Temperatures dropped into the 30s across eighteen states and fell to freezing in eight states.

Clear skies and cold air spread over Ohio on 30 June and 1 July. These conditions, combined with very dry soils and vegetation in extreme drought, caused the night air to lose heat rapidly. A low temperature of 34 degrees recorded six miles northwest of Caldwell (Noble County) matched the coldest July temperature ever recorded in Ohio. Most other Ohio weather stations fell into the upper 30s or 40s. In spite of the cold nights, highs were near 80 degrees during the "cold wave" and rose to 102 at Caldwell a week after the record cold morning. There was no widespread frost and, for most Ohioans, the cold morning of 1 July was a relief from the heat of the summer of 1988.

22 December 1989
Coldest December

This was the coldest December in most of Ohio and the Great Lakes region since such summaries were started in 1883. The cold started early in the month and continued without relief until the final two days of December.

As a prelude to the coldest weather, a general snowfall covered Ohio on Friday, 15 December. Heavy snow started before dawn in southwestern Ohio and spread northeast. Totals by evening were three to six inches in western and central Ohio, six to nine inches in the southern part of the state, and eight to fourteen inches across the northeastern region.

Circulation around this snowstorm pulled extremely cold arctic air southward in its wake to envelop the eastern two-thirds of the nation. The core of this cold-air mass settled over Ohio on 21 and 22 December. Highs climbed only to about 5 degrees, and lows fell to the coldest December readings ever known in some communities. The coldest among Ohio weather stations were -27 degrees at Delaware, -26 at Athens, and -24 at Millersburg, Dennison, New Lexington, Wilmington, and Xenia. The low temperature of -19 degrees at Toledo Express Airport exceeded the December record of -15 last reached in 1983 and was just 1 degree from the all-time cold record set on 21 January 1984. Ice formed early and was twelve inches thick by 22 December in Maumee Bay.

A temperature of -20 degrees at the Greater Cincinnati Airport on 22 December was the coldest ever recorded during December in that city. Daily temperature records were also established in other cities, with -20 degrees at Dayton, -17 at Mansfield and Columbus, -16 at Akron-Canton, and -15 at Cleveland. Clouds and lingering snow kept the eastern lakeshore relatively warm during the cold wave. The lowest temperature along the lake at Painesville and Conneaut was only -4 degrees, whereas fifteen miles inland it was -21 at Chardon and -22 at Dorset.

The early winter cold caused Lake Erie to freeze in the western basin by 15 December and across the central basin by Christmas. This was about two weeks earlier than usual and hampered late-season shipping. At least eight ships with cargos of iron ore, salt, or stone were struggling in the ice. The port of Conneaut reported a 310 percent increase in mechanical failures during the severe cold and snow, and conveyers were kept running to prevent freeze-ups (Schmidlin 1993a). On the positive side, ski areas in northeastern Ohio were open twenty-two to thirty-one days during this cold December, compared to only fourteen days in 1988. At one resort, December lift ticket sales were the best in twenty-seven years of operation and business more than doubled from 1988.

Temperatures remained cold through Christmas, but a mild January and February followed, so the winter of 1989–90 went into the records as mild, despite the record cold December.

22 June 1992
Latest Freeze

A low of 32 degrees was recorded at Dorset (Ashtabula County) on 22 June 1992. This is the latest official freezing temperature known in Ohio. Lows dropped into the upper 30s across most of eastern and northwestern Ohio. It was 33 degrees that morning at Millport, Warren, Chardon, and

Canfield. Frost occurred in scattered areas of the northeast, but no wide-spread damage was noted in gardens or on crops.

19 January 1994
Greatest Cold Wave

A cold wave to rival the Great Cold Wave of February 1899 covered Ohio during 18–21 January 1994. The coldest temperature recorded in Ohio during the 1994 cold wave was 2 degrees above the state cold record of -39 established in 1899, but a greater area of the state fell below -25 in 1994 than in 1899 (figs. 23 and 37). Temperatures under -30 degrees occurred only in the southeastern valleys during February 1899, but the cold wave

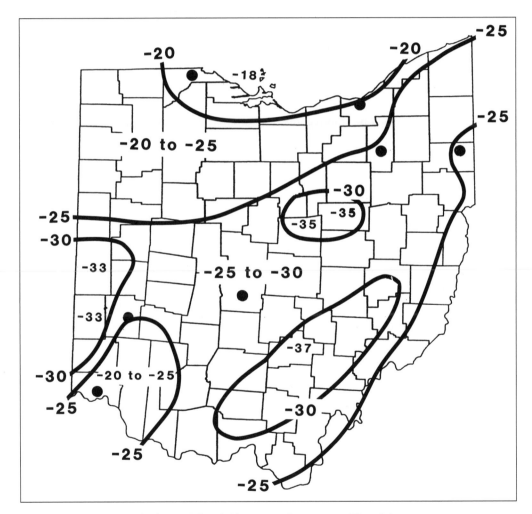

Fig. 37. Low temperatures (in degrees Fahrenheit) on 19–20 January 1994. The minimum of -37 degrees at Logan, Hocking County, on 19 January tied the state cold record for January and was the coldest temperature in Ohio since -37 degrees was recorded at Milligan on 13 January 1912.

of January 1994 brought official temperatures of -30 to -35 degrees to a wider area, including the north-central hills and in western Ohio. On this basis we can say that the 1994 cold wave was the greatest ever known in Ohio.

Comparing the two cold waves at Ohio's major cities is not easy, because in 1899 the official thermometers were in the city, while in 1994 they were located at airports, where temperatures are colder. Columbus, for example, recorded -20 degrees in February 1899 but established a new record with -22 degrees on 19 January 1994. The latter will stand as the all-time record for Columbus, but if the thermometer had been at the airport location in 1899 the low temperature may have been colder than -20 degrees.

Bitter cold air began flowing into Ohio over the weekend of 15–16 January, and many sites set records with temperatures of -10 to -15 degrees. A major snowstorm tracked up the Ohio Valley on 17 January. In the wake of this storm, the coldest air from arctic Canada moved southward to be centered over the Ohio Valley on 19 January. The rapid movement of this bitter air from the Arctic into Ohio over snow-covered ground prevented much warming.

All-time cold records were established at Cleveland, where the low of -20 degrees exceeded the January 1963 record of -19, and at Akron-Canton, where the temperature of -25 broke the old record of -24 set in 1985. A low of -22 degrees at Youngstown broke the station record of -20 set in 1985. The low of -22 degrees at Mansfield tied the station record set in January 1985, and -25 degrees at Dayton Airport established a record for the month of January.

The valleys of southeastern and north-central Ohio had the coldest temperatures (fig. 37). The coldest official temperature in Ohio during the cold wave was -37 degrees at Logan in Hocking County. This tied the state cold record for January set in January 1912 at Milligan in nearby Vinton County. Lows fell to -35 at New Lexington, Danville, and Millersburg, to -34 at Millport, and to -33 at Eaton and Greenville in western Ohio.

There were numerous unofficial reports of temperatures of -35 to -40 degrees on home thermometers hung on porches or posts. This is common during cold waves. A thermometer that has not been constructed and calibrated properly may read several degrees from the actual temperature. In addition, thermometers exposed to the open sky will cool several degrees below the air temperature on clear calm nights. For this reason, official thermometers are housed in shelters to prevent radiation from the thermometer to the sky. But it is also likely that an air temperature colder than -37 degrees occurred someplace in Ohio during January 1994 and was not recorded on any official thermometer.

As usual, the warmest locations during the extreme cold wave were along Lake Erie, where Put-in-Bay and Toledo Airport were "warmest" in Ohio with -18 degrees. Temperatures fell to -20 to -22 degrees in the wine-grape region along Lake Erie in Ashtabula County, killing buds on the premium grape vines. These temperatures were lower than ever known on the North Coast.

Most of Ohio endured fifty hours or more of subzero weather from Monday night until Thursday morning. At Columbus and Cleveland the official thermometers were below zero for fifty-six hours. Temperatures at noon Wednesday, 19 January among Ohio's major cities ranged from -5 at Cincinnati to -12 at Akron and Findlay. The high temperature at Youngstown on Wednesday was only -6 degrees, the coldest on record.

Monday, 17 January 1994 was a school holiday for Martin Luther King Day, but snow closed many schools in southern Ohio on 18 January and the extreme cold caused most other Ohio schools to shut down Wednesday and Thursday. Some schools opened Friday, often with low attendance, but others were closed the whole week. Most universities closed on 19 January, and Ohio University canceled classes for the entire week.

Manufacturing was stymied by the cold. Honda assembly plants at Marysville and Anna were shut down two days by the cold weather and lack of parts, idling 10,200 workers. Workers were forced to use vacation days while the plants were closed, according to the *Columbus Dispatch*. Ford plants in Lorain and Cleveland were on four-hour shifts for a day when natural-gas supplies could not meet their demand. Lake Erie ice provided a sturdy basis for fishing, but ice-fishing guides at South Bass Island canceled all trips Wednesday—it was too cold. Retail business was down in most areas; however, pizza delivery and video rentals were doing good business as people sought food and entertainment at home. The Akzo Salt Mine under Lake Erie at Cleveland was running twenty-four hours a day, six or seven days a week, to keep up with the regional demand for road salt.

CHAPTER FOUR

Heat

TEMPERATURES FAR ABOVE normal may occur any time of the year in Ohio when an air mass from the subtropics envelops the region and sunshine heats the surface and air. Winter heat waves bring welcomed relief from the cold, but temperatures of 110 degrees during Ohio's extreme summer heat waves have had disastrous effects on the state.

Heat waves during the cool season from November to March originate in the Gulf of Mexico. Winter air temperatures over that region are 75 to 85 degrees, and a strong flow of air from the Gulf can raise winter temperatures to 60 degrees in Ohio if there is no snow cover to chill the tropical air mass. Heat waves during this season are considered "good" weather because they assure the absence of snow and ice for a few days, reduce heating costs, and allow Ohioans to shed winter clothing. However, winter heat can reduce the cold-hardiness of plants and a subsequent cold wave may damage the buds of fruit trees, grapevines, and other vegetation.

Most ordinary summer heat waves also originate in the Gulf of Mexico as the Bermuda High Pressure strengthens and weather across Ohio becomes "tropical" for a few days. These heat waves are common and cause the temperature to reach 90 degrees on twenty to thirty-five days each year in southern Ohio and five to fifteen days a year in the north (fig. 38). Heat waves along the northeastern lakeshore are tempered by the cooler waters of central Lake Erie.

Extraordinary summer heat waves cause temperatures to rise above 100 degrees over most of Ohio and are rare events in this climate. Temperatures in the moist tropics of the Gulf of Mexico do not exceed 100 degrees, so the source of extreme summer heat over Ohio is the dry, hot southwestern states. With little moisture in the surface soil and vegetation, most of the sun's energy is converted to heat in the dry southwestern climates, enabling temperatures to rise to 115 degrees in summer. Heat

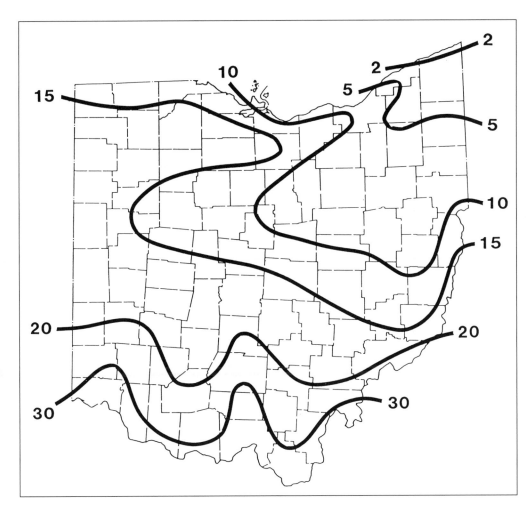

Fig. 38. Average annual number of days with a high temperature of 90 degrees or warmer.

waves with 110-degree temperatures often spread from the southwestern desert into the dry Great Plains of Texas, Oklahoma, Kansas, or even South Dakota. Heat of this intensity does not reach Ohio most years because the extensive crop and forest land east of the Great Plains provides so much water that evaporation from the moist surfaces cools the air mass. By the time air from the Southwest reaches Ohio it produces only a humid 95-degree day, uncomfortably hot, but not unusual.

A necessary condition for extreme summer heat in Ohio is a Midwest drought. Soils and vegetation are dry during these droughts, allowing the hot, dry air from the Southwest to enter Ohio without the cooling effects of evaporation. Under these drought conditions, temperatures have risen to 110 degrees in Ohio, peaking at 113 degrees in June 1934.

Extreme heat has widespread effects on human health, energy use, vegetation and crops, and the behavior of materials. Heat stress causes illness and death, especially among the elderly. In Ohio the deadly effects of heat begin as the temperatures rise above 90 degrees (Kalkstein and Davis 1989). In the great heat waves of the 1930s as many as fifty people a day died. Widespread use of air conditioning in homes, businesses, and public buildings has reduced the number of heat deaths (Rogot, Sorlie, and Backlund 1992), but for the elderly and others for whom cooling is not provided, the risk remains high.

Consumption of electricity peaks during heat waves, and Ohio utility companies may be forced to buy electricity out of state when demand exceeds their capacity to produce electricity. Crops and other vegetation wither in dry heat, and highway pavement may buckle as it expands under the hot sun. This chapter describes the outstanding heat waves in Ohio and their impacts on society.

4 July 1897
An Ohio Heat Record?

Official records show a temperature of 113 degrees was measured at Thurman, Gallia County, on Sunday, 4 July 1897. This temperature, the hottest ever recorded in Ohio, was later matched by a 113-degree reading near Gallipolis on 21 July 1934. A note by Alexander (1924, 291) concerning the temperature at Thurman casts doubt upon its validity. Alexander, referring to the data from Thurman, wrote, "The maximum temperatures from 1894 to 1901, inclusive, appear too high, due, perhaps, to improper exposure or a defective thermometer." On 4 July 1897, there was no other temperature in Ohio over 106 degrees, and Thurman was the only station east of the Mississippi River reporting a temperature as hot as 113.

The 9 July 1897 issue of the *Gallipolis Weekly Tribune* conveyed the news of a hot Independence Day, but no note was made of extraordinary temperatures. The *Tribune* editor wrote, "Sunday was a record breaker for heat. For two hours in the afternoon the mercury marked 99 degrees. We hoped to see it go to a hundred in the shade. We never have, but do not dispute it doing so." Given this statement, it seems unlikely a well-sheltered, accurate thermometer just fourteen miles away in Thurman could have read 113 degrees.

The absence of other temperatures near 113 degrees on 4 July 1897, Alexander's doubts about the record at Thurman, and a rather ordinary account of summer heat in the Gallipolis newspaper indicate that temperatures probably did not reach 113. We suggest that future references to Ohio's heat record of 113 degrees list it as having occurred only once, near Gallipolis on 21 July 1934.

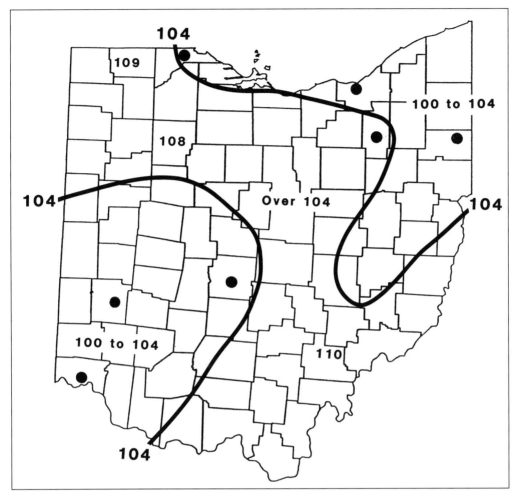

Fig. 39. High temperatures (in degrees Fahrenheit) on 5–6 August 1918. Maximum readings were 110 degrees in Athens County and 109 at Wauseon.

6 August 1918
August Heat

The greatest August heat wave known in Ohio extended from 4 to 14 August 1918 and culminated with extreme temperatures on Tuesday, 6 August. On that day, the average high temperature among forty-nine reporting stations in Ohio was 103.3 degrees (fig. 39). Most Ohio communities had their hottest day on record, although these records were eclipsed in the 1930s.

Amesville, ten miles northeast of Athens, recorded 110 degrees on 6 August 1918. Excluding the suspicious 113 degrees at Thurman in 1897, this was the hottest temperature recorded in Ohio up to that time, exceeding the previous record of 108 degrees at Pomeroy on 18 July 1887.

This record stood as Ohio's hottest temperature until 113 degrees was recorded near Gallipolis in the great heat wave of 1934.

Other extreme temperatures on 6 August 1918 included 109 degrees at Wauseon, west of Toledo, and 108 degrees at Findlay, McArthur, and Danbury. This was the hottest temperature recorded at Wauseon since records began in 1869. Longtime Wauseon observer Thomas Mikesell had recorded the previous heat record, 104.5 degrees on 7 July 1874. Even along the normally cool lakeshore, temperatures soared to 105 at Ashtabula and Sandusky and 103 at Toledo and Put-in-Bay.

Ohioans turned to the swimming holes, ice cream parlors, and parks to keep cool during the August 1918 heat. A record four thousand bathers crowded Toledo Beach, the greatest ever for a weekday, according to the *Toledo Blade*. The *Sandusky Register* reported Cedar Point also set a record for weekday bathers. The *Dayton Journal* reported "porch sleeping" was popular, and many spent the night on their fire escapes, lawns, or in parks to find relief from the stifling heat. In Dayton "men vied with women in the scantiness of dress . . . while everyone sought the shady side of the street."

There was much concern during the heat wave over a potential "ice famine." Ice companies could not keep up with the demand and many customers did not get ice as promised. In Dayton, where three hundred tons of ice was a normal consumption on a summer day, five hundred tons per day were being delivered, and that still was not enough. Dayton Mayor Jesse M. Switzer promised to look into the problems of the Miami Ice Delivery Company, which was not able to deliver ice to all consumers, causing "considerable inconvenience and some suffering." The *Dayton Journal* reported Miami Ice had nineteen delivery stations in the city and three thousand tons of ice in storage, but, even with drivers working eighteen-hour days and on Sunday, they could not keep up with the demand for ice. The company asked residents to come to an ice station and pick up ice themselves rather than wait for delivery. To speed delivery, all prisoners in the city workhouse were turned over to the ice company and were paid "regular ice company wages" until the crisis passed.

An ice famine existed in Lima, where fifteen hundred people waited through the night for a local ice plant to open in the morning. A general shortage of ice wagon drivers developed in Columbus. The *Columbus Evening Dispatch* reported that drivers were hired away from ice company jobs at thirty dollars per week by higher-paying government jobs. To alleviate the shortage, Crystal Ice Company in Columbus asked for workhouse prisoners to drive ice wagons. Despite the shortages of ice and trouble in deliveries, the *Sandusky Register* reported ice companies gave free ice to the poor of Ohio cities.

Factories in Toledo, Lorain, Warren, and other cities shut down when the men could no longer work in the extreme heat. Several dozen "heat prostrations" were reported around Ohio, and several deaths were attributed to the heat. It was widely reported that in Cleveland about thirty infants died from the heat.

A severe windstorm swept across Columbus near the end of the heat wave on 12 August. The Weather Bureau measured a one-minute wind speed of 102 miles an hour, and considerable damage was done to buildings and trees, especially on the Ohio State University campus.

1934
Hottest Summer

The summer of 1934 ranks as the hottest in Ohio since records began in 1883. The mean temperature of 75.7 degrees for the three summer months—June, July, and August—exceeded the previous record of 74.1 degrees set in 1901. Ohio's hottest summer since 1934 has thus far been 1949, with a mean temperature of 74.6 degrees, although 1936 was close behind at 74.5 degrees.

Warm and dry weather was a trademark of the early 1930s in Ohio and in much of the United States. In Ohio 1934 was the fifth consecutive year with average temperatures above normal and statewide precipitation below normal. Summer 1934 brought the hottest June and hottest July since at least 1883. August 1934 was only a little warmer than average. Every summer from 1930 to 1944 was warmer than average in Ohio (Rogers 1993), a period of heat that is unmatched in more than one hundred years of recordkeeping.

The dubious value of long-range weather predictions was illustrated that summer. Dr. James Scarr, head of the U.S. Weather Bureau office in New York City, was quoted in the 1 May 1934 *Canton Repository* as stating that the nation may be in for a cool summer in 1934 and "may even be facing another ice age." Dr. Scarr blamed the cold winter and spring of 1934 in the United States on the "cosmic dust" through which the earth was passing. This dust, he said, blocks the sun's rays and would cause the earth to be cool in the summer of 1934.

Cosmic dust or not, the summer 1934 was a record breaker. It was preceded in Ohio by the driest May in history, a rare 100-degree May temperature, and a general dust storm on 10 May. Dry conditions in Ohio and westward in the early 1930s contributed to the record heat in summer 1934. Dry soil and parched vegetation provided little water for evaporation, so surfaces heated to temperatures not normally experienced in the Heartland.

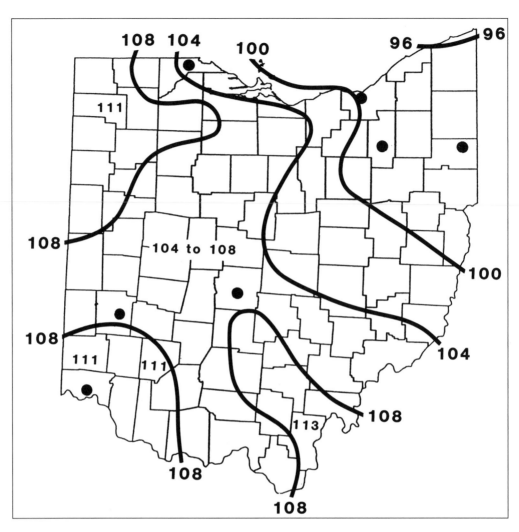

Fig. 40. High temperatures (in degrees Fahrenheit) during July 1934. A temperature of 113 near Gallipolis on 21 July 1934 remains as the hottest ever recorded in Ohio and the hottest temperature recorded so far east in the United States.

Temperatures during June 1934 were above normal on all but two or three days. Highs rose to 106 degrees at Hamilton, Paulding, and Defiance on 1 June. The warmest high of the month was 108 degrees at Germantown (Montgomery County) on 29 June. July 1934, with a mean temperature of 78.8 degrees, ranks as Ohio's hottest month. It exceeded the previous monthly heat record of July 1901 by .6 degree. The hottest month since July 1934 has been July 1955, with an average temperature of 77.5 degrees. Extreme heat during July crested across much of Ohio on the weekend of 21–22 July (fig. 40). Meteorologist William Alexander was quoted in Friday newspapers predicting that the "hottest weather the state has ever produced" would arrive for the weekend. He was right. Most cities in central and southern Ohio established records that have yet to be matched.

Temperatures began their rise to the weekend crest on Friday, 20 July as Toledo and Columbus reached 101 degrees, Fremont 103 degrees, and Cincinnati 105 degrees. That Friday night was one of the hottest in memory as temperatures cooled little from the afternoon highs. The heat wave continued for another week, but all-time heat records were set on Saturday, 21 July with 109 degrees at Cincinnati and 106 degrees at Columbus. Defiance reported 108 degrees, and Wilmington and Hamilton sizzled at 111. It was also on 21 July 1934 that the hottest temperature ever recorded in Ohio, 113 degrees, was measured near Gallipolis. This event is described in more detail below. Extreme heat continued through the weekend with 108 degrees at Cincinnati on Sunday. Thunderstorms rumbled across the state Sunday evening, damaging buildings and crops at Piqua, Newark, Gallipolis, and other communities.

The next wave of extreme heat came across Ohio on Tuesday and Wednesday 24–25 July, when the hottest temperatures were reported from northwestern counties. Defiance reported 111 degrees, Fremont reached an all-time record of 110, Findlay and Montpelier soared to 109, Bowling Green and Napoleon hit 107, and Lima reached 106. The high of 103 degrees at Toledo was the hottest temperature there since 1918, although this was exceeded by a record 105 degrees in July 1936. Farther east along the North Coast, Cleveland reached a July heat record with a relatively mild 99 degrees.

Heat continued in central Ohio on 25–26 July with 109 degrees at Chillicothe, 108 at Delaware, and 107 in Wilmington. The *Columbus Dispatch* reported expansion of pavement caused part of Route 7 to blow up near Marietta. A brick street exploded in Frankfort and damaged a poultry truck. The July heat wave ended when cooler air arrived on the evening of Thursday, 26 July.

Heat takes a great toll on human life, and although the exact number of deaths caused by heat is difficult to determine, some estimates were made for the 1934 heat wave. During the week 20–26 July 1934, it was estimated that 160 Ohioans died from the heat, according to the *Columbus Dispatch*. Half of those deaths were in Cincinnati.

Urban neighborhoods retain heat through the day and into the night, so cities may be much warmer than rural districts (Schmidlin 1989c). For example, an unofficial street-level thermometer on the Dispatch Building in Columbus showed 112 degrees on 22 July and was still 100 degrees at 8:30 P.M. that evening. The 25 July *Fremont Messenger* reported: "Tuesday night was the hottest night of the year and a sweating populace awoke unrefreshed after restless slumber to hear the discouraging word that no relief was in sight for at least another 24 hours."

Extreme heat withered crops in Ohio. The combination of heat and drought in the summer of 1934 resulted in water use restrictions for many communities. Toledo residents used a record 56 million gallons of water on 24 July, and residents were asked to limit lawn sprinkling. Springfield fire fighters ordered residents to stop all water use immediately whenever the fire siren sounded so that pressure was available for fighting the fire.

Extreme heat returned to Ohio in the summer of 1936, but between these two hot summers, bitter cold prevailed during January and February 1936.

Fig 41. Weather observer Edwin "Pete" McCormick at the government weather station on Route 588 near Gallipolis. McCormick recorded the hottest temperature in Ohio, 113 degrees, at this site on 21 July 1934. (Photograph courtesy of Alice Mossman)

21 July 1934
Ohio's Hottest Temperature

Temperatures during Ohio's hottest summer reached their peak from 21 to 25 July 1934. Highs across Ohio were the hottest ever known at many locations. At 3:00 P.M. on Saturday, 21 July 1934 a weather station near Gallipolis recorded a high of 113 degrees, the hottest temperature ever officially recorded in Ohio, and also the hottest temperature recorded so far east in the United States.

The previous Ohio heat record of 110 degrees at Amesville, Athens County, on 6 August 1918 was exceeded at three other Ohio stations, Defiance, Hamilton, and Wilmington, with highs of 111 degrees during the July 1934 heat wave. The hottest since 1934 was 111 degrees at Paulding on 14 July 1936 and at Napoleon on 6 August 1947.

Edwin "Pete" McCormick was the weather observer who recorded the 113-degree record (fig. 41). His home was about four miles northwest of Gallipolis on the north side of State Route 588, just west of the intersection with Mitchell Road at an elevation of 673 feet above sea level. Alice Mossman, Pete McCormick's niece and neighbor who occasionally took observations when McCormick was away, told us the thermometers were located in a shelter just off the driveway in Mr. McCormick's yard (letter to the authors, 9 June 1993). The shelter was 25 to 30 feet east of the house (Jonathan Louden, Gallia County Librarian, letter to the authors, 18 July 1988).

The 113-degree record was preceded by an uncomfortably hot night, and the temperature was up to 105 by noon. The 23 July 1934 *Gallipolis Daily Tribune* reported "even the Indians and Mound builders may never have known of temperatures ranging from 109 to 113 degrees in this sector." Depression politics continued in the extreme heat. Several hundred persons "were held in rapt attention and greatly impressed by the powerful speech" given from a Gallipolis park bench by Daniel Morgan, a contender for the Republican nomination for governor.

Gallipolis had some relief from the heat in the form of thunderstorms Sunday evening but paid a price. Storm winds flattened crops, destroyed barns and chimneys, and blew the roof from the Gallia Hotel. The *Gallipolis Daily Tribune* reported that, as a subject for conversation, the freakish weather over the weekend outweighed even the fatal shooting of John Dillinger by federal agents in Chicago.

8–15 July 1936
Most Intense Heat Wave

"Relief, like Mr. Hoover's prosperity, was still around the corner." This Depression-era quote of frustration appeared in the *Napoleon Northwest-*

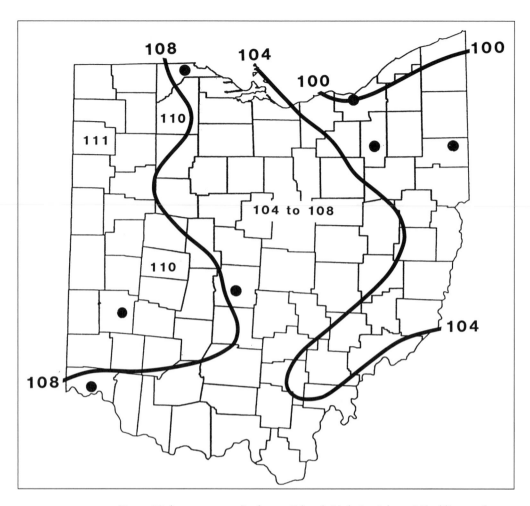

Fig. 42. High temperatures (in degrees Fahrenheit) during July 1936. Paulding was hottest with 111 degrees and several cities reached 110. Maximum temperatures of 106 at Columbus and 105 in Toledo on 14 July 1936 are the hottest ever recorded in those cities.

News after the temperature soared to 110 degrees in Napoleon during Ohio's longest heat wave. Outstanding weather with extreme drought, heat, and cold became a trademark of the early 1930s. This period of extreme weather culminated with an unprecedented July heat wave in 1936.

The eight days from 8 to 15 July 1936 were the hottest ever known in Ohio. Temperatures exceeded 100 degrees at most weather stations every day and reached extremes in many cities that still remain as all-time records sixty years later (fig. 42). Among the eighty-eight Ohio weather stations operating in 1936, only three, Cleveland, Bangorville (Richland County), and Demos (Belmont County), failed to reach 100 degrees during July 1936. Those three stations attained "only" 99 degrees.

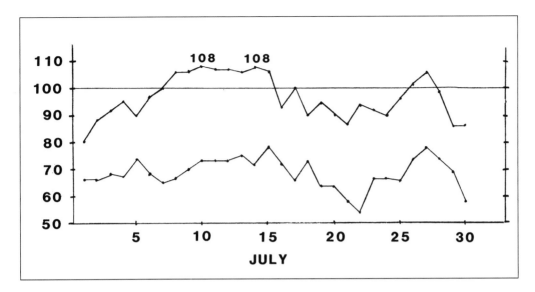

Fig. 43. Daily maximum (upper line) and minimum (lower line) temperatures (in degrees Fahrenheit) at Hamilton during July 1936. A horizontal line marks 100 degrees. The heat wave of 8–15 July was the most intense known in Ohio.

Ohio's heat record of 113 degrees set two years earlier near Gallipolis was not exceeded in July 1936, but the average temperatures across Ohio during 8–15 July 1936 were hotter than in any similar period in 1934. The average high temperature among Ohio weather stations during 8–15 July was 101.7 degrees. The hottest were Hamilton, with an eight-day average of 106.8 degrees (fig. 43), and Bowling Green, where highs averaged 106.4 degrees.

Heat intensity reached a peak on 14 July, with an average high temperature of 105 degrees among Ohio's weather stations. Paulding was Ohio's hottest site with 111 degrees, but Bowling Green, Napoleon, Urbana, and Van Wert were close behind with 110 degrees. Highs of 106 at Columbus and 105 at Toledo on 14 July are the maximum of record at those cities.

Although the impacts of extreme heat were felt throughout Ohio, the hottest temperatures and greatest suffering occurred in the northwest. Few homes or places of employment had air conditioning, so heat stress was common. One-half of the population of Henry County was sleeping in basements, on porches, or on lawns, according to the *Napoleon Northwest-News.* "Wearing apparel," the paper noted, "was cut down to the absolute minimum permitted by law, and ice cream and beer parlors were doing a land-office business." Stores in Napoleon were sold out of electric fans, and "the old-fashioned, hand-propelled fan was being swung with rare abandon in some of the best parlors in town." The *Defiance*

Crescent-News reported on 10 July that the "hospital is crowded with patients" and fire fighters flooded the hospital grounds and roof with water to reduce the "high temperatures in which patients sweltered." Infants and the elderly, especially those in frail health, were most vulnerable to heat stress.

Highways cracked and buckled as they expanded with heat, sending pavement flying into the air. Route 2 between Hicksville and Farmer exploded on 9 July. This fourteen-mile stretch of highway was plagued with six breaks in five days. Other pavement breaks were reported on Route 24 west of Defiance, on Route 33 in Napoleon, and on Route 115 near Holgate. A two-foot-wide strip of bricks on Main Street in Napoleon exploded. Automobile engines ran poorly. Mechanics explained that "excessive heat caused gasoline to run through the carburetors without vaporizing thoroughly." Water use was high during the heat wave. The Defiance water plant pumped 1,288,000 gallons on Saturday 11 July, 65 percent more than usual.

The extreme heat of July 1936 affected much of the country. The 11 July *Defiance Crescent-News* reported, "Half of America awoke again today to find itself prisoner for the eighth straight day in a titanic natural oven in which humans and cattle and crops slowly were having the life baked from them and money was melting by the hundreds of millions." The only 120-degree temperatures known outside the desert Southwest occurred in July 1936, with highs of 121 degrees in Kansas and North Dakota.

The record-breaking heat ended over Ohio late on 16 July, although temperatures remained in the 90s for the rest of the month and ascended to 100 degrees again at several sites on 27 July.

6 August 1947
Hottest August

The period from 3 August to 14 September 1947 was one of the longest periods of summer heat in Ohio. Temperatures at Columbus were above average for forty-three consecutive days, averaging 7.3 degrees warmer than normal and exceeding even the warmest period of the hot summers of the 1930s. This heat wave also goes into the record books for the hottest temperature ever recorded during August in Ohio—111 degrees recorded by observer Harry Knipp at Napoleon on Wednesday, 6 August 1947.

The extreme heat at Napoleon is somewhat puzzling, because the heat of 1947 was not generally marked by excessively high temperatures in Ohio, but rather by sustained moderate heat in the 90s. For example, only ten of eighty-seven reporting stations in Ohio reached 100 degrees during August 1947, and only Napoleon exceeded 105 degrees. On 14 July 1936, when Napoleon recorded 110 degrees, Bowling Green, Van Wert, and Urbana also recorded 110 and Paulding was 111 degrees. But in 1947, Napoleon stood alone with excessive heat. This may have been the result of a unique combination of still air and clear skies at Napoleon, slight warming of air as it descended the Maumee Valley, or a poor exposure of the thermometer at Napoleon that allowed poor ventilation or brief exposure to the sun.

With little air conditioning yet in 1947, the fifteen to twenty days in August with temperatures of more than 90 degrees created heat stress among Ohioans. The *Cleveland Plain Dealer* reported that 11 persons had died from the heat in Ohio through 8 August and the national death toll stood at 135. The 98-degree heat at Toledo on 6 August caused the Willys-Overland factory (now Jeep) to cancel the afternoon production on station wagon and truck lines and send 2,500 workers home. Lawn sprinkling was banned in several cities by 12 August to conserve municipal water pressures. This hot August followed a cold, wet spring and a cool July. For farmers, the heat of August provided quick crop growth, and the progress of corn and soybeans was described in the August 1947 issue of *Climatological Data—Ohio Section* as "spectacular and a little short of miraculous."

4 September 1953
Greatest September Heat

The longest and most intense late summer heat wave in Ohio history scorched the state for ten days in late August and early September 1953. Afternoon temperatures rose above 95 degrees by 25 August and were near 100 from 30 August to 4 September. This was the last great Ohio heat wave before air conditioning became common in offices, stores, and homes in the 1960s.

A high temperature of 107 degrees at Philo, Muskingum County, on 4 September equaled the September heat record for Ohio, set at Logan on 5 September 1899. Highs in early September reached 106 degrees at Coshocton and Milford and 105 degrees at Napoleon, Fremont, and Gallipolis. The "coolest" location in Ohio was the eastern lakeshore, where Painesville warmed to only 96 degrees.

Temperatures in Cincinnati were 100 to 103 degrees from Monday, 31 August to 2 September. Five hundred employees of the Union Central Life Insurance Company were sent home from their offices on 31 August. Fans were sought for the sixth floor courthouse jail in Cincinnati after temperatures reached 112 degrees in the cells. City pools closed for the summer on Tuesday, 1 September but were reopened the next day due to the extreme heat.

The Ohio State Fair ran in Columbus during the heat wave. A record one-day fair attendance of 124,408 was noted on Sunday, 30 August in spite of 100-degree heat at the Columbus Airport Weather Bureau office. Nearly 2,000 people received medical attention at the fair, and there were seventy-three ambulance runs to the fairgrounds. Judges of flower, vegetable, and fruit exhibits had to choose ribbon winners quickly before exhibits wilted in the heat. Vendors were pleased with ice cream and drink sales, which were well above normal. People, animals, and exhibits at the fair consumed a million gallons of water a day, causing a water shortage for the rest of Columbus.

Cleveland residents suffered through three consecutive days of 101-degree heat, the hottest ever in September and the first time that city had recorded two days in a row at 100 degrees. The acting police chief issued a "hot-weather order" directing police to give special attention to safety in city parks, where many residents were sleeping to beat the heat. Businesses and factories closed early, including the Federal Reserve Bank and the American Steel and Wire Company. Lead insulators on electric lines expanded and burst in the heat, cutting power to ten thousand Cleveland area residents. The *Cleveland Plain Dealer* reported that as of 4 September seven Clevelanders had died due to the heat.

Forecasters were expecting a cold front on 3 September and, for encouragement, noted that snow was falling in Wyoming. The front was delayed one day, but relief finally arrived in Ohio during the afternoon of Friday, 4 September in the form of cool air and rain. Temperatures were cool for the remainder of the month and frost was reported by 23 September.

2 December 1982
Warmest December Day

A storm system with strong southwest winds over the Plains and a jet stream of nearly one hundred miles an hour from Texas into the Midwest gave the warmest December temperatures ever observed in Ohio. Highs during 2–3 December reached 70 degrees in all but extreme northwestern Ohio. Temperatures in the middle 70s were common in the east and south. Highs of 80 degrees at Ironton and Gallipolis on 2 December and at Athens and Chillicothe on 3 December established new December heat records for Ohio, exceeding the previous December heat record of 79 degrees at Ironton on 9 December 1911. The *Ironton Tribune* story of the heat was headlined, "Weather undermines Christmas spirit." This was the beginning of the warmest December in Ohio since 1931, and it culminated with the warmest Christmas known in Ohio.

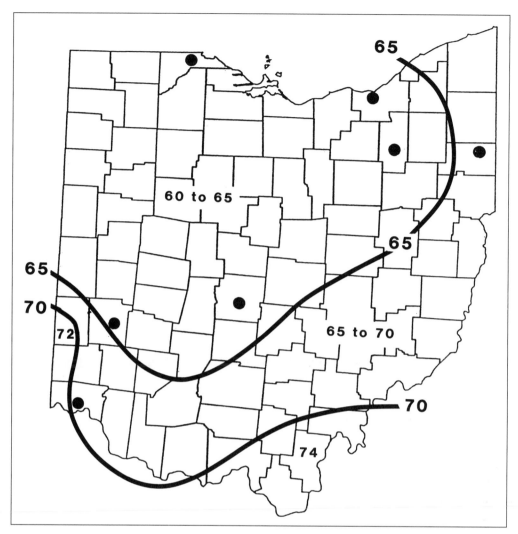

Fig. 44. High temperatures (in degrees Fahrenheit) on 25 December 1982, Ohio's hottest Christmas. Gallipolis was warmest with 74 degrees.

25 December 1982
Warmest Christmas

A strong storm system over the central Great Plains pulled springlike air over Ohio, making Christmas 1982 the warmest ever recorded in the state. The Plains storm also piled the deepest snow in seventy years on Denver, Colorado, closing the airport for thirty-six hours during the busy holiday travel period.

Temperatures started out at July levels across Ohio on Christmas morning. It was 60 degrees at dawn in Cleveland and 64 degrees by 10:00 A.M. in Cincinnati. Showers dampened the southwestern counties, but dry weather allowed heat records to fall by afternoon across the rest of Ohio.

Highs reached 60 degrees at all stations and exceeded 65 degrees in the east and south (fig. 44). Records for Christmas heat that had stood since 1893 fell at Toledo and Akron. The high of 66 at Cleveland broke that city's Christmas heat record set in 1932. The warmest temperatures occurred along the Ohio River, where Portsmouth, Ironton, and Gallipolis exceeded 70 degrees.

Just one year later, on Christmas 1983, one of the greatest cold waves of history swept the region. Temperatures across Ohio were below zero all day, some 70 degrees colder than enjoyed on Christmas 1982.

21 August 1983
Hottest since 1954

A hot summer month with temperatures 4 degrees above normal in Ohio culminated with a hot Sunday on 21 August 1983. Highs reached 100 degrees in western and southern Ohio and peaked at 107 at Meldahl Lock and Dam along the Ohio River west of Chilo. This was the hottest official temperature in Ohio since 107 degrees was recorded at the downtown Cincinnati Weather Bureau office on 12 July 1954. The 107-degree temperature has not been matched in Ohio since 1983. Other hot readings in August 1983 included 105 degrees at Chillicothe and 104 degrees at Hamilton and Cincinnati-Fernbank.

Ohio River communities reached 90 degrees on twenty or more days during August 1983, and some nights did not cool below 75 degrees. Heavy use of air conditioning created record electricity demand for Cincinnati Gas and Electric Company. The *Cincinnati Post* reported that twenty-three "cool centers" were opened in city neighborhoods for residents to escape from the heat. Unhealthy levels of air pollution accompanied the heat in Cincinnati and caused added stress to the elderly and those with respiratory problems.

25 June 1988
Hot Saturday

An early summer heat wave in the midst of the hot summer and drought of 1988 brought some of the hottest weather ever in far northern Ohio. This was Cleveland's hottest day since records began in 1871.

June had been hot and dry in Ohio and throughout the Midwest. Hot southwest summer winds from Texas and Mexico are usually modified by passing over green, moist forests and crops before reaching Ohio. But in June 1988, there was nothing but dry, parched ground between Texas and Ohio. The strong southwest wind on 25 June brought 100-degree air di-

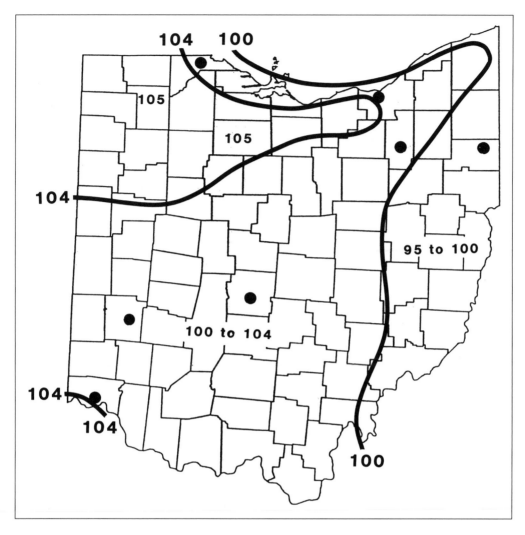

Fig. 45. High temperatures (in degrees Fahrenheit) on 25 June 1988. Readings of 104 degrees at Toledo and Cleveland were the hottest ever recorded in June and, at Cleveland, the hottest in that city's history.

rectly from the southern Plains. For some residents, it brought back haunting memories of the hot, dry winds of June 1934 and July 1936, when similar conditions prevailed.

Temperatures reached 95 degrees at every reporting station in Ohio and exceeded 100 degrees in most of the western and central counties (fig. 45). The hottest official reading in Ohio was 106 degrees at Cincinnati-Fernbank. This was the second hottest June temperature ever recorded in Ohio, exceeded only by 108 degrees at Germantown on 29 June 1934. Temperatures on this Hot Saturday reached 105 at Tiffin, Napoleon, and Hoytville.

The high of 104 degrees at Cleveland was the hottest temperature since records began at Cleveland in 1871, exceeding the previous record of 103 set on 27 July 1941. Toledo also recorded a high of 104, breaking the June heat record of 101 for Toledo but missing the all-time record of 105 set on 14 July 1936. Southwest winds of fifteen to twenty-five miles an hour, gusting to more than forty, combined with dry soil, low humidity, and drought-stunted crops to raise clouds of dust.

Much cooler air arrived on Sunday, 26 June, with temperatures 30 degrees cooler than on Saturday. By Monday morning, a record low of 45 degrees was recorded at Toledo, just forty hours after the hottest June day in more than one hundred years!

CHAPTER FIVE

Drought

DROUGHT IS A slow disaster. It comes gradually, without warning, over several weeks, affecting vegetation, water supplies, and society over large areas. Drought can be distinguished from "dry spells" by length and intensity. Dry spells occur frequently in Ohio. Sunshine and a lack of rain for three or four weeks turn lawns and gardens brown but allow uninterrupted outdoor activities and are usually considered "good" weather. These dry spells may reduce crop yields if they occur at critical times during the season, but dire predictions of reduced yields usually do not materialize. Dry spells end as normal rainfall returns after a few weeks, and there is little lasting effect.

Droughts occur because a persistent weather pattern blocks moisture from entering the region or because the mechanisms for producing precipitation are lacking. For example, a persistent flow of air from the west prevents moisture from the Gulf of Mexico from reaching Ohio. Strong and persistent high pressure inhibits convection and blocks weather fronts from the region. These conditions commonly occur for several short periods each year, but weather patterns producing "extreme" drought, the driest category in the Palmer Hydrological Drought Index (PHDI), occur only about every ten years in Ohio (Dickerson and Dethier 1970). Causes of drought are summarized by Namias (1983).

Notable early droughts were reported in Ohio in 1841, 1856, 1863, and 1870–72 (Mindling 1944; Rogers 1993). Values of the PHDI have been calculated back to 1895 for Ohio, and since that time the greatest droughts have been in 1895, 1930–31, 1934, 1953–54, 1963–64, and 1988. The characteristics and impacts of these six great Ohio droughts are described in this chapter.

1895
Drought

Rogers (1993) identified the three years from June 1893 to May 1896 as one of the most persistent periods of dry weather in Ohio during the past 140 years. Twenty-eight of thirty-six months were dry during this period, with the most intense dry weather occurring in the summer of 1895. Precipitation in Ohio from February to October 1895 averaged only 16.4 inches, compared to the nine-month normal of 29.5 inches. Heavy rains during November and December 1895 ended the drought, although some water supplies remained short into the spring of 1896.

All of Ohio was in severe or extreme drought during the summer and autumn of 1895. The 1895 agricultural season started out dry and there was little rain until late August. No hay was available for market in June, and some farmers were replanting hayfields with corn to be used for animal feed, according to the 15 June 1895 *Lima Times-Democrat*. Yields of oats, hay, wheat, and apples were diminished by the summer drought, but rains in late August improved the corn crop and brought growth to pastures.

Barge traffic on the Miami-Erie Canal was suspended between Defiance and Toledo by late June 1895 as the Maumee River fell to its lowest level in years. Many other smaller streams were dry by July. Municipal water supplies ran out in some parts of Ohio. The 1 August 1895 *Hamilton Daily Democrat* reported that Dayton banned all lawn and street sprinkling and Middletown began pumping canal water for consumers when the city wells ran dry. Effects of the drought were lessened by a cool July that reduced water demands, in contrast to the extreme heat that characterized droughts of the twentieth century.

1930
Drought

The 1930s were characterized by hot, dry summers and drought conditions in Ohio and much of the central United States. The period from April 1930 to March 1931 is the driest twelve months ever recorded in Ohio, with only 21.9 inches of precipitation, 16 inches below normal (Rogers 1993). July 1930 stands as the driest July in Ohio history, with a state average of 1.52 inches of rain, about 38 percent of average.

Following a dry spring and the record dry July, extreme drought prevailed all through Ohio from July 1930 to June 1931. The effects of drought were most evident in summer and autumn 1930. Temporary relief came with above-average precipitation in summer 1931 and winter 1931–32. The spring of 1933 was very wet, but drought developed again in the hot summer of 1934. The frequent droughts of the 1930s were finally alleviated with the record rains of January 1937.

Fig. 46. Sparse and stunted corn during the drought of 1930 in Fayette County. (Photograph courtesy of the Fayette County Historical Society)

Surface runoff stopped during the summer of 1930, causing the underground water supply to diminish rapidly (Devereaux 1930). Springs and creeks stopped flowing and wells failed. Rains in September 1930 revived pastures and gardens, but there was no runoff to start stream flow or improve municipal water supplies. Very dry conditions returned in October 1930 and lasted through January 1931.

Drought was intensified by temperatures that exceeded 100 degrees on several days during July and August 1930, reaching 109 degrees at Circleville on 20 July and 108 degrees at Fremont on the twenty-first. Ironton reported 106 degrees on 28 July, and Steubenville warmed to 106 degrees on 4 August. As usual during droughts, extreme heat was punctuated by record cold. At Wilmington, a July heat record of 102 degrees on 12 July was followed by a July cold record of 41 degrees on 15 July. The hottest and coldest July temperatures recorded in seventeen years came just three days apart! Frost was reported in some areas of Ohio on 15 July 1930.

Hot weather caused wheat to ripen two weeks earlier than normal. Harvest began on 21 June, according to the *Wilmington News-Journal,* but yields were only about 70 percent of normal. Milk production dropped as pastures turned brown. Sweet corn showed little growth, and some canning companies announced in late July that they would not be opening for the season (fig. 46). This affected not just growers of sweet corn but also hundreds who depended on the canneries for a few weeks of late summer work and income. Vegetable growers near Cleveland ran water lines to irrigate their fields, but the ponds and streams ran dry, cutting off the source of irrigation water.

As the agricultural crisis deepened, the Ohio Chamber of Commerce called a meeting of businessmen, bankers, and agricultural leaders in Columbus to survey effects of the drought and discuss measures of relief to agriculture. Governor Myers Cooper met with President Herbert Hoover early in August and announced a plan for farm relief in Ohio. Record numbers of cattle, dairy cows, and sheep arrived at Columbus auction houses in August, raising fears of a milk and meat shortage later in the year. In fact, although large numbers of animals were sold some weeks, overall deliveries of animals to market were only a little above normal and no shortages developed. By autumn it was announced that the corn production in Ohio was 69 percent of average, sugar beets 70 percent of average, and hay production just 58 percent of average. An excellent crop of tobacco was reported.

Reservoirs of the B&O Railroad ran dry in Clinton County by mid-July, and water had to be hauled from distant wells to supply the trains. Water was hauled to many rural families whose wells gave out in July. Pasture and woodland fires burned thousands of acres but caused little property damage. Several communities restricted water use, and the city of Canton, according to the *Wilmington News-Journal,* hired thirty men to patrol the city and prevent use of city water for lawn sprinkling, washing cars, and filling swimming pools.

1934
Drought

Ohio had recovered from the 1930–31 drought by the spring of 1933, when most of the state was wetter than normal. However, dry weather prevailed again during the summer of 1933 in central and northern Ohio, and drought had spread across the state again by the spring of 1934. With a statewide average precipitation of 26.7 inches, the year 1934 was 12 inches below average and the fourth driest twelve-month period since 1854 (Rogers 1993). The driest weather stations in 1934 were Put-in-Bay with 17.80 inches and Kenton with 18.79 inches. The period from mid-April to mid-June was especially dry, with only .5 to 1.5 inches of rain at many sites (Mindling 1944), far below the average of 6 to 8 inches.

Severe to extreme drought existed in most of Ohio from May 1934 to April 1935 (Karl and Knight 1985b). Summer 1934 was also the hottest summer in Ohio history (Rogers 1993), adding to the hardships caused by drought. By August 1934, flow in the Miami River at Dayton was only 109 cubic feet per second (cfs), compared to an annual average of about 1,000 cfs (Mindling 1944). The Little Miami River at Batavia was at its lowest level in more than thirty years by early June, according to the *Cincinnati Enquirer*. The press hailed this as the worst drought in many years in Ohio but, in fact, drought conditions were not as severe as in 1930.

Statewide average rainfall for May 1934 was only .78 inch, 20 percent of average and the driest on record (Rogers 1993). Blowing dust enveloped much of Ohio during 10–11 May, coating surfaces and giving a yellowish color to the sky, according to the *Norwalk Reflector-Herald*. Forest fires in mid-May destroyed more than ten thousand acres of timber in south-central Ohio. Homes were saved from the inferno by Civilian Conservation Corps workers, who cut away trees and lit backfires. Although dry spring weather was favorable for planting, by the end of May crops were stunted and water was being hauled for livestock all through Ohio.

A general rain provided some relief in mid-June, and in spite of continued extreme heat, crops were much improved by July. Rains were favorable through the rest of the summer, although the heat prevented water from penetrating the soil very deeply. Forecasts for Ohio crop production continued to be adjusted upward into October 1934 as the yields exceeded dire forecasts made early in the summer.

1953–54
Drought

Dry weather prevailed across Ohio during the summer and autumn of 1952, and the PHDI reached the "moderate" category by winter. Drought was alleviated somewhat by near-normal rainfall during the winter and spring of 1953, but twenty-three of the twenty-six months from May 1952 to July 1954 were below normal in precipitation (Rogers 1993). Extreme heat accompanied the very dry autumn of 1953, resulting in widespread consequences and creating extreme drought conditions the following winter. This drought, as with most droughts that affect Ohio, was felt across much of the nation. At its peak, the 1953–54 drought covered 51 percent of the United States (Heim 1988).

The primary impact of the drought was a reduced water supply in wells and reservoirs from autumn 1953 to the spring of 1954. Rural residents were especially stricken with dry wells. For example, the *Lancaster Eagle-Gazette* reported that Knox County farmers whose wells were empty were allowed to haul water from the Mt. Vernon city water system. The Oberlin College swim team could not practice in October 1953—there was not enough water to fill the pool.

Severe to extreme drought continued into the summer of 1954, but rainfall was sufficient to restore soil moisture and ensure normal crops during 1954. Deep-soil water supplies remained critically short into 1954, and it was not until autumn 1954 that water supplies in wells and reservoirs returned to normal.

1962–65
Drought

Drought prevailed in portions of Ohio from summer 1962 to the summer of 1965. For most of this time, mild to moderate drought conditions existed, especially in the north, but a very dry autumn 1963 and winter 1963–64 produced extreme drought statewide. A wet spring of 1964, including some floods, alleviated this drought, but a dry autumn again in 1964 returned portions of Ohio to severe drought in the winter of 1964–65.

Precipitation for Ohio in the year 1963 was only 26.5 inches. This was 12 inches less than average and the driest calendar year in Ohio since records began in 1854 (Rogers 1993). September and October 1963 were especially dry, with a two-month statewide total of just 1.15 inches, compared to the normal of 5.42 inches. Several stations received no measurable rainfall at all during October 1963. For September and October combined, Piqua had just .06 inch; Eaton, .09 inch; St. Marys, .14 inch; and Versailles and Dayton, only .17 inch. A weather station one mile south of Sidney had no measurable rainfall at all during September and October 1963!

Agricultural production was reduced in some areas, but overall production for Ohio was not severely affected in any of the years during this long dry period. A combination of adequate rains in portions of the state and timely rains when crops desperately need rain, during July for corn for example, contributed to the small impact on yields. Dry weather during planting and harvest seasons can actually be beneficial to crop yields. Impacts of the drought were primarily in Ohio forest lands and water supplies. Wells and reservoirs were at critically low levels and hundreds went dry. Forest and pasture fires were common across the state during October 1963 and in other seasons during the dry 1962–65 period.

1988
Drought

Unlike droughts of the 1950s and 1960s, which were focused in the autumn and winter seasons, the drought of 1988 occurred in spring and summer and had a widespread impact on agricultural production, in addition to reducing water supplies in streams, wells, and reservoirs. This was also the hottest summer in more than thirty years, and temperatures over 100 degrees enhanced the deleterious effects of the drought.

Drought developed across Ohio during autumn 1987 but near-average precipitation in the winter of 1987–88 kept the PHDI in the mild to moderate range into spring 1988. Very dry conditions during spring and early summer 1988 caused a worsening of the drought, so that most of Ohio was in "extreme" drought by summer (Rogers 1993). Ohio came out of the drought with a wet fall in 1988 and a wet spring in 1989. A dramatic reversal came in 1990, the wettest year known in Ohio, with a statewide average of 51.4 inches of rain (Rogers 1993). However, dry weather returned in the summer and autumn of 1991 and drought prevailed again in Ohio during winter 1991–92.

Severe or extreme drought enveloped 45 percent of the continental United States by July 1988, with the driest conditions in the northern Midwest and Ohio Valley (Heim 1988). During this drought in the Heartland, the usually dry American Southwest was getting record rainfall. Climatologists attributed this condition to an unusual pattern of air flow that prevailed for three months across the United States (Trenberth, Branstator, and Arkin 1988). A trough of low pressure in the far West gave storms and rains to the deserts while high pressure in the midcontinent forced the storm track far north into Canada and caused drought in the Midwest. By examining global weather, the climatologists traced this unusual pattern back to the tropical Pacific Ocean, where unusually warm waters early in 1988 had caused a change in the normal spring and summer flow in the atmosphere. These anomalies in the central Pacific extended eastward across North America.

Dry conditions in Ohio during April and May began to have an impact on crops by early June. Yields on the first cutting of hay were only 50 to 60 percent of normal in central and southern Ohio, according to the 2 June 1988 *Columbus Dispatch,* and newly emerged corn plants were wilting. Hay was being imported from other states by midsummer to feed Ohio livestock.

On 24 June, the Ohio Department of Agriculture forecast the Ohio corn crop would be 33 percent of normal and the soybean crop just 10 percent of normal, according to the 25 June *Columbus Dispatch.* Such early predictions were overly pessimistic, as usual during a drought. In fact, the 1988 Ohio corn and soybean crops were both about 75 percent of the average for the 1980s (Ohio Department of Agriculture 1993). This was still a significant reduction and had a major impact on the farm economy in Ohio. Yields were much lower than the state average in areas where rains did not come at critical periods in crop growth. On the other hand, yields were about normal where timely rains appeared.

Although the drought of 1988 hurt the overall economy of Ohio, some segments profited from the hot, dry summer. Air-conditioner sales were booming, air-conditioning repair businesses worked around the clock, ice plants were operating at capacity, and ice cream sales were above normal. Companies supplying bottled water had record sales and trucks were booked thirty days in advance to haul larger quantities of water. Another benefit of the drought was fewer mosquitoes in Ohio during June and early July.

State officials created a "drought task force" in June headed by Lt. Gov. Paul Leonard. The task force assessed the impact of the drought, made efforts to raise awareness of the situation, and coordinated government response to the crisis. A more celebrated effort to alleviate the drought occurred in Sandusky County, where, according to the *Columbus Dispatch,* a local florist paid one thousand dollars to bring a Sioux medicine man from the Rosebud Indian Reservation to begin a four-day rain-making ceremony on 19 June. Promoters may not have noticed that South Dakota, home of the medicine man, was also suffering from extreme drought. A little rain fell after the rain dance, but the drought continued.

A change of the weather patterns over North America brought general rains back to Ohio by late July, and the months of August and September 1988 had normal rainfall across the state. This alleviated the dryness in the surface soil and helped lawns and crops. However, little water penetrated into the deeper soil, so wells and reservoirs remained low until heavier rains returned in spring 1989.

CHAPTER SIX

Floods

OHIO STREAMS EFFICIENTLY carry runoff from precipitation south into the Ohio River and north to Lake Erie. Stream flow normally reaches a peak in spring, when soils are saturated and vegetation is not consuming water, and reaches a minimum in late summer, autumn, or winter. Smaller streams have a cover of ice in winter, and even the largest rivers freeze over during the coldest periods of winter, although water continues to flow beneath the ice.

Floods may be divided into two general categories, flash floods and regional floods. Flash floods are local events affecting one or two small watersheds. They are the result of intense local rainfall, usually during summer thunderstorms, and last just a few hours. There is little warning time for flash floods because they develop quickly and accurate forecasts for thunderstorm rainfall amounts are not yet possible. Most people in the path of a flash flood first become aware of the danger as they see the water rising.

Regional floods result from prolonged heavy rain over a large area. More than one major river may be affected by a regional flood. Weather systems producing large-scale rains are predictable, and the resulting regional floods develop over a day or two. Thus, there is generally a flood warning several hours or a day before regional floods develop, and there may be two or three days of preparation before the flood crests on the major rivers in Ohio.

Regional floods are most common in winter and spring, when the soil is saturated or frozen and there is little vegetation to intercept and transpire rainfall or slow the movement of water into streams. Large-scale weather systems producing heavy rain are most common during these seasons. If a snow cover exists it adds to the flood as it melts during a rainstorm. River ice breaks up during a flood and the broken ice may jam in narrow portions of the stream and against bridges. This "ice jam" acts as a temporary dam, creating higher water upstream from the jam and extensive damage downstream when the jam breaks apart. Ice jams may last a few hours or several days before washing downstream.

The Ohio River drains portions of eight states as it passes along Ohio's southern shore, so it responds to precipitation over a wide area. Heavy rains in Ohio may cause floods on the rivers flowing into the Ohio River, such as the Muskingum, Scioto, and Miami Rivers, without causing a large flood on the Ohio. On the other hand, heavy rains in Pennsylvania and West Virginia may cause a flood on the Ohio River even if heavy rain has not fallen over Ohio.

A special type of flood that affects Ohio's North Coast is the "wind setup" on Lake Erie. Gales from the northeast cause the lake water levels to rise in the western basin and fall at the eastern end of the lake. A wind setup develops after several hours of strong northeast winds and may increase lake levels by four feet or more from Port Clinton to Toledo. This floods the flat shoreline of western Lake Erie, and waves cause damage to homes and roads. As the winds stop or reverse their direction, a "seiche" develops in which the lake sloshes back and forth with oscillating water levels for the next day or two (Irish and Platzman 1962).

12 August 1861
The Elkton Flood

There were no flood watches from the government, no nervous television weathercasters pointing to flashing red radar echoes of heavy rain, and no sirens to blow as the water got too high in the streams of Columbiana County in August 1861. Formation of the United States Weather Bureau was still a decade away, and deadly weather, along with disease and accidents, was one of life's expected risks. The major news stories this week were war casualty reports—481 Union soldiers killed and 1,011 wounded in the Battle of Bull Run.

Rain began falling over Columbiana County about noon on Monday, 12 August, and became a downpour at 5:00 P.M. The 15 August 1861 *New Lisbon Buckeye State* reported, "A greater quantity of water was never known to fall in this region of the country, in so short a space of time." Cellars were flooded in New Lisbon, now simply called Lisbon, and streets were impassable with water and mud. A new bridge over Beavercreek at the east end of Lisbon was washed away, as were two bridges at West Point, five miles down the road toward East Liverpool.

The community of Elkton, four miles east of Lisbon, was flooded by Beaver Creek and Elk Run, a tributary from the north. Every home in

Elkton was damaged, and four persons drowned when one home was carried away in the churning floodwaters.

17 February 1867
Ice Jam Floods Toledo

The Maumee River, the largest river flowing into any of the Great Lakes, is often seized by ice jams. The flow of ice on 17 February 1867, "one of the most exciting days ever experienced by citizens of this city," according to the *Toledo Daily Blade,* was considered spectacular.

Ice had broken upstream in the river Saturday morning, 16 February and jammed against the bridge in Maumee, about ten miles above Toledo. Waters rose behind the ice and began tearing away flooring in the bridge. On Sunday, the ice still held fast in Toledo and was used as a convenient way to cross the river. However, unknown to Toledo residents, the ice jam at Maumee had given way and a flood of ice and water was pouring downstream. It swept into Toledo at about 10:00 A.M. Sunday.

The *Toledo Daily Blade* reported, "An immense field of broken ice came rushing down the river, plowing its way at a rate of five or six miles per hour, and following in its wake came with almost irresistible force broken ice thrown up in every conceivable shape, together with timber and driftwood."

The next obstruction across the river encountered by surging ice was a bridge at the site of the present Cherry Street Bridge. Mountains of ice piled against it, causing the water to rise again. By this time a crowd of ten thousand spectators lined the west bank of the Maumee at Toledo to watch the river's show of strength. Ice blocks carried in the flow were thirty feet square and twelve to fifteen inches thick with clear blue ice, each weighing about twenty-five tons. Pounding ice and rising waters caused the east end of the bridge to collapse and it was swept downstream.

"The yielding of the bridge produced the greatest excitement," according to the *Toledo Daily Blade.* Judge F. A. Jones and his wife were driving across the bridge when they felt it trembling. He "whipped up his horse" and barely reached the other side when the bridge was torn away. Persons could be seen scrambling to get off the shuddering bridge moments before it collapsed, but several were tossed into the ice and water as it went down. Apparently all reached shore.

Ice and water released at the destroyed bridge jammed again downstream at the foot of Elm Street. River water rose three feet in one-half hour behind this ice jam, flooding Water Street and docks and offices along the riverfront. The Middle Grounds were flooded to the axles of railcars and the Island House actually appeared as an island. The C&T

Railroad bridge withstood the battering as loaded railroad cars had been pulled onto the bridge to weigh it down in anticipation of the flood.

Once again the flood behind the ice jam built high enough to force a break in the jam and the flow continued downstream. The steamer *Belle* was ripped from her moorings and carried along with the ice. At 5:00 P.M. she was two miles downstream with ice piled to her upper deck. Men on board clambered over the ice to escape. The *Belle* was found three days later between Manhattan and Presque Isle and was towed to shore.

11 February 1881
The Maumee Rages through Toledo

The winter of 1880–81 had been exceptionally cold. The ice on the Maumee River and its tributaries was thick, and the countryside was quiet beneath a heavy coating of snow. The spring rains came, lasting several days, and the people waited.

Reports from upstream were bleak. Huge ice jams were holding the water back, flooding Grand Rapids. Water was being retained for a march into Toledo. Rain that had been falling for several days "descended in torrents" on the evening of 11 February, according to the *Toledo Blade*. This downpour made a flood imminent in Toledo. Merchants and residents along the Maumee scrambled to move belongings to upper floors.

Ice on the Maumee near Toledo began to break up and sweep toward downtown. Near 11:30 P.M. on 11 February, the ice had broken up as far as Madison Street. The *Toledo Blade* noted that "the noise made by the crashing ice and the rushing and roaring water, would have deadened the sound of contending battalions of artillery on the battlefield." Toledo residents lined the river to see docks being torn from their foundations and anything near the river's edge being swept to the bay. Many citizens stood on the Cherry Street Bridge and watched the approach of five schooners previously moored at the Wabash docks. They had torn from their moorings and were caught in the ice flow.

As the schooners neared, people ran from the bridge and the draw was opened. The *Toledo Blade* described the *Mediterranean* as floating through "majestically"; however, the stern rigging of the vessel caught the drawbridge and pulled it shut. The *Atmosphere* loomed in sight piloted by the mate. It struck the bridge, timbers fell, spars toppled, and planks splintered, but the mate stood at the wheel. The bridge fell and the *Atmosphere* continued downstream. It took a section of the bridge with it and struck a building next to the bridge. The remaining schooners, the *M. Stalker*, the *Benson*, and the *Dunford*, passed through without difficulty.

This impromptu regatta on the Maumee continued. The side-wheel steamer *Emerald* broke loose from the foot of LaGrange Street and struck the Pennsylvania Railroad bridge, sending timber and rails crashing into the water. The *Emerald* went on to strike a barge and set it loose. The schooners that passed through the Cherry Street Bridge were still on the rampage. They collided with the barge *Geo. W. Adams* and the propeller *W. T. Graves*. The *Lyman Casey*, the propeller *Salina*, and the barge *Agnes* were also damaged. The final view was a mass of boats haphazardly posed in the Maumee River, the Cherry Street Bridge and the Union Railroad and Pennsylvania Railroad bridges each missing a span.

In the city itself, great blocks of ice wedged everywhere Saturday morning, 12 February. Buildings along the river appeared as though they were packed in ice. Amid the water and ice were boats, lumber, merchandise, and debris of all types. The tracks at the Wabash Round House were under four to six feet of water. Water stood two feet deep on Perry and Monroe Streets and entered a nearby clothing store, a drug store, and several saloons. The ground floor of the police department was covered with eighteen inches of water, and prisoners had to be relocated to upper floors. The trestle work of the Toledo & Ann Arbor Railroad bridge bent under the force of the ice and water. The eight cars on it toppled and stuck fast in ice. In East Toledo, as on the west side of the river, merchants frantically worked through the night moving goods to higher places. The East Toledo Mills office was razed by a large cake of ice, as was the brick mill.

Temperatures dropped Saturday, and residents flocked to the riverside to view the "arctic" scene. Ice, some pieces as large as half an acre, were entangled in the river, cemented together when temperatures fell. Overall, damage was relatively small at Toledo, and the ice and water took with it millions of rats.

Elsewhere in the state, water was also rising. In Troy a reservoir burst and water inundated the town. Several levees on the Scioto near Circleville burst, and in Columbus, the Scioto River reached heights not seen in the previous twelve years. The lowlands to the west and the south of the city flooded, causing many families to leave their homes. Small creeks became rushing rivers, sweeping away large quantities of timber and some livestock.

Cleveland had a scare as an ice jam formed between piers at the mouth of the Cuyahoga River on 10 February. Residents stood by as thirty shells were fired from cannons placed on the pier. Tensions were relieved as the explosion broke the jam and water levels returned to normal.

The Blanchard River, a tributary of the Maumee, alarmed the citizens of Findlay as it rose to heights never before seen. The ice on the river broke and started moving out until a jam formed below the railroad bridge. Water backed up and flooded land along the river bottom and crossed over East Main Cross Street and East Front Street.

February 1883
Major Flooding Spreads across Ohio

Heavy rain falling on frozen ground caused extensive flooding across Ohio during February 1883. Average rainfall for the month was six and a half inches, and more than eight inches fell at Cincinnati and Lebanon. Much of the rain came on 3–4 February, when more than four inches, including some sleet and freezing rain, was recorded at several weather stations. Southern Ohio had another two inches on 7 February, and most of the state had one to two inches of rain again on the fourteenth. The result was that Ohio "rivers were flooded to an almost unprecedented extent," according to the February 1883 *Report of the Ohio Meteorological Bureau.*

The first period of heavy rain caused a breakup of ice and rapid rise on rivers from 3 to 5 February. In northwestern counties, snow followed by heavy freezing rain hampered travel and communication during 3–4 February but reduced runoff into the Maumee River and its tributaries. In spite of this, rain and thawing caused ice jams and high water on the Auglaize, Blanchard, Maumee, Portage, and Sandusky Rivers. Flooding forced hundreds of people from their homes and caused extensive damage at Napoleon, Defiance, Ottawa, Findlay, Elmore, and Fremont. This was the highest water known to that time at some locations in northwestern Ohio. Toledo escaped the flood of 3–4 February due to a two-mile-long ice jam on the Maumee River above the city.

A more serious flood came to the Maumee River and Toledo on 17–18 February as more rain and temperatures in the 60s caused the ice to finally melt. With the experience of 1881 to guide them, Toledo merchants and railroad men along the river prepared for high water, although on 15 February it was expected the ice would break up and flow harmlessly into Maumee Bay.

A large ice jam above Toledo broke loose at 11:30 A.M. on Saturday, 17 February, and the rush of impounded water from behind the ice flooded the Toledo riverfront. Water Street was covered five feet deep, and the Middle Grounds was inundated with three to six feet of river water. Basements, warehouses, and docks were flooded, although damage was reduced by the earlier preparations.

Of five bridges across the Maumee River at Toledo, only the Lake Shore Railroad bridge survived the flood. Two portions of the Wheeling and Lake Erie bridge were torn away, as was the approach to the Cherry Street

Fig. 47. A Maumee River ice jam swept away a span of the Cherry Street Bridge in Toledo on 17 February 1883. (Photograph courtesy of the Toledo–Lucas County Public Library)

Bridge (fig. 47). The Union Railroad bridge and Pennsylvania Railroad bridge were also knocked down. On the Pennsylvania Railroad bridge, seven railcars loaded with stone weighing thirty tons each were parked on the spans in an effort to anchor the bridge. As the ice gathered against the bridge, the spans and cars were all lifted and dumped into the river.

When the Maumee River ice jammed again downstream late on Saturday, 17 February, water rose to a record level, twenty-seven inches above the 1881 flood mark in Toledo and about fifteen feet above its normal level. There was extensive damage to lumber yards, riverboats, and warehouses along the shore, but not as much damage as expected for such high water. The gas supply was interrupted during the flood, so home and municipal lights were darkened. The *Toledo Blade* reported that during the gas shortage "the chief reliance was upon the electric lights. Those who had adopted the new idea considered themselves in luck."

To the east, more than three inches of rain on frozen, snow-covered ground caused the Cuyahoga River to flood the Flats of Cleveland on 3 and 4 February. The flood was the "most destructive ever known" up to 1883 in Cleveland. An estimated 23 million board feet of lumber and 15 million shingles were washed from lumber yards into the Cuyahoga River. The tug *Florence* tore loose and sank, and other vessels were tossed about but not seriously damaged. Water receded in the Cuyahoga on 6 February, and hundreds of men began clearing debris from the flooded areas.

A series of mishaps created a spectacular fire in the Standard Oil Works in the Cuyahoga Valley on Saturday morning, 3 February. The flood on Kingsbury Run carried oil from a "leaking still" of the Standard Oil Works into the boiler fires of the Great Western Oil Works. The floating oil ignited and surrounded a tank containing five thousand barrels of crude petroleum, which exploded, throwing flaming water and oil in all directions. This ignited the Merriam and Morgan paraffin works, which began to burn. The burning oil continued downstream on the flood to the main Standard Oil Works in the Cuyahoga Valley, where it ignited ten oil tanks holding about fifty thousand barrels of oil. The immense fire burned into the next day and attracted thousands of spectators, who crowded at the foot of Broadway hill and other vantage points.

Fears of a major flood on the Ohio River at Cincinnati began on 7 February, when the telegraph office and every business was reported under water upstream at Marietta. Lower portions of Steubenville, Pomeroy, and Portsmouth were also inundated. Cincinnati merchants began moving goods from the riverfront in preparation for a flood. By Sunday, 11 February, the water was the highest in thirty-six years. Barges were being run along Second Street in Cincinnati, firemen were pumping water from basements, all the transfer wagons in the city were moving goods to higher ground, and gas lights in the city went out when the Gas Works was submerged that evening. As the gas lights went out, candles and coal-oil lamps were used in homes and businesses. Hotels and theaters switched to electric lamps. Small boats were moving goods and ferrying persons "at enormous rates," and there was concern about evacuating the poor from tenement houses.

The crest on the Ohio River came at Cincinnati on 15 February 1883 with a level of 66.3 feet. This exceeded previous records of 64 feet in 1774 and 1832 (Mindling 1944) but was surpassed by a new record of 71.1 feet a year later. Most rail lines from Cincinnati were blocked, little mail moved, and livestock drowned along the river. Steamer traffic on the river was stopped and most bridges to Kentucky were closed. Coal barges were run up Central Avenue as far as Pearl Street, where wagons were loaded to make deliveries of coal. In spite of fears of burglaries and robbery in the darkened flooded district, there was "a most gratifying absence of crime."

14 February 1884
Second Highest Stage at Cincinnati

Cincinnatians might have wondered why their climate was changing in the early 1880s. Record floods occurred in February 1883 and again in February 1884 to culminate "nearly five years of great rains," according to Alexander (1924). Every year from 1879 to 1883 had much more rain than had been considered normal. The College Hill station recorded more than seventy-two inches of rain in 1880, among the highest totals known in Ohio.

Floods of February 1884 on the Ohio River were the result of heavy snows during December and January followed by heavy rains and warm weather during the first half of February. Snowfall of 27 inches at Cincinnati during December and January was more than the average for an entire winter. Six inches of rain and 60-degree temperatures in early February caused a rapid runoff into streams. The river stage at Cincinnati reached 71.1 feet on 14 February, exceeding the record set just one year earlier. Only the 80-foot stage in January 1937 brought higher water to Cincinnati.

Flood conditions developed statewide during 5–8 February 1884. Barns and small bridges were destroyed in the Maumee basin, Coshocton was under water up to Second Street, and there was minor damage along the "rushing roaring" Hocking River in Lancaster, according to the *Columbus Evening Dispatch*. Lowlands were submerged in Cleveland, Columbus, Youngstown, and Akron. Bridges over the Muskingum River were destroyed at Zanesville and McConnellsville.

Floodwaters from southward-flowing streams gathered into the Ohio River, resulting in floods in the upper Ohio Valley by 7 February and the record stage at Cincinnati a week later. Potteries were submerged in East Liverpool, and all riverfront mills and factories shut down at Steubenville.

The crest reached Marietta on 10 February. The *Marietta Register* reported water four feet deep on the Washington County courthouse floor, and the city beyond Fourth Street was called a "watery mess." Several commercial buildings and 450 homes and barns were moved from their foundations at Marietta (Mindling 1944). At least 150 Belpre buildings were submerged to the second floor and 40 more swept away, mostly below Main Street, according to the *Marietta Register.*

Extensive areas of Pomeroy, Gallipolis, Ironton, Portsmouth, and Ripley were under water as the crest moved downstream during 10–14 February. Riverfront buildings were submerged to their second floor in these communities, many families were evacuated, and railroad, mail, and telegraph service were interrupted. The flood exceeded the 1832 records at Portsmouth and Gallipolis and was not surpassed in that stretch of the Ohio River until March 1913. To add to the misery at Portsmouth, a windstorm on 13 February destroyed several flooded buildings.

Preparations were underway by 7 February for a major flood at Cincinnati. Rising waters cut electric service by the twelfth, and engines at the Water Works were flooded, raising fears of a "water famine" in the city. Grand Central Station was filled with water and "could better accommodate a good-sized steamboat rather than a locomotive," according to the *Cincinnati Enquirer.* About three thousand homes and other buildings were submerged, many of them carried away in the flood. Boats were everywhere, taking people where they wanted to go in the flooded district and "charging exorbitant prices." Thousands were forced from their homes, some of the homeless sheltered in empty railroad boxcars. Waters receded after 16 February, and the cleanup and relief efforts consumed the attention of Cincinnati and other riverfront communities.

24 June 1884
Twelve Inches of Rain in Eighty Minutes?

The *Ohio Meteorological Report* for June 1884 related the story of twelve inches of rain falling in about eighty minutes in southwestern Canton Township, Stark County. Although it has been repeated as fact by Alexander (1924, 715) and others, this is an extraordinary amount of rain and the estimate was probably an error. Mindling (1944) called this "probably the most intense rainfall of which any record exists in Ohio," although he noted it was not measured by means of any regular rain gauge but "was quite carefully investigated by competent men whose estimate was at least twelve inches."

The 25 June 1884 *Canton Repository* carried the preposterous headline "Four feet of water falling in three minutes," which may have made the estimate of twelve inches of rain in eighty minutes seem reasonable. In its only report of heavy rain that day, the *Canton Repository* told of a "waterspout" on the farm of Solomon Brown, four miles southwest of Canton. Forty acres of Brown's farm was reported to be covered with four and a half feet of water, which apparently inspired the headline of four feet of water falling in three minutes. However, several feet of water covering the field after heavy rain was probably the result of drainage into the lower portions of the field.

The claim of 12 inches of rain in eighty minutes may also be evaluated in the context of other heavy rainfalls in Ohio and elsewhere. Weather historian David Ludlum (1982) reported the greatest twenty-four-hour rainfall in Ohio was 10.51 inches at Sandusky on 12 July 1966. Miller and Hamilton (1969) gave "unofficial, but reliable reports" of 14.8 inches of rain in Chester Township, Wayne County, in twelve hours or more during the night of 4–5 July 1969, causing floods that killed fourteen people in that county. The greatest one-hour rainfall *in the world* was 12 inches at Holt, Missouri, on 22 June 1947, and at Kilauea, Hawaii, on 24–25 January 1956 (Riordan and Bourget 1985).

12 May 1886
The Xenia Flood

A flash flood killed twenty-eight people along Shawnee Creek in Xenia late on Wednesday, 12 May 1886. This was the greatest flood disaster known in Ohio up to that time and thus far has been exceeded in the number of deaths only by the March 1913 Flood.

There were also deadly tornadoes in Ohio during 12–14 May 1886, and early reports of the storms on 12 May attributed most of the deaths in Xenia to tornadoes. The 20 May 1886 *Findlay Hancock Courier,* for example, reported a "Xenia Tornado" and flooding with thirty-six dead. Even as late as 1944, Mindling reported no lives lost due to flooding in Xenia but twenty-seven deaths from a tornado. Tornadoes caused extensive damage on the night of the Xenia flood, but these reports of deaths from a Xenia tornado were incorrect. It was, however, an uncanny coincidence that eighty-eight years later, in 1974, a Xenia tornado would kill thirty-two people.

As is typical in localized deadly flash floods, there was no official rain gauge to measure how much rain fell to cause the flooding on Shawnee Creek. Rain gauges in Dayton, fifteen miles to the northwest, captured 4.5 inches of rain in just two hours (Mindling 1944). This was a very intense rainfall, and floods around Dayton damaged crops, bridges, and railroads and killed livestock. Estimates were given in the *Xenia Gazette* that 7 to 9 inches of rain fell "within the space of a little over an hour" along Shawnee Creek.

Runoff from this extraordinary rain poured down Shawnee Creek in a wall of water several feet high, knocking homes off their foundations and carrying them along in the current. Families were unaware of the

Fig. 48. A small building and other debris jammed against the Cincinnati Avenue Bridge in Xenia after the flood of 12 May 1886. (Photograph courtesy of the Greene County Historical Society)

impending disaster and waters rose too quickly for everyone to escape. The landscape along Shawnee Creek after the flood looked similar to the destruction along Wegee Creek at Shadyside after a flood killed twenty-six in 1990. Dozens of homes had been swept into the raging creek and piles of debris gathered at bridges (fig. 48).

Rumors at the time held that a railroad embankment with a debris-choked culvert acted like a dam, causing a large lake to form behind the embankment. Reports circulated that the railroad embankment failed and, like a failed dam, sent the deadly flood of water down Shawnee Creek. The *Xenia Gazette* noted that this theory was "not at all contradictable, as everyone in the flooded district says that it rose ten or fifteen feet in a moment."

It was true that debris from the flood blocked many culverts and jammed up behind bridges, causing a temporary rise in the floodwaters that washed downstream with renewed vigor when the debris or bridge gave way. But a letter published in the 18 May *Xenia Gazette* disputed the claim that a failed railroad embankment caused the great flood. The writer observed

Fig. 49. Funeral for eight members of the Powell family, drowned in Xenia after the flood of 12 May 1886. (Photograph courtesy of the Greene County Historical Society)

that the embankment was mostly intact after the flood and was lowered only fifteen inches by the flood that ran over it. Therefore, a "sudden release of gathered water . . . could not have caused the devastation." He reported that six inches of runoff from a ten-square-mile drainage area was sufficient to cause the flood: "This volume of water so suddenly hurled through the city, aggravated by the resulting gorges at the numerous bridges, did the awful work."

Rains began at 8:00 P.M. Wednesday evening and continued for three hours. The 14 May *Xenia Gazette* reported:

> The wind came in a continual gale, with an occasional gust which would break down trees, slam shutters and do other damage. . . . In the midst of the storm about 10 o'clock, the fire bells rang out their wild alarm . . . but directly the second alarm came and brought out the whole town. . . . The streets were dark and the rain coming down in torrents, but it was soon learned what the trouble was, that Shawnee Creek, that heretofore harmless little stream, had become mad and was out of its banks and sweeping everything before it.

The entire reach of Shawnee Creek through Xenia was flooded for a distance of one to two hundred yards on either side of Water Street, which ran along the creek. Several families were saved in heroic rescues after their homes were carried into the current. The Orrin Morris and William Powell families were not so lucky. Sixteen people died in these two homes. The Morris home on West Second Street was carried away toward the Main Street Bridge, where it was crushed and sank. The William Powell family met a similar fate when their home was carried from Detroit Street into the flood and fell apart (fig. 49). Several homes were swept away and five persons drowned in the lowlands along Shawnee Creek known as Barr's Bottom.

At least three hundred persons were homeless after the flood, many of them sleeping and eating for a few days at "the rink" in Xenia, where relief supplies were delivered. City council allowed fire engines to pump out wells in the flooded district and divided all unclaimed lumber among the needy. The council also advised the citizens along portions of Shawnee Creek of the city's plan to use that land to widen the channel, thus eliminating the need for property repairs. The Market Street Bridge was swept away, but debris from homes piled high behind the Main Street Bridge and took several days to remove. Western Union telegraph operators in Xenia were kept busy for two days sending and receiving messages about the flood.

Xenia residents had been generous in their assistance to Jamestown after the tornado there two years earlier, and now Jamestown residents were quick to respond to Xenia's disaster. A check for four hundred dollars arrived in Xenia from the residents of Jamestown within two days of the flood.

In other damage that night, a tornado destroyed homes, barns, and forests along a path north of Xenia near Goes, known then as Goe's Station. Wind and flood damage also struck Bellbrook and Clifton in Greene County, and two people were killed by a tornado near Carpenter in Meigs County (Grazulis 1990).

23 January 1904
Ice and Water Deluge Toledo

Mid-January thaws and heavy rains caused a breakup of ice on Ohio rivers in 1904 and created numerous floods as the broken ice jammed at bridges or narrow places in river channels. The ice jams, or "gorges" as they were sometimes called, greatly slowed the flow of water, and temporary "lakes" grew behind the jams.

Ice jams formed along many Ohio rivers on Saturday, 23 January 1904 and continued to form and break for the next two days. An ice jam against the Nickel Plate rail bridge over the Black River in Lorain caused floods that damaged machinery at the American Shipbuilding plant and carried away or crushed several tug boats, dredges, and other vessels docked in the Black River, according to the *Toledo Daily Blade*. The force of the ice caused the Nickel Plate bridge to collapse Saturday afternoon, leaving nothing but concrete supports and a portion of the draw span. Two people died on 23 January at Dover, where houses and bridges were washed away following 3.5 inches of rain (Mindling 1944). In southern Ohio, fifty feet of the Detroit Southern rail bridge over the Scioto River at Waverly was swept away by ice and high waters. Floodwaters on the Mahoning River forced the closure of industries, shut the Youngstown water plant, and flooded tracks of major railroads leading into the city.

The greatest damage from the ice jams and floods of January 1904 came along the Maumee River. The 23 January 1904 *Toledo Daily Blade* reported that the greatest flood since 1883 occurred that morning when an ice jam above Walbridge Park broke just after midnight and "the huge mass moved down past the city and lodged at the mouth of the river."

Thousands of large ice blocks pushed along by floodwaters caused much damage as they passed through Toledo. Lake vessels tied up for winter along the banks were swept away, shipyards and rail yards were flooded, railcars were pushed over, and riverfront industries were damaged. A portion of the Fassett Street Bridge was swept away, as were approaches to the Wheeling and Lake Erie rail bridge and the Terminal rail bridge downstream toward Maumee Bay.

Ice jammed again at Presque Isle, near the mouth of the river into Maumee Bay, and river water rose behind the temporary dam to flood lower portions of Toledo. River levels twelve feet above normal covered city streets and caused the backup of sewers into basements of many downtown office buildings. With water in the basements, heat, elevator, and electric services were cut and most offices closed for several days.

The ice jam at the mouth of the Maumee River held into midweek, and many industries remained closed and railroads blocked. Shortages of coal, gas, and other commodities began to appear. Frustration with the situation also increased. The general manager of the flooded Gendron Wheel Company, which employed 475 men, asked, "Why in thunder haven't we an ice crusher in Toledo? We are paying high enough taxes to give us some protection." A representative of American Shipbuilding, however, said that "there wasn't a boat in the world that could successfully break the jam."

Without an ice-breaking ship available, an effort was made to dislodge the jam with explosives. Mayor Samuel M. Jones and several members of Toledo government rode a bobsled drawn by four horses out to the ice jam in Maumee Bay on Wednesday, 27 January to witness the destruction of the ice jam by nitroglycerin. A hole ten by seven feet was blasted in the jam, but the remainder of the ice held fast. This mission was deemed a failure. Mayor Jones, after observing that explosives could not budge the ice jam, said, "That job belongs to God. It is His exclusively."

In showing the positive effects of the flood on Toledo, the 25 January *Toledo Daily Blade* reported, "The unemployed have had little trouble finding work along the river front today." A glut of steel on the markets had caused production and wages to be cut 10 percent at the American Bridge plants in Toledo. Now with bridges swept away all through the region, "the most permanent good will be to the bridge works and steel plants." And, noted the *Blade,* "bridge workmen will fare well during the next few months." No deaths or serious injuries were reported in the floods, although stories were told of many narrow escapes.

14–18 March 1907
Floods Sweep Southern Ohio

All rivers flowing south into the Ohio River reached flood stage during 14–17 March 1907. On many streams this was the highest water known, although greater floods in March 1913 would erase most of the 1907 records. More than four inches of rain fell across the southern third of Ohio during 12–14 March, with the heaviest rain, five to six inches, in a band from Cincinnati eastward through Circleville to Athens and into Noble County. Streams rose rapidly, and the major rivers reached flood stage by 14–15 March. The flood continued downstream into the Ohio River from 15 to 18 March.

Dozens of small bridges and several large bridges were washed out in central and southern Ohio, rail traffic was stopped by high water and washouts on tracks, and homes were swept into streams. Businesses, factories, and coal mines were damaged, causing great loss of income for workers and owners. Electric light plants and waterworks were submerged in many communities, cutting off those important services for several days. Landslides blocked roads, farm fields were covered in deep mud, and some rivers even changed their courses during the flood. Local militia patrolled many communities after the flood.

Fire bells began ringing in the Hocking Valley to warn of the impending flood on Wednesday, 13 March. The *Athens Journal* reported a great flood along the Hocking with several lives lost and a wide disruption of communication and transportation. Dozens of homes in Athens were swept away, overturned, or lifted off foundations. Telephone and telegraph wires were down and the waterworks and electric light plants were flooded. Rail lines all along the Hocking were cut by the raging river. Large areas of Athens were inundated, causing large losses among business and railroads.

Upstream on the Hocking River, the west and south sides of Lancaster were flooded and police and firemen were rescuing residents from roofs and second-floor windows. Several commercial buildings at Gloucester were lifted and washed away by Sunday Creek, including three grocery stores, a restaurant, and Will Reese's poolroom, according to the *Athens Journal*. Many homes and other businesses were damaged. The coal mines around Gloucester suffered heavy losses. Mine 256 was flooded, resulting in the loss of thirteen horses, machines, motors, cars, and other equipment. All homes in Trimble were flooded.

Paint Creek reached record flood levels in Chillicothe and flooded six hundred homes early Thursday, 14 March. The *Cincinnati Enquirer* reported boats patrolled the submerged areas of Chillicothe, providing food and fuel to residents. Crooked Creek flooded Waverly, washing away Water Street Bridge and damaging several industries and homes. The Scioto River reached the highest stage known at Waverly and washed away portions of every railroad serving the city.

Six hundred persons were forced from their homes at Zanesville and were cared for in schools, fire stations, and churches. South of Zanesville, water was five feet deep in the downtown streets of Roseville and hundreds of homes were flooded in Roseville, White Cottage, and Crooksville. Residents of those communities scrambled into the hills for safety, according to the *Cincinnati Enquirer*. Two hundred homes in Lima were flooded with three to five feet of water from the Ottawa River. Buck Creek flooded Springfield, forcing hundreds from their homes and blocking rail traffic. The water rose so fast Wednesday morning that eighteen families along Front Street in Springfield had to be rescued by boats.

Sidney was flooded on the upper reaches of the Miami River, and the flood continued downstream to Dayton, Miamisburg, and Hamilton. The flood along the Miami was near the highest known to that time, and there was major damage in some communities. This flood, however, was minor compared to the devastation that would come to the Miami Valley six years later. Most of Batavia was flooded by the East Fork of the Little Miami River, and only one road remained open out of town. The bridge across East Fork at Batavia was damaged when a large ice house was carried downstream and smashed against the bridge.

The flood on the Ohio River moved downstream from Pittsburgh, where it crested at the highest level known to that time early on 15 March. Lowlands, railroads, and many homes and businesses were covered at East Liverpool and Steubenville. The Ohio River rose 30 feet in two days at Marietta, reaching 50.6 feet, the highest level since 1884. About two-thirds of Marietta was under 10 feet of water on 15 March, leaving five thousand homeless. Portsmouth streets were full of moving vans on 15 March as residents and businesses rushed their goods to higher ground. On Sunday, 17 March, with temperatures near 70 degrees, the river reached nearly 61 feet at Portsmouth. Many Portsmouth residents had boats, and the *Cincinnati Enquirer* reported that "thousands took advantage of the fine weather to row about the city's streets."

The Ohio River rose 14 feet in twenty-four hours at Cincinnati to reach a crest of 62.1 feet late on 18 March. This was about the same level reached two months earlier, but the city was better prepared for this flood. Lower sections of Cincinnati were inundated, the greatest damage befalling the many large industries along Front and West Pearl Streets. Thousands of spectators were out in the warm weather on 17 March to view the flood from vantage points such as Second and Broadway. The greatest disruption at Cincinnati came when floodwaters of Mill Creek caused 120 feet of the Eighth Street Viaduct to collapse. This important bridge to Price Hill carried rail and streetcar traffic along with a water main and electric, telephone, and telegraph lines.

The 16 March 1907 *Cincinnati Enquirer* reported seventy-six dead in the Ohio Valley, including thirty-two in Ohio. Twelve were reported dead at Athens, six at Steubenville, four in Zanesville, three at Nelsonville, two each at Marietta, Circleville, and Chillicothe, and one at Sabina.

23–27 March 1913
Ohio's Greatest Weather Disaster

Four days of heavy rain falling onto saturated ground caused floods all across Ohio during 23–27 March 1913, killing 467 persons. This flood is "Ohio's Greatest Weather Disaster" because the extent of death and destruction exceeds all other weather events in the state's history. Never before 1913, and never since, has so much rain fallen over so much of the state in such a short time. The Flood of 1913 set the record water levels on many Ohio streams.

The direct cause of the Flood of 1913 was the coincidental path of two low pressure storm systems that moved from the Southwest through the Great Lakes region, the first on 24 March and the second on the twenty-sixth. Each storm system had an uncommonly large area of heavy rain "with the peculiar condition that one disturbance followed the other so closely that the rain areas of the two blended, concentrating over the same portion of the country" (Horton and Jackson 1913). Conditions prior to the heavy rains were favorable for flooding. Soils were saturated with wa-

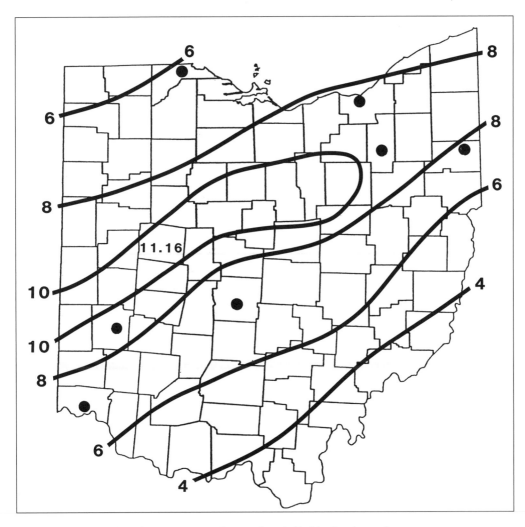

Fig. 50. Rainfall (in inches) during 23–27 March 1913. About half of the five-day total came on 25 March.

ter from earlier light rains and most rivers were running nearly full. This is a common condition of late winter and early spring in Ohio. Fortunately, the ground was not frozen and there was no snow cover to add to the floods.

Heavy rainfall began over Ohio during the evening of Easter Sunday, 23 March and continued until the last disturbance moved to the East Coast and temperatures fell below freezing, turning the rain to light snow on the twenty-seventh. Total rainfall from 23 to 27 March 1913 exceeded 6 inches, except in the southeast, and was heaviest in western and north-central Ohio (fig. 50). Four-day rainfall totals there were about 10 inches with as much as 11.16 inches at Bellefontaine and 10.61 inches at Marion.

Because the Flood of 1913 was caused by large atmospheric disturbances, the entire state was affected. In addition, the heaviest rains fell over the headwaters of the Miami, Scioto, and Muskingum Rivers, causing extreme floods along the entire lengths of Ohio's large rivers. It was along these rivers, and in the larger cities through which they flow, that most of the death and destruction occurred.

Heavy rains progressed from west to east, so the Miami was the first river to reach flood stage. At Dayton, the flood crest reached 29 feet at 1:00 A.M. on 26 March. This was 8 feet higher than the previous record flood of 1866. Downstream in Hamilton, the Miami crested just two hours after the high water mark was reached at Dayton, reaching a crest of 34.6 feet, 13.5 feet over the previous record of 1898. (River levels are measured above some local benchmark and cannot be compared from one city to another except in relative height above the previous record.)

On the Scioto River, the crest of 22.9 feet passed through Columbus at noon on 25 March. This was 1.6 feet above the previous peak in 1898. The crest of the Scioto floodwaters passed Chillicothe at 11:00 A.M. on 26 March, and here the crest of 37.8 feet was 9.5 feet higher than the 1898 record. Farther east on the Muskingum River, the state's largest tributary of the Ohio River, the flood passed Zanesville early on 27 March and reached Beverly later that day. Crests on the Muskingum River were 11 to 15 feet above all previous records.

As the crest of the Muskingum and other tributaries reached the Ohio River, new flood records five feet above previous records were set from Marietta downstream through Portsmouth to Maysville, Kentucky. Crests on the Ohio River below Maysville, including Cincinnati, did not reach a record in 1913. These March 1913 records on the Ohio River were exceeded downstream from Gallipolis in January 1937.

There is some importance in knowing the number of deaths in Ohio due to the Flood of 1913, as this is the deadliest weather disaster in Ohio history. Headlines in Ohio's largest newspapers on 26 March reported thousands were dead in Dayton and 100 to 150 dead in Columbus. Estimates were reduced through the week as more factual reports were received. Newspapers printed extensive lists of the dead and names of those previously reported dead but still living.

The press's initial gross exaggeration of the magnitude of the flood was a common occurrence. Sketchy and unreliable early field reports were compounded by the desire for dramatic headlines, which, naturally, proclaimed the worst scenario and most pessimistic numbers. Newspapers corrected these exaggerations in subsequent days but never in headlines

Fig. 51. The flood in Dayton during March 1913. (From the collections of the Montgomery County Historical Society)

the size of the initial false report. The public was ill served by such dooms-day reporting, and it made newspapers unreliable as historical documents in the first day following a major disaster. Faster communication has alleviated this problem somewhat in the late twentieth century, but the tendency remains for the press to seize the worst numbers available for headlines.

The final death toll of the Flood of 1913 remains open to discussion by historians. We accept the value of 467 dead estimated by meteorologist J. Warren Smith (Mindling 1944). To best describe the effects of this flood, the discussion below is divided by river basin and region.

Miami River. The most destructive and deadly portion of the Flood of 1913 occurred in the Miami Valley of western Ohio. Becker and Nolan (1988) reported 49 people dead at Piqua, 14 at Troy, 123 in Dayton, and 106 at Hamilton, for a total of 292 dead just among these four cities. These numbers do not agree entirely with those presented by Morgan (1917). Although both list 123 deaths in Dayton, Morgan gave 159 dead at Hamilton, 19 at Piqua, and 49 at Troy.

Fig. 52. Flood waters on South Ludlow and Fourth Street in Dayton in March 1913. The strength of the current is evident around poles and buildings. (From the collections of the Montgomery County Historical Society)

Conover (1917) summarized the desperate situation in Dayton on 25 March 1913: "A brown wave of water, six feet high, rolled its foaming crest westward on the streets and meeting at each corner a similar wave from the north, piled the water into a raging torrent which filled the streets with foam and wreckage." After heavy rains on Easter Sunday, flood warnings had been telegraphed on Monday, 24 March to cities along the Miami River by Weather Bureau officials in Columbus (Morgan 1917). The Dayton Weather Bureau telephoned persons living in lowlands that often flooded, but the magnitude of the coming flood was unknown on Monday. Whistles sounded at National Cash Register (NCR) Tuesday morning to warn Dayton residents of the flood, but still no one could expect such water as swept the city that day.

By evening on 25 March, fourteen square miles of Dayton were under water, much of it a swift current ten to fifteen feet deep (Becker and Nolan 1988) (figs. 51 and 52). The Miami River was eighteen feet deep in Dayton's Union Station, imprisoning six hundred people for three days. Water rose to eleven feet deep at Third and Main Street with a current that tore away lampposts and smashed store windows. Explosions and fires spread through several downtown buildings and caused several deaths as people who had sought refuge on rooftops were forced into the flood. A row of two- and

Fig. 53. High Street in Hamilton during the flood of March 1913. (From the collections of the Montgomery County Historical Society)

three-story buildings on both sides of Third Street from Jefferson to St. Clair burned down. St. Elizabeth's Hospital in the Edgemont neighborhood was surrounded by water and nuns carried dozens of patients to upper floors of the hospital. Water sixteen feet deep in the Dayton Public Library caused the loss of forty-five thousand books (Clatworthy 1913). Nearly fifteen hundred horses were estimated to have drowned in Dayton, creating a huge problem of disposal of carcasses (Becker and Nolan 1988).

Ohio National Guardsmen, eventually totaling one thousand, arrived in Dayton late on 26 March. Governor James Cox placed Dayton under martial law so troops could maintain order and enforce rules established to speed the rescue and cleanup operations (Conover 1917). Hundreds of men were made "special deputies" with authority to shoot thieves, although there was apparently little time or opportunity for thievery. No one was shot.

NCR, the largest employer in Dayton, converted its production to flat boats, "one of which was turned out every eight minutes," and launched

Fig. 54. Water of the Miami River surging against the High and Main Street Bridge in Hamilton at 12:10 P.M. on 25 March 1913. The bridge collapsed eighteen minutes later. (From the collections of the Montgomery County Historical Society)

to rescue people clinging to trees and roofs (Conover 1917). Company woodworkers produced three hundred boats in two days. John Patterson, scion of a pioneer Dayton family and president of NCR, became a local hero during the flood, according to the 25 March 1988 *Dayton Daily News*. The NCR factory and grounds were above the flood and were turned into a huge relief camp where the homeless slept and ate and doctors treated the injured. Patterson sent his seventy-one hundred employees out for relief work, ordered a train of medical supplies from New York, and sent a train to Toledo for food. Governor Cox appointed Patterson head of the Dayton Relief Committee.

Upstream from Dayton, damage was extensive at Piqua and Troy. A 1913 report by meteorologist J. Warren Smith reported forty-four deaths at Piqua, half of the city flooded, and one hundred homes destroyed (Mindling 1944). Water was six feet deep in the business district. Mindling

Fig. 55. Lowering baskets for food along Lower Plum Street in Cincinnati during the flood of March 1913. (From the collections of the Montgomery County Historical Society)

(1944) reported sixteen deaths in Troy, 75 percent of the city flooded, and fifty homes washed away.

Below Dayton on the Miami River, 25 percent of Middletown was flooded, six people drowned, and forty-one homes were destroyed. About half of Hamilton was flooded, and ninety-eight lives were lost there (Mindling 1944). Floodwaters reached four blocks into the west side of Hamilton and more than twenty blocks to the east, where the land was flatter. Water was ten to eighteen feet deep in residential sections of Hamilton (figs. 53 and 54), where as many as five hundred homes were destroyed. Washed out bridges in Hamilton County isolated several communities (fig. 55).

Fig. 56. A Dayton street buried in lumber carried with the flood of March 1913. (From the collections of the Montgomery County Historical Society)

By Friday, 28 March, the flood had receded from Dayton and the work of clearing debris was "progressing with marvelous speed and rapidity," according to the *Toledo Blade* (fig. 56). People who had been trapped in downtown Dayton for four days "made their way to the suburbs by the thousands." Removal of debris and cleaning of streets proceeded with good weather through the weekend, although drinking water and some other basic supplies were still short in Dayton.

Scioto River. Columbus was cut in half by the floodwaters of the Scioto River when a levee protecting the west side failed at 10:00 A.M. on Tuesday, 25 March. The rush of floodwaters through railroad underpasses created whirlpools and great rapids Tuesday night that scoured away nearly every building for four blocks on Glenwood and Central Avenues (Mindling 1944). It was in these areas that most of the ninety-three Columbus deaths occurred. Water was nine feet deep at Mound and

Fig. 57. Erosion of Hickory and Fourth Streets and portions of homes during the flood of March 1913 in Chillicothe. (Photograph courtesy of the Ross County Historical Society)

Glenwood, Broad and Glenwood, and Rich and Cypress, and seventeen feet deep at West Park and Sullivant Avenues.

The Weisheimer Bridge on Maple Grove Road north of Columbus washed out Tuesday morning. When the State Street Bridge collapsed Tuesday morning, debris was swept downstream and destroyed the Town Street Bridge. The *Columbus Evening Dispatch* reported electric wires snapped as the bridges fell and were hurled through the air in balls of fire.

Hundreds of Columbus residents clung to rooftops and trees for two days waiting for rescue. Thirteen people were rescued from a single tree. A cold wave Wednesday night caused many to lose their grip and drown in the floodwaters. By 26 March several thousand people were marooned without food, fresh water, or heat in Columbus, and the *Columbus Evening Dispatch* estimated that five thousand city residents had evacuated their homes. Nearly 300 homes and businesses were destroyed at Columbus and another 4,071 were damaged (Mindling 1944).

Upstream in Delaware, the Olentangy River reached 23 feet above flood stage and Sandusky Street was 8 feet under water, the first time this street was known to have been flooded. The Olentangy, normally 250 feet wide at Delaware, was up to 3,380 feet across at William Street. It swept away all the bridges in Delaware, destroyed thirty-three homes and drowned eighteen people. On the lower Scioto, 75 percent of Chillicothe was flooded and eighteen people lost their lives (fig. 57).

Muskingum River. In the upper reaches of the Muskingum basin, water was six feet deep in the business district of Clinton, one third of Massillon was flooded, and two hundred homes were flooded in Newcomerstown (Mindling 1944). Four persons drowned in Coshocton, where sixteen homes were washed away, three deaths were reported in Mt. Vernon, half of Dresden was inundated, and four hundred homes were flooded in Newark.

An especially thorough account of the flood at Zanesville was given by Lewis (1913). The Muskingum River crested twenty-seven feet above flood stage and seventeen feet above the 1898 record at Zanesville. Water was twenty feet deep at the intersections of North and Third Streets, Lee and Linden, West Main and State, and State and Blue.

Five of seven bridges at Zanesville were lost to the flood. The B&O Railroad bridge collapsed Wednesday morning, and the Sixth Street Bridge fell into the river soon after, when the Muskingum Woolen Mill floated into it. The Third Street Bridge fell at noon and was swept downstream to wreck the Putnam Bridge. The Pennsylvania Railroad bridge went into the river during the afternoon. An improvised foot bridge that was hung on cables to the Third Street Bridge piers was used by thousands of persons daily after the flood. Zanesville's famous Y-Bridge was topped by the flood, only the lampposts visible, but it withstood the tremendous stresses (Mindling 1944). More than 3,400 buildings were flooded in Zanesville, including 2,500 homes. About 150 buildings were swept away or carried off their foundations, especially on First, Second, and Third Streets below Main Street (Lewis 1913). The current there removed the sidewalk and street to a depth of ten feet. Miraculously, only two lives were lost at Zanesville.

Maumee River. Heavy rains moved into the Maumee basin of northwestern Ohio and northeastern Indiana early on Easter Sunday, 23 March. Total rainfall during 23–27 March was five to seven inches in the northern portion of the basin, whereas the southern portion, drained by the St. Marys River, received seven to nine inches. The *Toledo Blade* reported on 24 March that the Maumee rose twelve feet in twenty-four hours at Ft. Wayne and nine feet at Napoleon in the first day of the flood. Water continued to rise for three days as the floods on numerous smaller streams crossed the flatlands of northwestern Ohio into the Maumee. By 25 March, the river was ten feet above flood stage at Defiance and three feet above previous records. About one-third of Defiance was flooded, including 268 homes (Mindling 1944).

Near the mouth of the Maumee at Toledo, water reached the highest recorded except in brief ice jam floods. A portion of the old Cherry Street Bridge in Toledo collapsed in the flood and the new Cherry Street Bridge was opened for traffic. Ice had moved out of the Maumee two weeks earlier, so ice jams, a frequent obstruction to spring floodwaters on the Maumee, were not a problem in the Flood of 1913.

The Maumee flooded a thousand homes in Ft. Wayne, Indiana, where the crest occurred on Wednesday, 26 March. The town of Texas was flooded on Monday, and by Tuesday there were floods along the Maumee, Ten Mile Creek, and Swan Creek in Toledo. Cygnet was surrounded by floodwaters Sunday night and rail lines were blocked all through north-western Ohio. Findlay had its most disastrous flood in history on 25 March. The business section was flooded two feet deep by the Blanchard River, the electric power station was under six feet of water, and telegraph and telephone offices were flooded, cutting off communication. A Findlay police captain died in the flood. Floodwaters of the Maumee washed through Cheney Lumber in Defiance on Tuesday, carrying lumber downstream. On Wednesday, the Hopkins Street Bridge over the Auglaize River at Defiance collapsed and the State Bridge at Defiance fell into the Maumee.

Sandusky and North-Central Rivers. Rainfall over the Sandusky River basin was 7 to 8 inches in the lower reaches but 10.41 inches near the headwaters at Upper Sandusky. The Sandusky broke all previous flood records set in 1883 or 1904. Crests were 6 to 11 feet above flood stage at Upper Sandusky, Tiffin, and Fremont and exceeded the previous records by 3 to 5 feet. Four of five bridges in Fremont were washed away, according to the *Toledo Blade,* and food supplies were being shipped into the city from Toledo. Churches, hotels, and the county courthouse were used as hospitals and shelters for evacuees. Five hundred homes were flooded in Fremont and there were three deaths (Mindling 1944).

Houses, stores, and factories were destroyed by the flood at Tiffin. Hundreds were rescued from rooftops and trees, some by a "high power motor boat" sent from Sandusky. Many others could not be rescued before their homes collapsed. A total of nineteen people died at Tiffin (Mindling 1944), including six members of the Klingshirn family. Food was short in Tiffin as elsewhere, and local authorities confiscated meat from marooned railcars. The Portage River was higher than known before at Portage and Woodville with many buildings swept away.

Northeastern Rivers. The Cuyahoga River flooded lowlands in Cleveland causing great damage to docks, lumberyards, freight houses, trains, and rail yards. Swift currents tore the steamer *William H. Mack* from its moorings and lodged it against the West Third Street Bridge, which collapsed into the river. Small streams in the region, including Euclid Creek, Mill Creek, Dugway Creek, and Doan Brook became raging torrents pouring through streets and flooding homes. The Chagrin River was twelve hundred feet wide at Gates Mills, where cattle in fields could only poke their heads above water.

In Akron, where 9.65 inches of rain fell in four days, the Little Cuyahoga broke through the bank of East Reservoir, damaging the Goodyear Plant and carrying away more than fifteen houses and several bridges. One thousand people were homeless in Akron, electric power was out, and most industries closed. Seven locks were dynamited on the Ohio Canal at Akron to allow the floodwaters to pour into the Cuyahoga River, according to the *Cleveland Plain Dealer.*

Warren, Niles, and Youngstown were flooded to the highest levels known. Two people drowned in Warren and about 550 homes were flooded in the three cities. A freight train fell into a creek at Brighton in Lorain County, resulting in the death of three crewmen. High waters receded across northeastern Ohio by Friday, 28 March, and most roads, businesses, and schools reopened. Relief supplies began moving from northern Ohio cities to the more severely affected regions of Columbus, Dayton, and Hamilton.

Ohio River. Ohio River water backed up at Marietta as a great flood flow entered from the Muskingum River. The crest at Marietta was nearly six feet above the 1884 record and covered half the city. The fact that no one died in Marietta was attributed to "the large number of men at work who were familiar with river life and skilled in handling boats."

About 40 percent of Gallipolis was flooded (Mindling 1944) and water reached thirteen inches higher than the 1884 record at Ironton. Two-thirds of Ironton was inundated, the water supply was off for five days, and gas was shut off for twelve days. Mail, telephone, and telegraph service was cut for four days. One flooded block of Ironton burned to the water line on 30 March. Two hundred boats were seized by the Ohio National Guard to rescue persons from the flood and fires. A total of twenty-four homes were washed away at Ironton and another sixty-eight were pushed off their foundations.

Levees on the Scioto River and concrete walls along the Ohio River were topped by the flood at Portsmouth, flooding 75 percent of the city. Mindling (1944) reported water up to 9 feet deep in residential areas and forty-five hundred homes flooded. The Ohio River crested at Cincinnati on 1 April, about 2 feet below the February 1884 record, but the rise of 21.3 feet in twenty-four hours was unprecedented (Alexander 1924). The *Cincinnati Star Times* reported that although more people were affected by the Flood of 1913 than that of 1884, conditions were better in 1913 due to better relief and rescue operations at Cincinnati.

Summary. Meteorologist J. Warren Smith's estimates for the Flood of 1913 included 467 deaths, 40,637 homes flooded, and 2,200 homes destroyed (Mindling 1944). Losses totaled $113 million (1913 dollars), including about $78 million to buildings and personal property, $12 million to roads and bridges, $12 million to railroad property and the suspension of rail business, $6 million to crops, livestock, farm buildings, fences, and soil erosion, and $4 million to machinery.

Horton and Jackson (1913) suggested that the extreme magnitude of the Flood of 1913 was partly due to deforestation in Ohio and the spread of agricultural and municipal land. They also blamed encroachment onto the flood plain by structures, roads, and bridges. Horton and Jackson (1913) noted that reservoirs may be used for flood control but that they will not prevent floods, only lessen their impacts. The Miami Conservancy District established a wide-reaching flood control project in the years after the flood that became a model for similar projects in Ohio and nationwide (Bock 1918, Morgan 1951, Becker and Nolan 1989).

16 July 1914
Heavy Rains Soak Cambridge

The worst flood in twenty-five years in Guernsey County came in 1914 after a late Thursday thunderstorm. Wind uprooted trees and blew down silos, and hail the size of pigeon eggs fell. It was rain, however, that caused most of the damage. Alexander (1924, 306) called this "certainly one of the heaviest rainfalls in the history of the state." The official government gauge on Samuel Mehaffey's farm near Cambridge recorded 7.09 inches of rain between 5:30 and 7:00 P.M., most of it falling in just thirty minutes (Alexander 1924, 306). The rain was localized and centered on an oval area of about five square miles northwest of Cambridge. Little rain fell to the east at Lore City or Quaker City. Flash floods swept several streams and flooded most of Cambridge.

16 August 1920
Toledo Cloudburst

Overnight rainfall and an 8:00 A.M. Monday cloudburst flooded downtown Toledo. The twenty-four-hour rainfall of 4.48 inches with this storm was less than the 5.98 inches that fell on 4 September 1918. However, it was the intensity of this storm that made it so destructive. The Toledo rain gauge measured 1.25 inches in ten minutes and 3.58 inches in just one hour on 16 August 1920 (Hutter 1952).

Water poured through streets, its force tearing up thousands of paving blocks. Torrents of water and blocks flowed over curbs and sidewalks into buildings and basements. Passing cars and trucks made waves that hit buildings and poured into doors and windows. Downtown basements along Jefferson, Madison, and Erie Streets had up to eight feet of water and, in some cases, water was two feet deep in first floor offices and shops.

Fire department crews began pumping water from downtown basements Monday afternoon, and city crews began repairing and cleaning tattered streets. By 17 August, streetcars were running and streets and stores had been cleaned so the downtown looked normal again. However, tons of mud still lay in hundreds of basements. The *Toledo Blade* reported on Tuesday, "Thousands of scattered paving blocks gave the street the appearance of an Irish town after a Sinn Fein–Ulster argument."

26 February 1929
Miami River Flood

Two to three inches of rain, melting snow, and ice jams contributed to flood conditions across much of Ohio during the last week of February 1929. The Maumee River flooded behind an ice jam at Waterville, and similar ice jams inundated land along the Rocky River near Cleveland. The Kokosing River matched its 1913 flood level in Mt. Vernon, and a man drowned in Wheeling Creek at Bridgeport, south of Martins Ferry. Greatest flood levels occurred in southwestern Ohio, where the Great Miami and other rivers reached their highest levels since 1913. A flood disaster was averted by flood protection measures put in place by the Miami Conservancy after the 1913 flood.

The Miami River rose 10 feet in five hours at Hamilton early Tuesday, 26 February (Mindling 1944). The crest of 17.4 feet matched the 1913 flood crest, but the *Hamilton Evening Journal* reported, "There can be no comparison, however between a stage of 17 feet now and the same stage in 1913." Highway and train traffic were disrupted and lowland areas were under water, but there were no fatalities and no major damage to buildings.

Peck's Addition was flooded at Hamilton and about one hundred people were evacuated for several hours. Water also backed up into the village of New Miami north of Hamilton. Flooding at Middletown and Dayton was limited to cellars and low-lying roads. The Little Miami River south of Xenia reached a flood level higher than recorded in 1913.

More serious flooding occurred at Springfield, where Buck Creek and Mad River, tributaries of the Great Miami, overflowed into the business district and residential areas. Several hundred people were homeless until waters receded. Fires caused by short circuits also did extensive damage at Springfield (Mindling 1944).

21 March 1933
Ohio River Flood

Two periods of heavy rain during March 1933 brought the Ohio River to its highest level in twenty years at Cincinnati. The first rainstorm, from 13 to 15 March, resulted from low pressure tracking north of Ohio followed by another low crossing the state from the southwest (Buckley 1935). This brought three to four inches of rain to the upper Ohio basin centered on the Hocking and Muskingum Rivers. A second period of heavy rains, from 18 to 20 March, resulted from the slow movement of low pressure northward through western Ohio. More than two inches of rain fell in the southern half of Ohio, with three to five inches in the southwestern counties.

Widespread minor flooding followed the first rainstorm in southern Ohio. As tributaries to the Ohio River drained, the Ohio River reached flood stage from Pittsburgh downstream to Pomeroy on Thursday, 16 March. The flood from the first rainstorm reached Cincinnati about the same time that the second rainstorm began in southwestern Ohio on the eighteenth.

This unfortunate combination of heavy rains from 18 to 20 March and the arrival of the earlier flood from upstream brought the Ohio River at Cincinnati to the highest stage since 1913. The flood stage of 52 feet was reached on the eighteenth, and the crest of 63.6 feet came late on the twenty-first (Buckley 1935). This was about 8 feet below the 1884 record flood and 16 feet below the Great Flood that would come in January 1937.

Airplanes were removed from Lunken Airport and levees around the airport topped with sandbags to protect the property. The *Cincinnati Enquirer* reported the old Central Union Station was flooded, but train movement continued when the new Union Station, on higher ground and scheduled to open in April 1933, was opened early. Steamboat traffic came to a halt on the Ohio River when clearance was reduced under bridges.

A more disastrous flood was averted by the dry and unfrozen condition of soils in the Ohio Valley and the absence of snow cover prior to the two rainstorms. The *Cincinnati Enquirer* noted that the March 1933 flood was "nothing compared to what might have happened if the Miami Conservancy District Flood Works hadn't been on the job to hold in check the swirling waters of the Big Miami River." However, Buckley (1935) observed that three inches of rain fell upstream from the dams in the Miami River basin compared to more than five inches below the dams, thus "the Conservancy Dams were of little, if any, benefit in retarding the progress of the flood waters of the Ohio River." In fact, Buckley noted that "channel improvement on the Miami River south of Dayton speeded the runout of its waters, thus intensifying the flood of the Ohio River."

7 August 1935
Coshocton Flood

The greatest flood in Coshocton and adjacent counties since March 1913 came after heavy rains on the night of 6 August 1935. The rains were especially heavy over the Tuscarawas watershed, and by Wednesday, 7 August portions of Coshocton and Newcomerstown were inundated.

Even before these rains began, soils were saturated from rains during the past week. Rain lashed the county on Friday, 2 August, causing crop damage and washing out some roads and bridges. Both the Tuscarawas and Walhonding Rivers rose to within a few feet of flood stage on the fourth but receded without major damage.

The rains of 6–7 August were the greatest known in the region, "the most terrific cloudburst in local history." Coshocton weather observer Owen Popham recorded 7.1 inches overnight. Totals of 8.7 inches were recorded at Newcomerstown and 6.7 inches at Millersburg.

The torrential rain on wet soils resulted in quick runoff into streams. The Tuscarawas River at Coshocton rose 11 feet overnight on 6 August and reached a peak at 24.6 feet at 5:00 A.M. on the eighth. This was 13.6 feet above flood stage but 6 feet below the 1913 crest. Hundreds of shocks of wheat and oats and two live calves, swept from fields upstream, floated through Coshocton.

As is typical with flash floods, residents had little warning or opportunity to escape. As word of the flood spread in Coshocton, boats were readied to take people from flooded homes and farms. By 6:00 A.M. Wednesday, all available trucks were being used to move people and household goods through flooded streets to dry land. All boats were taken over by the city to prevent vandalism, and a police permit was required to operate a boat during the flood.

Among the heroes of this disaster was Dave Courtright, who rescued several people from their homes by boat. The *Coshocton Tribune* reported he was the son of Walter Courtright, former superintendent of the waterworks in Coshocton. The elder Courtright was called "the hero of the 1913 flood" for rescuing many people during that disaster twenty-two years earlier.

All homes along Water Street in Coshocton were flooded. Water rose to Vine and South Third and traffic was stopped below Third Street. More than two hundred Coshocton families were evacuated. The memory of the 1913 flood was fresh, and residents left their homes more willingly than in 1913. Some stayed with family outside the flooded area, but about two hundred people, thirty hogs, and twelve horses spent Thursday night at the county fairgrounds.

19 March 1936
Spring Flood on the Upper Ohio River

Snowmelt and heavy rains in western Pennsylvania and West Virginia caused record floods on the upper Ohio River from Pittsburgh to Steubenville. Forecasts on Tuesday, 17 March 1936 were for the Ohio to reach the 35-foot flood stage at Steubenville Wednesday morning. That level was reached, but the river continued to rise rapidly, reaching 45.3 feet Wednesday afternoon, and surpassed the 1884 record of 49.1 feet at 11:00 P.M. Wednesday, a rise of 20 feet in two days.

Homes were evacuated along Wells Street and the lower end of South Third, and the water eventually blocked Water, Market, Washington, and Adams Streets. Hotels were filled to capacity by Wednesday afternoon. To protect their investments, steel mills along the river shut down and workers dismantled equipment and moved what they could to higher ground. Preparations were also made for impending floods downstream in Marietta and Portsmouth. At the same time, northern Ohio was shut down by deep snowfalls and high winds.

The crest of 52.6 feet in Steubenville came at noon Thursday, 19 March 1936. Water swept through the plants of Wheeling Steel and Weirton Steel and into the lowlands all along the river. The Ohio Edison electric plant at Toronto was shut down as water rose into that facility. Homes and factories were flooded at East Liverpool, Wellsville, Steubenville, Mingo Junction, Brilliant, and Martins Ferry. Water was into the second floor of some homes in Brilliant and Mingo Junction. Boats and trucks were used to evacuate lowland residents from Empire and Stratton, north of Steubenville, but these methods proved too slow in the rapidly rising waters. Boxcars of the Pennsylvania Railroad were pushed into the flooded areas and five hundred stranded persons were carried to higher ground in Toronto. Transportation came nearly to a halt in the region Thursday as roads and railroads were covered by the Ohio River. Route 7 was covered by 15 feet of water when the river crested at Empire. Governor Martin Davey sent the Ohio National Guard to assist the rescue and cleanup in communities of the upper Ohio Valley.

26 January 1937
Greatest Flood on the Ohio River

The greatest volume of water ever known to pass along Ohio's southern shores flooded all Ohio River communities during the last two weeks of January 1937. Ohio River levels on 26–27 January were the highest known from Gallipolis downstream past Cincinnati to the confluence with the Mississippi River at Cairo, Illinois.

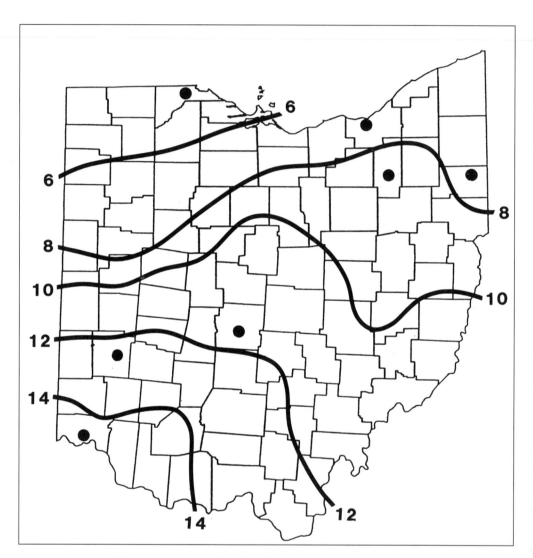

Fig. 58. Precipitation (in inches) during January 1937. A statewide average of 9.57 inches made this the wettest month since September 1866 in Ohio (Rogers 1993). About half of the total fell during 20–25 January. A station known as Fernbank along the Ohio River west of Cincinnati recorded 14.88 inches. Normal January precipitation is 2 to 3 inches.

Crests were 20 to 28 feet above flood stage from Gallipolis to Cincinnati and 4 to 9 feet above all previous records. The river level at Cincinnati crested 28 feet above flood stage and 8.9 feet above the February 1884 record. Flood levels above Gallipolis to Marietta, Martins Ferry, Steubenville, and East Liverpool were 10 to 20 feet over flood stages, but a few feet short of the record levels set in March 1913 and March 1936.

The meteorological conditions that caused the flood of January 1937 arose from persistent abnormal pressure patterns over North America (Brooks and Thiessen 1937). The "Bermuda High" of the western North Atlantic was stronger than usual for January and extended its influence westward into the southeastern United States. Circulation around the high sent huge amounts of tropical moisture northward into the Mississippi and Ohio River Valleys.

As usual in January, cold polar air resided over the Plains and Great Lakes regions. The boundary between these air masses, the "front," was often aligned from southwest to northeast along the Ohio Valley. Moist tropical air flowing northward was forced to rise over cold air north of this front and heavy rain developed, as described in the February 1937 issue of *Monthly Weather Review.*

It is not uncommon for this weather pattern to exist for a few days each winter, but the persistence of the pattern from 13 to 25 January 1937 was unprecedented. Six to 12 inches of rain fell in Ohio during this period, totals never before or since experienced over such large areas of the state (fig. 58). January 1937 remains as the wettest month in Ohio since 1866, with a state average rainfall of 9.57 inches (Rogers 1993). Cincinnati-Fernbank recorded the largest January total, 14.88 inches. Normal January precipitation in Ohio is 2 to 3 inches.

Rains during the last week of December 1936 had filled the Ohio River. Another 2 to 4 inches across the basin during the first twelve days of January 1937 kept water levels high, but the river remained within its banks. The first heavy rains arrived all across the Ohio River basin on 14 January, with 2 to 4 inches in a few hours. Rivers rose quickly. Newspapers expressed concern over the rising water but confidently predicted that colder weather would halt the rise and extensive flooding was unlikely.

Freezing weather did arrive on 16 January and most rivers fell slightly, but the destructive weather pattern was persistent, and heavy rain returned to southern Ohio on the eighteenth. The additional two inches of rain caused another rise in rivers and a crest near flood stage was expected on 19 January. This was not unusual, and river communities took the threat in stride. The 18 January 1937 *Portsmouth Times* reported, "Marietta, where residents take high water as a matter of course, repeated its periodic

process of boarding up store fronts and moving equipment to upper floors."
A major flood was not expected on 19 January, but the lives of thousands
of people would be changed by events of the next week.

A six-day siege of heavy rain from 20 to 25 January over the entire Ohio
River basin sent the river to all-time record flood levels below Gallipolis on
26–27 January. Rains of 4 to 6 inches were general, and Batavia received
8.10 inches. More than 7 inches fell in six days at Hillsboro, Cincinnati-
Fernbank, Chillicothe, and Hamilton. The entire Ohio River was over flood
stage from 22 to 28 January, and some stretches were above flood stage for
much longer (table 1). Flooding in the Mississippi River kept the lower
Ohio River above flood stage for fifty days at Cairo, Illinois.

Table 1
Flood Levels at Sites along the Ohio River in 1937

Site	Flood Stage	Crest	Date	Over Flood Stage (from)	(to)
Dam 13 Bellaire	45	52.0	26 Jan.	22 Jan.	28 Jan.
Belpre	36	55.4	26 Jan.	18 Jan.	31 Jan.
Dam 20 Belleville	45	59.1	27 Jan.	22 Jan.	30 Jan.
Dam 26 Gallipolis	50	70.3	27 Jan.	19 Jan.	1 Feb.
Dam 29 Ironton	51	73.6	27 Jan.	18 Jan.	2 Feb.
Portsmouth	50	74.1	27 Jan.	18 Jan.	3 Feb.
Dam 33 Aberdeen	50	75.3	27 Jan.	18 Jan.	4 Feb.
Cincinnati	52	80.0	26 Jan.	18 Jan.	5 Feb.

Note: Flood stages and crests are given in feet. Flood stages are local references so cannot
be compared among sites.

The development and impacts of the flood on the three major cities
affected, Cincinnati, Portsmouth, and Marietta, are discussed below.

Cincinnati. With water passing the predicted crest of sixty feet on 21 January, sixteen hundred Cincinnati houses were flooded, 170 people had been
evacuated, and traffic was being detoured from flooded roads. The *Cincinnati Enquirer* reported that each one-foot rise in water level flooded an
additional five thousand homes or businesses.

The river reached seventy feet at Cincinnati before noon on Friday, 22
January, forcing thirty-eight thousand from their homes. Rail traffic on
four of seven lines into the Union Terminal were blocked by high water,
and there were fears that electric service and water supply would be cut

for the city if the river continued to rise. It was announced that Cincinnati schools would be closed for the next week.

When the river reached nearly seventy-eight feet on 25 January, more than fifty thousand were homeless, water supply was shut off to the city except for four hours daily, and electricity was rationed. Streetcar service was suspended, only a few buses were operating, and the Suspension Bridge to Kentucky was closed. Banks and restaurants were open outside the flooded district, but stores, theaters, and factories closed throughout the city. Supplies of food, natural gas, gasoline, and coal were adequate. The sale of hard liquor was prohibited. A million gallons of gasoline that had spilled onto backwaters of the West End burst into flames and several buildings burned when firemen could not get through the flood.

Cincinnati's highest water came on Tuesday, 26 January with a crest of eighty feet, twenty-eight feet above flood stage and nearly nine feet above the 1884 record. About 10 percent of the city was under water. Drinking water was available, but its distribution was a problem and a boil order was given due to contamination. The city warned drastic measures would be taken unless drivers stayed off streets except "on authorized missions." Electricity was strictly rationed and available only for emergency needs. Food, milk, and coal were in good supply. Telephone and natural-gas service were not interrupted. The Suspension Bridge was reopened, but only for emergency traffic. Limited bus service was resumed.

Cincinnati recovered as the water slowly receded after 27 January. Water supply stations were set up at schools and stores were allowed to reopen outside the flooded areas. Floating gasoline posed a threat in several areas, but no new large fires broke out. Normal water supply resumed and bridges reopened on 2 February, and the Ohio River fell below flood stage at Cincinnati on 5 February.

Portsmouth. For twenty-four years Portsmouth had been the only "dry city" along the Ohio River, a result of the concrete flood wall erected after the 1913 flood. The wall was ten feet above the fifty-foot flood stage at Portsmouth, but it was evident by 21 January that the rising river would soon breech the wall that had protected Portsmouth for a generation. Officials feared water pouring over the wall would cause its catastrophic collapse, like a burst dam, and a flood would wash the city away.

Therefore, a quick, bold decision was made by City Manager Frank Sheehan to slowly and deliberately flood the city to save the flood wall and prevent a sweeping flood. It was announced on 21 January that factory and locomotive whistles would blow intermittently for one-half hour when the decision was made to open flood gates, and police, firemen, boy scouts, and volunteers would canvas the area to assure that everyone was out.

The sirens began wailing early on Friday, 22 January as the river approached the top of the flood wall. Gates were opened and water was released into Portsmouth. Three hours later the business district was covered with eight to ten feet of water with more to come. When the crest reached Portsmouth five days later, the Ohio River was twenty-four feet above flood stage and more than six feet above the 1913 record. River water was flowing fourteen feet deep over the top of the Portsmouth flood wall.

There was extensive damage to Portsmouth, but it was kept to a minimum by the prudent decision to allow the water to enter the city slowly, and the time allowed thousands of homeowners and businesses to remove goods and furnishings. No one died and only three injuries were reported.

Marietta. Marietta began preparing for a major flood on Thursday, 21 January. Store owners along Front and Greene Streets spent the night moving goods to storage at the Washington County Courthouse, and most stores were empty by Friday morning. School janitors removed chairs and desks from Marietta classrooms to make room for flood refugees. The city police department moved to the new City Hall.

The Ohio River crested at 55 feet at Marietta late on Tuesday, 26 January. This was 19 feet above flood stage and the second highest water level recorded at Marietta, just 3.5 feet below the record established in March 1913. The river remained above flood stage until Sunday, 31 January.

About one thousand homes were flooded in Marietta, and three thousand residents sought shelter. Downtown homes and businesses that had moved goods to second floors were forced to move up another floor or, in some cases, onto the roof to escape rising water. Gas and water service was cut off, but food supplies were maintained through the flood and there were no health problems. Sightseeing was restricted over the weekend, so the cleanup could proceed without interruption. Gas and water service was restored over the weekend, and most Marietta businesses that were not flooded reopened Monday, 1 February.

Flood damage occurred elsewhere along the Ohio River and on some interior streams during January 1937. Schools, businesses, and factories were closed as far upriver as East Liverpool. Closure of steel mills at Steubenville put 10,000 men out of work, but damage along the industrial waterfront was not severe. Streets were filled with water at Martins Ferry and 11,000 forced from their Belmont County homes, but the flood on the upper Ohio River did not reach the record stage of March 1936. Thousands of residents of the smaller communities downstream were forced from their homes. Water ran six feet deep in streets of Pomeroy and Ironton, and several thousand Brown County residents were homeless in Higginsport, Aberdeen, and Ripley. Another 2,250 people were homeless in Adams County.

All bridges in Zanesville were closed 26 January by floods on the Muskingum River, and about 1,000 were forced from their homes. High waters on the Mahoning River caused the evacuation of 140 people in Warren and closed the Youngstown steel mills for a day. The Licking River crested above its 1913 stage at Newark and washed away the Twenty-first Street Bridge. Flooding also forced several dozen people from homes and closed roads at Athens, Waverly, Coshocton, Ashland, Circleville, Lancaster, McConnelsville, Dover, and New Philadelphia.

Governor Martin Davey convened the Ohio legislature on Monday, 25 January to appropriate state funds for relief and rescue work in the Ohio Valley. More than five hundred National Guardsmen were on duty in communities between Marietta and Cincinnati, and another one thousand guardsmen were ordered into Cincinnati on 25 January. Trucks and men of the WPA were also sent into the Ohio Valley by national WPA administrator Harry Hopkins. The WPA cooperated with the Red Cross and supplied food and clothing from surplus warehouses in other states.

The American Red Cross mounted a huge rescue and relief effort in the twelve-state flooded region of the Ohio and Mississippi Valleys. In Ohio, 54,641 families were affected by the flood, the greatest numbers in Washington, Lawrence, Scioto, and Hamilton Counties (American Red Cross 1939). Red Cross statistics showed 10 people were killed and 16 injured by the flood in Ohio. This is an extraordinarily low number of casualties for a disaster of this magnitude and contrasts sharply with the 467 killed in the March 1913 floods.

The flood of 1937 was concentrated on the Ohio River, where waters rose over several days, giving time for preparations. Residents and communities there were accustomed to flooding, although not of the magnitude seen in 1937. The Flood of 1913, on the other hand, affected most of Ohio's rivers, including smaller tributaries, where waters rose rapidly and swept away many homes and people with little warning.

7 July 1943
Akron and Steubenville Floods

Cloudbursts dumped six to seven inches of rain in just a few hours during the afternoon of Wednesday, 7 July 1943, causing urban floods in Akron and Steubenville. The region between the cities also had heavy rains, but most damage was concentrated in the urban centers.

Nearly 6 inches of rain fell at the Akron Weather Bureau office, with 5.6 inches measured in the two hours ending at 3:50 P.M. Continuous lightning accompanying the cloudburst damaged roofs and chimneys and started several fires. It was floodwaters, however, that brought Akron, humming with wartime production, nearly to a standstill.

"Record Akron Storm Costs Nearly 300,000 Hours of War Work" was the headline of the *Akron Beacon Journal* Thursday afternoon. Water poured into the ground-level buildings at Goodyear Aircraft Company, halting second-shift production and causing cancellation of third-shift work. Production began again with the first shift the next morning. Electricity was shut off at Firestone Tire and Rubber when water surrounded the power plant and threatened to damage electrical equipment. Runways at Akron Municipal Airport were covered with a foot of water, as were the factory parking lots.

Seventy miles to the southeast, a steady afternoon rain became a torrential downpour at Steubenville, dumping 6.81 inches between 1:30 P.M. and 9:00 P.M. Water cascaded down the creeks and ravines of Jefferson County and swept away roads and homes and caused landslides. The flood came without warning, as though a dam burst.

The *Steubenville Herald-Star* reported two hundred homes were flooded in the Lincoln Avenue neighborhood, some up to their second floor. All 180 homes along Route 151 from Route 7 to New Alexandria were damaged and 7 were swept away by the flood on Georges Run. The Pennsylvania Railroad was blocked by a landslide near Mingo Junction, Route 7 was blocked by landslides both directions from Steubenville, and Route 22 was cut when a bridge was swept away by Cross Creek. On the north side of Steubenville, Wills Creek rose over its banks and swept 11 homes downstream.

16 June 1946
Wayne and Holmes County Floods

Floods of 16–17 June 1946 in Wayne and Holmes Counties actually had their origins with severe storms on the night of 12–13 June. A band of heavy rain extended west to east across southern Wayne County and northern Holmes County and dropped about four and a half inches at Fredericksburg. Floodwaters on Salt Creek covered crops and highways and washed out bridges in the vicinity of Fredericksburg. The major impact of heavy rains on 12–13 June was to saturate soils and fill streams, so that additional intense rainfall on the sixteenth quickly sent streams out of their banks.

Tropical air was over Ohio again on Sunday, 16 June after a warm front passed northeastward into New York and Pennsylvania (Cross 1947). Thunderstorms occurred in nearly all sections of Ohio, but severe storms and the heaviest rains affected northern Ohio from Toledo eastward. The Fredericksburg area of southern Wayne County received some of the heaviest rain, as on 12–13 June, but the rainfall of 16 June also extended southward across Holmes County and northward through Wooster to Medina

County. This north-south orientation of heaviest rains coincided almost perfectly with the drainage basin of Killbuck Creek and contributed to the flood on this stream.

Rains of more than 5 inches fell across 21.5 square miles between Fredericksburg and Wooster and in northwestern Wayne County. Cross (1947) estimated a rainfall of 7 inches near Burbank. The intensity of rain was extraordinary. Most of the rain fell in about ninety minutes between 7:30 P.M. and 9:00 P.M. Sunday. Recording rain gauges at Wooster, Overton, Charm, and Coshocton showed intensities of 3.5 to 4 inches in one hour. It is likely that rainfall in ungauged areas was more intense than this.

Damage to roads, bridges, and culverts was extensive. In Wayne County, twenty-seven bridges were seriously damaged and five bridges destroyed. Hundreds of culverts were damaged or filled with debris, requiring repair and cleaning. Similarly, twenty-eight bridges were seriously damaged or destroyed in Holmes County, but damage to roads and bridges was not as great as in the August 1935 flood.

The most spectacular damage caused on the night of 16 June was the wreck on the Erie Railroad between Burbank and Creston. An eastbound Erie locomotive pulling twenty-three freight cars approached a culvert at 10:00 P.M., traveling about thirty-five miles an hour. The culvert was weakened by the flood and collapsed as the train crossed (Cross 1947). All twenty-three cars were derailed and the engineer was killed.

8 June 1947
Flash Floods Tear through Southern Ohio

Flash floods swept several small streams in Adams, Lawrence, and Scioto Counties on the night of 7–8 June 1947. A cold front was moving southward across Ohio on 7 June and very unstable air with abundant tropical moisture was ahead of the front (Cross 1948). This volatile situation resulted in intense rainfall from slow-moving thunderstorms.

Official rainfall totals were two to four inches in the affected area. However, resultant floods indicated much more than four inches of rain fell in areas between official standard rain gauges. Therefore, a "bucket survey" was conducted after these floods to find containers, such as buckets, cans, and tubs, that caught rain during the storms (Cross 1948). The depth of rain water in containers was corrected for the shape and exposure of the containers to give estimates of rainfall.

The bucket survey showed that more than five inches of rain fell across 243 square miles of Adams, Scioto, and Lawrence Counties (Cross 1948). Peak rainfall totals were estimated to be about nine inches near Blue Creek in Adams County, near Buena Vista in southwestern Scioto County, and near Rock Camp in Lawrence County. Cross (1948) wrote it was "probable that more than five inches of rain occurred within an hour near the storm centers where the total rain was nine inches or more."

The flooded area of Lawrence County was greater than in Adams or Scioto Counties. Floodwaters entered nearly every home, along with churches and schools, in Rock Camp. Fifty homes were damaged and forty-five people were temporarily homeless in Lawrence County. More than thirty bridges, including some steel spans, were lost in the county. Crops and soils were damaged by flooding, erosion, and deep deposits of sand left by floodwaters.

The flood in Adams County was concentrated on the South Fork of Scioto Brush Creek, between Wamsley and Blue Creek and on small streams emptying into the Ohio River just south of this area. Travel on back roads was impossible for a week as more than twenty wooden bridges were destroyed and many gravel roads washed out.

Cross (1948) suggested that overall damage in Ohio was less than expected in a flood of this magnitude because of "the relatively low value of agricultural lands in this hilly area of small subsistence farms, together with the low cost type of road construction used on county and township roads."

21 March 1948
Northern Floods

Two days after violent winds swept Ohio, heavy rains sent the rivers of northern Ohio out of their banks late on Sunday, 21 March 1948. Thunderstorms ahead of a cold front dropped two to three inches of rain in a band from Van Wert through Findlay to Cleveland and Ashtabula. Most of the area had one-half inch of rain on 15 March and one inch on the nineteenth, with totals of four to five inches for the week (Cross 1949).

The Portage River reached its highest stage in more than sixteen years at Woodville and was within three feet of the stage set by the 1913 flood (Cross 1949). The Chagrin River at Willoughby and the Grand River near Madison also reached their highest stages in more than twenty years. The greatest damage occurred with urban flooding in the city of Cleveland and along the Chagrin River below Gates Mills. Twenty buildings were destroyed along the Chagrin River and another 153 buildings damaged. Several hundred residents were evacuated along the Chagrin River, and there was one injury (Cross 1949).

Big Creek overflowed at the Cleveland Zoo drowning fifty birds and mammals in their cages (Cross 1949). Cleveland streetcar tracks were submerged or blocked by dirt, idling more than fifty streetcars. All available city buses were pressed into service until streetcar lines were cleared on

Monday. Police were posted with lanterns to warn unwary motorists of gaping holes opened in streets where sewers collapsed.

16 June 1950
Crooksville Flood

One of the most intense cloudbursts in Ohio history caused flash floods on Moxahala Creek and its tributaries in Perry, Morgan, and Muskingum Counties. The Friday night floods inundated much of Crooksville, Roseville, Rose Farm, and Tropic. One life was lost, homes were destroyed, and the pottery industry of Crooksville was crippled. Cross (1950) called this the worst flood in Ohio since the Ohio River Flood of 1937.

The weather map for 16 June 1950 was a classic pattern for severe weather in Ohio, although no one could have anticipated the intense rainfall that caused flash floods that evening. A low pressure center was moving across southern Ontario and a strong cold front trailing from the low was crossing Ohio. A squall line of intense thunderstorms developed ahead of the cold front in northwestern Ohio and passed across the state Friday evening. Severe thunderstorms associated with this squall line gave extreme rainfall in the Moxahala Creek basin between 7:30 P.M. and 10:00 P.M.

Rainfall in official rain gauges totaled 4.92 inches at Crooksville, 5.84 inches at Thornville, and 3.94 inches at McConnellsville (Cross 1950). These are impressive totals for two and a half hours, but the heaviest rainfall did not occur over official rain gauges. The intensity of flooding indicated that the most intense rain fell along Black Fork, between these government weather stations.

A review of rain water caught in various containers gave rainfall estimates of 9 to 10 inches at Deavertown and at three locations near Sayre (Cross 1950). Maximum rainfall intensities along Black Fork were 4.6 inches in one hour and 8.2 inches in two hours. These values rank the Crooksville Flood as one of the most intense rainfalls ever known in Ohio.

Crooksville, a community of thirty-seven hundred, was hit hardest by the flood. One-quarter of the town was under water and floodwaters swept seven to eight feet deep through Main Street (Cross 1950). Crooksville's pottery works suffered great damage when hot kilns exploded as they were engulfed by floodwaters and firemen could not reach them. Acme Pottery, employing four hundred people, was totally destroyed by fire. Other potteries were damaged by the flood but escaped major fire damage.

Downstream from Crooksville, the community of Roseville was flooded to the second story of buildings. Water was six feet deep in the Municipal Building. More than half of Roseville's twelve hundred residents fled their homes, many driving into the hills to sleep in their cars all night.

Although the flood flows were not unprecedented, U.S. Geological Survey Engineer William Cross (1950) wrote, "The situation of several towns, all with considerable business and industrial development on the flood plains, located near the center of a cloudburst storm, made this one of the worst floods ever experienced in Ohio."

21 January 1959
Most Severe Statewide Flooding since 1913

Rains of three to six inches fell onto snow-covered frozen ground, producing the most destructive floods in Ohio since March 1913. All streams

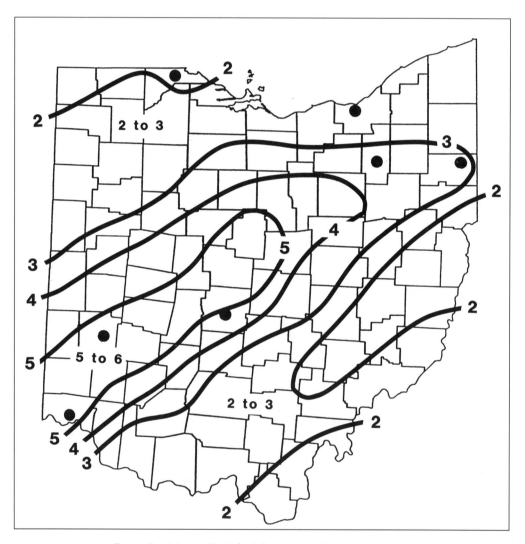

Fig. 59. Precipitation (in inches) during 19–22 January 1959.

reached flood stage from 21 to 24 January 1959, killing sixteen people in Ohio, forcing nearly forty-nine thousand people from their homes, and causing extensive damage to homes, businesses, roads, and bridges. A second flood was focused in northern Ohio on 10–11 February.

Classic winter flood conditions existed across Ohio during January 1959 (Kaser 1959). Soil frozen to a depth of six to eighteen inches was overlain by a shallow, dense snow cover containing one-quarter to three-quarters of an inch of water. High pressure centered over the northern Plains was pushing subzero air into the Great Lakes region while subtropical air was flowing northward from the Gulf of Mexico into the Ohio Valley. The confluence of these competing air masses, a stationary front, extended from New England to the Southwest and lay directly over Ohio from 19 to 21 January 1959.

The situation is not uncommon during Ohio winters, but the ordinary result is a cold winter rain that melts the snow cover, causes streams to fill, and makes for slushy walking. A final ingredient necessary for a major flood was a disturbance in the atmosphere that would create widespread heavy rains. This disturbance originated as a low pressure center over New Mexico on 19 January that intensified and passed just to the west of Ohio on the twenty-first (Kaser 1959).

Heavy rains fell across Ohio as the low passed by on 21 January (fig. 59). Two to three inches fell in northern and southeastern Ohio, but a band of three to six inches of rain extended from southwest to northeast across the state. Most of the rainfall came in an eighteen-hour period ending at 6:00 P.M. on 21 January and was concentrated on the headwaters of the state's major rivers. The alignment of this rainstorm was similar to that of March 1913, but rainfall totals in the March 1913 storm were about double the January 1959 totals.

Intense rainfall on 21 January combined with melting snow and frozen soil to create a rapid and almost total runoff of water into the streams of Ohio. This extraordinary amount of water was more than the normal stream channels could carry, and Ohio rivers overflowed onto roads and bridges, into communities and homes, and across farm fields.

In general, stream flood levels in January 1959 were the greatest since March 1913 and second or third highest of record. The January 1959 flood levels on Ohio's major rivers were several feet below the catastrophic levels reached in March 1913, although on some smaller watersheds the flood of January 1959 was higher than the March 1913 levels. These include the Kokosing River, Licking River, and Little Miami River from Fort Ancient to Morrow. On the other hand, the water levels in January 1959 were not particularly impressive on the lower Scioto and Muskingum Rivers or on the Maumee, where considerable ice held until the February flood.

Fig. 60. Chillicothe during the flood of 23 January 1959 (from Cross 1961). (Courtesy of the Ohio Department of Natural Resources)

Damage from the floods was second only to the March 1913 floods in Ohio. Cross (1961) reported 16 persons killed, 48,715 evacuated from their homes, and $100 million damage. Floodwaters destroyed 132 houses, caused major damage to 2,415 houses, and resulted in minor damage to another 14,534 homes. Fifty-five other buildings were destroyed and 1,145 were damaged. A total of 17,082 buildings were flooded. Thirty-one bridges were destroyed and hundreds of others damaged during the flood. Transportation was hampered by hundreds of closed state highways and city streets. National Guard troops assisted in many Ohio communities.

The streets of Mansfield were under four feet of water and industries were shut in Canton and Youngstown. Shelby was cut in half by the Black Fork of the Mohican River. Columbus was the most severely affected among Ohio's major cities, with many streets flooded, one hundred homes badly damaged, and thirty-two hundred evacuees cared for in Red Cross shelters. Greater damage was prevented at Columbus by Delaware Reservoir, which stored all the runoff from 381 square miles upstream on the Olentangy River.

Water plants at Newark, Newton Falls, Marion, Chillicothe, and numerous other communities were shut down as water surrounded plants and flooded pumps. Many community sewage treatment plants were also

Fig. 61. Forgotten laundry along Jefferson Avenue in Chillicothe on 24 January 1959. A water line on the house and clothes shows the height of water in the flood. (Photograph courtesy of the Ross County Historical Society)

knocked out of service for several days by high water. The reptile collection at the Cleveland Zoo was drowned as Big Creek flooded lower portions of the zoo grounds.

Mt. Vernon was inundated by the Kokosing River, forcing thirty-five hundred of the fifteen thousand residents from their homes and cutting off the water supply. Governor Michael DiSalle toured Mt. Vernon by army truck on 22 January. One-third of Chillicothe was flooded when the Scioto River broke through a levee of sandbags on 24 January (figs. 60 and 61). In Zanesville, the Licking River drove two thousand people from their homes (fig. 62).

High water and ice jams on the Sandusky River flooded Upper Sandusky, Tiffin, and Fremont. Fremont's business district remained flooded until

Fig. 62. Flood at Zanesville in January 1959 (from Cross 1961). The Muskingum River is flowing at right toward the bottom of the photo, and the Licking River enters from the left. The Y-Bridge is at the bottom center. (Photograph courtesy of the Ohio Department of Natural Resources)

25 January, and 1,353 residents were out of their homes, according to the *Toledo Blade*. Bulldozers pushed fifteen-foot piles of ice from Fremont streets back into the river. To the east, the Grand and Ashtabula Rivers reached the highest levels known, and there was extensive damage at Mentor, Fairport Harbor, and Geneva. Major roads in extreme northeastern Ohio were closed, including U.S. Routes 6 and 20.

Five retaining basins of the Miami Conservancy District prevented a major flood on the Miami River. Uncontrolled streams in the Miami basin caused damage to industries and homes at Springfield, Hamilton, and Middletown. Peak flow at Dayton during this flood was less than one-fourth of the flow on 25 March 1913 (Cross 1961).

The number of deaths and amount of damage were large but not as severe as during the March 1913 flood, due, in part, to the lesser intensity of the January 1959 flood. Other factors that contributed to reducing the casualties and damage in 1959 were the flood-control reservoirs built since 1913, better communication of warnings, organized rescue work, and more adequate design of bridges and other structures (Cross 1961).

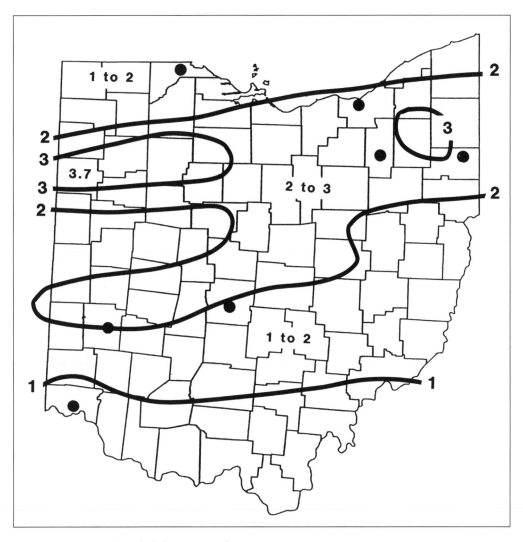

Fig. 63. Precipitation (in inches) during 9–11 February 1959.

A second flood developed on 10 February as a storm center moved north of Ohio, causing the familiar flood recipe of heavy rain onto frozen soil. With a storm track that was farther north than in the January storm, rainfall was heaviest in northern Ohio from Van Wert eastward across the headwaters of the Maumee, Sandusky, and Chagrin Rivers. Two to three and a half inches fell in this band while one to two inches fell in central and southern Ohio (fig. 63).

Some families were just returning to their homes after the January floods when they were forced out again on 11 February. Much of downtown Van Wert was under three feet of water in the worst flooding there since 1913. Main Street in Findlay was flooded by the Blanchard River and eight hundred Warren residents fled their homes as the Mahoning River covered the Flats section on 11 February. About twenty-five blocks of Fremont were flooded as water jammed behind broken ice downstream. At least two hundred Fremont residents had not returned to their homes following the January flood when their homes were flooded again in February (Cross 1961). The north side of Bucyrus was flooded by the Sandusky River, and Swan Creek flooded Swanton's emergency water pumps. Strong winds accompanying this rainstorm damaged homes and trees at Lima and Hillsboro.

The Toledo area, largely undamaged by the January flood, was severely affected in February. Ice broke on the Maumee River and huge ice jams formed at the Ohio Turnpike bridge and other locations causing concern over the safety of the structures. A turnpike spokesman reassured the public that the turnpike bridge was "built to withstand huge floods." Streets and homes were under water in several Toledo neighborhoods and in lowlands along the Maumee River in Waterville and Maumee. Several docks and other riverfront structures were swept away by the high water and ice floes in Toledo.

Without a protective cover of vegetation, the agricultural land of Ohio lost huge amounts of topsoil in these winter floods of 1959. Measurements showed the Maumee River carried 217,000 tons of sediment past Waterville on 12 February, or 34 tons of sediment per square mile in the Maumee River basin (Archer 1960).

5 June 1963
Cambridge Flood

Torrential rains fell overnight on 4–5 June 1963 across Guernsey County and portions of Coshocton and Muskingum Counties. A stationary front extended across the Great Lakes with moist tropical air to the south in Ohio. Two upper air lows over the central Appalachians joined and strengthened early on 5 June. They moved northwestward into Ohio, hovered over the state, and finally exited toward the east on the sixth (Cross 1964a).

The combination of tropical air, instability, and weak air motions led to severe thunderstorms that stagnated for many hours over the flood areas. Rains began at Cambridge at 3:00 P.M. on 4 June. A total of 7.95 inches was recorded in the sixteen hours between 3:00 P.M. and 7:00 A.M. at the official Cambridge Sewage Plant rain gauge. A bucket survey of fifty-three sites showed more than 13 inches of rain fell at two sites in the College Hill area west of Cambridge and also at four sites five miles northwest of Cambridge (Cross 1964a). A total of 20 inches was collected during 3–5 June at the Lewis Poleyn residence in southeastern Knox Township.

This flood occurred during a period of drought in Ohio, so soils absorbed more of the rainfall than under ordinary circumstances. In spite of this, floods of 5 June were the highest ever recorded on all streams in the affected area.

Flooding was most severe on Crooked Creek west of Cambridge. The bridge of the Baltimore and Ohio Railroad over Crooked Creek was destroyed, and all major highways were inundated by up to five feet of water. Route 40 was closed west of Cambridge for several days by damaged bridge approaches. Broken water mains or pollution interrupted municipal water supplies of Cambridge, Byesville, and Pleasant City. Several people were rescued by helicopter, but there were no fatalities.

10 March 1964
Floods End Drought

Two periods of heavy rain over southern and central Ohio from 4 to 10 March 1964 ended the severe 1963 drought but caused extensive damage, several deaths, and the evacuation of thousands of persons (Cross 1964b).

The first storm tracked from Arkansas to Michigan on 4–5 March and brought two to four inches of rain in a southwest-northeast band through Ohio. The greatest amounts were in the southwestern counties. Strong winds accompanying the thunderstorms caused one death at Zanesville and scattered wind damage through the state.

Soils were unfrozen and dry in southern Ohio and there was no snow cover, so much of the excessive rain of 4–5 March was absorbed into the soil or held in reservoirs. Although this rain caused no major flooding, it saturated soils in southern Ohio and brought most rivers to near flood levels. This set the stage for greater floods when more heavy rain arrived during 8–10 March.

A stationary front extended east-west across Ohio on 8 March, with cold air to the north and warm moist air to the south. It remained in that position for five days with only slight movements caused by passing low pressure waves. This weather pattern has been responsible for many of the great floods in Ohio. Extensive heavy rains developed as the moist tropical air from the south was forced to rise over the cooler air north of the front.

Rains associated with this front totaled three to six inches in southern and central Ohio during 8–10 March. This rain was not absorbed into the wet soils, and Ohio streams had little capacity after being filled by the heavy rain a few days earlier (fig. 64). As a result, all rivers in central and southern Ohio reached flood stage by 9 March and some exceeded long-standing records.

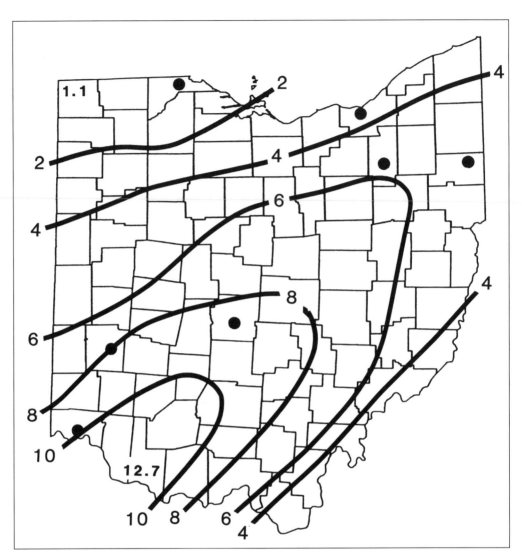

Fig. 64. Rainfall (in inches) during 4–10 March 1964.

The Hocking River had flooded Athens and Ohio University a year earlier and threatened with record high water again on Monday, 9 March. Athens County schools dismissed early to allow buses to deliver children home before roads were flooded by rising rivers, and Ohio University students removed their cars from basement garages at West Green dormitory. National Guard troops, firemen, and police worked through the night to evacuate residents of Rockbridge and South Logan upstream along the Hocking River.

The crest on the Hocking at Athens came late Wednesday morning at 24.15 feet (fig. 65). This was the highest water in Athens since 1907, exceeding even the 1913 flood stage. All schools and main highways were

Fig. 65. Ohio University, Athens, during the flood of 11 March 1964. (Photograph courtesy of the Ohio Department of Natural Resources)

closed in the region on Wednesday, mail delivery was curtailed, fifteen hundred Ohio University students were evacuated, and 380 Athens homes were flooded, according to the *Athens Messenger*. Water levels receded several feet by the next day, so roads and businesses reopened.

Elsewhere in central and southern Ohio, flooding caused extensive damage in the Muskingum, Scioto, and Miami river basins. Paint Creek exceeded 1913 stages and flooded Bainbridge, Bourneville, and Chillicothe. The East Fork of the Little Miami River exceeded the 1945 record stage at Perintown, and the communities of South Lebanon, Milford, and Batavia were partially inundated. Roads and schools were closed for a day or two in many communities.

Flooding also occurred along the entire Ohio River from Pittsburgh to the Mississippi River. The crest of 66.2 feet at Cincinnati on 11 March was the highest since 1945. All riverfront communities, except the few protected by floodwalls, were inundated, and several thousand people were evacuated. Water was 6 feet deep on Main Street in Pomeroy and businesses were closed for several days in most of the river communities.

Eight lives were lost in Ohio during these floods, eighty-four homes were destroyed, and eighty-two hundred homes damaged (Cross 1964b).

21 July 1964
Akron Flood

A cloudburst on Tuesday afternoon, 21 July 1964 overpowered Akron's sewer system and flooded streets, basements, and downtown parking lots in the greatest flood there since 1913. The focus of the heavy rain was in the center of the city and on the west side. One rain gauge in the flooded area recorded 3.05 inches between 2:20 P.M. and 3:35 P.M., although the distribution of rain was variable and some areas received more than was caught in the rain gauge. The Akron-Canton Airport had only .10 inch, and some areas of Bath reported no rainfall at all.

Urban runoff turned the Ohio Canal into a "raging river" through Akron. Buildings, bridges, and construction projects along the canal were damaged. The Bowery Street Bridge was damaged and a portion of a building on Bowery Street collapsed into the canal. Police ordered evacuation of the twelve-story Akron Savings and Loan Building as waters rose around it and poured into the basement. Hundreds of cars were submerged in parking lots, including many at the Akron Selle lot on South High Street. The North and Howard Streets area was flooded by the Ohio Canal and Little Cuyahoga River.

The most spectacular damage occurred when a thirty-six-inch sewer line collapsed under the Tallmadge Parkway (now Tallmadge Avenue), between Merriman and the Little Cuyahoga River, causing a huge hole to open in the eastbound lane. Three people died in the incident after dramatic rescue efforts held the attention of the community for forty-eight hours.

27 April 1966
Lake Erie Batters the Shoreline

Several hours of winds up to fifty-five miles an hour from the northeast pushed the western end of Lake Erie to its highest level in more than twenty-five years on 27 April 1966. The lake at Toledo reached 575.67 feet above sea level shortly after 11:00 A.M., a height that was not exceeded until November 1972.

The *Toledo Blade* reported that fifteen hundred persons were evacuated Wednesday as water sloshed over coastal roads and dikes and into homes in the Point Place section of Toledo and at Reno Beach and Howard Farms in eastern Lucas County. Heavy rains hampered the evacuation.

Waves seven to eight feet high rolled across dikes and battered lakefront homes at Reno Beach. The flood of lake water was a doubly cruel blow to some Edgewater Drive residents at Point Place. Their homes had recently been repaired from damage by the Palm Sunday Tornado a year earlier and were now two feet deep in Lake Erie.

Columbia Gas of Ohio shut off gas service to Point Place to reduce the chance of fires, and Toledo Edison cut electricity to Reno Beach. Lake levels remained high into the evening when winds shifted to the south, and the lake fell about three feet to normal levels. Sheriff's deputies and military police from the Ohio National Guard patrolled Reno Beach Wednesday night to protect property and direct traffic. Point Place was cordoned off by police into the next day, and large pumps moved water from neighborhoods back into Maumee Bay. Mailmen continued delivering mail at Point Place, sloshing through knee-deep water in high boots, according to the *Toledo Blade*. Most roads were reopened in the flooded areas Thursday and residents began returning to their damaged homes.

12 July 1966
Sandusky Flood

A week of severe weather across Ohio culminated in record rains over Erie, Ottawa, and Huron Counties on Tuesday, 12 July 1966. A line of storms with torrential rains remained nearly stationary for seven hours. At Sandusky, rainfall from 2:00 A.M. to 9:20 A.M. totaled 8.99 inches. Additional afternoon storms brought the total to 10.51 inches up to 9:30 P.M. This far exceeded the previous twenty-four-hour rainfall record of 5.95 inches at Sandusky set 24–25 June 1937. More than 5 inches of rain also fell at Fremont, Norwalk, and Put-in-Bay.

The results of a bucket survey at 162 sites showed 6 inches or more fell over an area of 260 square miles (Cross 1967). More than 12 inches of rain was estimated to have fallen in Huron, just south of Sandusky and near where Route 4 crosses the Ohio Turnpike. Total damages were about $5 million (Cross 1967), including $2.5 million in damage to twelve thousand homes and businesses in Sandusky.

23–27 May 1968
Rivers Run Wild in Southern Ohio

Two periods of heavy rain within five days sent rivers out of their banks in central and southern Ohio in 1968. The first deluge on 23–24 May was focused on southern Ohio, where three to six inches fell south of Interstate 70. Flash floods developed as the heavy rains fell onto soil saturated from wet weather earlier in May. Small streams overflowed their banks Thursday night, 23 May to cover roads, bridges, and crops. Ohio's larger rivers, including the Hocking, Scioto, and Little Miami, reached flood stage on 24 May.

The Hocking River reached 24.63 feet at Athens, more than 7 feet above flood stage and the highest since 1907. All communities along the Hocking were flooded, and roads, schools, businesses, and factories were closed throughout the river basin. Amesville businesses were flooded and, for the first time in memory, there was water on the floor of the First National Bank Building. Three feet of water in Amesville Nursing Home forced residents to the second floor. The *Athens Messenger* reported that a helicopter delivered food to the stranded nursing-home residents. Homes were evacuated and highways blocked in Nelsonville, Murray City, Logan, Rock Bridge, and Chauncey. The quick overnight arrival of the flood prevented residents from moving household goods to higher positions and, even when goods had been moved, they often had not been raised high enough.

The flood came at a time of tension on university campuses as students protested the Vietnam War. Ohio National Guardsmen were on duty at Ohio University as a precaution against civil unrest, but instead they saw duty in the flood. The *Athens Messenger* reported that "it was strange to see the Guardsmen and students working together in the flood" when only days before they had been antagonists.

The lower Scioto River flooded on 24–25 May, forcing more than two hundred Circleville families from their homes, according to the *Columbus Evening Dispatch.* Six bridges were swept away in Pickaway County as all tributaries of the Scioto went above flood stage. The entire village of Mooresville was flooded, and residents of Eagle Mills, on Salt Creek, were rescued from upper floors or the roofs of their homes. To the west, the Little Miami River rose six to eight feet above flood stage at Perintown, Kings Mills, and Milford. Mud was reported knee-deep in downtown Morrow, and more than one hundred families in Warren County lost all their possessions.

Additional rains of two to four inches in the flooded districts on 26–27 May caused a second rise in streams. Although the floods of 27 May were generally a few feet below the crests of previous days, continued high water hampered the recovery and repair of damaged structures. This second period of heavy rains extended into northern counties, where flooded fields caused extensive crop damage. Four deaths were reported in the Ohio floods of May 1968.

4 July 1969
Fourth of July Fireworks

The most devastating summer flooding in Ohio history struck north-central Ohio during the state's stormiest Independence Day. Severe thunderstorms moved from Lake Erie into North Coast communities between 7:30 P.M. and 8:00 P.M. on 4 July 1969. This line of storms became nearly stationary for more than eight hours, aligned from Toledo southeastward through Fremont, Norwalk, Ashland, and Wooster. Flooding, microburst winds up to one hundred miles an hour, tornadoes, and lightning caused 41 deaths and injured 559 persons, 51 of them hospitalized (Miller 1969a).

A special weather summary in the July 1969 issue of *Climatological Data—Ohio* reported damage totaling $65 million, with 32 homes destroyed and nearly 10,000 homes damaged. More than 300 mobile homes and 180 farm buildings were destroyed or damaged and 104 small businesses destroyed. Close to 700 boats were destroyed and 7,000 cars were destroyed or damaged. Among floods, only those of March 1913 and January 1959 caused more damage in Ohio than the 4 July 1969 storms.

Thousands of persons were outdoors on this Friday evening of the July Fourth holiday and would soon be treated to nature's fireworks. Forecasts early in the day had indicated that severe weather was possible during the evening, but little threatening weather was seen and many Ohio communities prepared for the traditional evening fireworks. Boats lined the lakeshore from Toledo to Cleveland and parks were jammed with spectators.

Severe weather developed over southern Michigan and Lake Erie after 6:00 P.M. and began moving southward toward the Ohio shore. Warnings of severe weather were issued by 7:45 P.M. as the Weather Bureau radar screens showed towering storms approaching the shore and a large ship in Lake Erie reported winds of one hundred miles an hour (ESSA 1969).

The line of severe thunderstorms, still growing, struck the shore between 7:40 P.M. and 8:00 P.M. with winds of more than eighty miles an hour, heavy rain, and intense lightning. Winds caused extensive damage to trees, wires, and homes along the shore in Lakewood. Two girls were killed under fallen trees in Lakewood Park, and a man died under a fallen tree at Cedar Point.

A tornado destroyed several homes and injured 40 persons when it touched down briefly at Perry (Lake County) (Grazulis 1990). Another tornado touched down near Delta (Fulton County), uprooting trees, destroying 2 barns, and damaging several homes. A tornado touched down north of Findlay, destroying barns, damaging 4 homes, and causing 1

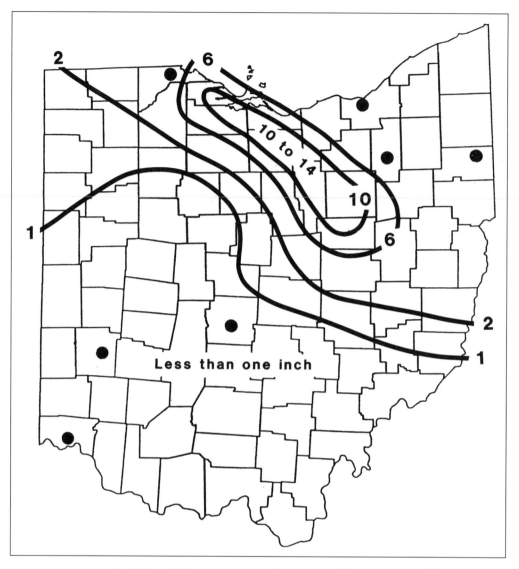

Fig. 66. Rainfall (in inches) on 4–5 July 1969. An official rain gauge at Wooster recorded 10.36 inches, and there were many unofficial reports of 11 to 12 inches. A site in Wayne County was estimated to have received 14.8 inches.

minor injury. Winds toppled 5,000 trees and damaged several homes in Toledo, where 75,000 homes were without electricity after the storms. Cleveland Electric Illuminating Company reported 175,000 customers in 5 northeastern counties were without power after the storm, according to the *Cleveland Plain Dealer*.

Hundreds of small pleasure boats were anchored just offshore in Lake Erie awaiting fireworks at Toledo, Sandusky, and Cleveland as the storms struck. Most made it to safe harbor, but U.S. Coast Guard ships and planes rescued one hundred boaters, according to the 10 July 1969 *Cleve-*

land Plain Dealer. Miraculously, only three persons died on Lake Erie. A man and woman were lost from a rubber raft off Geneva-on-the-Lake, and a boater was killed by lightning in Maumee Bay. Another boater drowned when his boat capsized on the Portage River near Port Clinton, according to the *Toledo Blade.*

Wind damage along the Lake Erie shore and inland was extensive, but most of the damage and deaths with these storms came as extreme rainfall developed inland late on 4 July and into 5 July 1969. Thunderstorms continued to form all night along the line from Toledo to Wheeling, West Virginia, and rainfall rates exceeded two inches per hour.

Total rainfall during the night of 4 July was ten to fourteen inches in a band one hundred miles long from Ottawa County to Wayne County (fig. 66). Most of this fell in less than twelve hours, causing excessive runoff into streams and rivers of north-central Ohio. Farmers watched as crops were destroyed. Floods, in some cases the greatest on record, enveloped the streams and dozens of communities along streams.

On the flat, poorly drained land of Ottawa and Sandusky Counties, fields were flooded as far as the eye could see. Homes and roads were inundated until the water slowly drained into Lake Erie several days later. Floodwaters in Fremont covered cars and stood 4 feet deep in homes along the Sandusky River. All roads leading into Huron County were blocked by high water or fallen trees after midnight (Miller and Hamilton 1969). Water moved 7 feet deep through the streets of Norwalk, and damage at the Norwalk power plant left the city without electricity or water for five days. Main Street in Greenwich was under 6 feet of water after a city dam broke, and water remained 3 feet deep in Bellevue a week after the flood began.

In Erie County, the Huron River reached a record flood at Milan, 7 feet above the previous high (Miller and Hamilton 1969). The Vermilion River was 13 feet over flood stage and 3.3 feet above the previous record at Vermilion. More than 4,800 persons were evacuated from their homes in Erie County. The Black River at Elyria exceeded its previous record level by 4.1 feet, and 440 homes were evacuated in Lorain County.

Northern Ashland County was isolated and without power for two days before waters receded. Thirty bridges were damaged in Ashland County, and the city of Ashland was without drinking water after the flood. Most of Wayne County had more than 10 inches of rain, and one location in Chester Township reported 14.8 inches overnight. All sections of Wayne County were flooded, and transportation in the county was blocked by 110 destroyed or damaged highway bridges. Wooster was isolated for the weekend, and the city water supply was not restored until 11 July. Two emergency water wells were drilled near Wooster Community Hospital Sunday, one to supply the hospital and the other to supplement water being trucked into Wooster. More than ten thousand Wayne County homes were without electric power Friday night. The *Ashland Times-Gazette* reported that Ohio Edison supplied electricity to Orrville after the Orrville Municipal System was lost to the flood.

Fourteen deaths were attributed to the flooding in Wayne County (Miller and Hamilton 1969). Some people drowned after being swept off flooded highways in their vehicles, others drowned after falling into deep water in their attempt to escape. Several bodies were not found until floodwaters receded four days later. Among the many heroic rescues, the *Ashland Times-Gazette* reported an Ohio Highway Patrol Officer and a truck driver pulled a family of four from their car after it was swept off Interstate 71 in Ashland County.

Killbuck Creek in Holmes County rose more than twenty feet to the maximum flood on record. Most of the village of Killbuck was flooded by the creek, and sixty-five bridges were damaged in Holmes County. Two hundred Killbuck residents spent several days living in the elementary school, along with Ohio National Guardsmen who had been called for duty. Major flooding was averted in Massillon when twelve men closed gates on the railroad opening between levees before the Tuscarawas River crested ten feet above flood stage.

Miller and Hamilton (1969) reported forty-one deaths attributed to the storms, including twenty-five by drowning, eight by falling trees, six electrocuted by fallen wires, one death from lightning, and one death from "storm related" injuries. A Weather Bureau report on the storms (ESSA 1969) reported five more deaths due to drowning by 21 July for a total of forty-six deaths in Ohio. Five persons were listed as missing.

14 November 1972
Lakeshore Flooding

The most damaging wind setup on the North Coast occurred early on Tuesday, 14 November 1972. Several hours of northeast gales flooded and battered the coast from Cedar Point westward to Toledo. Total damage in Ohio was estimated at $22 million and three thousand families were evacuated during the storm.

Winds at the Marblehead Coast Guard station averaged forty to forty-six miles an hour from the northeast overnight on 13 November and into the morning of the fourteenth. Winds up to seventy-three miles an hour were measured on commercial vessels over the open lake, and wave heights were 10 to 15 feet (Brazel and Phillips 1974). The northeast wind setup caused Lake Erie to rise about 3 feet at Toledo and fall 4 feet at Buffalo, a tilt of 7 feet toward the western end.

Water level at Toledo rose to 576 feet above sea level, establishing a new record high lake level, based on Toledo records beginning in 1940. This exceeded the previous record of 575.7 feet on 27 April 1966 (Brooks Widder NOAA/NOS Great Lakes Section; letter to authors, 8 July 1993). The 14 November 1972 lake level record has been exceeded several times at Toledo, and the present record is 576.7 feet, set on 14 April 1980.

The wind setup caused Lake Erie to invade the lowlands of Erie, Ottawa, and Lucas Counties. Houses were surrounded, roads and whole communities flooded, and dikes breached. North Bass, South Bass, and Kelleys Island suffered almost total inundation. Coastal buildings surrounded by the lake succumbed to several hours of battering by large waves. Coastal residents west of Huron were warned to evacuate homes as the water rose overnight. In the Reno Beach–Howard Farms area, two thousand persons evacuated five hundred homes. At Point Place in Toledo, seven hundred houses were flooded and hundreds of persons were forced out.

The Sand Beach–Locust Point area of Ottawa County was flooded before all residents could leave. An amphibious rescue vehicle entered the area but was driven back by nine-foot waves along the shore. The *Toledo Blade* reported two Coast Guard helicopters arrived and took all thirty to safety from the battered shore. The aerial rescue, the paper noted, was completed in weather "that even sea gulls would not fly in."

The wind setup of 14 November 1972 on Lake Erie was especially severe and set records for lake level at Toledo because several years of abnormal weather created higher than normal lake levels on Lake Erie. All of the Great Lakes had been rising since 1964 due to above-normal precipitation (Brazel and Phillips 1974). The year 1972 was wet and cool in the Lake Erie basin with less summer sunshine than usual. The increased rainfall and reduction in evaporation caused Lake Erie to rise several inches to its highest level since records began in 1860. Thus, the lake level was only one or two feet lower than coastal homes, roads, and dikes before the northeast gales began on 14 November, and these areas were inundated by the lake when wind setup caused an additional rise of three feet that day.

9 April 1973
Northeast Gales Whip the Lake

Residents of the Lake Erie shore continued to prepare for coastal flooding during the winter of 1972–73 but did not anticipate water above the flood of November 1972. Lowlands from Sandusky and Port Clinton to Toledo had been flooded in November as gales from the northeast piled already high lake waters into lakeshore communities.

Now, less than five months later, winds of forty-five miles an hour from the northeast were again pushing the lake into the western basin, and waves battered roads, homes, and dikes. Waves of 8 to 10 feet smashed homes and washed over dikes and other protective barriers. By 4:00 P.M. Monday, 9 April 1973, the lake level at Toledo was 576.67 feet above sea level, 6 feet above recent levels and 8 inches above the November 1972 flood. This was the highest lake level recorded to that date at Toledo and has been exceeded only once, by less than 1 inch, on 14 April 1980.

The often-flooded Point Place area of Toledo was hardest hit. City Manager James Daken reported that five square miles were inundated by Lake Erie and water in Point Place was twenty inches higher than in November 1972, according to the *Toledo Blade*. Columbia Gas of Ohio and Toledo Edison shut off utility service to more than six hundred Point Place homes to eliminate the danger of gas explosions and short circuits. Telephone service was also disrupted as terminals were flooded.

Lowlands at Sand Beach, Willow Beach, and Asher Beach west of Port Clinton were flooded by the lake, and some farms were surrounded by water. Perry Street in Port Clinton was under water, but businesses had used sandbags to keep water from merchandise. Water also rose up to Second Street past Port Clinton's downtown intersection of Madison and Perry. Several dozen persons were evacuated, but most returned to their homes Tuesday. Route 2 was closed west of Port Clinton, as was Route 269.

Damage was minor on the Bass islands, although the *Toledo Blade* reported that South Bass Island became two islands for a time Monday as water rolled waist deep over the narrow neck of land at Perry's Monument. A few roads were flooded on the islands and east-facing beaches were damaged.

Cleanup of flood damage continued for several days as residents moved back into soaked homes through debris-littered streets. Water thrown over dikes or into farm fields a mile inland remained for days, its path back to the lake blocked by dikes.

Some flooded residents again speculated that the federal government was responsible for the prevailing high lake levels, that Lake Erie was being held artificially high to allow heavier loads in commercial vessels. And once again, government officials had to explain that there is virtually no control possible over the level of Lake Erie. Water flows freely into the lake from Lake Michigan and Lake Huron and freely out of the lake into the Niagara River. Lake Erie is high when several years of wet weather prevails, and the lake is low after several years of dry weather in a natural cycle of fluctuations. Northeast gales during periods of high water will always threaten homes and roads along the lakeshore.

14 September 1979
Hurricane Frederic

Ohio is not considered to be in the "hurricane belt" of the United States, but the remains of a hurricane occasionally bring heavy rain and winds to the state. Hurricane Frederic came ashore from the Gulf of Mexico at Mobile, Alabama, on Wednesday, 12 September 1979, with winds of 132 miles an hour, becoming the costliest hurricane to strike the United States to that date. The storm weakened as it moved north through Alabama and Tennessee, and, as wind speeds fell below seventy-five miles an hour, it was downgraded to a tropical storm.

The heavy rains of Hurricane Frederic passed over Ohio from southwest to northeast late on 13 September and into the morning of the fourteenth. Rainfall totaled four to six inches in a broad band across Ohio from Cincinnati and Dayton to Columbus, Akron, Cleveland, and Youngstown. Southeastern counties had two to four inches, and less than two inches fell in the northwest. Streams and rivers overflowed their banks on Friday, 14 September all through the region of heaviest rains. Roads, industries, and low-lying homes were flooded. Damage to crops was extensive throughout the state.

Columbus schools closed Friday and state offices delayed opening until 10:00 A.M. to give employees time to get around flooded roads and through stalled traffic. Blacklick Creek flooded the Municipal Building in Reynoldsburg and topped a levee to flood three hundred homes at Blacklick Estates in Madison Township Friday afternoon, according to the *Columbus Dispatch*.

Water flowed a foot deep through downtown Grove City and flooded several homes. Thirty people were evacuated from mobile home parks in Millersburg, fifty persons were evacuated at Rittman, the Hocking River flooded south of Lancaster, and two bridges were washed out on Route 13 between Newark and Mt. Vernon.

In northeastern Ohio, the Cuyahoga River flooded and caused evacuations in Valley View and Independence. The flood level of 22.1 feet on the Cuyahoga at Valley View was the second highest on record, reported the *Cleveland Plain Dealer*, just 4 inches below the record set on 22 January 1959.

12 March 1982
Northwestern Ohio Floods

Northwestern Ohioans remember the flood of 1982 as occurring on 12 March, but the scene was set months before in the autumn of 1981.

Autumn precipitation was above average and soil was moist when the first significant snow fell on northwestern Ohio in mid-December. Snow continued to fall throughout December, leaving a cover of six to fifteen inches.

Early January brought temperatures above 40 degrees, and the already moist ground received even more moisture from melting snow. Temperatures were extremely cold in mid-January, freezing exposed soils up to three feet deep. Moderate to heavy rainfall in the last week of January saturated the snowpack, and again a return to cold temperatures created ice layers in the snowpack. February brought milder temperatures, which further compacted the snow.

This serious potential for a flood did not go unnoticed. In February the National Weather Service began issuing the first of several flood watches. The first nine days of March added even more snow and rain. It was this five-month history of rain, excessive snowfall, and extremely low temperatures that set the stage for the flooding that began on Friday, 12 March (Glatfelter and Chin 1988). Seven to ten inches of snow and ice covered the ground in northwestern Ohio when the rains began falling on the twelfth. Although two inches of rainfall was not excessive, it brought with it warmer temperatures and provided additional moisture to the already saturated snow cover.

By Saturday, 13 March, temperatures in northwestern Ohio were above 50 degrees. Most of the snow cover was gone and melted snow and rain had already started its disastrous descent into the local river basins. The National Weather Service issued a flood warning predicting near-record flooding in northwestern Ohio, and the flooding that followed was the worst since March 1913.

Moisture started flowing into the network of rivers that comprise the Maumee River basin. The St. Joseph, St. Marys, Tiffin, Maumee, Auglaize, Blanchard, and Ottawa Rivers along with countless other streams and drainage ditches began to swell on 13 March. Five days later, on the seventeenth, the Maumee River crested at 25.9 feet in Fort Wayne, Indiana, only three inches lower than in the great flood of March 1913.

The Tiffin River crested on 15 March with a record high of 18.3 feet in Stryker, and the Blanchard River crested on 13 March at 12.4 feet near Findlay. The Auglaize crested near Fort Jennings at 15 feet on 13 March, and the Ottawa River near Allentown reached 8.7 feet on 12 March. Most rivers had not seen crests this high since January 1959 or earlier.

Water poured into Grand Rapids, and by Sunday, 14 March, the main streets were five to seven feet deep. The Post Office moved to the Wesleyan Church and the Fire Department moved to the Junior High. Across northwestern Ohio, communities gathered together, filling sandbags in an attempt to forestall the rising waters. The National Guard was called to several communities to assist in traffic control and maintain order. Governor James Rhodes visited the area on 14 March and surveyed the extent of the damage. President Ronald Reagan made a similar visit several days later to Fort Wayne, Indiana.

Ten days later the water subsided. Nature's wild party was over and northwestern Ohioans were left as the cleanup crew. Defiance, Paulding, Wood, Henry, Putnam, and Lucas Counties were declared disaster areas. There was major damage to roads, bridges, businesses, private property, and agricultural lands. Twelve homes were destroyed, two hundred others damaged, and hundreds of people were temporarily homeless. Damage was estimated at more than $11 million. Defiance County appeared hardest hit, with $8 million in damages.

14 June 1990
Shadyside Flood

The deadliest Ohio flood since 1969 occurred in the steep Appalachian valleys of Belmont County late on Thursday, 14 June 1990. The lives of twenty-six persons were lost in this brief flash flood on Wegee Creek and Pipe Creek near Shadyside (NOAA 1991).

Conditions were ripe for flooding across Ohio on 14 June. Soils were saturated with water from a very wet month of May, which meant that additional rains would run off quickly into streams. Tropical air was flowing northward from the Gulf of Mexico early on the fourteenth, and the temperature and humidity in Ohio were the same as in Tampa, Florida. This abundant moisture and an approaching cold front led forecasters to expect thunderstorms on the fourteenth, but these large-scale weather conditions gave no clue as to the extreme rainfall that would fall over Belmont County. The clues to the impending flood, largely unavailable to the forecasters that day, were in the mesoscale features in the atmosphere, weather systems less than one hundred miles across that are not seen on normal weather maps.

Mesoscale convective systems (MCS), large, long-lived clusters of thunderstorms that are often responsible for severe weather, had crossed the Great Plains into Michigan the previous night. Air flowing out of the MCS had formed weather fronts that crossed Ohio from the west and north on 14 June (NOAA 1991). Thunderstorms developed along this outflow boundary in western Ohio during the morning. These storms produced 2 to 3 inches of rain in a few hours in Columbus, Newark, and other portions of Ohio during the afternoon, with as much as 3.75 inches in Holmes County. Urban and small stream flooding forced dozens of Newark residents from their homes, but the storms were

Fig. 67. Mobile home carried along and destroyed in the Shadyside flood of 14 June 1990. (Photograph courtesy of the National Weather Service, Cleveland)

Fig. 68. A car, mobile home, and other debris left by the Shadyside flood of 14 June 1990. (Photograph courtesy of the National Weather Service, Cleveland)

Fig. 69. Flood destruction at Shadyside on 14 June 1990. (Photograph courtesy of the National Weather Service, Cleveland)

moving southeastward at twenty to thirty miles an hour and no major damage occurred.

More thunderstorms developed along the old MCS outflow boundary over western Pennsylvania on the evening of 14 June. These thunderstorms increased in coverage and intensity dramatically after 7:00 P.M. and began moving or developing toward the southwest, into Belmont County, Ohio. The line of storms moving from the west merged with these storms by about 9:00 P.M., contributing to intense rainfall in Belmont and Jefferson Counties.

Heavy rain from these combined storms began falling over the watersheds of Pipe Creek and Wegee Creek at about 8:30 P.M. and ended by 10:00 P.M. There were no rain gauges in the flooded areas, but a National Weather Service investigative team estimated that 3 to 4 inches of rain fell in a little over one hour (NOAA 1991). Total rainfall may have been 5.5 inches between 7:30 and 10:30 P.M.

Rainfall of this magnitude is always dangerous, but under normal conditions it does not produce catastrophic flash floods in Ohio. However, the narrow, steep-sided valleys and saturated soils along Pipe Creek and Wegee Creek on 14 June 1990 caused nearly all of the rain that fell to run off quickly into the creeks.

No warning could be given to residents of the area. The National Weather Service issued a flood watch for southeastern Ohio, including Belmont County, at 7:41 P.M., about two hours before flooding began, to indicate that flooding rains were possible. However, flood watches are not uncommon during summer in Ohio and the residents were not prepared for the wall of water that would sweep down their narrow valleys.

Flash flooding began at 9:30 P.M. and was over in thirty minutes. In that time, a wall of water generally six feet high, but reported at some spots to be more than twenty feet high, poured down the creeks at seven to ten miles an hour. Debris such as trees, cars, and collapsed buildings carried in the flow created dams at bridges along the creeks, causing higher flood levels and greater flows as they broke. The creeks were not gauged but were estimated to flow at thirteen to fifteen thousand cubic feet per second during the peak of the flood (NOAA 1991).

Most homes in the steep Appalachian valleys of southeastern Ohio are clustered in the narrow flat area in the bottom of the valleys. This placed the residents along Pipe Creek and Wegee Creek right in the path of the flood. The road also follows the stream, so there was no option for escape from a flash flood in these valleys except by climbing up the hills.

In the village of Shadyside, at the mouth of Wegee Creek, Fire Chief Mark Badia took a call at about 9:20 P.M. for assistance in flooding several miles upstream. Two fire trucks and an ambulance responded but found their way blocked by water on the road as they rushed upstream. The roar of the approaching wall of water could be heard, so they parked the vehicles on high ground and ran from house to house warning people of the impending flood.

The wall of water advanced too quickly for many residents to escape to higher ground. Houses and mobile homes were pushed from their foundations and floated downstream, only to collapse in the turbulent waters. On well-anchored structures, the flood pushed in the upstream wall and poured right through the building. Some homes floated some distance and were deposited intact on lawns or in the road. Several dozen residents were rescued from trees or from the attics of their displaced homes. About 80 frame houses and mobile homes were destroyed in the flood and another 250 homes damaged (NOAA 1991). Many vehicles were destroyed, rolled and crumpled in the debris, wrapped around trees, or left high in fields (figs. 67, 68, and 69).

Debris continued downstream with the flood into the Ohio River and was carried thirty miles downstream to the Hannibal Dam, where it formed a raft of fifteen acres. Refrigerators, furniture, tires, toys, dead livestock, and portions of mobile homes mixed with hundreds of trees in the debris, according to the *Cleveland Plain Dealer*. Propane tanks and drums filled with unknown chemicals raised fears of an explosion. The June 1990 issue of *Storm Data* reported two bodies were found in this debris. The hunt for survivors and bodies continued through the night and into the next several days. Fifteen bodies were found in the first two days, but it was a week before all were found. In all, twenty-six persons died in the flood (NOAA 1991). Thirteen persons died along Pipe Creek. Eleven of those bodies were found downstream along the banks of the Ohio River. Another eleven died along Wegee Creek, with nine of the bodies washed into the Ohio River.

Relief poured into Shadyside Thursday night and Friday. Neighboring police and sheriff departments, the U.S. Coast Guard, and the Ohio Department of Transportation provided personnel and equipment to search for survivors and bodies and to remove debris. The *Cleveland Plain Dealer* reported that five hundred National Guard and Army Reserve troops came from Ohio and West Virginia. Red Cross and Salvation Army workers arrived soon to attend to the immediate needs of survivors.

Attention focused immediately on why a flood warning was not issued to residents to alert them to the impending disaster. Most residents were aware of the flood watch issued at 7:41 P.M. through radio or television. But flood warnings were issued by the National Weather Service only if satellite or radar images showed intense rainfall or if a report of flooding was received from local authorities.

Satellites estimated only 1.4 to 1.8 inches of rainfall in Belmont County, and this information was not available to forecasters until after the flood (NOAA 1991). National Weather Service radars at Akron-Canton and Pittsburgh underestimated the intensity of rainfall due, in part, to the distance of the storms from the radars. No one in the flooded areas of Belmont County reported flooding to the National Weather Service. In fact, it was nearly four hours after the flood ended that forecasters knew of the flooding.

Even if a warning could have been issued, it is doubtful whether it could have been disseminated to residents along Wegee and Pipe Creeks in time for them to escape the rapidly building flood. The valleys of Belmont County had no flood-warning sirens to alert residents, and reception of NOAA weather radio, an instrument for immediate dissemination of warnings, was poor in Belmont County. One may also wonder whether residents along Pipe and Wegee Creeks, where no major floods are known to have occurred before 14 June 1990, would have immediately climbed to high ground in the pouring rain if a flood warning had been issued.

One way to protect residents of Appalachian valleys from floods is to install a flood gauge and siren system, whereby high water upstream triggers sirens that alert residents downstream. Even these systems give only a few minutes warning of floods.

31 December 1990
Statewide Floods End the Wettest Year

Ohio's wettest year ended with the wettest December in history and extensive flooding on New Year's Eve. Precipitation for 1990 averaged 51.38 inches across Ohio, 13 inches above average, and the greatest since records began in 1854 (Rogers 1993). Several cities, including Akron, Cleveland, and Columbus, also set records for annual precipitation in 1990. Precipitation of 65.7 inches for 1990 at Akron-Canton Airport was touted in the 2 January 1991 *Cleveland Plain Dealer* as a record one-year total for any weather station in Ohio. However, Sanderson (1950) reported 70.48 inches at Kings Mills (Warren County) in 1926.

December 1990 was the wettest December on record, with a statewide average precipitation of 7.64 inches. Ironically, this record wet year came between the Ohio droughts of 1988 and 1992. December was a mild month, but snow and near-zero temperatures prevailed for several days at Christmas. When heavy rain and sixty-degree temperatures returned on 29 December, frozen ground and melting snow contributed to a rapid runoff into Ohio streams from 30 December 1990 to 2 January 1991. The December 1990 issue of *Storm Data* reported $50 million damage from the floods in Ohio. Greatest losses were in northwestern counties and along the Ohio River, although flooding occurred on virtually all streams.

The Maumee River crested five to seven feet above flood stage from Defiance downstream to Toledo. Elsewhere in northwestern Ohio, Woodville was flooded by the Portage River, one hundred persons were evacuated at Delphos, and the Blanchard River flooded streets and closed several bridges at Findlay. The Tiffin and St. Joseph Rivers were five to six feet above flood stage in Williams County.

River crests two to five feet above flood stage on 30 and 31 December caused damage along other rivers, including the Scioto, Cuyahoga, Chagrin, Sandusky, Mahoning, Great Miami, and Hocking.

CHAPTER SEVEN

Damaging Winds and Tornadoes

DAMAGING WINDS OCCUR many times each year in Ohio, although the chance of such winds at any location is rather small. Minor damage to property and vegetation begins with winds of 45 to 50 mph. Some trees are uprooted by winds of 60 to 70 mph, other trees may be snapped off, shingles are blown from roofs, windows are broken, electric and telephone wires are blown down, and mobile homes may be pushed off foundations or overturned. If winds exceed 100 mph, large trees are uprooted or snapped off, moving cars are blown off roads, mobile homes are demolished, and roofs are blown from frame houses. Winds of more than 150 mph tear roofs and walls from well-built frame homes, toss cars through the air, and topple entire forests.

Damaging winds occur in three types in Ohio: large-scale, microbursts, and tornadoes. Large-scale winds of more than 50 mph may occur around an intense low pressure system, typically behind the cold front associated with an intense low. Winds of this type cover the entire state, although some areas may be affected to a greater extent, and may last for several hours. Microbursts are small areas of very strong downdraft winds produced by thunderstorms. These complex features were first described as a hazard to airliners by Fujita and Caracena (1977) and Fujita and Byers (1977). Microbursts are about a mile wide and two to three miles long, although they can be much smaller. Microburst winds descend from a thunderstorm, strike the ground, and spread out, causing fan-shaped damage outward from the center of the microburst.

There is no weather event that captures the attention and interest of Ohioans more than the tornado. Brief, violent, and random, the tornado allows only a few minutes warning. It may strike at any location and move over any terrain. The words "tornado warning" and the wail of community sirens bring our society to a halt as families huddle in basements or

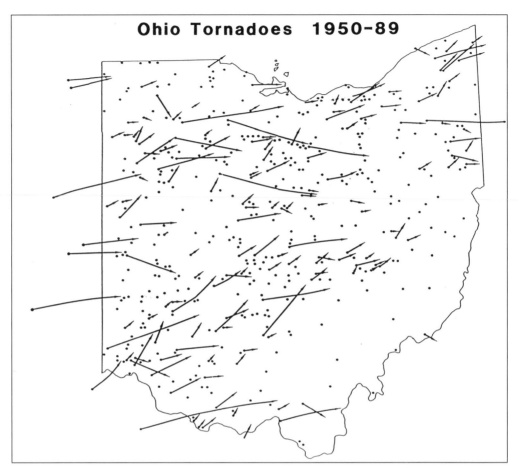

Ohio Tornadoes 1950–89

Fig. 70. There were nearly five hundred tornadoes reported in Ohio during 1950–89. Lines represent paths of the tornadoes, although the damage paths may have been sporadic. Paths less than two miles long are given as dots. Data used to map the paths were provided by the National Severe Storms Forecast Center.

crowd into closets, schoolchildren crouch in hallways, and drivers pull off the road for shelter. Fortunately, only about thirteen tornadoes strike Ohio each year and most of these cause little damage (Schmidlin 1988).

All portions of Ohio have had tornadoes, but they are most common in western and northern Ohio at the eastern edge of the North American "tornado alley" (fig. 70). Most tornadoes are small and may go unreported if they strike only rural wooded areas. Large tornadoes, on the other hand, are almost certainly recorded. The reported frequency of tornadoes is greatest where the population is greatest, as in Ohio's urban counties. In these counties, even the smallest tornadoes are reported to authorities.

Most (75 percent) Ohio tornadoes occur from April to July, when severe thunderstorms are most numerous over the Heartland, although tornadoes have also touched down in every other month. The most common hours of occurrence follow the general trend of afternoon and evening thunderstorms. About 75 percent of Ohio tornadoes touch down between 2:00 P.M. and 10:00 P.M.

Huge, violent tornadoes get most of the attention, but the typical tornado is only one hundred yards wide, on the ground for about one mile, and has maximum winds of less than one hundred mph (Schmidlin 1988). These tornadoes, comprising about two-thirds of Ohio tornadoes, rank F0 or F1 on the Fujita scale of tornado strength and damage. (The Fujita scale ranks tornadoes, on a scale from F0 to F5, according to maximum estimated wind speeds.)

About 30 percent of Ohio tornadoes were ranked F2 or F3 on the Fujita scale, indicating a maximum wind speed of 113 to 206 mph. The maximum wind speed occurs in a very small portion of the total tornado path. These tornadoes are on the ground for several miles and may be several hundred yards wide. The most dangerous tornadoes are the rare F4 and F5 storms that comprise only 3 percent of all Ohio tornadoes. These tornadoes have wind speeds of 207 to 318 mph, are on the ground for about thirty miles, and may be one-quarter to one-half of a mile wide. Although these storms are rare, they cause 75 percent of the tornado injuries and deaths in Ohio.

Early reports of tornadoes often described a path more than one hundred miles long with sporadic tornado damage along the path. The sporadic damage was attributed to the "skipping" motion of the tornado. However, aerial inspection of tornado damage paths and recent research through videotapes of tornadoes revealed that these long-path tornadoes are usually "families" of several tornadoes from one thunderstorm. A severe thunderstorm may produce several tornadoes over a period of one to two hours. Individual tornadoes may be on the ground for five to twenty-five miles. As one tornado dissipates, another soon forms, causing a damage path that is very long but has breaks between tornadoes in the family.

Rotation in the base of a thunderstorm cloud may indicate that a tornado is forming. Funnel clouds are appendages at the bottom of a cloud and indicate a tornado may touch down soon. The approach of a tornado is marked by a roar sounding like a dozen jet airplanes or freight trains. Large hail often falls near a tornado, and the storm may be accompanied by intense lightning.

About 20 percent of Ohio tornadoes occur after dark, and many are surrounded by heavy rain and thus are not visible as they approach. Those that are visible take on many different shapes and colors. Most are shaped like a funnel, but others are cylindrical or ropelike. The tornado usually evolves through several shapes during its short lifetime. Depending on the viewer's position with respect to the clouds, the tornado may appear white, a shade of gray, or almost black. Greenish clouds are sometimes noted prior to a tornado.

The National Weather Service relies on trained severe storm spotters and law enforcement agencies to notify them of a tornado on the ground. Detection of tornadoes by Doppler radar may allow a few additional minutes of warning (Burgess, Donaldson, and Desrochers 1993).

27 June 1812
First Tornado Deaths

The first recorded tornado deaths since European-American settlement in Ohio occurred north of Dayton on Saturday, 27 June 1812. A tornado began in Darke County and moved southeast across southern Miami County into northern Montgomery County (Grazulis 1993).

A story from Dayton in the 1 July 1812 issue of the *Chillicothe Ohio Sentinel* related, "On Saturday last the country above us was visited by one of the most dreadful tornadoes ever experienced in this state. It passed about 8 miles north of this town and extended its ravages from a quarter to half a mile wide. We have heard of several lives lost, and an immensity of damage in the destruction of houses, out houses, fences, timber, and grain."

Grazulis (1993) reported two children died in their destroyed home along Ludlow Creek, "probably in Montgomery County." However, the deaths along Ludlow Creek were most likely in Miami County (Mindling 1944). About twenty persons were injured.

18 May 1825
Burlington Tornado

The Burlington Tornado of 18 May 1825 was one of the most violent storms experienced by Ohio pioneers and, as such, was widely described in early histories. Atwater (1838, 101) reported the tornado struck Urbana, lifted for many miles, and then struck again across Licking and Knox Counties, passing a few miles south of Kenyon College. Grazulis (1993) reported a path fifty miles long beginning in Delaware County and ending in Coshocton County. The storm lifted several times along its path and may have been several separate tornadoes from the same thunderstorm.

In a history of Licking County, Hill (1881, 406–7) described the passage of the storm through Bennington and Burlington Townships and just north of Utica into Knox County. Damage across Licking and Knox Counties was up to one mile wide and "it prostrated every forest tree, or stripped it of its limbs and left it standing as a monument of its inexorable wrath" (Atwater 1838). Most of the damage was near the village of Burlington, now called Homer, along present Route 661, in northern Licking County. Burlington, according to the 26 May 1825 *Newark Advocate,* was "literally swept from the ground." Three persons were killed.

A dark black cloud was seen to the west of Burlington with trees and limbs "flying in every direction in the air," according to the *Newark Advocate.* All forty log homes and several brick buildings in Burlington were destroyed (Grazulis 1993). Log houses, down to the very lowest logs, were carried away. Fallen trees lay in every direction, "so that the course of the storm could not be determined from the position of the fallen trees" (Hill 1881).

22 March 1830
Urbana Tornado

Four persons were killed in one house when a tornado destroyed much of Urbana at 1:30 P.M. on Monday, 22 March 1830. The 27 March 1830 issue of the *Urbana Mad River Courant* reported the tornado touched down six miles southwest of the city then moved directly through Urbana and to the northeast. Its path was about one hundred yards wide. A clear rotary motion was evident in the damage, and it "was highly charged with the electric fluid which formed very brilliant appearances."

Seventy buildings were damaged in Urbana, including thirty-one homes. Several frame and brick homes were blown down entirely and swept away, and personal possessions were found several miles to the northeast. Two churches were destroyed and other buildings were unroofed or lost chimneys or porches.

Town council met that evening to express sympathy to those who lost homes in the tornado and to ask for relief supplies from those who were not affected. This request was "most cheerfully and promptly complied with." Roofs were replaced, and, by Friday, houses had "risen from their own ruins," according to the *Urbana Mad River Courant.* Clothing and other necessities were generously provided to those who lost all.

20 January 1854
Brandon Tornado

The July 1854 issue of the *American Journal of Science and Arts* contained a description of a rare January tornado by Orange N. Stoddard, professor of chemistry and natural philosophy at Miami University. Temperatures warmed to springlike levels across Ohio on 19 and 20 January. It was 70 degrees at noon at Cincinnati, but pressure was falling rapidly at Oxford.

Violent rains, vivid lightning, and large hail were common across Ohio that afternoon.

The tornado first touched down at 2:00 P.M. in southwestern Miller Township (Knox County) and then moved at 40 to 45 mph northeast toward Brandon. Five buildings were demolished along the south side of what is now Route 27, on the west side of Brandon. These included a house and barn, a brick church, a brick schoolhouse, and a log house. All were "swept from their foundations" with debris strewn toward the north.

The tornado continued another eleven miles to near Gambier, where its damage track disappeared. Professor Stoddard's survey of the direction that debris was blown and the direction trees fell in forests east of Brandon showed a clear tornado circulation. Trees near the center of the path fell to the left, nearly perpendicular to the path, whereas those on the right margin fell forward and those on the left fell inward toward the center of the path but against the direction of the tornado. More than fifty thousand trees were felled by the tornado. Professor Stoddard estimated a minimum wind speed of 173 mph was required to fell a large solid oak not in leaf. He also found a board driven three inches into an oak stump and a shingle buried one inch into an oak tree.

The observations by Professor Stoddard that "a secondary or double whirl existed," and "a secondary whirl about 60 rods (330 yds) in diameter, lagging a little behind the more extended one on the right, seems undeniable," may have been an early recognition of multiple suction vortices in tornadoes formally identified by other scientists more than a century later.

21 May 1860
Microbursts Destroy Southern Ohio

A forty-mile-wide area of numerous microburst winds with some possible tornadoes extended for 250 miles from Louisville, Kentucky, to Portsmouth, Ohio, Monday afternoon, 21 May 1860 (Grazulis 1993). Damage in Ohio was focused on Cincinnati, which was hit about 3:00 P.M., and Portsmouth, where the destructive winds arrived an hour later.

The *Cincinnati Enquirer* called this the "most violent and destructive tornado ever witnessed in this latitude." Although much of the damage may have been straight microburst winds from the southwest, the *Cincinnati Enquirer* reported the storm was "a whirlwind" with some damage at right angles to the main body of wind. Trees, awnings, chimneys, and signposts were destroyed by the thousands in the Cincinnati area. Five Cincinnati churches sustained heavy damage from the winds. One student died when a school on Baymiller between Dayton and Bank was unroofed.

Severe winds caused difficulties for boats on the Ohio River. The steamer *Virginia Home* capsized two miles above Cincinnati, and two cabin boys were still missing the next day. Additional wind damage was reported at Lawrenceburg and Cumminsville.

Similar destruction swept Portsmouth. The 26 May 1860 *Portsmouth Times,* not to be outdone by the *Cincinnati Enquirer* in its superlatives, reported "a terrible tornado swept over this city and vicinity, surpassing in violence all storms ever experienced in Ohio." In fact this may have been exaggerated very little as it was the deadliest windstorm up to that time in Ohio.

Destruction at Portsmouth began at "the point," the extreme southern edge of town. The *Portsmouth Times* reported the "air was filled and literally darkened with timbers, rafters, shingles, bricks and mortar, tin roofing . . . whirling and eddying above." Severe damage occurred along Front Street, with many buildings having their second and third floors entirely carried away. The Presbyterian Church on Court Street lost its roof and steeple, including the bell tower and town clock. As if guided by a divine hand, the steeple crashed to the ground within a four-foot space between two occupied houses. Other destroyed buildings included a machine shop on Mill Street and Gaylord's rolling mill. Three people were killed in Portsmouth.

4 March 1880
Toledo's Tornado

The only tornado to cause significant damage to downtown Toledo came just before midnight on Thursday, 4 March 1880, rather early in the spring for tornadoes in northern Ohio.

Under a headline of "Toledo's Tornado," the 5 March 1880 *Toledo Blade* reported, "Last night this city and vicinity was visited by what was probably the most terrific and destructive storm on record, and which has also been peculiar on account of the limited locality in which it spent its force." The report also noted that the wind damage was mostly from the west but at other places along the damage track "the debris indicat[ed] that it was from the north, and even from the east." The U.S. Signal Office at Toledo officially classified the storm as a tornado.

Damage to buildings was widespread downtown and across the Maumee River in east Toledo, concentrated between the present High Level and Craig Memorial Bridges. Many buildings were unroofed. Debris from Westminster Church fell through a roof at 46 Locust Street. Roofs were off buildings on Magnolia and Ontario Streets and the Island House at the Middle Grounds. The roof was also blown from Armada Mills and Everett School. Trees and wires were down and wooden sidewalks torn up.

The greatest damage occurred at the Buckeye Brewery. A seventy-five-foot brick chimney fell down into the engine room where three men were sitting. The night watchman for the brewery escaped with injuries but two visitors were killed.

25 March 1884
Southwestern Tornadoes

A very active day of tornado weather from South Carolina and Georgia northward through Kentucky and into Indiana and Ohio produced dozens of tornadoes throughout the region, killing at least thirty people and injuring two hundred. On 25 March 1884 two killer tornadoes touched down in southwestern Ohio.

The first tornado formed just north of Lebanon at about 4:00 P.M. and traveled twenty-five miles to Beavercreek (then called Zimmerman) in Greene County (Grazulis 1990). The *Dayton Daily Journal* related that passengers on a train from Lebanon to Dayton saw the large cloud "rising and falling" and the train was later stopped at Oak Ridge (where Bigger Road presently crosses Interstate 675) by fallen trees. Thirty buildings were destroyed along the path, including many at Oak Ridge, and two people were killed by this storm east of Ridgeville in Warren County. A man near a bridge over the Little Miami River at Beaver's Station saw the tornado "swoop down upon the river, the tongue striking the water and licking it up like a huge monster and blowing it high in the air." He reported the entire bridge flew into the air, some large timbers swirling one hundred feet above the ground.

A second tornado touched down a few minutes later in Indiana just west of the stateline community of Scipio. The tornado moved through Scipio, where present routes 126 and 129 converge in Butler County, and the town was destroyed, reported the *Cleveland Plain Dealer*. Two people were killed at Scipio (or Philanthropy, as it was also known). The Scipio tornado continued destroying farms as it moved northeast into central Butler County. A reported death from hail at Scipio during this storm (Mindling 1944, 70) was not confirmed in our research.

27 April 1884
Jamestown Tornado

The first of two strong tornados formed about 4:30 P.M. Sunday afternoon, 27 April 1884 near the west bank of the Miami River eight miles south of Dayton. These two twisters traveled on a total path forty miles long across Greene County and into Fayette County just west of

Jeffersonville. The *Xenia Gazette* reported this was "not an extra high wind, but one of your regular Western cyclones, funnel shaped and with all of the other destructive equipments." Most of the damage and all fatalities occurred toward the end of the path at Jamestown.

The April 1884 *Report of the Ohio Meteorological Bureau* contained a detailed summary of the Jamestown Tornado, its path, appearance, and damages. At the request of Director T. C. Mendenhall, Mr. E. H. Mark, secretary of the bureau, made a survey of the path beginning 29 April and for about one week traveled on foot and horseback talking to eyewitnesses and examining the character of damage. His report is among the most detailed ever made along the path of an Ohio tornado.

Near the beginning of the storm, according to Mark, water from the Miami River and the nearby Miami Canal was thrown "in a whirl 50 feet high." Barns and tobacco sheds collapsed between the river and canal. At some points the ground was "swept as clean as it could have been done with a broom," and even the corn stubs were pulled from the ground (Mark 1884). Witnesses reported the lower end of the tornado swung back and forth like an elephant's trunk and a dense cloud of "black smoke" was rolling up from the small end of the funnel. The two-room brick School House No. 9 along the Dayton and Lebanon Pike (Route 48) near Woodburn was unroofed, the roof carried several hundred feet, and the walls blown in.

A second tornado formed about three-quarters of a mile north of the Ed Wheatley farm and moved east-southeast, crossing the path of the first tornado near the Dayton and Lebanon Pike. John Ridenour reported he could see both tornadoes distinctly from his house. Damage from the first tornado continued a few hundred yards past this point, but after a path of seven miles across southeastern Montgomery County, this funnel seemed to lift and Mark (1884) found no more damage along its path.

The second tornado had a skipping path for the next eleven miles into Greene County, touching the ground occasionally and damaging trees and farm buildings. It touched down again three-quarters of a mile south of Xenia and damage was mostly continuous from there to Jamestown.

The Soldiers and Sailors Orphan Home was struck by the tornado near Xenia. The roof was stripped from the brick hospital, but miraculously no fatalities occurred to the children. A long veranda porch, a plank walk, and many large trees were all blown away. A greater disaster was avoided by the Sunday occurrence of this storm, according to the *Xenia Gazette*. The destroyed porch at the Orphan's Home would have been filled with 350 children on a weekday, but Sunday supper was served twenty minutes earlier so all children were safely in the dining room when the tornado swept the porch away. The tornado then followed the Toledo,

Cincinnati, and St. Louis rail line toward Jamestown. A train of fifteen cars stopped just west of the trestle across Caesar Creek and was struck by the tornado. Seven coal cars were blown from the center of the train into the field.

The tornado hit Jamestown, then a community of seven hundred, about 5:00 P.M., leaving it a "wind-wrecked tornado tossed and storm struck town," according to the *Xenia Gazette*. More than half of the residents were left homeless, and that portion of town north of Main Street was mostly destroyed. Damage began at the fairgrounds, just across the Jamestown and Xenia Pike (Route 35), and continued eastward along Xenia Avenue through town. Of 115 houses along Xenia Avenue, 95 were destroyed or badly damaged (Mark 1884).

The track of destruction through Jamestown was about three hundred feet wide and half a mile long. Most homes along this path were "crushed into atoms and then thrown to the winds," according to the *Xenia Gazette*. Homes that were not blown apart were battered and punctured by timbers and debris. Mark (1884) reported 186 houses were destroyed or damaged. Several timbers ten to twelve feet long, possibly carried from the fairgrounds, were "driven endwise into houses as though shot out of a cannon." Jamestown's two-story brick public school on Main Street was leveled to the ground. Baptist, Catholic, and African Methodist Episcopal churches were damaged. The roof from the United Presbyterian Church on Main Street was blown off and landed on the east side of the church while the belfry landed on the west side. Several other commercial buildings were damaged along Main Street. The Jamestown city building collapsed onto the Geisler Bakery. The total number of fatalities at Jamestown was seven, including three in one house.

The second tornado continued for another seven and a half miles to the east of Jamestown, destroying several more homes and farm buildings. The last damage was found by Mark about one mile west of Jeffersonville in Fayette County, about thirty miles from the formation of this tornado.

8 September 1885
Washington Court House Tornado

Skies over Fayette County darkened from the west for more than an hour before the heavy rains set in just before 8:00 P.M. on 8 September 1885. A tornado had formed seven miles west of Washington Court House and, with little warning to the residents, slammed into the city at 8:07 P.M.

Much of the city was destroyed as the tornado cut a path one hundred yards wide through the middle of the city. The 9 September 1885 *Fayette*

Fig 71. Damage at the corner of Main and East Streets in Washington Court House after the tornado of 8 September 1885. (Photograph courtesy of the Fayette County Historical Society)

Republican reported the "firmest and largest buildings in the city cracked and crumbled away and fell into vast heaps" and "ladies shrieked in terror and strong men trembled like infants." The 16 September issue of the *Fayette Republican* proclaimed this to have been "one of the most disastrous and fatal tornadoes in the history of the world," an obvious exaggeration that ignored numerous deadlier tornadoes, including one that killed ninety-nine in Missouri in 1880.

The streets of Washington Court House were piled with wrecked buildings, roofs of homes, trees, and telegraph poles. Grazulis (1990) reported three hundred buildings damaged or destroyed, including two hundred homes, the new county courthouse, and all forty businesses on the square (figs. 71 and 72). The Catholic and Baptist churches collapsed, the Odd Fellows Hall was destroyed, and the Ohio Southern Railroad Depot was ruined. Six people were killed by the tornado at Washington Court House, including two children in a family that had moved from Jamestown after that city was wrecked by a tornado the year before.

Jesse Bush's farm three miles west of Washington Court House showed evidence of extreme winds. It was mowed clear of all vegetation, the corn

Fig. 72. Destruction of the Baptist church, corner of North and East Streets in Washington Court House, during the tornado of 8 September 1885. Large-span roofs in churches, factories, and schools are vulnerable in strong winds. (Photograph courtesy of the Fayette County Historical Society)

flattened and pulled right out of the ground. Here was the source of the "straw story" circulating around Fayette County but "swallowed with a big grain of allowance," according to the *Fayette Republican.* However, a reporter visited the Bush farm to verify the story and saw many pieces of wood from trees with thousands of blades of hay "blown endwise in to a depth of one-quarter inch." The reporter collected several examples and invited readers to come to the newspaper office and see for themselves evidence of the straw story.

Cleanup proceeded slowly after the Tuesday tornado. Governor George Hoadly visited the next day and issued an appeal to the state for assistance to the city (Galbreath 1925, 636). Sheriff A. B. Rankin called out Company B of the Sixth Regiment militia for duty Tuesday night "to stop plundering." The militia remained on duty for a week, keeping order and assisting after the disaster.

News of the tornado spread through the week, and by Sunday visitors were pouring in on all rail lines. The *Fayette Republican* related that thirty-two coaches full of sightseers came from the east on the Columbus and

Cincinnati Midland, and eleven cars came from the west on the same line. Nine more cars came from the west and eighteen from the east on the Cincinnati and Muskingum Valley Railroad. The Ohio Southern Railroad brought forty passenger cars from Springfield, Chillicothe, and Indianapolis. In all, thirty thousand visitors came that Sunday to see the destruction at Washington Court House.

Strong tornadoes struck other parts of Ohio the evening of 8 September 1885. Homes, barns, and a school were destroyed along a twenty-five-mile path in Miami and Clark Counties (Grazulis 1990). Another tornado skipped across Crawford County, blowing a train off the tracks and destroying a church. Other wind or tornado damage was reported from Napoleon and Portsmouth, and in Pickaway, Fairfield, and Portage Counties.

14 May 1886
Deadliest Tornadoes of the Nineteenth Century

The deadliest weather Ohio had experienced up to that date came on 12 and 14 May 1886. Floods killed twenty-eight at Xenia on 12 May 1886 and a tornado killed two people near Carpenter in Meigs County the same evening.

Two days later, on Friday, 14 May 1886, Ohio's deadliest tornado outbreak of the nineteenth century occurred. A pair of tornadoes killed about seventeen people in western Ohio and a third caused great destruction in Seneca County. Press reports at the time and Mindling (1944) attributed all the damage along 110 miles to a single tornado; however, Grazulis (1990) reported three separate tornadoes along the path.

The three major tornadoes of 14 May appear to have been part of a tornado family from a thunderstorm as it moved northeast from Portland, Indiana, into north-central Ohio near Tiffin. The destruction was impressive and prompted the *Cleveland Plain Dealer* to proclaim, "Nothing like it has ever been known in the history of Ohio, or perhaps in the country before."

The first tornado entered Ohio just after 10:00 P.M. north of Fort Recovery and ended north of Celina in Mercer County. The *Findlay Hancock Courier* reported one person was killed in a farmhouse near the state line and three churches, a school, and several houses were blown down near Ft. Recovery. Another five people died in farmhouses that were leveled by the tornado northwest of Celina (Grazulis 1990). Press reports of 16 May 1886 put the number of fatalities in Mercer County at thirty, but estimates were revised downward the next day.

The Mercer County tornado lifted and another touched down at 11:30 P.M. at Dunkirk in Hardin County and traveled twenty miles through

Forest and Wharton to just south of Cary. A brick school, dozens of farm homes, and many barns were leveled along the path. Press reports at the time were vague, listing several people killed and others as "fatally injured." Grazulis (1990) reported that "as many as eight people" died near Dunkirk and another five were killed at Cary but gave a total of eleven dead.

The third member of this tornado family touched down at midnight three miles west of Attica in Seneca County destroying homes and damaging other structures. The *Cleveland Plain Dealer* reported that a gravestone was hurled against a barn one-quarter mile away from the cemetery, fence rails were driven six feet into the ground, and whole orchards were uprooted in Seneca County.

2 May 1887
Fulton County Tornado

Fifteen students and their teacher were in the school at Clinton Center, two miles southwest of Wauseon, on 2 May 1887. The temperature had reached 82 degrees by noon and only a very light breeze provided relief. Just after noon a very dark cloud with a "whirling white mass in the center" approached the school from the southwest. The tornado wrecked a barn and stable then passed directly over the school.

According to the *Wauseon Republican*, the school at Clinton Center was a "substantial brick structure and considered one of the strongest school buildings in the township." The school was demolished. The upper portion of the south wall was blown inward and all other walls fell outward. Portions of the roof were blown toward the northeast and other segments were sent toward the northwest. The falling structure fatally injured a thirteen-year-old boy. This is the only verified tornado death in an Ohio school. Longtime Wauseon weather observer and naturalist Thomas Mikesell verified that this was a tornado. He noted that a rail fence was unscathed just across the street from the destroyed school.

17 May 1894
Kunkle Tornado

A large, violent tornado swept across Williams County as part of an unusually powerful spring storm across the Great Lakes. Temperatures soared to 90 degrees before the storm but dropped to freezing with a gale-driven snow the next day. The cold gales across the Great Lakes in the wake of the storm destroyed or damaged thirty-five lake vessels with the loss of twenty-seven men (Swayze 1992a).

The *Toledo Daily Blade* described the Kunkle Tornado of 17 May 1894 as a "genuine Kansas tornado" and "the most disastrous wind ripper that ever visited the state of Ohio." Few of the five hundred residents of Kunkle had ever seen a tornado or knew much about them. Yet when this storm made its appearance, "even the most ignorant could not fail to guess its significance."

People of Kunkle were startled at about 4:00 P.M. to hear rumblings of thunder to the west that were unusually loud and of long duration. The sky had been sunny and the day the hottest of the spring. The thunder continued without abatement for fifteen minutes as the blackness of the western sky convinced viewers that "they were about to witness something unusual." Hail swept across the town, some the size of hens' eggs, and broke many windows.

The tornado was clearly visible as it approached Kunkle, in spite of the hail. Confusion reigned through the town, people standing in the streets with no clear idea of what should be done. Some were convinced that the end of the world had arrived. The confusion in the streets was followed by a rush toward houses and cellars as the tornado approached.

The main part of the tornado passed just south of the Wabash Railroad tracks that passed through Kunkle. Every building south of the tracks was destroyed, including six frame houses, two brick houses, and several barns and outbuildings. At least four persons died at a farm one-half mile south of Kunkle.

News of the disaster spread overnight, and from 5:00 A.M. to 9:00 A.M. the next day a steady stream of 250 buggies and wagons came from several counties. More than one thousand people milled around the town at dawn. They saw a path one-quarter mile wide cleared entirely on both sides of Kunkle.

Toledo Weather Bureau Observer Hanner was quoted in the 18 May *Toledo Daily Blade* describing the circumstances that led to the storm: "The condition yesterday morning was very favorable with the occurrence of severe local thunder storms and tornadoes. The best authorities in this country on tornadoes state that they always occur in the southeast quadrant of a cyclonic storm. This placed Ohio in that quadrant yesterday morning. We never predict tornadoes, only severe local storms. The word 'tornado' frightens people, so we do not use it."

20 April 1896
Sandusky County

A special dispatch from Fremont to the *Cleveland Plain Dealer* reported, "Never in the knowledge of the oldest settler of Sandusky county has a windstorm struck this vicinity so hard as that which traversed the major portions of Sandusky and Rice, two of the richest townships in Sandusky county, this afternoon."

The tornado appeared about 3:00 P.M., 20 April 1896, to the west of Fremont and moved on a six-mile path to Booktown north of Fremont. The damage path was one-half mile wide. Grazulis (1990) listed this as a violent F4 storm.

Few structures in the path of the tornado survived. Two men were killed, entire forests were flattened, farm homes and barns were demolished, fences scattered, and livestock killed. The iron bridge of the Wheeling and Lake Erie Railroad over Muscalonge Creek (now Muskellunge) was hit and twisted out of shape. A train had the misfortune of passing into the path of the tornado. A tree fell onto the caboose, crushing it and injuring one trainman.

Booktown, on the west bank of the Sandusky River just south of the present Ohio Turnpike, was heavily damaged. Of perhaps greatest importance, the "sole saloon, was blown away," according to the *Cleveland Plain Dealer*. Several other buildings, including a schoolhouse near town, were also destroyed. Students were on a vacation for the week so no injuries occurred in the school, which "was crushed like paper." On the Oak Harbor Road (Route 19), near the destroyed Greene farms, a brick schoolhouse with fifty students in it escaped damage, although everything around it was destroyed.

25 June 1902
Marietta Tornado

"Never in 114 years of Marietta's life has the historic city been visited by as destructive a cyclone as swept over the city at 8 o'clock tonight," began the story dated 25 June 1902 in the *Cleveland Plain Dealer*.

Buildings of the Ohio Valley Wagon Company, Acme Brick, Cisler's Brick, and the Parkersburg and Interurban Street Car Company were leveled by the winds. Dozens of homes were demolished, as was the Central Christian Church. Roofs were torn from homes, chimneys blown down, windows smashed, and trees uprooted. Small buildings were carried many yards. Marietta streetcar traffic was suspended and the electric plant was shut down. One person died in a collapsed home on the east side of town.

The *Marietta Daily Register* described it as a tornado that swept out of the heavy rain and lightning on Wednesday evening. It came from the northwest over the hill on the west side of the Muskingum River opposite the fairgrounds and swept down to the river. The sawmill of the Marietta Chair Company on the river was wrecked. The one-hundred-yard-wide storm then moved across the Muskingum River onto Second Street to Sixth Street over Mound Cemetery and to the suburban area then called Glendale. Trees were stripped of their leaves at Mound Cemetery.

One of Marietta's most prominent landmarks, the willow tree on the Warren property at Washington and Second Streets, was broken over by the winds. It had been planted one hundred years earlier by Governor Return J. Meigs, Jr., reported the *Marietta Daily Register.*

21 April 1909
Lake Erie Coast Battered by Wind

Weather forecaster James Kenealy referred to it as "a thunderstorm of exceptional violence" but noted that it lacked most of the characteristics of a real tornado. Whatever the term used for the wind that ravaged the North Coast on 21 April 1909, area residents trembled as the roar went through. It carved a track of destruction from Elyria to Ashtabula and south to Medina and Akron.

According to the *Cleveland Plain Dealer,* a moderate wind began Wednesday at 7:00 A.M. and increased until 9:00 A.M. A mild thunderstorm generated 43 mph winds at 10:35 A.M., and then winds fell to 20

Fig. 73. Home damaged on Vega Avenue in Cleveland during the 21 April 1909 windstorm. (Photograph courtesy of the Western Reserve Historical Society)

Fig. 74. St. Stanislas Church in Cleveland after the windstorm of 21 April 1909. The church was repaired and still stands at the corner of Forman Avenue, S.E., and East 65th Street. (Photograph courtesy of the Western Reserve Historical Society)

mph until 12:30 P.M., when a severe storm struck Cleveland. For the following five minutes, the average wind measured at the Weather Bureau's downtown office was 66 mph (Kenealy 1909). The one-minute average wind speed reached 84 mph and gusts may have been stronger. These high winds were accompanied by a severe thunderstorm and heavy rain. It lasted five minutes and, according to the Weather Bureau, it was the longest wind of such velocity recorded up to that time in Cleveland.

The wind cut a diagonal path one to two miles wide and six miles long through Cleveland, from the gullies on the south side into the residential district on the east side. The *Cleveland Plain Dealer* documented scores of buildings, churches, schools, and homes that were damaged (figs. 73 and 74). Fifty homes were destroyed and twelve churches were heavily damaged, many having their steeples and gables mercilessly battered. Stained-glass windows shattered as bricks and stones crashed through them. Seventeen schools were damaged, some struck by lightning, others lost roofs and windows. Classrooms were flooded with the heavy rain, and many schools were forced to close their doors for several days.

Damage was estimated to be close to $1 million. Major damage was done to the Leisy Brewing Company, Cleveland Co-operative Stove Company, Standard Tool Company, Wellman-Seaver-Morgan Engineering Company, National Safe and Lock Company, and Central Cartage and

Storage Company. More than twenty-five other firms suffered losses. Eighty people were injured and eight people died in the windstorm. Injuries included twenty-two people at the Wellman-Seaver-Morgan plant and seven at Standard Tool. At the general office of Wellman-Seaver-Morgan, money filled the air of the payroll office where clerks were preparing the payroll. The windows of the office blew inward, scattering $20,000 in all denominations across the room. A third of Cleveland was dark that evening because of heavy damage to electric lines. Telephone service was interrupted as well as streetcar service.

The *Cleveland Plain Dealer* also noted damage on the waterfront. Two Brown Hoist ore carriers at the Nypano dock were carried away and destroyed as the winds dashed them into the ground. Four other nearby ore carriers were also damaged.

16 June 1912
Zanesville Tornado

Threatening weather had reduced attendance at early mass of St. Thomas Catholic Church on Sunday, 16 June 1912. Still, six hundred were in the church on North Fifth Street in Zanesville when Father Roach heard a roar of wind and noticed plaster falling from the roof. He avoided panic by calmly asking the congregation to come to the front of the church and then file outside. The tornado struck before the crowd moved far.

St. Thomas was the oldest and one of the most beautiful of Zanesville's churches, according to the *Zanesville Weekly Courier*. Its steeple began 92 feet above the street and extended 160 feet into the air, topped by a 10-foot cross.

The huge steeple was blown over by the wind. It "fell with the swiftness of a darting arrow and pinned down everything in its path," according to the *Zanesville Signal*, crashing through the roof of the church and onto the congregation. A crumbling mass of mortar, stones, steel, and wood fell into the choir pit and destroyed their magnificent organ. Dust was thrown over members of the congregation and settled on them like a mask so that friends were unable to recognize each other. Two people of the congregation were killed and several injured by the fallen steeple and roof.

The tornado was accompanied by a deluge of rain and "electrical accompaniments." Wind blew chimneys and roofs from houses, uprooted trees, and curled tin roofs downtown. Damage was greatest along a three-hundred-foot-wide path from Belknap Street, Ridge Avenue, Chapman, West Main, and Market Street. Additional damage came up the hill on Greenwood, Eastman, Beulah, and Fox Avenues.

Every building along Market between Fifth and Sixth Avenues was heavily damaged, according to the *Zanesville Signal*. Besides the tragedy at St. Thomas Church, a coffin factory lost its roof, the Franklin Hotel lost part of its roof and was twisted, and chimneys blew off the Palace Hotel. Downtown windows were smashed by flying bricks, tin roofing, slate, and timbers. Streets were littered with rain-soaked debris.

21 March 1913
Worst Statewide Windstorm

The most destructive statewide windstorm in Ohio history hit on Good Friday, 21 March 1913, the first day of spring. All areas of the state were affected, but most damage was in the northwestern region of the state. This storm was a prelude to the catastrophic floods of the last week of March 1913 that killed 467 people in Ohio.

High winds hit western Ohio between 6:00 A.M. and 10:00 A.M. Friday morning, 21 March and swept into the eastern counties by noon. Wind speeds measured by the Weather Bureau on top of the Nicolas Building in Toledo averaged 71 mph between 8:00 A.M. and 10:00 A.M. and peaked at 84 mph, according to the *Toledo Blade*. This exceeded previous wind records of 72 mph at Toledo on 20 January 1907 and 7 April 1909 and stood as the record until 87 mph was recorded in 1948.

The Weather Bureau in Cleveland clocked winds of 64 mph on top of a building two hundred feet above Public Square. Most other wind measurements that day were unofficial readings or estimates. It was widely reported that winds blew 85 mph at Findlay and 90 mph at nearby McComb. Estimates of 70 to 80 mph were common across northwestern and central Ohio.

Wind speeds may sometimes be exaggerated, but damage reports on 21 March were consistent with the extreme wind estimates. From nearly every community in Ohio came reports of some damage. In some, where winds probably peaked at no more than 50 mph, damage was limited to signs, branches, windows, and utility wires. In other communities, where winds blew over 70 mph for several hours, extensive structural damage resulted. Large chimneys and church steeples were toppled, homes and factories unroofed, trees snapped or uprooted, and miles of wires brought down. Wagons and carriages with passengers were flung from roads into fields.

Northwestern Ohio took the most severe battering. Winds at Toledo gusted over hurricane force for several hours through Friday morning. Temperatures fell from 60 degrees at dawn to 43 degrees at 10:30 A.M. and 24 degrees on Saturday morning. All telephone and telegraph communication in Toledo was cut by fallen wires. Traffic on interurban and train lines was stopped by fallen trees, wires, and other debris on the lines. Injuries in Toledo, typical of those statewide, were caused by upset wagons, flying glass, falling debris, and being knocked down by wind. Dozens of Toledo homes lost roofs and hundreds lost windows or chimneys. Two homes were completely demolished. The southwest gale blew water out of Maumee Bay, grounding several boats and a tug near the Cherry Street Bridge.

In a perceptive comment on the vulnerability of modern society, the *Toledo Blade* reported damage was more severe in this windstorm than in previous storms, because on earlier occasions "the city was not liberally supplied with tall buildings, susceptible electric signs; such liable lots as electric lights, telephone and telegraph wires, with which the wind might vent its wrath."

Elsewhere in northwestern Ohio, a ninety-foot smokestack on the Seneca County Infirmary in Tiffin collapsed into a reading room, injuring nine men and killing one. An eleven-year old girl was killed by the falling cupola from Kimmer School, four miles northwest of Wauseon. The Lenox Rural School at Marion was damaged Friday morning before students arrived, and a regulator house of Marion Gas Works was wrecked. Roofs were blown from two buildings of the Ohio Cultivator Company, Coliseum Theater, and Evangelical Church in Bellevue.

Winds blew the roof and one wall off the Monarch Underwear Company in Bowling Green, and roofs were blown off many buildings in Sandusky and Napoleon. Winds destroyed the grandstand roof at the Napoleon Fair Grounds and demolished seventy horse stalls. Napoleon's Episcopal Church lost its spire. An operator at Napoleon Telephone Company, when told of poles fallen on railroad tracks, ran to stop a Wabash passenger train as it left the station, perhaps saving a wreck on the blocked tracks. At Findlay, the Pittsburg Glass Company was damaged and the roof blown from the Sheppard Sanitarium. The *Cleveland Plain Dealer* reported every building in McComb was damaged and many people injured in Lima, where the Methodist Church was wrecked. The *Cincinnati Enquirer* reported that "Wyandot County was practically unroofed."

Damage at Cleveland included trees, telegraph, telephone, and light wires down all through the city. Falling trees snapped trolley wires and obstructed traffic on the tracks. Some of the greatest damage at Cleveland came when the thirty-foot chimney at the four-story Alhambra Apartments, at East Eighty-sixth and Wade Park Avenue, crashed down through all floors and into the basement. Eight apartments were destroyed but, miraculously, there were no serious injuries.

In southern Ohio, the wind was not as strong or consistent as in the north but still caused damage and inconvenience. Oil derricks were toppled at Marietta and several people were injured at Ironton. A dozen homes in Ironton lost their roofs, and the *Cincinnati Enquirer* reported two-thirds of the barns within ten miles of Ironton were razed by the wind. A fallen smokestack wrecked Kelly Iron and Nail Company. The roof of the Cincinnati, Hamilton, and Dayton Railroad building in Ironton fell into the street and blocked streetcar traffic for two hours. Two churches were also unroofed in Ironton.

This windstorm was caused by an extraordinarily strong gradient of air pressure between a deep low pressure (29.1 inches of mercury) centered one hundred miles west of Toledo Friday morning and cold high pressure that was strengthening from the west. The western high moved into Indiana by Saturday morning with a pressure of more than 30.7 inches. As this pattern of very low and very high pressure passed across Ohio, the barometer at Toledo rose 1.42 inches in twenty-four hours beginning Friday morning. The result was a southwest gale across the state, with the strongest winds closest to the lowest pressure in northwestern Ohio.

7 July 1915
Cincinnati's Deadliest Wind

A vicious wind and rain storm swept southwestern Ohio on the evening of Wednesday, 7 July 1915. It hit Cincinnati at 9:30 P.M. and lasted about five minutes. The death toll of thirty-eight at Cincinnati is the greatest known in Ohio for a windstorm in which no tornadoes were involved. Twelve people were reported as missing, perhaps lost in the Ohio River (Mindling 1944). Devereaux (1919) reported "about 40" persons dead.

The wind caused extensive damage throughout Cincinnati and in nearby communities. There was no report of tornadoes, and the wind damage was all toward one direction, so the wind was presumed to have been the result of severe thunderstorm microbursts. The *Cincinnati Enquirer* consulted Weather Bureau forecaster W. B. Schlomer and reported that "notwithstanding the popular belief that Wednesday night's storm was a tornado, he has seen no evidence to verify this belief." An official one-minute average wind speed of 62 mph was measured by the Weather Bureau on the Federal Building (Devereaux 1919), but much stronger gusts may have occurred elsewhere.

Homes, apartment houses, and commercial buildings in Cincinnati were demolished or unroofed by the winds. Wires, signs, trees, cars, and streetcars were blown over downtown and in several suburbs, including Walnut Hills, Avondale, and Clifton. Every Cincinnati hotel had some wind damage. Most of the deaths came in collapsed buildings, although several were killed in a train wreck at Terrace Park, and an uncertain number of people, perhaps fifteen, drowned when boats overturned in the Ohio River.

The greatest tragedies developed in the collapse of buildings along West Sixth Street and a house on West Eighth. The *Cincinnati Enquirer* reported eighteen people died in the collapse of five buildings in the 500 block of Sixth Street near Mound. Nearby, eleven persons died when two homes collapsed.

Three men died when a train carrying race horses blew off the Pennsylvania Railroad tracks at Terrace Park. To collect insurance on their valuable horses killed in the wreck, horse owners claimed the wreck was not caused by wind but that the railroad was at fault for using defective cars. However, the crew testified at a coroner's inquest on 14 July 1915 that five cars derailed from the eleven-car train. A horse car was blown completely out of the train and down an embankment. It was clear that a strong wind was required to blow the car out of the train. The men who died were trapped in the derailed car with several panicked horses and could not be rescued unless the horses were shot: none of the crew wanted to be responsible for shooting horses worth up to twenty thousand dollars! After some delay, the surviving horses were shot, but the men had already died, presumably crushed by the horses.

The coroner also held an inquest into the eighteen deaths in the five collapsed buildings on Sixth Street. The Cincinnati Building Commissioner testified that building owners should not be held responsible for the collapse of the buildings. The buildings were fifty to sixty years old and dependent on each other for support. When one building collapsed in strong winds, all five went down with tragic results.

Outside of Cincinnati, the wind at Washington Court House was reported the most severe since the tornado of September 1885. Barns, trees, miles of fences, and a thousand acres of corn were blown down in Fayette County. Several buildings in Washington Court House were unroofed and some houses destroyed. A school was damaged in Wilmington, and the cemetery was heavily damaged with uprooted trees, broken monuments, and exposed coffins. More than one hundred small bridges were damaged by floods associated with the storms in Montgomery County. Other wind damage occurred in Clermont and Warren Counties.

20 October 1916
Deadly Lake Erie Gales

The deadliest winds known on Lake Erie took the lives of fifty-eight sailors on four vessels on Friday evening, 20 October 1916. This wind had its origins with a strong hurricane that struck Alabama on Wednesday, 18

October and moved north to near Chicago by the twentieth. Although no longer a hurricane, it remained a very strong low pressure storm center and gave several hours of winds of 60 to 75 mph over Lake Erie as it passed across Michigan Friday night. Storm warnings had been issued Friday morning for the Great Lakes, but some vessels continued their work. Four boats sank and several others struggled in the "hurricane" seas of Lake Erie.

The *James B. Colgate,* a 302-foot steel whaleback, was steaming west from Buffalo with a load of coal for Lake Superior when it went down Friday evening off Long Point, Ontario, northeast of Ashtabula (Swayze 1992b). Of the twenty-six men on board, only the skipper survived. In the same area, the 360-foot bulk freighter *Merida* was bound for Buffalo with a load of iron ore from Lake Superior when it went down with the loss of all twenty-six men (Swayze 1992b). Some bodies were picked up by other boats Sunday morning.

At the western end of Lake Erie the 161-foot schooner *D. L. Filer* sank off Bar Point near the mouth of the Detroit River with the loss of six of the seven men on board. On the barge *Bell,* a man was swept overboard and drowned as the barge was battered by the storm Friday evening off Bar Point. The *Cleveland Plain Dealer* reported the 164-foot *Marshall F. Butters* also sank in western Lake Erie when its load of shingles and lumber shifted. Its crew was picked up by several other boats in heroic rescues and there was no loss of life on the *Butters.* Strong winds were commonplace across Ohio Friday evening, causing scattered damage to property, fruit crops, and communication. Snow fell late Friday night in northern Ohio.

11 March 1917
Cincinnati and Montgomery County Tornadoes

Several strong or violent tornadoes occurred in eastern Indiana and southwestern Ohio between 3:00 P.M. and 7:30 P.M. on 11 March 1917. The deadliest swept a twenty-mile-long path eastward from New Castle, Indiana, where twenty-four were killed. An hour later another tornado touched down in Montgomery County, Ohio, probably spawned by the same thunderstorm that caused the New Castle tornado. A smaller tornado followed a parallel path four miles to the south through Montgomery County. A third Ohio tornado touched down in Madison and Fayette Counties. Finally, about three hours later, Cincinnati's first documented tornado swept the South Hyde Park section of that city.

Montgomery County Tornadoes. The Montgomery County tornado, classed F4 by Grazulis (1990), was as powerful as the New Castle tornado, but it passed through rural landscape, so the destruction was less than in the

Indiana storm. The path was nine miles long from three miles southwest of Brookville to two miles southeast of Trotwood. Damage occurred again two miles to the east on the west edge of Dayton, although it is not clear that it was this tornado that touched down again. Damage was continuous for a width of five to six hundred feet along the path in Perry and Madison Townships. Buildings on at least twenty-four rural properties were damaged.

The funnel was visible to everyone within five or six miles and was reported to have a gray color with a reddish glow (Young 1917). No rain accompanied the tornado, but heavy rain fell immediately after and severe hail fell three to four miles north of the path. The noise was described in typical tornado terms, "freight trains, a thousand airplanes, etc.," and was heard by some persons ten minutes before the tornado struck.

Several people had minor injuries and one person was killed. The number of injuries and deaths was surprisingly small given the strength of the storm and length of the path. The city of Dayton would have sustained enormous damage if the tornado had continued just a few more miles to the east.

A smaller tornado moved along a three-mile path about one mile south of Johnsville and New Lebanon at about 4:00 P.M. No one was injured, but several homes lost roofs and large trees were snapped. The Madison County tornado touched down about 5:30 P.M. and followed the Fayette County line eastward for seven miles from Bookwalter to Wesley Chapel. Several farm homes and a church were destroyed with some debris carried for three miles. Ten persons were injured (Grazulis 1990).

Cincinnati Tornado. The Cincinnati tornado was the first well-defined tornado to occur in the Queen City (Devereaux 1917). The weather had been unseasonably warm in advance of a cold front approaching from the northwest. A squall line ahead of the front crossed Cincinnati between 7:00 P.M. and 7:30 P.M. and spawned a tornado over the eastern sections of the city known as South Hyde Park or Mt. Lookout. This neighborhood was one of the "city's show places," with some houses valued at ten to twenty-five thousand dollars.

The first damage came at about 7:20 P.M. at the corner of Fairfax and Cinnamon Streets, where a small home was blown down. This initial damage was sporadic. The next effects were two blocks east at Lavinia Street, where a tree and small building were damaged, and another block east at Madison Street, where electric cables of the Cincinnati Traction Company and signboards were blown over. It then passed for a mile across the Cincinnati golf grounds without doing much damage.

The path of greatest damage began at the head of Morton Street and continued for about three-quarters of a mile to Delta Avenue, passing through the intersection of Grace and Griest Avenues. The damage path here was fifty to three hundred feet wide, and three persons were fatally injured.

Nearly all buildings and trees directly in the path of the tornado from Morton Street to Grace Avenue were destroyed. One exception was the Kessing House, "an exceptionally well-constructed building." Much of the house damage came from the loss of roofs. The roof of one house on Morton Street came apart in halves. The north half of the roof on the left side of the tornado was carried three hundred feet to the north over a row of houses and dropped in a yard. The south half of the roof on the right side of the tornado was carried five hundred feet to the south and smashed against a hill.

Thousands of trees were blown over by the wind. Those to the left of the path generally fell to the south, whereas those to the right of the path fell to the north, indicating the cyclonic circulation of the strongest winds.

Damage diminished east of Grace Avenue, but the path was visible beyond Ault Park, a distance of three and one-quarter miles from the first damage. Rainfall with the storm was light, but lightning was continuous and there was a tremendous roaring, hissing noise.

28 March 1920
Western Tornadoes

The Palm Sunday 1920 outbreak of thirty tornadoes across eight states killed 153 persons, ranking it as among the deadliest tornado outbreaks in U.S. history (Grazulis 1990). A strong (28.96 inches) low pressure center over Iowa early on 28 March pulled a warm air mass northward across Ohio. Strong west winds aloft led to ideal conditions for a large outbreak of severe weather (Mitchell 1920).

Four killer tornadoes moved into Ohio from Indiana and another moved across Wood and Ottawa Counties. The first crossed into Paulding County at about 6:00 P.M. and swept northeastward to Lucas County. It was a skipping path and may actually have been more than one tornado (Grazulis 1990). Thirteen people had been killed by this tornado in Indiana and another ten died in Ohio. Hardest hit in Ohio were the communities of Brunersburg, at the junction of Routes 15 and 18 on the northwestern edge of Defiance, and Raab's Corners, at the intersection of Bancroft and Raab Roads, twelve miles west of Toledo.

A community of 100 people at Renolett, west of Defiance, was hit first. The *Toledo Daily Blade* reported that every building in Renolett was leveled and 3 persons were killed. The tornado then passed through

Brunersburg, a community of 130 people. Most of the thirty-six homes in Brunersburg were heavily damaged and 3 people were killed. Several people were injured and 3 killed as the tornado then skipped across northern Henry County and leveled several homes and barns. In western Lucas County, damage was reported again near Swanton. Near the end of the tornado path, the small community of Raab's Corners was virtually leveled and 4 persons killed. Many farms in the Sylvania area were damaged and there were about 21 people injured. Another tornado, possibly beginning at Bowling Green, moved through Ottawa County at 7:30 P.M. In Genoa, 2 people were killed, 20 injured, and 20 homes and businesses destroyed.

A tornado that had killed fourteen in Indiana entered Mercer County at about 6:30 P.M. and passed northeastward into Van Wert County, killing two persons in a destroyed farmhouse.

A third tornado moved from Indiana and across Darke County south of Union City and Lightsville at about 7:30 P.M. Several farms were destroyed and four people died. From Lightsville the tornado continued to New Weston, where eight homes, a grain elevator, a school, and a church were demolished. Thefts were reported from damaged homes in Darke County with people saving souvenirs from the wreckage. The county sheriff immediately prohibited parking autos within two hundred feet of any damaged house.

A few minutes later, another, stronger tornado followed a parallel path through Darke County about eight miles south of the first Darke County tornado. This storm intensified to a violent tornado twelve hundred feet wide as it entered Ohio. Many homes and farms were destroyed along a path that ended three miles northwest of Greenville. Eight persons were killed near Nashville, three miles north of Palestine, and near Greenville. The Linamude School on Union City Pike, called a Darke County landmark by the *Dayton Daily News,* was "torn brick from brick" by the tornado. A new auto with its top torn off was still being driven after the storm and a Ford truck was found sitting high on a barn. Electric power and phone service was cut between Greenville and Union City. Merchants and businessmen of Greenville met on Tuesday, 30 March to create a relief fund for those who lost family and property in the tornadoes.

The small community of Moulton west of Wapakoneta was leveled, with only one building left standing and three deaths in the community. Grazulis (1990) did not indicate a significant tornado there, but Moulton is northeast of the track of the Darke County tornadoes and damage indicates a tornado did occur. The United Brethren Church was blown away with only the foundation left.

28 June 1924
Lorain Tornado

The deadliest tornado in Ohio history struck Lorain and Sandusky on Saturday, 28 June 1924. This was not the largest or strongest tornado to occur in Ohio, but, like the 1974 Xenia Tornado that killed thirty-two, this violent storm struck an urban center where thousands of people were put at risk. The number of fatalities will never be known with certainty, but an accepted figure is eighty-five dead (Grazulis 1990), seventy-two of whom were killed at Lorain, a city of thirty-seven thousand. A detailed account of the storms is given in the June 1924 and July 1924 issues of *Climatological Data—Ohio Section* and by Hunter (1924).

At the time of the storm, this was the second greatest loss of life reported from a tornado so far north in the United States, exceeded only by the New Richmond, Wisconsin, tornado that killed 117 in June 1899. Since 1924, only the Flint, Michigan, and Worcester, Massachusetts, tornadoes of June 1953 killed more at such a northern latitude (Grazulis 1990).

On this day of several tornadoes, high winds, and heavy rains across northern Ohio, at least four tornadoes touched down and wind and flood damage were widespread. Low pressure was passing eastward from northern Iowa through southern Michigan and into Ontario during the day. Temperatures were warm, near 80 degrees, but not unusual for June. Showers had passed through the lakeshore counties during the morning, but there seems to have been no indication that severe weather was coming later in the afternoon.

The place of first touchdown of the Lorain Tornado is uncertain. It was first observed just north of Sandusky, a city of twenty-three thousand, but Grazulis (1990) placed the beginning point to the west over Sandusky Bay. In any case, the first damage occurred as the tornado struck the northeastern edge of Sandusky at 4:35 P.M.

Damage at Sandusky was greatest along nine city blocks, an area about one-quarter mile wide and one-half mile long. The damaged area was bounded roughly by Market Street, Adams Street, Washington Park, and the waterfront. In that region, the *Sandusky Star Journal* reported that one hundred homes and twenty-five factories or businesses were destroyed, and eight persons were killed and about one hundred injured. The waterfront had heavy damage and the Sandusky Yacht Club building was swept into the bay. The three-story Groch Coal Company building collapsed, killing a bookkeeper and a driver. A watchman in a shanty at the Baltimore and Ohio rail yard was found dead several yards away, but the shanty was nowhere to be seen. Another B&O employee was crushed between two rail freight cars blown together by the wind.

Six autos were blown into Sandusky Bay from the ferry dock at the foot of Jackson Street. The steamer *Boeckling* was tied up at the Cedar Point dock with twelve hundred passengers. Captain Harry Wichter saw the storm and ordered everyone to stay in their seats. The passengers looked on with awe as the Sandusky waterfront was torn apart. The tornado then cut across Cedar Point about four miles south of the resort at its tip and then out over Lake Erie. Six cottages were blown down on Cedar Point, according to the *Toledo Blade*.

The U.S. Weather Bureau had an office in downtown Sandusky in 1924, and meteorologist C. C. Cooper reported large cumulus clouds were visible to the west and southwest soon after 3:00 P.M. Light rain began to fall at 4:15 P.M., and by 4:30 P.M. streams of clouds from the southwest and northwest seemed to be meeting over the lake north of Sandusky. Where they met, the clouds presented a "bluish-black appearance and a cloud-whirl was plainly seen." The barometer had been falling rapidly all after-noon, but it plunged .2 inch in five minutes and then rose .2 inch again as the tornado passed one thousand feet north of the Weather Bureau office. Winds had been from the southeast at the Weather Bureau as the storm approached but swung around to the northwest and increased to storm force. From 4:35 P.M. to 4:40 P.M. the wind averaged 72 mph and reached a maximum of 77 mph. Rainfall from 4:35 P.M. to 8:15 P.M. totaled 1.31 inches, and the temperature fell from 83 to 69 degrees.

Water service was knocked out for more than twenty-four hours in Sandusky, and when it was turned on again the residents were asked to boil the water. Advertisements in the *Sandusky Star Journal* hawked dis-tilled drinking water, tornado insurance, and window and auto glass. National Guard troops moved into Sandusky to maintain order, direct traffic, and assist in the cleanup after the tornado, but by Monday some residents were protesting the continued presence of the Guard and the requirement to obtain passes to get into damaged neighborhoods. How-ever, the 2 July *Sandusky Star Tribune* expressed appreciation for efforts of the Guard and thanked Governor Alvin Donahey for sending the troops.

The history of the tornado over the twenty-five miles of Lake Erie between Cedar Point and Lorain is not known. It is possible the tornado that came ashore in Lorain at 5:08 P.M. was not the same funnel that left Sandusky twenty-five minutes earlier. It is clear from reports along the shore and from boats offshore that a severe storm continued over the lake between the two cities. Gale force winds occurred at Vermilion as the storm passed, first from the south, then west, and then northwest. Large waves damaged cottages along the shore.

The ninety-one-ton yacht *Oswichee* motoring from Rocky River to Put-in-Bay encountered the tornado five miles offshore and six miles west of Lorain. A passenger, Dr. M. L. Combes, reported a black funnel cloud one-half mile wide at the water and much wider at the top. He believed the yacht passed near the center of the tornado at about 5:00 P.M. The captain, with fifty years of ocean experience, estimated winds at 90 to 100 mph. There was tremendous downward pressure and the water whirled counterclockwise. Lightning was continuous, but the roar of the wind was so great that they could not hear thunder. During the height of the storm they were in complete darkness, which was followed by a "dirty, yellowish, amber glare."

The massive funnel came ashore at the Lorain Municipal Bath House in Lakeview Park and tore a three-mile path through downtown Lorain in about three minutes. Its width varied from four thousand to five hundred feet, apparently becoming narrower as it progressed eastward. The tornado lifted east of the city and set down again at Sheffield and Avon.

Damage in Lorain was greatest from West Erie Avenue south to Seventh Street and along Broadway south to Eighth Street. Buildings were damaged for thirty-five blocks along Broadway, and at least two hundred automobiles sat buried in bricks and other debris. A smashed Ford found on Broadway had apparently been blown against the fourth story of a building where oil and paint were found on the bricks above the wreckage.

More than one thousand homes were damaged and five hundred destroyed at Lorain (DeWeese 1924). All downtown businesses sustained some damage, and two hundred businesses were destroyed. Most of the destroyed downtown buildings were not of modern construction, as reported by E. H. Emery, Weather Bureau meteorologist in Cleveland. For example, the modern Antlers Hotel, of steel construction, had only a corner of its roof damaged, although it was directly in the path of the tornado.

Initial reports in the 29 June *Cleveland Plain Dealer* listed "300 dead in Lorain," but this was gradually revised downward to seventy-two by 1 July. The State Theater collapsed onto about eighty patrons viewing a Saturday matinee musical. Initial reports from Lorain in the 29 June *Plain Dealer* indicated that eighty bodies were taken from the theater, but the final tally was fifteen dead in the theater, many of them teenagers. This is the largest tornado death toll in one building known in Ohio.

Most of the other deaths were in collapsed buildings. Seven or eight persons were killed in the collapse of the Bath House as bathers scrambled for shelter. Five people died at the home of attorney C. E. van Duesen on West Fifth Street, two died in the Crystal Restaurant on Broadway, two in the Dinery Restaurant on Erie Avenue, and one died in the Mills Seed

Store on Broadway (DeWeese 1924). Others were killed in their homes or in crushed cars.

Eight autos were blown into the lake at the municipal beach, and a canoe was found wrapped around a tree. Some homes had their roofs removed, on others the second story was swept away, some "roofs squatted grotesquely over the cellars," and other homes were entirely collapsed down to the foundation, according to the *Cleveland Plain Dealer*. On the east side of Lorain, sixty-two cars of a freight train were "scattered on both sides of the railroad" and some were carried thirty feet by the tornado winds. A bridge over the Black River was jarred four feet when the large freighter *Henry Ford II,* under construction at American Ship Building, was torn from its moorings and rammed the bridge. Business letters, checks, and other papers from Lorain fell from the sky later that evening sixty to ninety miles east in Ashtabula and Geauga Counties.

The steamer *City of Erie* left from Cleveland loaded with medical supplies for Lorain soon after the tornado while roads were still blocked. This vessel anchored in the Black River and became a base hospital until Monday, when it traveled back to Cleveland with fifty of the injured. Dozens of doctors and hundreds of nurses arrived by rail, auto, and boat from Cleveland and most worked twenty-four hours straight through Sunday afternoon treating the injured at Lorain. Fresh medical personnel arrived Sunday evening. Surgical supplies such as antiseptics, ether, alcohol, and bandages were taken from Lorain drugstores but soon were in short supply and were driven in from neighboring cities. American Red Cross personnel and supplies arrived quickly and hundreds of Boy Scouts came from Cleveland to keep sightseers out of Lorain.

Most of the homeless in Lorain stayed with relatives or neighbors, but others slept on cots in Red Cross tents. Limited radio and telephone communication was established Monday morning. The local telephone system was owned by Lorain County Telephone Company, but it was Ohio Bell Telephone Company linemen who worked through the night Sunday to restore a line to Cleveland. Distilled water was carried to hospitals in trucks, but the general population experienced shortages for two days. Electric service was out so the rescue and medical teams worked first by candles and then by the light of acetylene lamps. Cleveland Railway Company placed their facilities and crews at the service of the Red Cross to provide transportation and assistance in the cleanup of Lorain.

The 30 June *Cleveland Plain Dealer* reported that four hundred Ohio National Guardsmen under the command of Brig. Gen. John McQuigg "with drawn revolvers and bayonets fixed in their guns" took control of the west and east ends of Lorain while police from Cleveland patrolled the business district. The police in their strict control "recognized absolutely no papers, military or otherwise, and were bold in saying that not even President Coolidge could write a pass to get anybody into the ruined district."

Most debris was cleared from Lorain streets by Monday, 30 June, but buildings were still being searched for bodies. Thirteen more were found Monday, bringing the death toll at Lorain to seventy-two. Everyone had food and a place to sleep provided by the Red Cross, Salvation Army, or ordinary citizens. Some businesses reopened Monday or Tuesday and banks opened temporary offices in the Antlers Hotel to disperse funds to customers. Electricity, gas, and telephone service were restored in most of Lorain by Tuesday, 1 July but a night curfew remained downtown.

A second tornado touched down in Sandusky County west of Vickery ten minutes after the Lorain Tornado first hit Sandusky. This tornado moved eastward along the road to Castalia for thirteen miles, passed south of Castalia, then lifted and reformed in Huron Township (Erie County).

A third tornado touched down at 6:00 P.M. near Geauga Lake and traveled for twenty miles through northern Portage County. It is possible that this tornado formed from the same tornado family that produced the Lorain Tornado. It was milking time and three farmers were killed in three milking barns north of Mantua. The tornado continued eastward, passing one-half mile north of Hiram and striking Nelson, where every building in town was damaged (Grazulis 1990). Professor George Colton of Hiram reported the storm passed Hiram at 6:15 P.M. and produced a well-defined track one-third mile wide across the county. Tens of thousands of trees were broken or uprooted, including many orchards and sugar groves. Debris from destroyed homes was carried four hundred feet or more. Evidence of counterclockwise motion was clear. Trees to the right of the path lay to the east, whereas trees to the left of the path lay toward the west. A rafter from a barn eighty feet southwest of a house was blown around the house and into a window on the east side of the house. Lightning was constant during the storm, and more than two inches of rain fell at Hiram in one hour.

13 May 1933
The First Xenia Tornado

The first two weeks of May 1933 brought active tornado weather with dozens of powerful storms killing 192 persons in the Great Plains, South, and Midwest (Grazulis 1990).

Ohio escaped most of the severe weather, but in the predawn hours of Saturday, 13 May 1933 a tornado cut a two-mile-long swath through the eastern portion of Xenia. It leveled fifty to seventy-five "small frame houses of fragile construction" in a section known as Frogtown Hollow. Two persons were killed and about twenty-five injured.

Doctors and nurses converged on the area after dawn and National Guardsmen took charge of the rescue and cleanup. Heavy rain after the tornado hampered the effort and damaged many personal goods. The National Guard Armory in Xenia was set up for the homeless and was used by twenty-five persons Saturday night. Assistance was provided by the Red Cross and American Legion.

Relief efforts continued into the next week, including numerous clothing drives and collection of a tornado fund for victims. Many of the victims did not leave the scene but stayed with friends near their destroyed homes. A registration office was set up in the neighborhood so that residents could indicate the type of relief needed after the storm.

Xenia entered tornado legends forty-one years later when a violent tornado destroyed much of the city and killed thirty-two persons. A third tornado struck the city in 1989.

27 April 1943
Akron Tornado

Of 171 tornadoes in the United States during 1943, the Akron Tornado was judged at the time to have been the strongest (Baldwin 1943). Grazulis (1990) listed this as one of six violent F4 tornadoes in the United States during the year. The Akron Tornado, along with several others striking northern Ohio Tuesday evening, 27 April, occurred along a squall line ahead of a cold front passing across the lower Great Lakes region. This is the typical scenario for severe weather, but World War II limited public access to atmospheric conditions. Cleveland Weather Bureau forecaster C. George Andrus was quoted in the *Cleveland Plain Dealer* as saying, "Conditions causing the tornadoes here cannot be revealed because of censorship regulations on weather."

The Akron Tornado touched down near Wadsworth about 8:00 P.M. and traveled eastward twenty miles through the center of Akron to Mogadore. Before the tornado moved into Akron, the Mills Brothers Circus tent was blown down in Wadsworth and six homes and several barns were blown down in Copley. Farm homes were also damaged along Route 21.

The path through Akron was just south of West Exchange and north of East Market through the industrial heart of the city. War production was near a peak in 1943, and thousands were employed in the city's factories—ten thousand at B. F. Goodrich alone. The Goodrich plant sustained $250,000 damage, including hundreds of broken windows. A water tower on the Goodyear factory crashed into the company garage next door. Many other factories, especially those near High and Chestnut Streets, were damaged by the tornado. Industrial production in Akron was also hindered for a day or two by lack of electricity and rail lines blocked by debris in the area. Most larger factories were back to full production within two days, and smaller plants recovered within the week.

Residential areas of Akron were also battered by the tornado. Homes were destroyed along Pickford Avenue, Flint Drive, and Kenneth Place. Mail carriers completed a survey of residential damage two days after the tornado for the Akron Chamber of Commerce Tornado Relief Committee. Results reported in the 1 May *Akron Beacon Journal* showed 37 homes destroyed, 1,147 homes damaged, and 546 garages damaged or destroyed.

Auxiliary firemen of the Akron civil defense forces worked quickly to cover damaged roofs and walls with tar paper and tarps to prevent further damage by rain. Persons made homeless in the storm found shelter with friends and relatives. Rebuilding was a concern because lumber and other construction material was strictly controlled by the federal government through the war production board. Requests to the government for lumber were coordinated by the Red Cross and pleas made to prominent politicians. Building materials and workers were generally available soon after the storm.

One-third of Akron's taxicabs were damaged when winds blew the roof and side from the City Cab Company garage at Bowery and Wooster Avenue. Downtown stores had broken windows, and looters carried some goods away before police and civil defense patrols arrived. Akron hospitals were not seriously damaged, but electricity was out and nurses held flashlights and candles during a few surgeries before emergency power came on.

Several hundred men of the Akron Civil Defense were called for duty clearing debris and assisting with traffic and rescues during the disaster. They received high praise in the *Akron Beacon Journal* and reassured residents that their civil defense force was prepared in case of a war attack on Akron.

Given the strength of the Akron Tornado, its path through one of Ohio's largest cities, and occurrence with little warning, a large death toll would be expected. In fact, no one was killed. The *Akron Beacon Journal* reported that sixty-two persons were treated at Akron hospitals for tornado injuries.

Storms also occurred elsewhere in northern Ohio on 27 April 1943. A tornado traced a fifteen-mile path across central Medina County (Grazulis 1990), where two boys died in a collapsed barn. Three tornadoes skipped along a fourteen-mile path through Cleveland between 8:30 P.M. and 9:00

P.M. Damage began on the west side in an area bounded by Lorain Avenue, Madison Avenue, West Forty-first Street, and West Eighty-ninth Street, as described in the *Cleveland Plain Dealer*. The tornadoes passed eastward just two miles south of Cleveland Public Square and continued into the east side, where homes were damaged on East Ninety-first, East 131st, Harvard Avenue, Miles Avenue S.E., and Cullen Drive S.E. Downtown streets were flooded by rain and signs were blown off buildings. About one hundred homes were severely damaged by the Cleveland tornadoes and one hundred persons injured (Grazulis 1990). Neighborhoods were patrolled by air raid wardens and auxiliary police and firemen to prevent looting and keep sightseers away.

In explaining the tornado damage, the *Cleveland Plain Dealer* quoted Cleveland Weather Bureau forecaster C. George Andrus: "Pressure drop accounts for most of the damage a tornado brings. This causes air inside houses seeking a way out causing most of the damage from shattered glass." This "exploding house" theory of tornado damage was disputed as early as 1897 but persisted for many years and led to the dangerous suggestion of opening windows as a tornado approaches. We now know that pressure differences are not a significant cause of damage and opening windows accomplishes no more than a delay in getting to shelter.

13 August 1943
Canton Tornado

Tornadoes struck northwestern Ohio early in the evening on 13 August 1943. Barns were blown down and homes unroofed north of Defiance at 5:30 P.M. (Grazulis 1990). A tornado ninety minutes later in Erie County killed one person as it destroyed two homes at Vermilion. Three homes were destroyed but no one injured by a brief touchdown at Olmsted Falls in Cuyahoga County. Just before 9:00 P.M., another tornado damaged forty-six homes, killed an infant, and injured twenty-eight people when it touched down at Leavittsburg, west of Warren.

As the Leavittsburg Tornado was dissipating over Trumbull County, a large tornado formed over Massillon in Stark County. It touched down during heavy rain along Lincoln Way, called Route 30 in 1943, near the intersection with Genoa Road west of Canton. The path of destruction continued eastward for ten miles through Reedurban, West Manor, and the south side of Canton. War production was near its peak in the factories of Canton, and this storm, like the Akron Tornado of 27 April 1943, interrupted that production for a few precious days.

Friday the thirteenth was certainly unlucky for those along the path of the Canton Tornado. Eleven homes and 36 other buildings were destroyed by the tornado and 350 buildings were damaged (Grazulis 1990). There was one death. The Diebold plant at Navarre and Clarendon lost a portion of its roof and siding. The tornado did most of its damage as it struck industrial complexes at the intersection of Fifteenth Street and Henry Avenue and Fifteenth and Cleveland Avenue. Carnegie-Illinois Steel lost a yard crane and two 125-foot smokestacks. The south end of Barium Stainless Steel plant was twisted and wrecked, the powerhouse demolished, and the company garage leveled. Damage continued eastward to the homes of the 1500 block of South Market and across southeastern Canton.

Canton mayor Albert Fromm declared the area within one-quarter mile of the intersection of Fifteenth Street and Henry Avenue to be a "restricted zone" in order to prevent looting and assist in the cleanup and repair of damaged factories.

Industries returned to near normal production by Monday morning after a busy weekend of repairs. Spun Steel employees worked under the sky until the factory roof could be replaced. Wartime rationing of construction materials was eased for those who needed repairs to roofing and windows. However, it was feared that home appliances lost in the tornado would not be replaced anytime soon due to shortages. The normal ten-day waiting period for replacing lost ration coupon books was waived for those who lost coupons in the storm.

7 June 1947
Trumbull County Tornado

A violent tornado killed four persons as it tore a path across fifteen miles of southern Trumbull County before smashing into Sharon, Pennsylvania. It touched down in the DeForest area between Warren and Niles about 2:30 P.M. Saturday, 7 June 1947 and moved east along the southern portions of Howland, Vienna, and Brookfield Townships.

At the Youngstown Airport north of Vienna, personnel observed a "huge black cone-shaped" cloud to the south and airplanes were punctured by two-inch diameter hail. In Newton Falls, heavily damaged by a tornado on 31 May 1985, this storm passed to the north, but it was so dark that street lights and car headlights were on in midafternoon.

Most of the damage in Ohio was along Niles-Warren Road, Niles-Vienna Road, Youngstown-Vienna Road, and Smith-Stewart Road. A two-story apartment and store was leveled at DeForest and Niles-Warren Roads and a home demolished on nearby Orchard Avenue. A parked car was blown off Orchard Avenue and set down upright seventy-five yards away. Another home was destroyed on Mines Road and the tornado destroyed twenty-five homes as it crossed Niles-Vienna Road. A telephone pole was snapped off and driven through a cement block home. The tornado then passed along Smith-Stewart Road and crossed Youngstown-Vienna Road. Earlier damage west of the tornado path in Cuyahoga Falls and at the Ravenna Arsenal (then called the Ordnance Plant) may have been related to this tornado. Trees, power lines, and small buildings were blown down along a narrow path at the Arsenal.

The path of this tornado was remarkably similar to the deadly storm of 31 May 1985. Both caused initial damage at the Ravenna Arsenal and passed eastward into Pennsylvania. The path of the 1985 tornado was through Newton Falls and Niles, just three miles south of the 1947 tornado.

19 March 1948
Winds Flatten Northwestern Ohio

Wind damage was widespread across Ohio this warm Good Friday afternoon in 1948, although it was focused in the northwestern counties. News accounts at the time attributed most of the Ohio damage to straight-line winds, but Grazulis (1990) listed six strong tornadoes in Ohio that afternoon and some of the damage was caused by tornadoes.

Damaging winds hit northwestern Ohio and the Toledo area at about 1:00 P.M. on 19 March. The gust to 87 mph at the U.S. Weather Bureau office at Toledo Municipal Airport was a record for Toledo and is one of the highest winds officially measured in Ohio. At Woodville, a few miles southeast of the airport, five twenty-seven-ton boxcars were blown off their tracks. Seventeen empty boxcars were blown one-quarter mile down the Wheeling and Lake Erie tracks from Lallendorf Road into Pearson Park.

Homes, barns, and garages were leveled in the area. The capstone of the chimney fell through the roof of the Worth Clegg Funeral Home on East Broadway in Toledo as a funeral service was in progress. The *Toledo Blade* reported that Reverend Harold Davis continued his sermon as rain poured through the hole in the roof. The *Toledo Blade* reported at least thirty persons in the Toledo area were injured by flying glass, trees, and other debris.

In suburban Toledo, the Rossford Ordnance Depot was severely damaged, with eight unoccupied barracks demolished, windows smashed in thirteen warehouses, and dozens of semitrailers flipped over. Just east of Toledo, three transmitter towers of WSPD radio were blown down on Oregon Road and several cottages were leveled at Reno Beach. Other northwestern Ohio communities with serious damage were Wauseon, Delta, and Gibsonburg. The *Toledo Blade* quoted Don Coleman, chief of the Weather Bureau in Toledo, reporting it was a line-squall that passed through the city, but also showed evidence of the twisting action of tornadoes. Grazulis (1990) did not list any significant tornadoes in the Toledo area this day.

To the south a tornado traveled a skipping path from Ohio City in Van Wert County to near Columbus Grove in Putnam County. The *Lima News* reported 85 percent of the homes and businesses in Ohio City were damaged. Six miles north of Ohio City, winds demolished a hangar and wrecked six planes at the Van Wert Airport.

The greatest tragedy of this stormy Good Friday occurred as the tornado passed through Landeck, a community of two hundred, three miles southwest of Delphos. Two altar boys at St. Johns Catholic Church were killed when the steeple blew over and fell into the destroyed church. The *Lima News* reported the church would have been filled with children fifteen minutes later. Across the street from the church, ninety-three children in the two-story Landeck School crouched in the hallway as the wind shattered windows and covered the classroom floors with glass. There were no serious injuries at the school.

Elsewhere in northwestern Ohio, barns were blown down through much of Putnam County, windows were blown out and trees and wires down at Lima, planes were wrecked at the Fremont airport, and schools damaged at Benton Ridge and Cloverdale. The *Cleveland Plain Dealer* reported fifty barns destroyed in Wood County. Ohio Highway Patrol communications were interrupted at Findlay when their 220-foot tower toppled in the wind just as emergency calls were being received. The roof of the Campbell School in Sandusky collapsed under a toppled smokestack, injuring seven of thirty-five students in a sixth-grade classroom.

Scattered damage and widespread power failures were reported from the Cleveland area. Two DC-3 airplanes were lifted and moved at Cleveland Airport and a smaller plane was flipped over. High winds from noon until 3:00 P.M. also caused minor damage in Columbus with power outages and trees and signs down. At Newark, the 332-foot tower of WCLT radio was toppled, and St. Paul's Methodist Church was damaged. A Fayette County tornado unroofed a dozen homes at Bloomingburg (Grazulis 1990). The *Columbus Evening Dispatch* reported the Bloomingburg Methodist Church and Masonic Hall were severely damaged.

19 July 1950
Lima Tornado

Homes and factories of Lima sustained heavy damage in the tornado of Wednesday afternoon, 19 July 1950. There were no fatalities, but at least thirty people were injured and six were admitted to hospitals. Total damage in Lima was estimated at $1.5 million.

The tornado touched down near the Sharon Drive-In on West Elm at 4:50 P.M., tracked northeast across the city, and lifted before touching down again southwest of Beaverdam. The path of greatest damage was three miles long and about two blocks wide. The tornado was visible to Lima residents as a black funnel with house roofs and other debris swirling in the air.

Three homes on Murphy Street and at the corner of Collett and Delphos were demolished. About one hundred more lost all or part of their roofs and several hundred homes were damaged by wind and flying debris. Walls were ripped off homes on West Grand Avenue and a house on Marian Avenue was moved twenty feet off its foundation.

Extensive damage occurred at the Lennox Furnace Company on North Baxter. All windows were broken, one-fourth of the roof removed, and the smokestack damaged. Several people were injured in the Lennox Furnace parking lot. Three buildings were also destroyed at the Western Condensing Company on East Murphy.

Another tornado occurred in Ridge Township, three miles south of Van Wert, a few minutes before the Lima Tornado. Several farms were damaged and the Bethel Methodist Church was lifted seventy-five feet into the air and disintegrated. Pieces of the frame church were scattered over a wide area. There were no injuries.

8 June 1953
Northern Tornadoes

Ohio's deadliest tornadoes between 1924 and 1965 crossed the northern counties Monday evening, 8 June 1953, killing 17 people from near Bowling Green to Cleveland. Ohio was not the only state affected by this violent weather pattern. Another tornado the same evening killed 115 people at Flint, Michigan, and about 90 died in a tornado the next afternoon at Worcester, Massachusetts. These are the deadliest tornadoes ever known in the northeastern United States, and the Flint Tornado was the last single tornado to kill more than 100 people in the United States.

The first of three killer tornadoes in Ohio touched down at 7:00 P.M. northwest of Deshler in Henry County. This violent storm ravaged a twenty-mile-long path across Wood County and into Sandusky County, lifting as the next member of the tornado family touched down in Erie County half an hour later. Twenty-one homes were destroyed and sixteen others damaged in Wood County.

Five members of one family were killed when their farm was destroyed near Cygnet, south of Bowling Green, and three others were killed on Wood County farms. An eye-witness watched the tornado for ten minutes before it hit Jerry City and described it in the *Cleveland Plain Dealer* as "a

Fig. 75. Damage on the west side of Cleveland from the 8 June 1953 tornado. The roof and portions of the second story were removed from this house. (Photograph by Al Schaefer, courtesy of the National Weather Service, Cleveland)

long, white cloud that just kept coming toward me. It made a terrible noise." Tractor-trailers were blown off Route 25 and a car was hurled three hundred yards by the tornado. Livestock was killed along the path near Cygnet. Hogs covered one road "as if a giant had hurled them about by their tails." From Cygnet and Jerry City, the tornado moved through Wayne and into Sandusky County, where less damage was done.

As the Cygnet Tornado lifted, a second tornado touched down at 7:30 P.M. in Erie County along Thomas Road between Kimball and Avery. It moved to Ceylon and along the lakeshore before ending near Vermilion. Greenhouses crumbled with the winds at Ceylon and homes were destroyed along Poorman Road outside Vermilion. About twenty-three people were injured along the path and two persons died.

A third tornado caused panic through much of Cleveland when tornado warnings were broadcast over all radio and television stations at 8:55 P.M. The U.S. Weather Bureau had only recently begun issuing tornado warnings to the public and this was among the first such warnings issued in Ohio. Most people were uncertain of what action to take.

Coming at a time when tens of thousands of Cleveland homes were tuned to radio and television, the warning reached virtually the entire population. Widespread power blackouts soon after they heard the warning increased anxiety among Clevelanders. Callers jammed switchboards at newspapers, police stations, Cleveland Electric Illuminating, and City Hall inquiring about the storm. Cleveland police radio issued a statement advising residents "to take to their basements." This tornado warning by the Weather Bureau and prompt distribution through radio and television probably saved many lives in Cleveland.

The Cleveland Tornado touched down in Lorain County south of Elyria and perhaps as far west as the Erie County line (Grazulis 1990). It passed across the northwestern edge of Cleveland Hopkins Airport at about 9:45 P.M. and then did most of its damage from the airport across western Cleveland. The tornado passed into Lake Erie near East Fortieth Street, a mile from Public Square.

About one hundred homes were demolished in western Cleveland. Severe damage occurred at Bosworth and Thrush, West Twenty-eighth and Franklin, West 117th and Wayland Avenue, West 117th and Bellaire, on Lorain Avenue from West 117th eastward, and along West Twenty-fifth from the Detroit-Superior Bridge to Franklin (fig. 75). Five persons died in a collapsed house on West Twenty-eighth Street and two others were killed on Cleveland's west side.

Thirteen Cleveland schools were damaged along the tornado path, but its late evening occurrence prevented tragedy in the schools. Much of the damage was from fallen chimneys. However, the roof crashed into the second floor at Gordon School and the superintendent estimated at least one classroom of children would have been killed there in a daytime tornado strike. A wall was blown in at Waverly School. Five of the damaged schools reopened two days later, but eight schools remained closed longer for repairs.

Another violent tornado touched down at Temperance, Michigan, about three miles north of Toledo, and killed four people along East Temperance Road and Telegraph Road in Michigan. It continued over Lake Erie as a waterspout, entered Ohio waters, and passed about four miles north of West Sister Island. Its thirty-mile path as a waterspout, much of it in Ohio, is among the longest on record (Grazulis 1990).

Our society seeks to answer why severe or unusual weather occurs and we often blame ourselves. In 1953, the public and pseudo-scientists were quick to blame the rash of deadly tornadoes on atomic tests conducted in recent years in the Nevada desert. Politicians responded with calls for action. U.S representative James E. Van Zandt (R-Pa.), a member of the atomic energy committee, was quoted in the *Cleveland Plain Dealer:* "The recent tornadoes could definitely be traced to atomic tests in Nevada." Representative Ray J. Madden (D-Ind.) pressed for a congressional investigation to determine if atomic tests were causing more severe tornadoes.

Climatologist Jerome Namias, then head of the Weather Bureau's extended forecast division, "pooh-poohed the very idea" and observed the death toll was high this year only because tornadoes had hit populated areas. He said, "This freak weather is abnormal. But that's not strange, because its abnormal someplace all the time." Cleveland forecaster C. George Andrus also sought to reassure citizens that the tornadoes were perfectly natural and formed without the assistance of any human activity. He reminded people that violent weather had also been blamed on radio transmissions and airplane propellers when they were first introduced and were still novel ideas to the public.

5 April 1957
Hurricane Force Winds Hit Toledo

The stormy first week of April 1957 brought an ice storm to northwestern Ohio on 3 April and a snowstorm to the state on 7–8 April. Between the winter storms, hurricane-force winds hit Toledo and vicinity on the afternoon of Friday, 5 April.

High winds and heavy rain swept across Toledo at about 2:30 P.M. with wind speeds of 81 mph measured at Toledo Express Airport and 90 mph at the Toledo Edison Acme Plant, according to the *Toledo Blade*. The 604-foot freighter *Champlain* docked on the Maumee River was buffeted by the winds and snapped twelve steel mooring lines holding her to the Baltimore and Ohio Railroad docks. Harold Humphrey, bridge tender on the Fassett Street Bridge, was in his control cab atop the draw span when he saw the *Champlain* drifting downstream toward the bridge. Humphrey telephoned authorities to warn them of the impending collision and asked that auto traffic be held off the bridge.

Moments later the freighter collided with the bridge, causing six hundred feet of the mile-long structure to collapse into the Maumee River. No cars were on the collapsed sections and Humphrey escaped without injury, as did the twenty-five men aboard the *Champlain*. The Fassett Street Bridge carried twelve thousand cars daily and its loss was felt especially by employees of the Libbey-Owens-Ford Glass plant in Rossford and Rossford Ordnance workers who had to take long detours.

Wind damage was widespread elsewhere in Toledo and northwestern Ohio. Three men were injured when a crane blew over at the Willys Motors factory (now Jeep). Two broadcast towers of WWNG radio were toppled east of Bowling Green. Trees and wires were blown down and windows broken throughout Toledo and at Paulding, Wauseon, Wapakoneta, Napoleon, and Findlay.

25 April 1961
Eaton and Clinton County Tornadoes

The damage that occurred in Eaton was the end of a violent tornado that swept a thirty-mile path through Indiana into Preble County, Ohio (Grazulis 1990). The tornado struck Eaton just before 4:00 P.M. on 25 April 1961, a day that also brought two deaths from a tornado in Clinton County.

Several Preble County farms were damaged as the tornado approached Eaton from the west. The house and barn on the James Turner farm were demolished and a canceled check from the Turner home drifted from the sky seven miles to the east. Most of the damage occurred at the Reilane Subdivision off Richmond Pike. Four homes were destroyed here and many others lost roofs or were severely damaged. The tornado continued into Eaton and lifted east of town.

Houses were destroyed on North Maple and North Franklin. Other homes were damaged on East Decatur, and four garages were destroyed between Main and Somers Streets. One man died from injuries received in a collapsed barn. Several commercial buildings were damaged. The Eaton Tire Supply on North Barron lost its upper floor. As the upper floor of the City Building was battered, illegal pinball machines confiscated two years earlier were blown out and deposited on North Barron. Parks IGA grocery lost its roof and was closed until 9 May.

Damage in Preble County was estimated at $1 million, and fifteen families were left homeless by the tornado. Numerous relief organizations, including local churches, were giving assistance in the week following the tornado. Ohio National Guardsmen and Eaton police and fire crews patrolled and assisted in the cleanup. Eaton City Council voted on 2 May to raze the damaged ninety-one-year-old City Building and build a new structure for the town hall.

Another tornado and microburst winds swept through Clinton County and northern Highland County at about 4:30 P.M. Wind gusts to 115 mph were measured at the Clinton County Air Force Base, reported the *Wilmington News-Journal,* and air traffic controllers were forced to abandon the ninety-foot observation tower. Barns, garages, trees, and wires were blown down by a narrow, skipping tornado from Blanchester to Martinsville, New Vienna, Leesburg, and Greenfield. Sheet metal was torn from the Clinton County Courthouse in Wilmington, the steeple was toppled at the Leesburg Methodist Church, and a greenhouse and drive-in movie screen were flattened at Greenfield. Two persons died in collapsed barns in Martinsville.

20 August 1962
Cleveland Windstorm

A violent thunderstorm raked Cleveland and the eastern suburbs at 10:30 P.M. on 20 August 1962, knocking down power lines and thousands of trees and damaging several buildings from Lakewood to Euclid and inland to North Olmsted and Shaker Heights.

Winds gusted to 110 mph at Burke Lakefront Airport, and speeds of 75 mph continued for five minutes at the airport, according to the *Cleveland Plain Dealer*. Winds of 83 mph were recorded on the twenty-two-story Illuminating Building, and gusts to 63 mph were measured on the harbor breakwall. Winds at Hopkins Airport did not exceed 47 mph.

A tornado associated with this severe storm skipped across Cleveland, touching down first in the 9000 block of Detroit Avenue N.W. and again in Shaker Heights (Grazulis 1990). Three men died when a fifty-thousand-gallon water tower of the Monarch Aluminum Manufacturing Company at 9215 Detroit crashed through five floors of the building. Four others were injured at the facility. A home was unroofed at the second touchdown in Shaker Heights. Another Cleveland man died the next day after touching a live wire.

Although there were doubts about whether there was a tornado or just straight-line winds, Weather Bureau forecaster Harold Burke confirmed in the 22 August 1962 *Cleveland Plain Dealer* that there were "one or more funnels that did not touch the ground but created counter-clockwise spirals of high wind on the ground."

11 April 1965
Palm Sunday Tornadoes

A wide outbreak of thirty-seven tornadoes killed 256 persons, mostly in Ohio, Michigan, and Indiana, on Palm Sunday, 11 April 1965. This was the deadliest tornado outbreak in thirty-three years in the United States and has been exceeded only by the 3–4 April 1974 outbreak. The fifty-five persons killed in Ohio on 11 April made this the second deadliest tornado day in Ohio history.

Fujita, Bradbury, and van Thullenar (1970) identified eighteen separate tornado families across six states during this outbreak, with six tornado families affecting Ohio. Strong low pressure was intensifying over Iowa Sunday afternoon and moved into southern Michigan by evening. The

Fig. 76. Homes were swept away in the Fuller Creekside addition at Toledo on 11 April 1965. (Photograph courtesy of the Toledo–Lucas County Public Library)

clash between warm, moist air from the Gulf of Mexico and cool, dry air from the west triggered thunderstorms along a front Sunday afternoon and evening. In addition, a jet stream with winds of 140 to 180 mph was passing directly over the area of thunderstorm development, causing rapid intensification of the storms.

These conditions prompted Weather Bureau personnel to issue tornado forecasts for the affected area from early afternoon into the evening. In fact, most of the tornadoes occurred in areas forecast to have severe weather. The great death toll resulted from the numerous long-track violent tornadoes and perhaps from a lack of attention to radio and television on this balmy spring Sunday, the first nice day of the season in most areas (USWB 1965).

To facilitate description of these tornadoes, individual tornadoes or families are described separately below.

Toledo. The only tornado on 11 April 1965 to hit a large Ohio city, the Toledo Tornado touched down about 9:30 P.M. on a six-mile track across the northern edge of the city. First damage was in the vicinity of Secor Road and Sylvania Avenue, where greenhouses were leveled on Violet Road and buildings blown down at Monroe and Secor and on Stannard. Roofs were blown off and windows smashed in buildings along Sylvania Avenue between Monroe and Secor. A mile to the east, a department store was destroyed at Sylvania and Douglas and roofs ripped from homes near Blessed Sacrament Church at Castlewood and Bellevue. The Du Pont paint factory at Upton and Tremainsville was heavily damaged, with three buildings destroyed and a tall smokestack blown over. Garages were destroyed, homes unroofed, and trees uprooted along Eleanor Avenue between North Haven and Westway.

The greatest damage from the Toledo Tornado occurred near the end of its path as it crossed Interstate 75 and destroyed homes in the Fuller Creekside addition. Vehicles were tossed about on the interstate just south of the Michigan line. A Short-Way Lines bus was struck by the tornado near the Suder Avenue overpass on Interstate 75. It was lifted into the air and smashed upside-down back onto the roadway, its top crushed down to the windows, killing five persons. Ironically, the bus had been chartered to take New York Central Railroad employees and passengers to Detroit to meet a Toledo-bound train that had been rerouted due to tornado damage in Indiana. Several trucks and cars were also tossed off the interstate and one other motorist was killed.

After crossing the interstate, the tornado, now a violent F4 storm, devastated dozens of homes in the Fuller Creekside addition (fig. 76). Homes on Vistamar and Terramar were leveled, swept clean to their foundations and debris scattered for hundreds of yards. Five persons died in the Fuller addition and dozens were injured. As the storm continued east, a man was killed in a destroyed home on Summit, just north of Shoreland, and two women died in their homes on Edgewater near 145th Street. One of those fatally injured, Erma Jean Lashaway, was Miss Toledo in 1937.

Willshire to Strongsville. Four separate tornadoes touched down from a cluster of thunderstorms as they crossed northwestern and north-central Ohio between 9:00 P.M. and 11:30 P.M. This family of four violent tornadoes killed 34 people in Ohio and injured about 350 (Grazulis 1990). The history of this tornado family actually began at 7:00 P.M. over western Indiana, where 44 people were injured in Clinton County by the first tornado in the family. The second tornado in this family touched down in central Indiana about 7:30 and killed 25 people along a forty-seven-mile path.

The third tornado in the family appeared over eastern Indiana at 8:20 P.M. and entered Mercer County, Ohio, two miles south of Willshire. A farm home on Winkler Road was leveled by the tornado and two residents killed. The tornado continued across northern Mercer County into southern Van Wert County south of Ohio City. Ten homes and several barns were destroyed along Winkler Road and on Route 33 just south of the county line.

Fig. 77. Destruction along Route 65 near Cairo from the tornado of 11 April 1965. Two boys drowned in this ditch when their family car was demolished. (Photograph courtesy of the *Lima News*)

Moments later, the fourth violent twister in this family touched the ground six miles northwest of Lima and continued for twenty-five miles, lifting eight miles east of Bluffton. It passed across the northern edge of Cairo and about one mile south of Bluffton. Much damage was done at the intersection of Routes 103 and 235 (then Route 69) east of Bluffton. The tornado blew several cars and trucks from Interstate 75 as it crossed the highway between Beaverdam and Bluffton, according to the *Lima News*. Six persons were killed by this tornado near Cairo and seven others near Bluffton (fig. 77).

Soon after this funnel lifted back to the clouds over Hancock County, a fifth violent tornado formed and touched down southwest of Tiffin at 10:15 P.M. It followed a twenty-mile path to Reed Township. The only significant damage from this tornado was in the community of Rockaway on Route 224 three miles southwest of Republic. Four homes were leveled and one person killed. This tornado crossed Route 19 south of Republic at nearly the same spot another tornado killed a motorist on 10 May 1973 before hitting Willard.

The sixth and final member of this tornado family was also the most violent of the Palm Sunday Tornadoes in Ohio. This twister touched down southwest of Oberlin at about 11:00 P.M. and went through Pittsfield, Grafton, and Lagrange before ending at Strongsville in suburban Cleveland. The damage path was continuous and one-half mile wide, ending just before crossing the Ohio Turnpike at Strongsville (Fujita, Bradbury, and van Thullenar 1970).

Fig. 78. The Civil War monument was all that remained standing in Pittsfield after the tornado of 11 April 1965. General Sherman lies at the base. (*Cleveland Plain Dealer*, Cleveland, Ohio)

The community of Pittsfield, three miles south of Oberlin at the intersection of Routes 303 and 58, was devastated by winds estimated at more than 250 mph. All buildings in the town were leveled to the ground, including twelve homes, two churches, the town hall, and a combination grocery store and gas station. Every tree in Pittsfield was broken. The only thing left standing in Pittsfield was the Civil War Monument, and even there the soldier was blown from his platform (fig. 78).

At the Pittsfield Congregational Church, Reverend Elmer Novak with his wife and two children took shelter in the basement of the parsonage behind the church. As the tornado struck, they were sucked out of the parsonage, blown through the church, and dropped on the front lawn. They were hospitalized for their injuries.

Seven Pittsfield residents died in their destroyed homes and two motorists were killed when the tornado hit their cars while they were driving. Five more fatalities occurred near Lagrange, where twenty homes were demolished. Homes were also leveled along Route 82 near Columbia Center in eastern Lorain County, and three deaths occurred on Royalton Road and South Boone Road. Near the end of the path, eighteen homes were leveled in Strongsville, nine of them on Carlyle Drive. As this exceptional tornado was lifting in Strongsville, another tornado followed a six-mile path through Brunswick, destroying several homes and injuring six people.

Shelby County. At about the same time tornadoes were ripping through Lucas and Allen Counties, another tornado tore a twenty-mile path through rural Shelby County from near Ft. Loramie to just north of Maplewood. The *Sidney Daily News* reported damage was concentrated along Ft. Loramie-Swanders Road and Meranda Road and could have been much worse had the tornado not missed the communities of Anna, Swanders, and Maplewood. There were three fatalities and about fifty injuries in Shelby County.

The 14 April 1965 *Sidney Daily News* reported twenty-four homes, thirty-eight barns, and eighty-eight other farm buildings destroyed by this tornado. In addition, two Ft. Loramie businesses were wrecked and 225 cattle and hogs were killed on farms. A sixty-eight-car train encountered the tornado on the B&O tracks north of Swanders, resulting in the derailment of fifty-three cars (Grazulis 1990). Traffic was stopped for a time on Interstate 75 between Anna and Sidney after high tension lines fell across the highway.

Delaware and Morrow Counties. Northern Delaware County and western Morrow County were struck by a tornado just after 11:00 P.M. Most of the damage was in Radnor, where three people died, and across Delaware Reservoir in Westfield. About forty people were injured at Radnor and twenty-two at Westfield, and twenty-five homes were destroyed along this twenty-mile path (Grazulis 1990).

Pickaway and Fairfield Counties. The last significant tornado of the Palm Sunday outbreak occurred just after midnight along a twenty-eight-mile path north of Ashville and Lancaster. About twenty persons were injured and numerous farm buildings were blown down. A dozen trailers were destroyed on a lot north of Lancaster (Grazulis 1990).

Other tornadoes occurred during the Palm Sunday outbreak in Preble County at 11:30 P.M., in Greene County just before midnight, and in Harrison County at 1:00 A.M. on 12 April.

The cleanup began immediately Sunday night and continued for several days. The initial focus in every community was on a house-to-house search through the darkness for casualties. Some persons trapped in wreckage or blown from their homes into fields were not discovered for hours. Electric and telephone failures hampered communication Sunday night and Monday. Electricity was not restored in some areas until Tuesday. Debris on roads also slowed the rescue and recovery. A dozen Allen County trucks were equipped with snow plows to clear housing debris, trees, and mud from highways.

Farm families assisted each other in collecting scattered belongings, repairing homes, and gathering livestock. Cattle, hogs, and horses found wandering in fields and along roads were collected in barns to await their owners. High school and college students volunteered their time to assist neighbors. Five hundred students of Ohio Northern University were dismissed from classes Tuesday and Wednesday to help clean up the farms of Allen County. Hundreds of high school students in Bluffton and other towns were also dismissed for a day to help their communities recover from the disaster.

Affected areas in Ohio were quickly declared disaster areas, and national attention focused on the damage in Ohio, Indiana, and Illinois. Ohio Governor James Rhodes spent thirteen hours Monday touring the damaged areas of northern Ohio. President Lyndon Johnson toured tornado and flood damage across the Midwest, stopping at Toledo Wednesday afternoon. President Johnson spoke to about twenty-five hundred people at Toledo Airport and then toured the destruction of the Fuller Creekside addition.

23 April 1968
Ohio River Tornadoes

Two long-path violent tornadoes crossed the Ohio River from Kentucky and two others formed within Ohio on the stormy afternoon of Tuesday, 23 April 1968. The first crossed the Ohio River between Ripley and Levanna at about 2:15 P.M. and continued through Brown, Adams, and northern Scioto Counties. This tornado caused massive destruction to Falmouth and Dover, Kentucky. In the Ripley area, one person died, thirty homes were damaged, and forty barns were destroyed (Grazulis 1990). Many Civil War-era homes were damaged at Ripley, and the U.S. Shoe Plant and Independent Tobacco Warehouse sustained heavy damage. To the northeast, seventeen barns were destroyed near Decatur and twenty-five homes and barns damaged in Adams County. In addition, golfball-sized hail and three inches of rain pelted Ripley.

As the Ripley tornado was crossing the Ohio River, another tornado touched down six miles west of Batavia in Clermont County on a twenty-five-mile path to near Midland in Clinton County. It destroyed several homes as it passed east of Perintown toward Newtonsville. When the tornado passed east of Newtonsville, it was a violent storm with a damage path three thousand feet wide and winds estimated at over 200 mph. It was responsible for the death of one boy and damage to thirty homes (Grazulis 1990).

A tornado touched down south of Minford, Scioto County, at 3:30 P.M. Its five-mile path took it across the Scioto County Airport, where five planes were destroyed and another seven damaged. Several buildings were damaged and one man seriously injured in a collapsed concrete block barn. Golfball-sized hail covered the ground along this path.

The next tornado crossed into Ohio at 4:00 P.M. near Wheelersburg, a Scioto County community of seven thousand. Seven people were killed along its path. This violent storm immediately hit a commercial district and crossed a railroad and highways. It hit Reinhardt Transfer Company and Boll's Farm Supply, blew eleven cars of a freight train off the Norfolk and Western tracks, and rolled several cars on Route 52. Boll's Farm Supply building collapsed and two employees were killed. Eight people in Reinhardt Transfer escaped serious injury in that collapsed building. Rockwell Greenhouse was destroyed and the roof was removed from William Furniture.

After crossing Route 52 and tossing cars and the train, the tornado ascended a hill and wrecked the old Wheelersburg Cemetery. Four persons were killed in destroyed homes near Wheelersburg.

The tornado then tore across the rugged terrain of eastern Scioto County, northern Lawrence County, and into Gallia County, finally ending near Gallipolis. Ridge tops and valleys alike showed damage along the path. Dogwood Ridge, four miles east of Wheelersburg, was especially hard hit, and one person was killed. Damage also occurred at Sunshine, Flat Hollow, Little White, Oak, East Tygart, and Siloam Bottoms. The Sunshine Elementary School sustained heavy damage. Damage occurred to eight homes, six mobile homes, and four farm buildings along Chillicothe and McCormick Roads in the Gallipolis area (Grazulis 1990). Fifteen buildings were damaged at the Gallipolis State Institute.

In the aftermath of the storm, a medical team from Scioto Memorial Hospital set up an emergency treatment facility in the basement of Wheelersburg Methodist Church. Ninety-two people were injured by the tornado and thirteen remained hospitalized two days later. The Scioto County Engineer reported on 27 April that 97 structures were destroyed in Porter Township, including 69 homes and 28 barns, stores, or other buildings. A total of 476 buildings had some damage in Porter Township. Governor James Rhodes visited the region Tuesday night and sent one hundred Ohio National Guardsmen to prevent looting and control traffic.

Severe weather swept other parts of Ohio also, with high winds, hail, heavy rain, and power failures. A tornado damaged several farms and a school along a seven-mile path in Licking County, and a small tornado damaged a barn and power lines in Fulton County. Strong straight-line winds damaged homes, barns, businesses, and power lines in several counties.

8 May 1969
Tappan Lake Tornado

At about 8:30 P.M. on 8 May 1969 a tornado touched down on the west side of Tappan Lake (Harrison County). Initial damage was limited to treetops, but greater destruction from this strong (F3) storm occurred after it crossed the lake. Three brick and frame homes were destroyed, as were several cottages and mobile homes. Twenty-one persons were injured and one died. The tornado's total path was about two miles long.

Another tornado near Dayton earlier on 8 May destroyed thirteen homes and caused major damage to another sixty-three. An apartment complex sustained major damage. Its three-mile path from Kettering to Beavercreek caused $3 million damage and injured twenty-eight people. Less damaging tornadoes also occurred in Monroe and Marion Counties on 8 May.

Severe weather returned to Ohio on 10 May with tornadoes in Butler, Marion, and Stark Counties. The Butler County tornado crossed the county from Okeana to Monroe on its skipping thirty-five-mile path. It first touched down near Okeana at 4:10 P.M. Later touchdowns occurred in the south end of Hamilton at 4:25 P.M. and along a ten-mile continuous path in the eastern portion of Butler County. Damage amounted to $1 million, and twenty-six persons were injured in this 10 May tornado.

Golfball-sized hail accompanied the tornado in Hamilton and some wind damage continued across Warren and Clinton Counties east of the tornado track.

9 August 1969
Cincinnati Tornado

Cincinnati residents had been on alert for severe weather on Saturday afternoon and evening, 9 August 1969. National Weather Service radar had tracked a large severe thunderstorm across Indiana, and a tornado watch was issued for southwestern Ohio at 4:00 P.M.

As severe weather swept into Hamilton County, a deadly tornado touched down about 7:15 P.M. on Galbraith Road in the northern suburb of Hartwell. It ripped a seven-mile skipping path eastward across Interstate 75 into Arlington Heights, Deer Park, Madeira, Silverton, and Milford. From there it continued another fifteen miles across Clermont County with less damage.

Most of the destruction was concentrated along Galbraith Road and for a block or two on either side of Galbraith. The *Cincinnati Enquirer* reported a caboose was blown from a train into a field at Galbraith and Vine. A mother and two sons were killed in a collapsed apartment building.

A Hartwell shopping center was damaged at Vine and Compton, and a restaurant and other commercial buildings destroyed on Reading Road near Galbraith just east of Interstate 75. A motorist died when her car was demolished by the tornado. Mobile homes were toppled at the Arlington Trailer Park on Elliot Avenue, and 15 homes were severely damaged at Elliot and Olden Avenues. Meier's Wine Cellars in Silverton had minor damage. The tornado struck the St. Gertrude's Festival on Miami Road in Madeira. The *Cincinnati Enquirer* reported 31 booths and 2 large tents collapsed onto 250 people, injuring 30 and sending 3 to hospitals. More than 2,500 buildings were damaged and 27 homes destroyed along the path, leaving 1,500 people temporarily homeless. In addition to the 4 deaths, about 250 people were injured, 42 of them admitted to hospitals.

Cleanup began immediately Saturday night, involving police, fire, and utility crews and hundreds of volunteers. Governor James Rhodes ordered seven hundred Ohio National Guardsmen to assist the cleanup and maintain order. The governor toured the area Monday and most of the National Guard troops were withdrawn Tuesday. Streets clogged with debris and hundreds of sightseers hampered the cleanup Sunday. Many roads were closed until Sunday evening, including the Galbraith exit from Interstate 75, and electricity was not restored to all areas until Monday.

10 May 1973
Willard Tornado

Tornadoes have a reputation for seeking out mobile home parks, which are so vulnerable to destruction in strong winds. Only 9 percent of Ohio tornado fatalities since 1950 were in mobile homes (Schmidlin 1993b), but the Willard Tornado and others on 10 May 1973 fit the stereotype of the mobile home-seeking twister.

The Willard Tornado began its fifty-mile path just north of Fostoria and moved eastward passing just north of Tiffin and south of Republic (Grazulis 1990). Homes and farms were damaged along this path. As it crossed Route 19, a car was lifted from the road and carried several hundred yards. The driver died of multiple injuries. The tornado continued on, passing just north of Attica and into Willard at 6:00 P.M. Its path through Willard was along Route 224 on the southern edge of town.

On a path that varied from one hundred to two hundred yards wide, the tornado destroyed three mobile home parks, two car dealerships, and the Triangle Motel in Willard. It missed Willard High School and Junior High School by just one block. Sales receipts, work orders, and other papers from the Merkle Ford dealer were found more than fifty miles to the east in Akron.

The greatest damage occurred at the Briarwood Estates, Coble Village, and Willard mobile home parks. About 160 mobile homes were destroyed among 190 homes in the three parks, leaving more than three hundred persons homeless. Most residents could only gather an armload of their belongings from the ruins. The *Akron Beacon Journal* reported most of the homeless found shelter with friends and relatives and only eleven of the homeless were at Red Cross shelters.

Four persons died in the destroyed mobile homes and dozens were injured. Willard Area Hospital admitted twenty-three injured persons and transferred five to Norwalk and two to Mansfield hospitals. Another one hundred persons were treated for injuries at Willard Area Hospital, where a power failure required emergency power for forty-five minutes. Ohio National Guard troops based at the Junior High School distributed passes to residents for admittance into the damaged area.

Other tornado damage occurred at Bellville, where seven houses were flattened in a 7:15 P.M. storm. A three-block area centered at Bell and South Main was hardest hit. Eleven persons were treated at Mansfield General Hospital, and three others admitted for their injuries. The *Mansfield News Journal* reported that chickens were found embedded in telephone poles at Bellville. The Bellville Tornado continued east along Route 97 and damaged thirty homes at the Clear Fork Mobile Home Park.

A tornado at Kenton injured twelve at a mobile home park at about 6:30 P.M. and cut power to much of Hardin County. A furniture store was destroyed when a double-wide mobile home was lifted and thrown into the store. Trees were blown into houses and roofs blown away.

Another tornado skipped along a twenty-five-mile path in northern Ashland and Wayne Counties, damaging several houses and ten mobile homes in Savannah. Additional damage occurred along the path at West Salem and near Rittman. Yet another tornado skipped for fifty miles from near Springfield to the south edge of Columbus, where fourteen homes were destroyed and more than eighty damaged (Grazulis 1990).

3 April 1974
Xenia Tornado

The Xenia Tornado was a benchmark weather event for Ohioans. "Xenia" became a word synonymous with tornado destruction, not only in Ohio, but nationally. Not since the Lorain Tornado fifty years earlier had so many been killed by one tornado and an Ohio city so devastated as Xenia in 1974.

The tornado "superoutbreak" of 3–4 April 1974 resulted in 148 tornadoes in 13 states. Across the United States, 315 people were killed, more than 6,000 were injured, and 27,000 families suffered property losses (NOAA 1974). The Xenia Tornado caused the most deaths and damage of all tornadoes in the superoutbreak. In Ohio, twelve tornadoes touched down late on 3 April 1974 (Grazulis 1990) killing 36 people. The American Red Cross reported 2,100 injured in Ohio and nearly 7,000 families suffering some losses (NOAA 1974). More than 4,300 homes and 639 businesses were destroyed or had major damage in Ohio.

Meteorologists at the National Severe Storms Forecast Center in Kansas City recognized the potential for severe weather early on 3 April 1974. Low pressure tracked from Kansas early in the day to northern Illinois that evening. Cold, dry air circulating around the west side of the low clashed with moist unstable tropical air over the Ohio Valley causing widespread severe weather. A "severe thunderstorm watch" was issued for much of southern Ohio at 9:30 A.M. through 3:00 P.M. on 3 April (NOAA 1974). Additional severe weather watches were issued through the afternoon and evening.

The first line of thunderstorms, a squall line, passed across Ohio during the early afternoon. Skies cleared behind these storms and allowed the air to warm in the afternoon sunshine. This created more unstable air, and when the second squall line approached southwestern Ohio at 4:00 P.M., thunderstorm tops were at sixty thousand feet, indicating huge severe storms. These were the thunderstorms that produced deadly tornadoes in Ohio.

Fig. 79. Neighborhoods were filled with debris after the tornado in Xenia on 3 April 1974. (Photograph courtesy of the American Red Cross)

Fig. 80. Residents searched for personal belongings in the rubble of their homes after the Xenia tornado of 3 April 1974. (Photograph courtesy of the American Red Cross)

Fig. 81. Aerial view of a residential area of Xenia destroyed by the tornado of 3 April 1974. (Photograph courtesy of the American Red Cross)

Xenia Tornado. The Xenia Tornado was the first and most destructive of the Ohio tornadoes on 3 April 1974. It touched down at 4:30 P.M. (eastern daylight time) near the intersection of Centerville and Waynesville Roads about nine miles southwest of Xenia. The tornado entered Xenia at 4:40 P.M., cutting a path through the city of twenty-seven thousand and continuing northeast through Wilberforce before ending north of South Charleston in Clark County, a path of thirty-two miles. The Xenia Tornado killed thirty-two persons from Xenia to Wilberforce. Other sources list different totals, some including individuals who died of causes other than the tornado.

Extensive damage occurred to the downtown and residential areas of Xenia. About half of the buildings in the city were damaged and three hundred homes destroyed (figs. 79 and 80). Much of the damage to homes occurred in the Windsor Park and Arrowhead subdivisions of southwestern Xenia, where the homes were mostly built on slabs without basements (fig. 81). Eleven persons were killed in these two subdivisions and many others seriously injured. After the tornado destroyed Simon Kenton School and passed through Cherry Grove Cemetery, it destroyed several older homes and killed five persons along Trumbull Street, according to the *Dayton Daily News.*

Ten persons were killed in commercial buildings near downtown Xenia. Five died when an A&W Root Beer stand was destroyed at 62 Dayton Avenue, a block north of Main Street. Twelve persons huddled inside the cement block building when they saw the tornado approach. The toll of five killed at the A&W was the largest number killed in one building by an Ohio tornado since a Wood County family of five perished in a farm home on 8 June 1953.

Six blocks along Detroit Street were devastated in downtown Xenia. Nine Xenia churches were destroyed, including St. Brigid's Catholic Church, a Xenia landmark for 123 years (Smith 1982). The roof blew from the Greene County Courthouse and most windows were broken. Roofs were also peeled from the Armory and Red Cross Building, the masonic lodge lost its top story, a wall blew out of the library, and debris filled the city streets. Much of the old Xenia Hotel was destroyed, but enough remained to protect the many persons who took shelter there. The tornado unroofed the Galloway Log House, a remnant of Xenia pioneers.

Kroehler Manufacturing, employing 250 persons on West Second Street, was destroyed. Some Kroehler semitrailers were found in a nearby bowling alley. There was also extensive damage at KSH Plastics, Landmark, Marmac Company, Polymer Dispersion, Kroger Grocery Store, and the Super Valu warehouse on Bellbrook Avenue. All that remained at the Mr. Donut Shop in North Allison was three stools sitting on the slab floor. A forty-seven-car freight train was passing through Xenia on the Penn Central tracks just as the tornado struck. Seven of the cars were blown off the tracks as the train crossed Main Street, blocking that road.

After the tornado crossed downtown Xenia, it passed less than one-quarter mile south of Greene Memorial Hospital and destroyed homes along Marshall and Louise Drives. Two persons were killed on Louise.

The tornado continued in a northeasterly direction, killing one motorist on Route 42 before hitting Wilberforce and Central State University. Wilberforce was struck directly by the tornado resulting in three more deaths and damaging most of the buildings at Central State University.

Many of those who died in the tornado at Xenia had taken proper shelter in basements of the older homes on Trumbull Street or in hallways or closets of homes without basements in Windsor Park and Arrowhead subdivisions. The fact that many died in spite of their correct actions is not surprising, nor does it diminish the value of shelter in basements, hallways, or closets. The Xenia Tornado was a rare violent storm, much stronger than most tornadoes, with winds that completely leveled well-built homes. Even a modern well-built home cannot provide safe shelter during such a violent tornado. Perhaps more surprising is the number of people who survived. Thousands of people heard the warnings or saw the

Fig. 82. Destruction of school buses and Xenia High School in the tornado of 3 April 1974. (Photograph courtesy of the Greene County Historical Society)

tornado coming and sought shelter. These actions saved hundreds of lives even in homes without basements.

Seven of twelve Xenia schools were destroyed or damaged but, fortunately, classes had dismissed about an hour earlier and none of the 8,310 students were injured in the schools (Riedel 1974). Xenia High School, at the site of the present Central Junior High, was demolished. Students rehearsing a play saw the tornado coming and took shelter in a hallway at the high school. The students and their teacher were buried in debris but survived. School buses were blown into the school and were found on the stage where the students had been standing moments earlier (Smith 1982) (fig. 82). Central Junior High School, then located across from the present YWCA, remained standing but was so badly damaged that it was rebuilt at the site of the destroyed high school. Xenia schools reopened Monday, 22 April, with students attending double shifts at the five remaining Xenia schools and attending Beaver Creek schools from 3:00 P.M. to 8:00 P.M.

The emergency response was rapid and generous. American Red Cross workers were assisting Xenia within an hour of the tornado, and twenty-four hundred persons were provided temporary shelter that night (Riedel

1974). Several hundred Ohio National Guard troops moved into Xenia for three weeks to assist in the rescue and cleanup. Two of the guardsmen, of the 178th Tactical Fighter Group, died four days after the tornado in a fire while guarding a furniture store.

The Greene County YMCA in Xenia was an important assistance center for the community. It was one of the few intact buildings left in Xenia. At the YMCA, the tornado victims were provided with temporary housing, bathing, and meals. It also became an important recreational facility for the children and others in the city after the disaster. Several state and federal agencies and relief agencies set up offices in the YMCA after the tornado. Radio station WGIC abandoned normal programming and commercial messages for several days to provide a communication link in Xenia. Air time was used to exchange information among family members, provide health and traffic updates, give information on insurance and relief agencies, and relay notices about utility repairs. Governor John Gilligan toured the area Wednesday evening and returned with President Richard Nixon for a two-hour visit on Monday, 8 April.

Greene Memorial Hospital was nearly struck by the tornado but escaped with a power outage and minor damage. In the hours after the tornado, hundreds of injured filled the rooms, hallways, and even administrative offices of the hospital. Off-duty doctors and nurses, some still dressed in sport clothes or pajamas, came to the hospital as soon as possible Wednesday evening. A convoy of four ambulances and four buses carrying seven doctors and forty-four Air Force corpsmen left Wright-Patterson Air Force Base for Xenia shortly after the tornado struck (Riedel 1974). Doctors, nurses, and medical equipment were taken from Dayton to Xenia by police cars when helicopters could not fly early in the evening. Several helicopters from Wright-Patterson were pressed into service delivering supplies and personnel as the weather cleared later that evening. The *Dayton Journal Herald* reported a Union 76 fuel tank truck outside Greene Memorial Hospital pumped gasoline into hospital generators and filled the tanks of ambulances arriving with the injured. Overall, thirteen hundred persons were treated at Greene Memorial Hospital and eighty-five were admitted for injuries. Many of the seriously injured from Xenia were taken to hospitals in Dayton, Springfield, or Wright-Patterson. More than one hundred doctors responded to a call for assistance at Miami Valley Hospital in Dayton.

McDonalds and Ponderosa restaurants handed out thousands of free meals late Wednesday and Thursday to the rescue workers in Xenia. Galliger's Supper Club remained open continuously for three weeks after the tornado, serving forty-five thousand free meals with employees volunteering their time (Riedel 1974). Truckloads of household merchandise came from Rike's Department Store and Lazarus in Columbus. Groups of Mennonites came from all over Ohio and asked at local churches to find who in the community needed their help. They spent thousands of hours cleaning up the debris and rebuilding homes. Generators, floodlights, bulldozers, and dump trucks arrived by convoy from Wright-Patterson. Local contractors quickly volunteered heavy equipment and workers to remove debris blocking roads and covering the injured. University of Dayton students traveled in carpools to donate blood at Wright-Patterson Air Force Base, where a blood donation center was established.

At Wilberforce, the new dining hall was leveled at Central State University and the campus bookstore was destroyed. Several other university buildings were severely damaged, including the library and President Lionel Newsom's home, which lost roofs. About twenty students were injured but none killed at the campus. Classes resumed at Central State University on 15 April. Wilberforce University, adjacent to Central State, was also struck causing the destruction of several buildings. Four miles to the east in Cedarville, the roof was peeled from Patterson Hall at Cedarville College but there were no injuries. There was little if any outside help at Central State University until area roads were cleared five hours after the tornado struck, according to the 5 April *Dayton Journal Herald*. In the absence of other help, university faculty and students organized their own rescue and relief teams.

The next in the family of tornadoes that included the Xenia Tornado touched down in southeastern Clark County about twenty minutes after Xenia was struck. Downtown London was heavily damaged, but no serious injuries were reported. The final tornado in this family touched down at 6:00 P.M., thirty miles to the northeast near New Albany, in northwestern Franklin County. It destroyed a home and three barns and damaged twenty other homes along a five-mile path.

The 1974 tornado was the second of three to strike Xenia in the twentieth century. The first was in 1933 and the third destroyed six homes in the Shawnee Village neighborhood on 25 April 1989. Ernie and Phyllis Hopper lost their house in the 1974 tornado and moved to northeastern Xenia, where their new home was destroyed by the 1989 tornado, according to the *Dayton Daily News*.

Cincinnati Tornadoes. As the Xenia Tornado was churning through Greene and Clark Counties, a tristate tornado touched down at 5:10 P.M. near Rising Sun, Indiana, and traveled across the Ohio River to Kentucky. It passed about four miles west of Greater Cincinnati Airport and then crossed the river again to enter Ohio at 5:45 P.M. This was the fourth of six tornadoes in a family that swept across 230 miles in three hours. Its 21-mile path crossed several steep hills before ending near Dent, west of Cincinnati.

This violent (F5) tornado was as strong as the Xenia Tornado and swept homes away in the Nieman Estate neighborhood of Saylor Park (NOAA 1974; Grazulis 1990). It killed two persons and injured about 200 in Ohio. The wail of 125 tornado warning sirens covering 70 percent of Hamilton County's population undoubtedly saved many lives (NOAA 1974).

The next in this tornado family set down in the Elmwood Place neighborhood along Interstate 75 northeast of downtown Cincinnati at 5:30 P.M. and traveled twenty miles to Mason in Warren County. The *Cincinnati Enquirer* reported this tornado took a skipping path, injuring thirty in Elmwood Place and damaging the town hall, then ripping roofs from apartments along Summit Avenue in Roselawn and damaging businesses along Reading Road.

Near the beginning of the track, a patient at Longview State Hospital (now Pauline Warfield Lewis Center) died when a portion of the wall from the fourth floor was blown onto him. One hundred homes were damaged or destroyed near Mason, mostly in the Sherman Terrace area south of Mason and east of Route 42. Thirty employees and customers in the Mason Thrift Store crowded into a cold storage locker as the tornado approached. This small, sturdy room protected its occupants from injury as the store was destroyed around them. Grazulis (1990) reported two people killed in a mobile home near Mason, but this was not reported in *Storm Data* or newspapers. A death near Withrow High School in Hyde Park was caused by microburst winds, rather than the tornado.

The final tornado in this family touched down at 6:00 P.M. and traveled ten miles from Lebanon to Pekin, destroying barns and mobile homes and damaging several homes. Nine people were injured (Grazulis 1990). A day after these tornadoes ripped through Cincinnati, the Cincinnati Reds opened the 1974 baseball season hosting the Atlanta Braves. Henry Aaron hit his 714th career home run in his first at-bat to tie Babe Ruth's record.

Other Ohio Tornadoes of 3 April 1974. A tornado in Adams County traveled sixteen miles from west of West Union to just east of Peebles beginning at about 8:05 P.M. (Grazulis 1990). Five houses and several farm buildings were destroyed and one person was killed. Weak tornadoes touched down in southern Brown County and Pickaway County.

Three strong tornadoes struck Paulding County between 7:45 P.M. and 9:00 P.M. The first destroyed a house, some garages, and two barns on a ten-mile path from south of Oakwood to a mile northwest of Continental. The second touched down an hour later southwest of Melrose and lifted off north of Oakwood. It destroyed five mobile homes on its eight-mile path. As this tornado ended, another touched down on a seven-mile track between Payne and Paulding. A home and two barns were destroyed. The three Paulding County tornadoes had the potential for great damage but, fortunately, did not strike populated areas and injured only one person.

30 June 1977
Fremont Tornado

A stormy night in north-central Ohio resulted in several strong tornadoes in 1977. The first and most damaging of the storms struck Fremont on 30 June at 7:20 P.M. Its damage path nearly one-half mile wide struck residential and downtown sections of Fremont, causing about $4 million damage. Twenty-seven homes were heavily damaged and eighteen persons injured.

Downtown businesses were battered by tornado winds with roofing, bricks, signs, and other debris littering State Street after the storm. The steeple of the Presbyterian Church across from the Sandusky County courthouse fell into the street.

Disaster was averted when the tornado struck the Sandusky County Nursing Home at Fremont. The *Sandusky Register* reported the roof was blown away, windows broken, and brick facing torn from the walls, but none of the 136 residents were injured. After the storm passed, residents were evacuated to other nearby nursing homes.

The Fremont Tornado ended just east of the city, but the storm continued to the northeast, striking the Cedar Point Amusement Park with a small tornado about one-half hour later. The Frontier Town train depot was demolished and Camper Village hit, damaging fifteen vehicles and injuring nine persons, according to the *Sandusky Register*. All rides had been shut down before the storm struck.

Other damage occurred later that evening in separate tornadoes. Two homes were destroyed a mile north of Bellevue, a farm complex was destroyed south of Greenwich, several homes were blown down east of Bucyrus, and a house was demolished west of Shelby in Richland County (Grazulis 1990).

13 June 1981
Cardington Tornado

With unfortunate precision, a tornado that might have passed almost unnoticed through rural Ohio struck right through the center of Cardington in Morrow County on 13 June 1981. The entire nine-block business district was damaged. Four persons were killed and fifty-six injured.

The four-mile path began at 3:23 P.M. Saturday southwest of Cardington, where apartments, homes, and industries were torn apart. The tornado then entered the Cardington business district, passing just south of the intersection of Route 529 and Main Street, and followed Route 42 out of town to the northeast.

About half of the thirty-two units in the Carding Mills apartments were demolished, according to the 18 June 1981 *Morrow County Sentinel.* Four people died, fifty-four persons were taken to Morrow County Hospital in Mt. Gilead, and several others were transported to nearby hospitals. The *Morrow County Sentinel* reported ten people were admitted to hospitals for their injuries.

About 100 of the 620 homes in Cardington were destroyed or heavily damaged. Fifty businesses were destroyed, including Carl Funeral Home. The historic Wornstaff Hotel was heavily damaged. Cardington's Police Station was smashed, and all three Cardington fire trucks were crushed under the roof of the fire station. Downtown buildings lost their second and third floors. Cranes were busy Sunday removing upper portions of damaged buildings along Main Street to prevent further collapse and damage.

Cardington's largest employer, Stahl Truck Body plant, sustained heavy damage, and there were initial fears of major job losses. However, Stahl called their sixty employees to work Monday morning to assist in the cleanup and repair and expected to be in full production ten days later.

National Guard troops arrived in Cardington Saturday evening to assist in cleanup and rescue operations. Governor James Rhodes also arrived Saturday evening to inspect the damage and to plea for state and federal aid. Relief in the form of labor, money, clothing, and food arrived quickly from the Salvation Army, Red Cross, and churches of central Ohio. Residents of Xenia, remembering the generosity of Ohioans following their tornado disaster seven years earlier, responded with aid for the victims in Cardington.

Elsewhere in Ohio on this stormy Saturday, heavy rains associated with severe thunderstorms caused flooding in northwestern and north-central counties, drowning one man along the Vermilion River. High winds destroyed a street festival in Versailles and damaged buildings in Columbus. Two men were killed by lightning in Ohio, and other tornadoes touched down in Montgomery, Muskingum, and Perry Counties.

2 May 1983
Weston and Broadview Heights Tornadoes

Severe weather pounded northern Ohio from noon until 6:00 P.M. Monday afternoon, 2 May 1983, with damaging winds, heavy rain, and hail.

Fig. 83. The Weston tornado as it passed near Patrick Henry High School in Henry County on 2 May 1983. R.E. Bowman of Hamler took this photograph as he chased the tornado for several miles.

Most of the damage was at Weston, in Wood County, and at Broadview Heights in suburban Cleveland, where tornadoes touched down in populated areas and killed two persons.

The Weston Tornado was first sighted near Patrick Henry High School, on Route 18 east of Hamler in Henry County (fig. 83). It did little damage until the end of its twenty-mile path, when it struck Weston before crossing Route 6 west of Bowling Green. Two mobile home parks on the north side of Weston were demolished shortly after 1:00 P.M. Fifty-six mobile homes were destroyed and twenty-five damaged in Lawndale Mobile Home Plaza and Locust Lane Court. Witnesses reported the homes were lifted and rolled "through the park like a giant tumbleweed." One man died in his mobile home and fifteen others were injured at Weston. A helicopter from St. Vincent Hospital in Toledo arrived at Weston soon after the tornado to assist in evacuation of the injured. The *Toledo Blade* reported Ohio National Guard troops were on duty in Weston overnight and Governor Richard Celeste toured the damage Tuesday morning.

Storms continued eastward through Monday afternoon causing wind damage near Northwood, Huron, Greenwich, Norwalk, Findlay, and Put-in-Bay. Classes were dismissed at the Mount Blanchard Elementary School south of Findlay after winds and hail shattered two hundred windows. Cars were damaged by hail on the Ohio Turnpike in Lorain County.

Another tornado skipped twelve miles across Broadview Heights, Bedford Heights, Walton Hills, and Solon in Cuyahoga County at about 5:00 P.M. Twenty-five homes were destroyed and about one hundred damaged. One woman died in the destruction of her home in Broadview Heights. Another twenty-five people were injured. A portion of one home landed near Interstate 77, one-eighth mile away. One car was flipped over as the tornado crossed Interstate 77, and a truck driver was injured when debris crashed through his windshield. Continuing to the northeast, the tornado destroyed two commercial buildings on Krick Road in Walton Hills and damaged the roof and walls of the AAV Company in Solon.

31 May 1985
Northeastern Tornadoes

An extraordinary outbreak of forty-one tornadoes, including fourteen killer tornadoes, struck northeastern Ohio, western Pennsylvania, and southern Ontario on Friday, 31 May 1985. This region, far northeast of America's "tornado alley," had never experienced such a large outbreak of tornadoes. Seventy-five deaths in the United States made this the deadliest tornado outbreak nationally since 1974. With eleven dead in Trumbull County, this was also Ohio's deadliest tornado outbreak since the Xenia Tornado of 1974.

Ohioans had been put on notice all day of the possibility of severe weather. National Weather Service forecasts issued at 4:00 A.M., more than twelve hours before the tornadoes, included a flash flood watch and a statement that severe thunderstorms were possible in northeastern Ohio later in the day (NOAA 1985). Updated forecasts issued at 11:00 A.M. repeated the possibility of severe weather, and at 4:25 P.M., two hours before the first killer tornado in Ohio, the National Severe Storms Forecast Center issued a tornado watch for eastern Ohio and western Pennsylvania to become effective at 5:00 P.M.

In spite of all-day forecasts for severe weather, there was little if any warning for the tornadoes that actually touched down in Ohio. The repeated forecasts for severe weather seemed out of touch with reality. Sunny skies and fair weather prevailed most of the day, and even National Weather Service forecasters were puzzled by the lack of thunderstorms over Ohio Friday afternoon (NOAA 1985). The public seemed to assume fair weather through the afternoon meant severe storms were not going to develop.

However, National Weather Service forecasters had correctly identified conditions that would lead to "a significant severe weather episode" twelve hours in advance (NOAA 1985). Thunderstorms developed near Cleveland just before 4:00 P.M. and grew explosively, pulled upward ten miles by a 140-mph jet stream over northeastern Ohio. The next three hours would provide the most tornadoes ever experienced in one day in northeastern Ohio.

The first severe weather was identified on the National Weather Service radar at Cleveland and was given to the public as a "severe thunderstorm warning" for Ashtabula County at 4:10 P.M. Hail and 60-mph winds hit the region thirty minutes later. The first tornado touched down at 5:00 P.M. in Ashtabula County near Monroe Center just two miles from the Pennsylvania border. It damaged ten mobile homes in Ohio before it entered Pennsylvania and killed twelve persons in Albion and Cranesville (Grazulis 1990). Two more tornadoes developed in this tornado family during the next hour across western Pennsylvania and New York.

A severe thunderstorm warning issued at 4:45 P.M. for Trumbull County preceded the next tornado. It struck at 5:05 P.M. along a fifteen-mile track in Trumbull and Ashtabula Counties from Mesopotamia to Orwell. Forty homes were destroyed and at least thirty people injured. As the tornado lifted near Orwell, the next member of this tornado family touched down just a few hundred yards inside Ohio east of Kinsman and traveled fifty-six miles to Tionesta, Pennsylvania, where it killed sixteen people.

A fourth Ohio tornado touched down at 5:30 P.M. just north of Dorset and traveled ten miles across Ashtabula County, ending southeast of Pierpont. Several homes and farms were damaged and about fifteen persons were injured. Electric and telephone communication were cut all along the path. Four more tornadoes occurred in this family during the next hour in western Pennsylvania.

The most famous Ohio tornado of this outbreak touched down in Portage County at about 6:30 P.M. and cut a forty-seven-mile path through Newton Falls, Niles, and Hubbard before entering Pennsylvania. It was an F5 "maxitornado," with winds along a portion of the path estimated at more than 250 mph, and became the deadliest Ohio tornado in eleven years. This was the only F5 tornado in the United States during 1985.

This extraordinary tornado touched down in the Ravenna Arsenal, a wooded military storage facility, but caused little damage except to trees. A few miles to the east, the tornado entered populated areas of Trumbull County and took a path through the middle of Newton Falls, a community of five thousand people.

Years of tornado preparedness paid off in Newton Falls. A tornado warning siren system was in place and the Newton Falls Police and Fire Departments and the Public Safety Reserve, a volunteer organization, had instructed residents how to react if they heard the sirens. Members of the

Public Safety Reserve, trained by the National Weather Service, watched the sky from the top of City Hall to act as storm spotters for the community whenever a severe weather watch was in effect.

When the tornado watch was issued for eastern Ohio at 5:00 P.M., police captain Clayton Reakes climbed to the top of the Public Safety Building to watch for approaching severe weather (Witten 1985). Captain Reakes spotted the tornado headed for Newton Falls at 6:38 P.M. and, using a walkie-talkie, radioed for the sirens to be turned on. Sirens wailed a warning to residents of Newton Falls for about sixty seconds before the tornado struck.

The *Youngstown Vindicator* reported about four hundred homes destroyed or severely damaged in Newton Falls, but there were no deaths, a testament to efficient tornado preparedness and warning. After hitting a residential district along West Broad, the tornado caused damage along Broad and Canal Streets in Newton Falls' historic downtown. The school and post office were damaged and a service station and drug store destroyed. Homes along Warren, Ophelia, and Columbia Avenues were then destroyed as the tornado headed toward Lordstown. About one hundred people at a wedding in the fellowship hall of First Church of God on Broad Street escaped injury when the tornado ripped a thirty-five-foot wide hole in the sanctuary roof. Down the road, the First Congregational Church was damaged by the tornado then burned early the next day. Bulldozers were brought in to clear streets and a medical triage area was set up in front of the bank at Broad and Canal. To the east, one woman was killed on South Leavitt and ten homes were destroyed along Layer, Palmyra, Tait, and Highland Roads on the north side of Lordstown.

The greatest destruction occurred as this tornado passed through Niles. It moved into the northern sections of Niles wrecking the Ashland Oil and Refining Terminal along Niles Road. The tornado then passed to Woodglen and St. John Avenues, Susan Court, and the Cynthia development before passing over Niles Union Cemetery on Vienna Road. Trees were flattened in the cemetery and a concrete crypt ripped open. Contrary to initial reports, the crypt held no bodies. Across from the cemetery on Niles-Cortland Road (Route 46), a convenience store, auto repair shop, and Niles Monument Company were flattened. One person died on Cynthia Avenue and another in the convenience store.

The tornado then demolished several homes in the Shadow Ridge neighborhood and crossed Youngstown-Warren Road (Route 422), where it destroyed the Niles Park Plaza, the Top of the Strip roller skating rink, and a 100-bed nursing home scheduled to open the next week. Seven deaths occurred in this region. Much greater tragedies were averted by the timing of the huge tornado. The skating rink was nearly empty but would have held 150 to 200 young skaters an hour later. Eastwood Mall, just one-half mile from the destruction, was not seriously damaged. Niles fire lieutenant John Hughes reported in the 2 June *Youngstown Vindicator* that 62 homes and 21 apartment units were destroyed and 110 other homes and 61 apartments were damaged.

From Niles, the tornado continued east through northern Hubbard Township and into Pennsylvania. Two persons were killed and about eighty homes were damaged in the area of Chestnut Ridge, Thomas, and Masury Roads.

Six other tornadoes touched down in Ohio between 7:00 P.M. and 9:00 P.M. Friday, with the storm activity shifting into central Ohio. A strong tornado traveled a twenty-nine-mile path beginning at 7:15 P.M. across northern Licking County into Coshocton County before ending near West Carlisle. Several homes were destroyed, twenty people injured, and one man died in a destroyed house. A second tornado struck the same area at 8:00 P.M., causing a few injuries. Another strong tornado destroyed several homes and farms and injured twenty people along a fifteen-mile path from near Salem to New Waterford in Columbiana County. Small tornadoes caused minor damage west of London in Madison County, near East Sparta in Stark County, and along Ohio Brush Creek in Adams County.

10 March 1986
Late Winter Tornadoes

Tornado Safety Week was coming later in the month, but the atmosphere threw an early dose of spring storms across Ohio this Monday afternoon of 10 March 1986.

A line of severe thunderstorms entered western Ohio about 4:00 P.M. and swept across the state by 8:00 P.M. About half of Ohio's eighty-eight counties reported severe weather: strong winds, hail, or tornadoes. Winds measured at 60 to 70 mph destroyed barns, sheds, mobile homes, and vehicles, took the roofs from several homes, and downed thousands of trees. A wind gust of 106 mph was measured at the Marion Airport at 5:30 P.M. Air traffic controllers at Greater Cincinnati Airport in Kentucky took refuge in an auxiliary tower after windows were blown out of the main control tower.

Tornadoes caused extensive damage and killed three persons, all in mobile homes. Ten people were injured in Wilmington, where two homes were destroyed and six others badly damaged by a tornado. Thirty mobile homes were blown over. Another tornado touched down in Fayette County and ended near Derby in Pickaway County. One man died in a destroyed mobile home near Washington Court House and ten others were injured in the destruction of a frame home, ten mobile homes, and five farm buildings.

In Brown County, the east side of Ripley was badly damaged by a tornado. No injuries occurred but two tobacco warehouses were destroyed and a restaurant, the high school, and many homes were badly damaged. To the north in Huron County, a six-mile tornado track ended near Olena, on Route 250 south of Norwalk. Six frame homes and three mobile homes were destroyed along the path and one person was killed.

Just before 8:00 P.M. a final tornado touched down south of Norwich and crossed Interstate 70 before ending at New Concord. A woman died in a mobile home south of Norwich and one other home was destroyed. Two persons were injured on the Muskingum College campus. Other tornadoes unroofed apartments in Butler County, damaged one hundred homes in Mercer County, destroyed a barn in Hardin County, and unroofed a home in Crawford County.

2 June 1990
Harrison/Fairfield Tornado

The third largest tornado outbreak in United States history hit nine midwestern states from the early afternoon until past midnight on Saturday, 2 June 1990. A total of sixty-six tornadoes killed 9 people and injured 244 nationally (Grazulis 1993). Most of the tornadoes occurred in southern Illinois and Indiana, but this outbreak ended in southwestern Ohio between 10:00 P.M. and 1:00 A.M.

A violent (F4) tornado from Indiana swept into Harrison, Ohio, at 11:13 P.M. and continued for twenty-five miles across northern Hamilton County into southeastern Butler County. There were no fatalities in this tornado, but about sixteen people were injured in Ohio. The tornado in Ohio destroyed fifty-one homes, five businesses, and four mobile homes. At least nine hundred homes, thirty-one businesses, twenty-two mobile homes, 5 apartments, and 3 schools were damaged (Grazulis 1993).

The tornado entered Harrison near the bridge on South State Street, as reported by the *Cincinnati Enquirer,* and traced a path across the city to the Harrison Airport. More than three hundred homes in the Whitewater Meadows subdivision at Harrison sustained damage and some were leveled to the ground. Two hangers collapsed at the airport and eleven small airplanes were destroyed. A 75-foot-tall sign supported by 18-inch-wide, 5/8-inch-thick steel I beams was bent over to the ground at the Waffle House restaurant in Harrison. The June 1990 issue of *Storm Data* reported the sign was engineered to withstand 250-mph straight-line winds. Miraculously, there were only five minor injuries at Harrison.

Harrison High School graduation ceremonies were held as scheduled on 5 June, but were moved from the debris-filled stadium to the school auditorium. Families whose homes were swept away had to borrow clothes to attend the emotional ceremonies.

The tornado's path continued east, passing less than one mile south of the uranium processing plant at Fernald. In Colerain Township, nine homes were heavily damaged on Cranbrook Drive and four were unroofed. Pleasant Run Middle School lost part of its roof and five stores were demolished at the Pleasant Run Shopping Center at the corner of Kemper and Hamilton Roads. More damage occurred on Broadbent Road and Galloway Court in Pleasant Run.

Seventy-seven homes, five apartments, and twenty-six mobile homes were destroyed or damaged in southern sections of Fairfield and to the east in Union Township. Seven of the destroyed trailers were in the Port Union Trailer Court on Route 747. The tornado crossed Interstate 75 at Tylersville Road, where a Knights Inn motel and two restaurants were damaged. The final damage was in Warren County west of Mason.

The absence of deaths and low number of injuries is amazing for a violent tornado through populated areas. Much of the credit for the low number of casualties can be given to the tornado warning siren system in Hamilton County and in Fairfield. The *Cincinnati Enquirer* reported sirens began blowing in Hamilton County at 11:14 P.M. as the tornado entered Harrison, giving persons to the east in Colerain Township several minutes to take shelter. The 157 Hamilton County sirens were installed in the 1960s, according to the *Cincinnati Enquirer,* and the Fairfield sirens were installed after the 1974 Xenia Tornado. Each siren can be heard for about one mile.

Another tornado touched down just before 2:00 A.M. that night in southern Clermont County, where three mobile homes and several barns were destroyed. There were no injuries.

27 March 1991
Nettle Lake Tornado

Several tornadoes in Michigan, Illinois, Indiana, and Wisconsin caused millions of dollars damage and killed two persons on Wednesday, 27 March 1991. One of those touched down in northeastern Indiana and crossed the northwest corner of Ohio on a twenty-one-mile path that ended just across the state line in Michigan (Grazulis 1993).

The tornado entered Ohio near Columbia, crossed Route 49, and struck the residential and vacation community at the south end of Nettle Lake at 8:30 P.M. Several barns and hundreds of trees were blown down on the six-mile-long skipping path in Ohio. The damage path was about two hundred yards wide. Route 49 was closed by a barn that was blown onto the highway, and two persons were injured when their car was blown from the roadway and overturned.

Homes and cottages at Nettle Lake sustained extensive damage. An Ohio Emergency Management Agency summary in the 30 March *Toledo Blade* showed twenty frame homes destroyed, twenty-four frame homes with heavy damage, and eighty-eight homes with minor damage. Sixteen mobile homes were destroyed and thirty-two damaged. Century-old Nettle Lake United Brethren Church was "swept away," the pulpit and piano found in a nearby field. Shady Shores Campground was also destroyed. Damage in Ohio totaled $12 million.

Many homes at Nettle Lake were summer cottages and unoccupied in late March. Similar damage on a crowded summer weekend could have been tragic. Still, there were sixteen people injured at Nettle Lake, none seriously. According to the *Toledo Blade,* the National Weather Service at Fort Wayne had issued a severe thunderstorm warning for Williams County but the area was not under a tornado warning when the storm struck.

Volunteers from the tristate area converged on Nettle Lake soon after the storm struck with chain saws, bulldozers, and front-end loaders to remove debris and clear roads. By 2:00 A.M. all roads were opened in the area. Williams County commissioners declared a state of emergency Thursday morning as a first step in acquiring state and federal aid.

18 February 1992
Violent Winter Tornado

The outstanding tornado year of 1992 started early, with three February tornadoes. A weak tornado at 2:30 P.M. on 15 February destroyed a mobile home and some barns on a path 70 feet wide and .3 mile long near Alger in Hardin County. Three days later a rare violent (F4) winter tornado churned along a path 200 feet wide and 2.8 miles long in Van Wert County. Moments later another tornado touched down briefly in an open field on Landeck Road south of Delphos in Allen County.

The violent tornado touched down at 6:10 P.M. on Tuesday, 18 February about one-half mile west of Route 127 in Van Wert County, just north of the Mercer County line. The family living in the first house struck by this tornado were two-time victims. Their previous house, one and one-half miles away, had been destroyed in the 1965 Palm Sunday Tornado.

Four houses were destroyed by the tornado. One was completely leveled, indicating winds of more than 200 mph and justifying the "violent" rating. A metal bed frame was embedded in a tree next to the leveled house. There were also pieces of glass, blades of grass, and wire embedded in trees. A mobile home was destroyed, and two cars parked next to the mobile home were lifted and thrown seventy-five yards into a field. Six other homes had severe damage. Six persons were treated for cuts and bruises at Van Wert Community Hospital.

The *Cleveland Plain Dealer* reported there was no warning of the storm either from citizens, police, or radar screens. The lack of severe injuries or deaths was fortunate, given the lack of warning and the violent nature of this winter tornado. Its occurrence was a reminder that devastating tornadoes may occur during any season in Ohio.

12 July 1992
Most Tornadoes in One Day

The twenty-eight tornadoes that occurred in Ohio on Sunday, 12 July 1992 went into the record books as the most recorded in a single day. They also contributed to the July 1992 record of forty-four tornadoes in one month and a record annual total of sixty-one (Crowther 1993). The average number of tornadoes for an entire year in Ohio is thirteen, and the previous annual record was forty-three tornadoes in 1973 (Schmidlin 1988).

Frequent tornadoes and heavy rains in Ohio during July 1992 were the result of a stationary weather front that lay across the state on several days. This front acted as a catalyst for thunderstorms. Fortunately, summer tornadoes tend to be weaker than spring storms and none of the forty-four Ohio tornadoes during July 1992 were violent. This contributed to the absence of fatalities and only thirty-six injuries.

A line of damage from several tornadoes on 12 July stretched across northwestern Ohio, from Pettisville in Fulton County, across Lucas, Wood, and Ottawa Counties, to Sandusky. A tornado hit west of Pettisville at about 5:00 P.M. and continued for two miles between County Roads 18 and 20. Twenty-four buildings were damaged, including an apartment complex, and eight persons were injured. Vehicles were flipped and the *Toledo Blade* reported a sheet of plywood was driven ten inches into a tree.

A tornado in Lucas County cut a swath from Whitehouse through Waterville Township to Dutch and River Roads north of Waterville and ended south of Perrysburg. About twelve homes had serious damage at Whitehouse. Anthony Wayne High School sustained major damage. The gymnasium roof was ripped away from the school as was the flat roof over classrooms. Walls of the cafeteria and some classrooms collapsed. Toledo Express Airport was closed for several hours Sunday evening as electricity went out and heavy rain, golfball-sized hail, 66-mph winds, and fog enveloped the facility.

Numerous homes were damaged after the tornado crossed the Maumee River, passed through Perrysburg Township, and lifted three miles south of Perrysburg. Near the Route 25 exit off Interstate 475, a wall collapsed at Smith Equipment Company and barns lost roofs or were blown down completely near Roachton Road. Another tornado destroyed two homes and injured five persons one mile south of Perrysburg.

Farther south in Wood County, a tractor-trailer was lifted from Interstate 75 near Bowling Green and dropped onto a minivan traveling to its left. It took rescuers more than an hour to remove the four occupants of the van, but only minor injuries resulted. A house and barn were blown down at the Islamic Center of Greater Toledo, a prominent landmark on the flat Wood County landscape. The mosque was not damaged, but a six-thousand-pound copper covered wooden dome stored behind the barn was found in a cornfield three miles away. Fallen utility poles and wires dangled over many Wood County roads.

One or possibly two tornadoes touched down in Ottawa County, the first cutting a swath along Hellwig Road in Clay Township just west of Genoa at 5:45 P.M. The *Toledo Blade* reported that trucks parked near the intersection of Hellwig Road and Route 51 were flipped over and homes and garages were destroyed.

To the east, a tornado swept across Elliston Cemetery, uprooting and snapping trees and breaking tombstones. The tornado then entered Graytown, where many homes were damaged, some losing roofs, siding, antennas, and trees. Another tornado damaged homes and injured three persons at Woodville and Lindsey in Sandusky County.

Heavy damage occurred in the vicinity of Route 250 and Route 2 in Perkins Township, south of Sandusky. At least ten homes were destroyed and another twenty-five heavily damaged. A motor home with six people was blown over on Route 250, and the Baywinds Athletic Club was left a mass of twisted steel. Perkins Township police chief Richard Burrows was processing three prisoners when the tornado blew doors off the police station. This region was crowded with tourists visiting Cedar Point, and several had more thrills than they expected from the visit. Guests at the Holiday Inn huddled under mattresses in a banquet room. Doors and signs were blown from the motel.

Elsewhere in western Ohio on 12 July tornadoes took the roof off a home two miles west of Napoleon, destroyed farm buildings at Wilshire, destroyed a barn and mobile home twelve miles northwest of Celina, took the roof from two buildings at Celina, destroyed several buildings east of St. Marys, and damaged buildings at Wapakoneta. A house and two cars were damaged at Marengo (Morrow County).

Farther east that evening, four tornadoes struck Lorain County. They destroyed eight houses and damaged several others at Lagrange, damaged homes and a high school at Amherst, and damaged homes at North Ridgeville. Five persons were injured in the county. In Cuyahoga County, a tornado over the NASA Lewis Research Center was visible from the control tower at Cleveland Hopkins Airport as it destroyed a mobile home, antennas, and trees. Several buildings were damaged in Portage County, including a Goodyear blimp hangar. Farm, tree, and utility line damage was caused by tornadoes near New London, Auburn Center, Brunswick, and Kent. Extensive damage was caused eight miles northwest of Medina, where thirty homes were destroyed and miles of utility lines were blown down. Four people were injured.

A tornado in Summit County passed through eight miles of industrial, commercial, and residential sections of Cuyahoga Falls and Stow. It touched down at about 9:30 P.M. along Bath Road and struck the Remington Industrial Park at State and Steels Corners Roads. The tornado caused more than a million dollars damage to industries and put several hundred people out of work. About one hundred vehicles were damaged or destroyed at a Ford dealership on State Road. The Northampton Center School on Bath Road, an 1875 one-room schoolhouse used as a museum, was destroyed, with only antique books, dishes, and clothing salvaged the next day. In the same area, the Northampton United Methodist Church lost its roof. Just to the east in Stow, the *Akron Beacon Journal* reported that about fifty homes were damaged and most of the city lost power. Stow streets were blocked by hundreds of fallen trees.

Eight more tornadoes struck on 13 July and four more were confirmed on 14 July, all with minor damage. The thunderstorms responsible for three days of tornadoes also caused extensive damage with straight-line winds over 60 mph, hail, and flooding. Several persons were injured by lightning, thousands of trees were blown down across the state, and there was widespread wind damage to homes and other buildings. About fifty thousand persons lost electric power in Cuyahoga County on 14 July.

22 November 1992
The Arcanum Tornado

The Arcanum Tornado and other severe weather on Sunday, 22 November capped a memorable year in Ohio tornado history. It brought the total number of tornadoes in Ohio to sixty-one during 1992 (Crowther 1993), exceeding the previous record of forty-three in 1973. While autumn and winter tornadoes have occurred in Ohio, the extent and severity of storms on 22 November made this an unusual event. This was the northern portion of an outbreak of violent tornadoes that killed 17 and injured 270 in Mississippi and Georgia the same day (Crowther 1993).

A variety of severe weather affected southern Ohio, but the most extensive damage was in Arcanum, a Darke County community of twenty-five hundred residents. Western Ohio had been placed under a tornado watch at 5:22 P.M. As storms approached from Indiana, a severe thunderstorm warning was issued for Preble County at 5:43 P.M. and for Darke County at 6:05 P.M.

The Arcanum Tornado touched down at 6:00 P.M. in Preble County near Campbellstown. It moved across northern Preble County north of West Manchester and into Darke County toward Arcanum. In Preble County the tornado destroyed several homes and businesses and a Monroe Township building on Kimmel Road. The *Dayton Daily News* reported three homes were demolished near the corner of Route 726 and Shurley Road and traffic was blocked by trucks blown over on Interstate 70. Eight persons received minor injuries in Preble County.

The tornado continued into Darke County, causing injuries near Ithaca and ripping into Arcanum at 6:28 P.M. At Arcanum, fifty-four homes suffered moderate to heavy damage, seventeen businesses had heavy damage, and fourteen vehicles were destroyed in the path five blocks wide. Trees and power lines were down through the village and appliances littered the streets. Aluminum siding was strewn through the remaining trees, and pink fiberglass insulation from the destroyed Carter Lumber Company littered the community. Another thirty buildings were heavily damaged along the path in rural areas of Darke County.

Farther east at 6:15 P.M., a small tornado destroyed two barns and several garages on a one-mile path just south of New Harmony in Brown County. It also caused severe damage to four mobile homes. There were no injuries. Golfball-sized hail damaged several cars in Hillsboro at 8:00 P.M. Hail and minor building damage occurred that evening in Shelby, Miami, and Montgomery Counties.

Although it did not enter Ohio, a rare violent (F4) November tornado was visible at about 5:00 P.M. from thirty miles away at the Greater Cincinnati Airport. It carved a twenty-two-mile-long path through Indiana and Kentucky southwest of the airport and lifted just fifteen miles from Cincinnati.

CHAPTER EIGHT

Hail and Other Outstanding Weather Events

HAIL FORMS IN thunderstorms through the accumulation of supercooled water droplets onto pellets of ice. Temperatures are far below freezing above eighteen thousand feet, even on the hottest summer days in Ohio, and large thunderstorms extend thirty thousand feet or more into the atmosphere, yielding abundant opportunities for hail.

Strong updrafts are required to sustain hailstones in the thunderstorm and allow the continued growth of ice. Examination of hailstones reveals concentric rings of ice accumulation with alternating clear and opaque layers. All thunderstorms contain hail, but most thunderstorms do not produce hail at the surface because small hail will melt in the lower portions of the cloud before they reach the surface.

Large hail will survive the trip from the frigid upper portions of a thunderstorm into Ohio's summer heat and pelt the surface. A thunderstorm may produce hail at the surface for several minutes, leaving a "hailstreak" one-half mile or more wide and several miles long. A slow-moving thunderstorm can produce hail for ten to twenty minutes at one location, covering the ground with ice and producing drifts of hail a foot deep.

Any location in Ohio may expect hail on about two days each year (Baldwin 1973), generally in spring and summer when thunderstorms are most numerous. Fortunately, most hail is small, perhaps pea-sized, and causes no damage except bruising of fruit or vegetable crops. Hail one inch or more in diameter can cause extensive damage. Cars and aluminum siding are dented, windows broken, awnings pierced, trees stripped of leaves, and crops battered. Animals have been killed by large hail in Ohio, and persons have sustained minor injuries when caught outside in a hailstorm.

The largest hailstone recorded in the United States fell in Kansas and was 5.5 inches in diameter and weighed 1.6 pounds (Ludlum 1982). Other examples of very large hailstones may actually be two or more stones that froze together in the cloud. Several cases of Ohio hailstones more than 3 inches in diameter are described in this chapter, along with other interesting and unusual Ohio weather events.

23 June 1882
Mystery Wave at the Cleveland Lakefront

Large waves arriving from a calm Lake Erie have hit the North Coast at least twice in recorded history, the first on 23 June 1882 and the second on 31 May 1942. Seven people were drowned by the 1942 wave, reported to be up to fifteen feet high along sixty miles of the coast from Bay Village to Geneva.

The 23 June 1882 *Cleveland Plain Dealer* reported that a "tidal wave" more than eight feet high "with the water back of the incline as high as the crest" came ashore at 6:20 A.M. "carrying before it everything movable and some things supposed immovable." The wave was reported from Erie Street on the east to the Cleveland breakwater on the west, a distance of about two miles, although it may have extended farther along the lake.

Engineers at the Life Saving Station reported the high water mark there was eight feet and ten inches above the lake level before and after the wave and the pier was submerged by four feet. Sheds at the station were torn apart, and several persons were injured when they were tossed about by the wave. Huge logs were carried hundreds of feet inland, fires extinguished at the Lake Erie rolling mill, barges tossed onto dry ground, and mooring lines snapped from ships. Buildings were damaged and tracks torn up at the Union Depot. Fishing was reported to be excellent on land without bait or hook as hundreds of fish were left stranded after the wave receded. One drowning was reported.

The *Cleveland Plain Dealer* reported that distant thunder was heard offshore ten minutes before the wave hit. A heavy cloud was observed over the lake parallel to shore, "the lower part of which looked like a large, heavy curtain hanging over the water, above it a contorted, angry looking conglomeration of cloud." A signal officer noticed the wave about one-quarter mile offshore and said it "appeared like a great green wall perhaps ten feet high." The lake was calm and the approaching wave swept along silently until it reached shallow water, where it made a loud "swishing noise and broke on the shore with a great roar." Two "recoil waves" followed close together. Small boats offshore reported a sudden rise of water, but none of the vessels were tipped. No strong wind was reported that morning from shore, and only a brief shower of rain fell a few minutes after the wave. After the wave, the lake "relapsed into a state of placid repose."

This type of large wave from a calm lake may be caused by a strong wind, by a shift of the lake bottom possibly due to an earthquake, or by the impact of a large object hitting the lake. A similar large, unexpected wave on Lake Michigan drowned six persons at Chicago on 26 June 1954 (Ewing et al. 1954). Another large, single wave caused extreme damage at Daytona Beach, Florida, on 4 July 1992 (Churchill et al. 1995). At both Chicago and Daytona Beach, a line of thunderstorms offshore was held responsible for generating the large waves. On 23 June 1882 there was no report of a wave at Toledo, according to the *Toledo Blade,* and no indications of an earthquake in the region. Because there was no known earthquake or impact, it seems likely that violent thunderstorm winds several miles offshore created a large wave that moved toward the shore. A similar explanation may apply to the 31 May 1942 North Coast wave, as lightning was observed for several hours offshore, according to the *Cleveland Plain Dealer.*

25 March 1884
Scipio Hailstorm

The hailstorm of 25 March 1884 merits attention due to the claim by Mindling (1944, 70) that a man was killed by the hail. Human fatalities in hail are extremely rare in the United States, although animals are commonly killed. Only two authentic cases of deaths in hailstorms are known from the twentieth century. A thirty-nine-year-old farmer was killed by hail on 13 May 1939 near Lubbock, Texas, and an infant in its mother's arms was killed by hail at Fort Collins, Colorado, on 30 July 1979 (Ludlum 1982, 153).

A severe storm including two tornadoes struck southwestern Ohio on the afternoon of Tuesday, 25 March 1884. The 3 April 1884 *Butler County Democrat* reported that a black cloud approached Scipio from the southwest, turned greenish, and then hit the small town with severe wind and hail, wind causing most of the damage. Many homes and barns were unroofed, some barns were destroyed, and one man was killed when his store collapsed. The *Butler County Democrat* gave this account of a man injured by the hail: "During the storm of Tuesday week hailstones of immense size fell in many parts of the county. William Wyncoop, of Reily Township, was in town a few days afterward and was covered with numerous contusions and bruises that were received by being caught in the storm." This research revealed no evidence of a man being killed by the hail at Scipio.

17 May 1894
Hail Pelts Northern Ohio

A very strong cold front triggered severe storms across Ohio on Thursday, 17 May 1894. The deadliest storm was the Kunkle Tornado, but these thunderstorms also produced one of the most widespread occurrences of hail known in northern Ohio.

Damaging hail fell in many communities but was especially severe at Cleveland and Canton. The *Cleveland Plain Dealer* reported that the day was sultry and "humanity in Cleveland was perspiring freely" before hail the size of oranges, about two to three inches across, pelted the city at 2:45 P.M. Hailstones striking the stone pavements sounded like "the rattle of musketry" and caused horses to bolt. People rushed out from stores after the storm to pick up and measure the hailstones. "It was an ordinary sight," according to the *Cleveland Plain Dealer,* "to see usually solemn citizens scamper across the sidewalk and pick up a record breaker."

Greenhouses and plants were destroyed by the hail, and lawns and sidewalks along Euclid Avenue were littered with broken tree branches. More than 350 windows were shattered at the Tyler Wire Works factory, and most homes on the east side had broken windows. Skylights broke in dozens of buildings sending hail, rain, and glass into parlors and shops. Even streetcar windows broke from the pelting of ice.

Cleveland schools were not seriously damaged, but the hail certainly caused a disruption. According to the 18 May 1894 *Cleveland Plain Dealer,* "The school children had a picnic. The first thing the storm did was break the skylights and scare the teachers. The youngsters were animated with a desire to rush out and gather the hail stones. . . . The teachers could not control the children."

Widespread wind and hail damage occurred in Stark County as the storm swept through at 4:00 P.M. Hail the size of hens eggs destroyed greenhouses, skylights, and nursery stock. Hundreds of windows were broken on homes and factories, according to the *Canton Evening Repository.* South School also lost many windows. "Such a storm never visited Canton before," according to the *Repository,* and similar sentiments were expressed in Navarre and Alliance.

11 July 1900
Three-Inch Hail at Elyria

Rain showers had passed north and south of Elyria on Wednesday afternoon, 11 July 1900, when, at 2:30 P.M., there came without warning a "tremendous downpour of large balls of ice." The *Elyria Democrat* reported the hailstones were "all unusually large"—most were two to two and a half inches in diameter and many were three and a half inches across. The *Democrat* reported that the hailstones weighed up to five ounces, but the *Elyria Republican* reported more conservatively that the "average weight of the icy missiles was between three and four ounces." Spherical hail two and a half inches in diameter would weigh about four ounces. A hailstone at North Ridgeville was said to have been four inches in diameter.

The five-minute barrage of hail caused extensive damage in Elyria. Skylights were riddled all over the city, glass one-quarter inch thick "penetrated as easily as if it were paper." Tin roofs were penetrated, slate roofs demolished, trees stripped of leaves, and greenhouses wrecked. The hail came with a west wind, so hundreds of windows were smashed on the west side of Elyria homes.

19 August 1903
Black Rain in Clermont County

Dr. Julius Abbott of Bethel reported three episodes of black rain in Clermont County during 1903. On the occasion of the third black rain, on 19 August, he sent a sample to J. Warren Smith of the Weather Bureau. Smith sent a sample to a soil scientist.

Rain with an uncommon color has been known from many places. In this case, the soil scientist found the sample contained an "extremely fine soil with a considerable portion of organic matter," according to the November 1903 issue of *Monthly Weather Review*. It seems that a drought had lowered the Ohio River so that banks of fine black mud were exposed and dried west of Bethel. Strong winds in thunderstorms had swept the black dust into the clouds and it fell with rain ten to twenty miles to the east. Dr. Abbott reported the rain left a black scum on creek banks and grass.

14 April 1912
Spring Hail in the Northwest

Sunday, 14 April 1912 is remembered worldwide as the evening the Titanic struck an iceberg and sank off Newfoundland with the loss of 1,490 lives. It was ice of another sort that startled residents of northwestern Ohio. Thunderstorms rumbled across the region with heavy rain, high winds, and damaging hail.

The *Toledo Blade* reported that hail the size of hickory nuts (one inch) lay several inches deep in a mile-wide path on the city's east side and in Bay View Park. As it fell, the hail "produced a tremendous roar and gave everyone a nervous feeling." There was little damage in Toledo because the cold spring had kept fruit trees from budding and most Toledo greenhouses were on the west side of the city out of the hail path.

Greater damage occurred south of Toledo, where hail stripped branches from trees, killed hundreds of chickens, and destroyed glass in greenhouses and homes. Mindling (1944) reported that some hailstones that fell near Fremont were two inches across. Windows were smashed in Marion and a woman was seriously injured by flying glass in Fostoria.

The *Toledo Blade* reported a man was cut by glass when hail broke all the windows on one side of an Erie Railroad passenger train between Kenton and Marion.

9 July 1913
Columbus Hail

Temperatures had already risen to 89 degrees by noon on Wednesday, 9 July 1913, when storms swept across the southern side of Columbus. The 9 July *Columbus Evening Dispatch* reported a hailstone five and a half inches in diameter, although the 10 July issue reported the largest stones were about three inches. A single extreme report of hail size should be treated with caution. Smaller hail may freeze together in the cloud and fall as a small clump of ice, the largest dimension of which may be much larger than the size of individual stones. Simple exaggeration may account for some reports of extremely large hail.

Whatever the size of the largest hailstone, the deluge of three-inch hail caused extensive damage along the path of the hail fall. As usual, greenhouses and the plants inside were destroyed by the barrage. An employee at the Columbus Floral Company Greenhouse was slightly injured by shattering glass. Ordinary windows on homes, schools, stores, and hospitals were broken by the hundreds in south Columbus and in the Briggsdale neighborhood. It was said to be the worst hailstorm known up to the time in Columbus. Fields of corn were cut to pieces and flattened, and hundreds of chickens were killed when struck by the ice. Large hail also fell in Harrison and Guernsey Counties.

26 August 1923
Cincinnati Hail

> "Sunshine faded into murkiness. A few
> drops of rain fell. A moment and white
> streaks were mingled with the downpour.
> Then came a patter of machine gun fire,
> a booming of thunder, and the city was
> being pelted with ice."

Such was the beginning of this 1923 hailstorm, as described by the *Cincinnati Enquirer*. Beginning on Sunday, 26 August at about 3:30 P.M. and lasting ten to twenty minutes, it swept for ten miles along a four-mile-wide path across Cincinnati and adjacent Covington, Kentucky. The heaviest hail fell from Fifteenth Street southward. Nearby farms were spared the damage inflicted on the city.

The size of the largest hailstones was generally about one inch in diameter, although, as the *Cincinnati Enquirer* reported, "accounts of the size of the hail stones grew with each retelling, until some persons were insistent they had seen pieces as large as goose eggs." Hail was most commonly described as "walnut-sized."

Hailstones smashed thousands of windows along the storm's path and accumulated to a depth of two inches. Trees were stripped of foliage, awnings collapsed, auto tops pierced, and small plants "hammered to the ground." Traffic stopped on Cincinnati streets and pedestrians ran for cover. Electric signs were broken and seventy-five boulevard lights smashed. Snow shovels were brought out to remove the ice. Some enterprising residents scooped up the hailstones to replenish the Sunday ice supply in their refrigerators.

The *Cincinnati Enquirer* reported that "never in the memory of early residents of Cincinnati had the city received such a pelting of ice." This was verified by W. B. Schlomer, head of the Weather Bureau office in Cincinnati. Schlomer also noted that the metal cups of the anemometer on the roof of the Government Building had eighteen indentations from hail, some one-quarter inch deep.

26 January 1927
Highest Pressure

The highest barometric pressure measured in Ohio was 31.04 inches (1051 millibars) at Toledo on Wednesday, 26 January 1927. High pressure creates good weather, and record high pressure, which creates even better weather, goes largely unnoticed. The record high pressure is included here for its meteorological significance.

A large area with pressure of more than 31 inches was centered in the northern Great Lakes region Wednesday morning. The Weather Bureau description of the daily weather map noted that "an area of high pressure of great magnitude has overspread the Hudson Bay region, Ontario, Quebec, and the greater part of the United States from the Rocky Mountains eastward." The highest pressure at 8:00 A.M. on the 26 January 1927 weather map was 31.06 inches at Sault St. Marie, Michigan, where the temperature was -32 degrees. A colder reading of -50 degrees was reported just to the north at White River, Ontario.

At Toledo, temperatures were at -1 degree Wednesday morning with a brisk north wind and a rising pressure of 30.82 inches. The high pressure center drifted southeast from the northern lakes across Ohio during the day. Pressure peaked at 31.04 inches at Toledo that evening to establish the state record. Although a state record, this was well below the North

American record pressure of 31.53 inches at Mayo, Yukon Territory, Canada, on New Year's Day 1974 (Ludlum 1982).

As is typical with winter high pressure, cold weather continued through the day and overnight with a high of only 8 degrees and a low of -1 again Thursday morning. By Thursday morning, the high was centered over Albany, New York, and pressure had fallen to 30.90 inches at Toledo with the prospect of warmer weather.

The fair, cold weather during this record high pressure was in sharp contrast to the weather at the time of the state low pressure record. Exactly fifty-one years later, on 26 January 1978, the National Weather Service at Cleveland measured 28.28 inches pressure during a severe blizzard that paralyzed Ohio for four days.

5 June 1933
Great Hailstorm at Martins Ferry

June 1933 was remarkable as the hottest, driest, and sunniest June in Ohio since records began in 1883. This month's title as the hottest June stood for only one year, but the "driest June" title held until June 1988. It was also remarkable for what Ohio meteorologist William Alexander called the "Great Hailstorm" at Martins Ferry on 5 June.

The hail swath extended about twenty miles across northern Belmont County. The lion's share of damage was in Martins Ferry, where the hail lasted for about twelve minutes beginning at 11:00 P.M. It was said to be the most destructive hailstorm in eastern Ohio since 27 September 1850, surpassing even that of April 1891. According to the *Martins Ferry Daily Times,* "Tales told by old residents about the hail storm of 42 years ago had been accepted with reservations by younger generations until last night when it was demonstrated that balls of ice two and even three inches in diameter do fall from the sky."

When the pounding stopped, stunned residents quietly left their homes and wandered the ice-covered landscape of destruction. Martins Ferry looked like a "war-zone" after the storm. An "eerie and dangerous mist" filled the midnight air over the melting ice and made driving risky. Street lights were smashed, thousands of windows shattered, scores of autos ruined, awnings shredded, and tree limbs broken. The hail pierced metal car roofs, metal gutters, and even roofs of homes.

The size of the stones was reported to be generally the size of a hen's egg (two inches), but some were the size of a man's fist (three to four inches). Numerous claims were made of tennis ball size, and one hailstone reportedly weighed six ounces. Hailstones are ripe for exaggeration, but damage in the Martins Ferry storm, such as the penetration of car roofs, attests to the stones "unprecedented and prodigious size." Lawns were pitted two inches deep, paint chipped off houses, and branches torn from trees. Leaves and branches were piled a foot deep in streets. Ice remaining the next morning was shoveled into iceboxes and drifts of hail a foot deep did not melt for two days.

Damage to windows occurred mostly on the south and west sides of buildings. Art windows were smashed in churches without regard for denomination—First Baptist, Welsh Church, St. Mary's Catholic, and the Lutheran church. Ferry Hospital suffered seventy-one broken windows and the high school lost two hundred windows.

Tar-paper roofs were torn apart and hail penetrated three-eighths-inch sheeting underneath. Wood shingle roofs were "chewed apart" by the stones, and even slate roofs were broken and leaking. Many homes suffered water damage as rain poured through holes punched by hailstones. Flat roofs were damaged most, whereas pitched roofs generally deflected the stones. Window repair was well underway the next day, with glass shipped in from surrounding towns. Much roof damage was not discovered until closer inspection and was expected to take weeks to repair.

Most losses were not covered by insurance, as hail damage was not covered by standard storm insurance. However, local insurance agencies were eager to capitalize on residents' newfound awareness. Advertisements in the 6 June issue of the *Martins Ferry Daily Times* proclaimed, "Hail insurance for a small additional cost." The paper also contained several advertisements by roofing companies.

The *Martins Ferry Daily Times* reported a political story: "A Republican asked a Democratic friend whether this was part of the New Deal. The Roosevelt adherent stopped the argument by stating that the iceball shower was due to Republicans still controlling the Weather Bureau."

13 November 1933
Dust Storms of 1933–1935

Although the Dust Bowl was to the west in Oklahoma, widespread drought in the early 1930s also brought occasional dust storms as far east as Ohio. Dust carried from the Plains states reduced visibility to a mile or so at Columbus early on 13 November 1933 and produced an odor similar to "freshly plowed earth," according to the November 1933 issue of *Climatological Data—Ohio Section*. This was the driest November in a decade in Ohio, and the region to the west had been in a moderate or severe drought since summer. Strong west winds ahead of a cold front carried the dust into southwestern and central Ohio, at times so thick that air traffic was delayed. Several persons in Cincinnati awakened to a choking sensation.

A thick coating of light brown dust covered exposed surfaces in Columbus.

Dust was reported heavy in Ohio during 1935 on 5–6 March, 21–22 March, and 28–30 March, with the first episode reported to be the worst. The sun had a silvery appearance and shone only dimly on the afternoon of 5 March. Visibility was greatly reduced. Air traffic was hindered and balloons disappeared from sight at three thousand feet. The Weather Bureau at Cleveland reported the dust could be felt and tasted in throats and coated all outdoor objects.

24 September 1950
Dark Sunday

Smoke from extensive forest fires in northwestern Canada was channeled into Ohio, causing "almost midnight blackness through the entire state," according to the *Cleveland Plain Dealer*. It became so dark from noon until 3:00 P.M. on 24 September 1950 that thousands of people jammed phone circuits, calling to "find the cause of the eerie phenomenon." Weather Bureau forecaster C. George Andrus made several radio broadcasts to assure Cleveland that the midday darkness was perfectly natural and not related to war or the supernatural.

During the height of the darkness, automobile headlights were on, landing lights came on at Cleveland Airport, and the afternoon game between the Indians and Detroit Tigers was played under the lights at Cleveland Stadium. Even birds were fooled. Thousands went to roost as though night had come. Temperatures responded as if night had arrived at Cleveland, cooling from 50 degrees at 9:30 A.M. on Sunday to 44 degrees by 2:00 P.M. The ocher sky raised fearful memories for some Ohioans as it reminded them of the sky before the Lorain Tornado of 1924.

11 July 1959
Hardin and Hancock County Hail

Several swaths of hail flattened and shredded crops across portions of four counties late on Saturday, 11 July 1959. The damaged area extended from western Logan County, where two thousand acres of corn, soybeans, and oats were damaged, across western and southern Hardin County, into southern Hancock County and western Wyandot County. Large hail was also reported in Fremont. As usual in these severe thunderstorms, the hail was accompanied by heavy rain and high winds.

The greatest hail damage occurred in Hardin and Hancock Counties. One swath of hail two miles wide extended from south of Mt. Blanchard northeast toward Carey. Crops on several farms were ruined by hailstones to the size of golfballs. The hail fell for thirty minutes in some areas, beginning at about 7:30 P.M. Ice piled into drifts two feet deep and remained in shaded areas through the next day.

In Hancock County, seven to ten thousand acres of corn, soybeans, and tomatoes were destroyed or severely damaged. Wheat was already harvested so generally escaped damage. The toll was greater in Hardin County, where eighteen thousand acres of crops were destroyed south and west of Kenton.

19 July 1961
Fatal Lightning at Salt Fork Dam

One of the deadliest lightning bolts known in Ohio killed four men during the construction of Salt Fork Dam north of Cambridge on 19 July 1961. A "howling thunderstorm" at 3:20 P.M. caught eleven men in the open, according to the *Cambridge Daily Jeffersonian.* Several of the men sought shelter under rocks or in a truck, but four stood under a large sycamore tree to escape the downpour. That proved to be a fatal mistake as a bolt of lightning struck the tree, ripped bark from the trunk, and killed the men. Ironically, the sycamore that carried the fatal bolt to the men had been scheduled to be cut down that morning but rain had delayed the task.

18 March 1968
North Coast Fog

A persistent and disruptive fog enveloped the Lake Erie shore communities from Sandusky eastward on Sunday, 17 March and Monday, 18 March 1968. Fog was present statewide Sunday morning. It cleared across the state except along the North Coast, where temperatures in the 30s allowed the fog to persist through the day. Cleveland Hopkins Airport was closed from 1:00 to 11:00 A.M. Sunday, with flights routed to Detroit or Pittsburgh. Light Sunday highway traffic was not affected much by the fog, and Cleveland's St. Patrick's Day Parade was held as scheduled.

Fog on Monday morning was much more disruptive as thousands attempted to drive to work. Commuters were advised to leave for work at least an hour early, to avoid lake shore routes, and to use public transportation. Cleveland freeways were clogged by traffic jams for hours Monday morning. Traffic moved at less than twenty-five miles an hour, there were numerous accidents, and buses ran late. Some people were three to four hours late for work.

Chain-reaction accidents were common in the poor visibility. Police closed the Shoreway for three hours after twenty-two cars piled up at the Main Avenue Bridge and ten more collided at West Twenty-eighth. There were thirty-one collisions between 5:40 and 7:15 A.M. on the Abbey Road Bridge near West Fourteenth Street, and the *Cleveland Plain Dealer* reported police were still taking accident reports from those motorists at 3:00 P.M. No serious injuries resulted. Hopkins Airport was closed for five hours Monday morning and again after 5:40 P.M. Burke Lakefront Airport was closed all day.

11 May 1980
Hail Strikes Franklin County

Hail as large as baseballs caused more than $10 million damage across southern Franklin County late on Sunday, 11 May 1980. Severe thunderstorms dropped heavy rain and spread high winds across Ohio too, but it was large hail that caused most of the destruction. Grove City and Reynoldsburg had the most damage, but the south side of Columbus and neighboring counties were also pelted by ice.

Hail smashed windows in homes, offices, schools, and cars. Aluminum siding was dented and ripped away, awnings collapsed, and roofs damaged. Six of Grove City's eight new police cars had smashed windows and dented roofs. Ten motorists were stranded on Interstate 71 when their windshields were shattered by hail. The windshield of a small airplane was smashed in midair, causing an emergency landing at Port Columbus Airport. Greenhouses, always at risk in hailstorms, suffered greatly. The *Columbus Dispatch* reported that more than six thousand panes of glass were shattered at River Bend Gardens on Noe-Bixby Road. Four elementary schools and a middle school in the South-Western City School District were closed Monday for repairs to broken windows. Buckeye Junior High in Columbus was also closed Monday for repairs to seventy-five broken windows.

Average Temperature and Precipitation

Average daily maximum (MAX), minimum (MIN), and mean (NORMAL) temperature and median precipitation (PRECIP) for the period 1961–90 are given for eighty-eight Ohio weather stations in Appendix 1. Data are taken from Owenby and Ezell (1992). Temperatures are adjusted to a midnight observation time, so they may be compared among stations. Station locations are shown in figure 84.

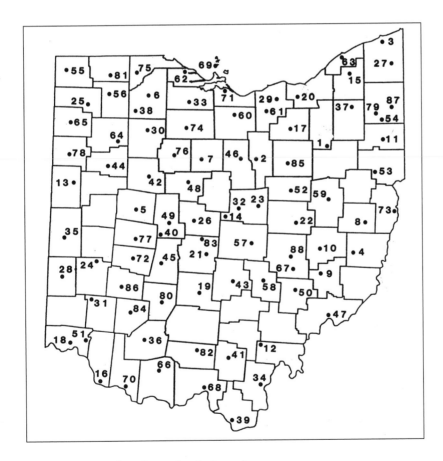

Fig. 84. Locations of weather stations in Appendix 1.

STATION		JAN.	FEB.	MAR.	APR.	MAY	JUN.	JUL.	AUG.	SEPT.	OCT.	NOV.	DEC.	ANNUAL
1. Akron-Canton Airport	Max	32.6	35.9	47.3	59.1	69.7	78.5	82.3	80.4	73.7	62.1	49.7	37.7	59.08
	Min	16.9	18.9	28.6	37.9	48.2	57.0	61.5	60.1	53.7	42.7	34.2	23.6	40.28
	Normal	24.8	27.4	38.0	48.5	59.0	67.8	71.9	70.3	63.7	52.4	42.0	30.7	49.68
	Precip	1.89	2.13	3.03	2.90	3.43	2.85	3.46	3.03	3.09	2.07	2.83	2.68	35.55
2. Ashland	Max	30.2	32.8	43.9	56.8	69.4	78.4	82.5	79.8	73.4	60.5	47.6	34.4	57.48
	Min	13.8	15.3	24.8	34.5	45.9	55.0	59.3	57.0	50.8	39.5	30.8	20.4	37.26
	Normal	22.0	24.1	34.4	45.7	57.7	66.7	70.9	68.4	62.1	50.0	39.2	27.4	47.37
	Precip	2.12	1.88	2.95	3.23	3.86	3.10	3.56	3.63	2.96	2.06	3.10	2.70	38.28
3. Ashtabula	Max	30.8	32.7	42.5	55.3	67.7	77.1	81.2	79.2	73.3	61.1	49.3	36.6	57.23
	Min	17.0	17.1	26.6	36.4	46.8	56.3	61.2	60.0	53.5	43.2	35.0	24.4	39.79
	Normal	23.9	24.9	34.6	45.9	57.3	66.7	71.2	69.6	63.4	52.2	42.2	30.5	48.51
	Precip	1.70	1.78	2.29	2.98	2.66	3.57	3.99	3.43	3.48	3.14	3.57	3.06	38.55
4. Barnesville	Max	33.1	35.8	47.3	58.8	70.3	78.3	82.0	80.2	74.5	62.2	50.0	38.3	59.23
	Min	14.5	16.0	26.3	34.7	44.9	53.9	58.7	56.6	49.9	37.7	30.5	21.6	37.11
	Normal	23.8	25.9	36.8	46.8	57.6	66.1	70.4	68.4	62.2	50.0	40.3	30.0	48.17
	Precip	2.38	2.70	3.55	3.81	4.13	4.23	4.21	3.29	2.78	2.73	2.99	2.90	42.27
5. Bellefontaine	Max	29.7	33.5	44.9	57.5	70.2	78.9	82.5	79.9	74.4	61.7	48.4	35.9	58.13
	Min	14.0	16.3	26.4	36.9	48.6	57.5	61.6	59.3	52.9	41.2	31.5	20.9	38.93
	Normal	21.9	24.9	35.7	47.2	59.4	68.2	72.1	69.6	63.6	51.5	40.0	28.4	48.53
	Precip	1.60	1.84	2.68	3.62	3.67	3.52	3.48	3.37	2.43	2.12	2.73	2.86	36.65
6. Bowling Green	Max	30.0	32.5	44.3	57.9	71.4	80.9	84.7	81.4	75.4	62.5	48.6	35.8	58.78
	Min	14.3	15.6	25.3	35.4	47.5	57.3	61.4	58.6	51.9	40.1	31.2	20.6	38.27
	Normal	22.2	24.1	34.8	46.7	59.5	69.1	73.1	70.0	63.7	51.3	39.9	28.2	48.53
	Precip	1.44	1.34	2.32	2.91	3.50	3.39	3.30	2.68	2.35	1.60	2.32	2.58	32.89
7. Bucyrus	Max	30.4	32.8	44.0	57.2	70.0	79.4	83.1	80.4	74.2	61.3	48.2	35.8	58.07
	Min	14.7	15.9	25.8	35.4	46.3	56.0	60.4	57.9	51.2	40.0	31.5	21.3	38.03
	Normal	22.6	24.4	34.9	46.3	58.2	67.7	71.8	69.2	62.7	50.7	39.9	28.6	48.05
	Precip	1.61	1.87	2.85	3.15	4.05	3.64	3.82	3.22	3.11	1.97	2.62	2.78	38.89
8. Cadiz	Max	32.2	36.7	47.9	60.0	71.2	78.9	82.5	80.8	75.3	63.2	50.6	38.2	59.79
	Min	16.2	18.3	27.8	38.4	49.2	57.7	62.1	60.4	54.1	41.9	32.8	22.5	40.12
	Normal	24.2	27.5	37.9	49.2	60.2	68.3	72.3	70.6	64.7	52.6	41.7	30.4	49.95
	Precip	2.08	2.35	3.03	3.26	3.88	4.08	3.87	3.30	2.55	2.55	2.64	2.74	37.41

STATION		JAN.	FEB.	MAR.	APR.	MAY	JUN.	JUL.	AUG.	SEPT.	OCT.	NOV.	DEC.	ANNUAL
9. Caldwell	Max	38.8	43.1	55.2	65.7	74.9	82.3	85.1	83.9	78.6	67.6	55.4	43.2	64.48
	Min	19.2	21.3	31.7	40.6	48.9	56.7	60.3	59.1	52.9	42.0	33.8	24.3	40.90
	Normal	29.0	32.2	43.5	53.2	61.9	69.5	72.7	71.5	65.8	54.8	44.6	33.8	52.69
	Precip	1.66	1.98	2.67	3.21	3.79	3.91	4.08	3.10	2.73	2.39	2.73	2.55	37.55
10. Cambridge	Max	38.1	42.3	54.4	65.4	75.2	82.6	85.5	84.3	78.4	67.3	54.7	42.6	64.23
	Min	19.9	22.0	31.9	40.3	49.0	57.6	61.8	60.8	54.2	42.5	34.5	25.4	41.66
	Normal	29.0	32.2	43.2	52.9	62.1	70.1	73.7	72.6	66.3	54.9	44.6	34.0	52.95
	Precip	2.18	2.29	3.42	3.08	3.82	3.62	3.76	3.10	2.65	2.16	2.78	2.72	39.01
11. Canfield	Max	35.0	38.5	49.7	61.6	72.2	80.3	83.7	82.3	76.3	65.1	51.9	39.2	61.32
	Min	16.9	18.0	28.4	37.5	46.5	55.2	58.5	57.4	51.3	40.6	33.0	22.6	38.83
	Normal	26.0	28.3	39.1	49.6	59.4	67.8	71.1	69.9	63.8	52.9	42.5	30.9	50.07
	Precip	1.60	1.68	2.73	2.85	3.18	3.31	3.60	3.29	3.30	2.37	2.93	2.21	36.18
12. Carpenter	Max	36.4	40.9	52.3	64.1	74.5	81.9	84.9	83.3	77.6	66.1	54.1	41.8	63.16
	Min	16.9	19.4	28.8	38.7	48.3	56.4	60.7	59.4	52.3	39.2	32.0	23.2	39.61
	Normal	26.7	30.2	40.6	51.4	61.4	69.2	72.8	71.4	65.0	52.7	43.1	32.5	51.38
	Precip	2.32	2.08	2.99	3.27	3.82	3.71	4.67	3.12	3.09	2.38	2.74	2.73	40.45
13. Celina	Max	33.6	37.8	49.9	62.8	73.8	82.4	85.2	83.4	78.1	66.0	51.8	38.4	61.93
	Min	17.8	20.9	31.4	41.4	51.3	60.3	63.8	61.8	55.5	44.8	35.1	23.8	42.33
	Normal	25.7	29.4	40.7	52.1	62.6	71.4	74.5	72.6	66.8	55.4	43.5	31.1	52.13
	Precip	1.55	1.96	3.40	3.08	3.34	3.38	3.39	3.02	2.61	2.15	2.40	2.62	35.38
14. Centerburg	Max	30.3	34.7	45.9	59.0	70.5	78.8	82.3	80.6	74.6	62.2	49.3	36.1	58.69
	Min	13.9	16.8	27.1	37.1	47.4	56.1	60.3	58.6	52.0	40.3	31.8	20.8	38.52
	Normal	22.1	25.8	36.5	48.1	59.0	67.5	71.3	69.6	63.3	51.3	40.6	28.4	48.60
	Precip	1.90	1.73	2.81	3.33	3.63	3.99	4.13	3.38	2.88	2.31	3.73	2.78	39.98
15. Chardon	Max	29.5	32.6	42.5	55.8	67.9	76.6	80.5	78.5	72.3	60.2	47.8	35.2	56.62
	Min	13.0	13.5	23.6	33.6	44.3	53.4	58.1	56.6	50.1	39.7	31.7	20.6	36.52
	Normal	21.3	23.1	33.1	44.7	56.1	65.0	69.3	67.6	61.2	50.0	39.8	27.9	46.57
	Precip	2.64	2.51	3.33	3.55	3.57	4.18	3.53	3.61	3.75	3.75	4.05	3.79	45.45
16. Chilo	Max	37.1	40.4	51.3	63.6	74.7	82.7	86.6	85.2	79.1	67.0	54.4	42.6	63.73
	Min	18.8	21.1	30.6	39.5	49.7	58.6	63.6	62.3	55.9	43.4	34.7	25.2	41.95
	Normal	28.0	30.8	41.0	51.6	62.2	70.7	75.1	73.8	67.5	55.2	44.6	33.9	52.84
	Precip	2.55	2.80	4.13	3.66	4.03	3.28	3.94	3.88	2.83	2.39	3.68	3.54	43.10

STATION		JAN.	FEB.	MAR.	APR.	MAY	JUN.	JUL.	AUG.	SEPT.	OCT.	NOV.	DEC.	ANNUAL
17. Chippewa Lake	Max	30.0	33.7	44.5	58.0	70.1	78.8	82.8	80.4	74.4	62.0	49.0	35.8	58.29
	Min	13.4	14.7	24.7	34.6	45.4	54.4	58.7	56.8	50.7	39.1	31.2	20.6	37.03
	Normal	21.7	24.2	34.6	46.3	57.8	66.6	70.8	68.6	62.6	50.6	40.1	28.2	47.66
	Precip	1.83	1.98	3.12	3.13	4.05	3.36	3.85	2.95	3.23	2.01	3.19	2.95	36.28
18. Cincinnati Airport	Max	38.4	42.8	54.4	65.5	75.2	83.3	86.6	85.1	78.8	67.5	54.8	43.1	64.63
	Min	21.2	24.4	34.2	43.0	52.7	61.5	66.1	64.2	57.2	44.6	35.9	26.7	44.31
	Normal	29.8	33.6	44.3	54.3	64.0	72.4	76.4	74.7	68.0	56.1	45.4	34.9	54.47
	Precip	2.33	2.07	3.92	3.66	4.30	3.06	3.63	3.28	2.40	2.65	3.41	2.97	40.57
19. Circleville	Max	34.0	37.9	49.3	61.2	73.2	81.4	85.1	83.2	77.2	65.0	52.0	39.6	61.59
	Min	17.7	19.4	29.2	38.6	49.7	58.4	62.9	60.4	53.5	41.3	33.0	24.2	40.69
	Normal	25.9	28.7	39.3	49.9	61.5	69.9	74.0	71.8	65.4	53.2	42.5	31.9	51.14
	Precip	1.81	2.08	2.90	3.39	4.23	3.59	3.78	3.53	2.72	2.30	3.02	2.67	37.99
20. Cleveland Airport	Max	31.9	35.0	46.3	57.9	68.6	78.3	82.4	80.5	73.6	62.1	50.0	37.4	58.67
	Min	17.6	19.3	28.2	37.3	47.3	56.8	61.4	60.3	54.2	43.5	35.0	24.5	40.45
	Normal	24.8	27.2	37.3	47.6	58.0	67.6	71.9	70.4	63.9	52.8	42.5	31.0	49.56
	Precip	1.86	2.33	2.90	3.10	3.18	3.43	3.42	3.49	3.13	2.35	2.87	2.94	36.51
21. Columbus Airport	Max	34.1	38.0	50.5	62.0	72.3	80.4	83.7	82.1	76.2	64.5	51.4	39.2	61.20
	Min	18.5	21.2	31.2	40.0	50.1	58.0	62.7	60.8	54.8	42.9	34.3	24.6	41.59
	Normal	26.3	29.6	40.9	51.0	61.2	69.2	73.2	71.5	65.5	53.7	42.9	31.9	51.40
	Precip	1.90	2.00	2.99	3.10	3.51	4.00	3.89	3.22	2.73	1.99	3.11	2.75	37.78
22. Coshocton	Max	35.4	39.3	51.3	62.3	72.7	80.7	84.0	82.4	76.4	65.2	52.5	40.2	61.87
	Min	16.7	19.1	28.7	37.3	47.3	56.0	60.2	58.6	51.8	39.7	31.9	22.7	39.17
	Normal	26.1	29.2	40.0	49.8	60.0	68.4	72.1	70.5	64.1	52.5	42.2	31.5	50.52
	Precip	1.95	2.38	3.01	3.66	3.81	3.66	4.50	3.15	2.81	2.53	3.00	3.03	39.73
23. Danville	Max	30.9	34.5	46.2	58.3	70.8	79.5	83.8	81.1	74.9	62.4	49.3	36.7	59.03
	Min	13.0	14.5	24.3	32.8	43.8	52.9	57.5	55.3	48.5	36.2	28.9	19.9	35.63
	Normal	22.0	24.5	35.3	45.6	57.3	66.2	70.7	68.2	61.7	49.3	39.1	28.3	47.33
	Precip	1.95	2.04	3.16	3.32	3.78	3.77	3.91	3.25	3.08	2.03	3.33	2.84	39.36
24. Dayton Airport	Max	34.1	38.0	50.0	61.9	72.5	81.6	84.9	83.0	76.5	64.5	51.3	39.1	61.45
	Min	17.9	20.8	31.0	40.5	51.0	59.2	63.4	61.3	55.1	43.6	34.4	24.0	41.85
	Normal	26.0	29.4	40.5	51.2	61.8	70.4	74.2	72.2	65.8	54.1	42.9	31.6	51.65
	Precip	1.65	1.93	3.19	3.50	3.52	3.38	3.59	3.00	2.66	2.24	2.90	2.86	35.90

STATION		JAN.	FEB.	MAR.	APR.	MAY	JUN.	JUL.	AUG.	SEPT.	OCT.	NOV.	DEC.	ANNUAL
25. Defiance	Max	29.7	32.4	43.7	57.7	71.2	80.9	84.6	82.0	75.2	62.3	48.2	35.6	58.63
	Min	13.0	14.5	25.0	35.4	46.1	56.0	60.4	58.0	51.4	39.6	30.9	19.7	37.50
	Normal	21.4	23.5	34.4	46.6	58.7	68.5	72.5	70.0	63.3	51.0	39.6	27.7	48.06
	Precip	1.56	1.46	2.40	3.09	3.53	3.22	3.74	2.25	2.98	2.16	2.80	2.48	34.70
26. Delaware	Max	32.0	34.8	46.3	59.2	71.3	80.1	84.0	81.9	75.7	63.1	49.5	37.3	59.60
	Min	14.5	16.7	26.7	36.4	46.7	56.1	60.6	58.2	51.3	39.2	31.0	21.3	38.23
	Normal	23.3	25.8	36.5	47.8	59.0	68.1	72.3	70.1	63.5	51.2	40.3	29.3	48.91
	Precip	1.60	1.70	2.56	3.29	3.75	3.70	3.97	3.21	2.77	2.02	3.34	2.62	37.31
27. Dorset	Max	29.6	32.5	42.9	56.2	68.5	77.2	81.6	79.6	73.5	61.0	48.4	35.3	57.19
	Min	13.2	13.4	24.0	33.6	43.4	52.8	57.1	55.7	49.6	39.2	31.7	20.9	36.22
	Normal	21.4	23.0	33.5	44.9	56.0	65.0	69.4	67.7	61.6	50.1	40.1	28.1	46.70
	Precip	2.13	2.03	2.95	3.28	3.46	4.04	3.52	3.97	3.88	3.69	3.65	3.05	42.61
28. Eaton	Max	32.4	36.9	48.7	61.9	73.6	82.1	85.6	83.8	78.0	64.8	51.2	37.8	61.40
	Min	13.7	16.6	27.2	37.1	47.2	56.0	60.2	58.5	51.5	39.2	31.0	20.5	38.23
	Normal	23.1	26.8	38.0	49.5	60.4	69.1	72.9	71.2	64.8	52.0	41.1	29.2	49.81
	Precip	2.28	2.23	3.42	3.50	4.00	3.60	3.81	3.08	2.76	2.93	2.92	3.45	39.65
29. Elyria	Max	35.5	38.6	49.8	62.3	73.2	82.2	85.5	83.8	78.0	66.6	53.2	39.9	62.38
	Min	19.6	21.0	31.1	40.6	49.8	59.0	62.7	61.9	56.0	45.2	36.5	25.6	42.42
	Normal	27.6	29.8	40.5	51.5	61.5	70.6	74.1	72.9	67.0	55.9	44.9	32.8	52.40
	Precip	1.83	1.85	2.80	2.82	3.51	3.76	3.39	3.00	3.03	2.30	3.14	3.05	36.49
30. Findlay	Max	30.7	34.2	46.3	59.0	70.7	79.9	83.4	81.0	74.4	62.2	48.3	35.4	58.79
	Min	15.9	18.4	28.2	38.2	49.1	58.4	62.4	60.0	53.4	42.0	32.7	21.7	40.03
	Normal	23.3	26.3	37.3	48.6	59.9	69.2	72.9	70.5	63.9	52.1	40.5	28.6	49.41
	Precip	1.56	1.81	2.73	2.88	4.00	3.44	4.20	3.00	2.70	1.91	2.53	2.90	36.49
31. Franklin	Max	34.4	38.5	50.0	62.6	73.6	82.2	85.9	84.2	78.3	65.6	52.7	40.0	62.33
	Min	17.3	19.5	30.0	39.8	49.4	58.8	63.0	60.4	53.0	40.6	33.1	23.6	40.71
	Normal	25.9	29.0	40.0	51.2	61.5	70.5	74.5	72.3	65.7	53.1	42.9	31.8	51.52
	Precip	1.92	2.35	3.34	3.80	4.30	3.13	4.33	2.98	3.01	3.00	3.20	2.88	38.91
32. Fredericktown	Max	31.3	34.9	46.5	59.7	71.3	80.1	83.9	82.2	75.9	63.1	49.9	36.6	59.62
	Min	12.7	14.7	25.7	35.3	45.1	54.4	57.9	55.8	48.7	37.4	29.9	19.7	36.44
	Normal	22.0	24.8	36.1	47.5	58.2	67.3	70.9	69.0	62.3	50.3	39.9	28.2	48.03
	Precip	2.11	2.15	3.04	3.49	4.23	4.14	3.64	3.06	3.27	2.06	3.08	3.05	38.63

STATION		JAN.	FEB.	MAR.	APR.	MAY	JUN.	JUL.	AUG.	SEPT.	OCT.	NOV.	DEC.	ANNUAL
33. Fremont	Max	30.0	33.0	43.9	57.9	70.4	79.9	84.0	81.5	75.2	62.4	49.1	35.7	58.58
	Min	14.9	16.9	26.9	37.3	47.9	57.9	62.0	59.5	52.6	40.5	32.5	21.3	39.18
	Normal	22.5	25.0	35.4	47.6	59.2	68.9	73.0	70.5	63.9	51.5	40.8	28.5	48.88
	Precip	1.57	1.43	2.56	3.06	3.55	3.90	3.34	3.00	2.86	2.10	2.59	2.80	35.14
34. Gallipolis	Max	44.1	48.9	60.3	70.3	78.9	85.6	88.0	86.9	81.8	71.7	60.2	48.5	68.77
	Min	23.7	26.1	35.3	43.3	51.9	60.2	64.3	63.0	57.1	45.3	37.1	28.4	44.64
	Normal	33.9	37.5	47.8	56.8	65.4	72.9	76.2	75.0	69.5	58.5	48.7	38.5	56.70
	Precip	2.35	2.65	3.34	3.12	3.68	3.39	4.63	3.68	2.64	2.40	2.86	2.83	41.12
35. Greenville	Max	30.9	34.0	46.9	60.4	72.1	81.2	84.5	82.6	77.0	63.7	50.2	36.6	60.01
	Min	13.5	15.5	26.9	36.7	47.1	56.6	60.4	57.4	50.2	38.4	30.6	20.0	37.78
	Normal	22.2	24.8	36.9	48.6	59.6	68.9	72.5	70.0	63.6	51.1	40.4	28.3	48.89
	Precip	1.58	1.87	2.73	3.42	3.65	3.19	3.93	2.94	2.90	2.48	2.20	2.79	35.93
36. Hillsboro	Max	33.6	38.2	49.7	62.0	72.3	80.1	83.6	82.0	76.7	64.6	52.3	39.4	61.21
	Min	17.7	20.8	31.2	41.6	51.3	59.9	64.2	62.2	55.8	44.1	34.9	24.0	42.31
	Normal	25.7	29.5	40.5	51.8	61.8	70.0	73.9	72.1	66.3	54.4	43.6	31.7	51.76
	Precip	2.30	2.33	3.94	3.89	4.34	3.44	4.26	3.90	2.76	2.48	3.09	3.13	41.88
37. Hiram	Max	31.5	35.1	46.2	58.3	69.2	77.3	81.2	79.3	72.9	61.4	49.0	36.4	58.15
	Min	15.5	17.1	27.0	36.9	47.3	55.7	60.4	59.0	52.7	41.8	32.6	21.7	38.98
	Normal	23.5	26.1	36.6	47.6	58.3	66.5	70.8	69.2	62.8	51.6	40.8	29.1	48.56
	Precip	2.16	2.17	3.38	3.20	3.83	3.88	3.35	3.26	3.81	3.14	3.59	3.46	41.50
38. Hoytville	Max	29.5	32.6	44.4	58.9	71.4	80.6	84.0	81.3	75.4	62.6	48.6	35.0	58.69
	Min	13.8	15.9	26.0	36.3	47.2	57.2	61.1	58.3	51.7	40.1	32.2	20.7	38.38
	Normal	21.7	24.3	35.2	47.6	59.3	68.9	72.6	69.8	63.6	51.4	40.4	27.9	48.53
	Precip	1.30	1.37	2.20	3.00	3.46	3.50	3.67	2.95	2.79	2.03	2.38	2.48	33.35
39. Ironton	Max	40.5	45.8	57.5	68.6	78.0	85.3	88.0	86.9	80.6	69.6	57.5	45.9	67.02
	Min	20.8	23.7	33.2	42.0	51.2	59.9	64.2	63.2	56.3	43.9	35.4	26.7	43.38
	Normal	30.7	34.8	45.4	55.3	64.6	72.6	76.1	75.1	68.5	56.8	46.5	36.3	55.20
	Precip	2.55	2.78	3.06	3.50	3.98	3.57	4.58	3.77	2.59	2.80	2.93	3.13	40.93
40. Irwin	Max	35.7	40.1	52.4	64.6	75.1	83.2	86.0	84.7	79.2	67.8	53.5	40.3	63.55
	Min	18.2	20.7	31.2	40.6	50.2	58.3	61.5	59.6	53.1	42.5	33.9	23.8	41.13
	Normal	26.9	30.4	41.8	52.6	62.6	70.8	73.8	72.2	66.2	55.2	43.7	32.1	52.34
	Precip	1.76	1.63	2.66	3.20	3.68	3.92	4.08	3.29	2.60	1.85	2.89	2.54	37.57

STATION		JAN.	FEB.	MAR.	APR.	MAY	JUN.	JUL.	AUG.	SEPT.	OCT.	NOV.	DEC.	ANNUAL
41. Jackson	Max	36.7	40.8	52.3	64.6	74.8	82.1	85.3	83.9	78.0	66.3	54.4	41.8	63.42
	Min	16.4	18.9	28.9	37.3	46.9	55.8	60.8	59.2	51.9	38.9	31.3	22.4	39.06
	Normal	26.6	29.9	40.6	51.0	60.9	69.0	73.1	71.6	65.0	52.6	42.9	32.1	51.24
	Precip	2.34	2.23	3.32	3.22	4.01	3.35	3.83	3.79	2.68	2.33	2.65	3.02	41.43
42. Kenton	Max	30.8	34.7	45.9	59.6	72.0	81.0	84.8	82.6	76.3	63.2	49.6	36.1	59.72
	Min	14.0	16.5	26.7	37.1	47.9	57.1	61.4	58.9	52.1	40.2	31.7	20.3	38.66
	Normal	22.4	25.6	36.3	48.4	60.0	69.1	73.1	70.8	64.2	51.7	40.7	28.2	49.19
	Precip	1.82	1.68	2.73	3.31	4.09	3.50	3.41	2.82	2.83	1.70	2.69	2.78	36.08
43. Lancaster	Max	33.5	36.3	48.2	60.2	72.2	80.8	84.8	82.6	76.9	65.4	51.4	38.7	60.92
	Min	15.8	18.0	28.0	37.0	47.1	56.4	60.9	58.9	52.0	39.9	32.1	22.1	39.02
	Normal	24.7	27.2	38.1	48.6	59.7	68.6	72.9	70.8	64.5	52.7	41.8	30.4	49.97
	Precip	1.77	1.86	2.44	2.73	3.42	3.20	3.44	3.28	2.35	2.05	2.66	2.49	36.20
44. Lima	Max	30.9	33.8	45.2	58.3	71.6	80.7	84.5	81.5	75.5	62.7	49.3	36.8	59.23
	Min	15.0	16.7	26.9	37.1	49.0	58.3	62.8	60.1	53.8	41.8	32.5	22.0	39.67
	Normal	23.0	25.3	36.1	47.7	60.3	69.5	73.7	70.8	64.7	52.3	40.9	29.4	49.45
	Precip	1.75	1.59	2.65	3.03	3.79	3.09	3.44	2.67	2.95	1.95	2.51	2.50	36.13
45. London	Max	31.6	35.5	47.1	59.4	72.2	80.7	84.4	81.5	75.7	63.2	50.0	37.7	59.92
	Min	15.1	16.9	26.9	36.3	47.9	56.7	61.1	58.3	51.7	39.4	31.3	22.0	38.63
	Normal	23.4	26.2	37.0	47.9	60.1	68.7	72.8	69.9	63.7	51.3	40.7	29.9	49.28
	Precip	1.56	2.30	2.64	3.38	3.61	3.48	3.72	3.63	2.21	2.00	3.10	2.68	37.05
46. Mansfield Airport	Max	32.1	35.0	46.6	58.6	69.3	78.2	82.1	80.1	73.7	62.3	49.2	36.8	58.67
	Min	16.8	18.9	28.6	38.2	48.3	57.3	62.0	60.4	54.0	43.1	33.9	22.7	40.35
	Normal	24.5	27.0	37.6	48.4	58.8	67.8	72.1	70.3	63.9	52.7	41.6	29.8	49.51
	Precip	1.65	1.66	2.88	3.43	4.15	3.68	3.67	4.00	3.25	2.08	3.12	2.82	38.92
47. Marietta	Max	38.8	42.7	54.4	64.8	75.0	82.5	85.7	84.4	78.3	67.2	55.1	43.7	64.38
	Min	20.5	22.4	31.9	40.3	50.0	58.6	63.3	62.1	55.2	43.1	34.9	26.1	42.37
	Normal	29.7	32.6	43.2	52.6	62.5	70.6	74.5	73.3	66.8	55.2	45.0	34.9	53.38
	Precip	2.36	2.49	3.11	2.84	3.62	3.64	3.90	3.33	3.01	2.69	2.77	2.91	39.00
48. Marion	Max	31.3	34.1	45.6	58.9	71.5	80.9	84.6	82.2	75.7	62.8	49.2	36.5	59.44
	Min	14.1	15.6	25.8	35.5	47.1	56.5	60.6	57.7	51.0	39.5	31.0	21.0	37.95
	Normal	22.7	24.9	35.7	47.2	59.3	68.7	72.6	70.0	63.4	51.2	40.1	28.8	48.70
	Precip	1.91	1.53	2.50	3.37	4.03	3.47	3.51	3.05	3.00	2.31	2.73	2.67	36.61

STATION		JAN.	FEB.	MAR.	APR.	MAY	JUN.	JUL.	AUG.	SEPT.	OCT.	NOV.	DEC.	ANNUA
49. Marysville	Max	33.0	36.8	49.0	61.1	71.8	80.5	83.8	82.1	75.5	63.5	50.2	37.7	60.42
	Min	16.0	18.6	28.7	38.3	48.8	57.4	61.6	59.6	52.9	41.5	32.6	22.3	39.86
	Normal	24.5	27.7	38.9	49.7	60.3	69.0	72.7	70.8	64.2	52.5	41.4	30.0	50.14
	Precip	1.73	1.80	2.60	2.74	3.74	3.53	3.48	2.62	2.64	2.04	2.95	2.66	35.60
50. McConnelsville	Max	36.8	40.6	52.6	64.8	75.5	82.8	86.1	84.8	79.0	66.7	54.7	41.9	64.11
	Min	15.5	18.0	28.0	37.3	47.0	55.9	60.9	59.7	52.5	39.6	31.6	22.2	39.14
	Normal	26.9	30.0	41.1	51.2	61.1	69.2	73.3	72.2	65.6	53.3	43.4	32.5	51.63
	Precip	2.74	2.33	3.22	3.28	4.05	3.85	4.73	3.56	2.84	2.65	2.74	3.04	40.61
51. Milford	Max	35.0	38.2	50.1	63.1	74.6	82.8	86.6	84.7	78.2	65.8	52.6	40.8	62.71
	Min	16.7	18.9	28.8	37.7	47.7	56.6	61.8	59.9	53.0	40.0	31.5	23.0	39.63
	Normal	25.9	28.6	39.5	50.4	61.1	69.7	74.2	72.3	65.6	52.9	42.1	31.9	51.17
	Precip	2.42	2.25	3.80	3.87	4.62	3.66	4.13	3.61	2.76	2.75	3.43	3.33	43.21
52. Millersburg	Max	32.3	35.4	46.8	58.7	70.8	79.2	83.0	80.5	74.6	62.5	49.7	37.8	59.28
	Min	14.8	16.3	25.9	35.4	46.4	55.1	59.5	57.4	51.3	39.5	31.2	21.5	37.86
	Normal	23.6	25.9	36.4	47.1	58.6	67.2	71.3	69.0	63.0	51.0	40.5	29.7	48.57
	Precip	1.64	2.08	2.69	3.20	4.04	3.87	3.56	3.28	3.20	2.22	2.94	2.42	37.13
53. Millport	Max	34.7	38.6	49.9	61.3	71.4	79.9	83.3	81.9	75.6	64.2	51.6	39.2	60.97
	Min	16.3	18.1	28.2	36.6	45.6	54.1	58.1	56.9	50.2	39.3	31.9	22.4	38.14
	Normal	25.5	28.4	39.1	49.0	58.5	67.0	70.7	69.4	62.9	51.8	41.8	30.8	49.55
	Precip	2.02	2.41	3.08	3.23	3.84	3.23	3.96	2.83	2.90	2.35	2.96	2.95	37.87
54. Mineral Ridge	Max	35.8	39.7	50.9	63.2	74.2	82.3	85.7	84.1	78.1	66.7	53.3	40.2	62.85
	Min	18.9	20.3	30.0	39.1	48.2	56.8	60.7	59.9	53.9	43.1	35.1	25.1	40.93
	Normal	27.4	30.0	40.5	51.2	61.2	69.6	73.2	72.0	66.0	54.9	44.2	32.7	51.89
	Precip	1.43	1.72	2.75	2.74	3.49	3.60	3.60	3.08	3.39	2.46	2.65	2.50	36.58
55. Montpelier	Max	28.7	31.6	43.0	56.9	70.3	79.7	83.6	81.1	74.3	61.2	47.3	34.5	57.68
	Min	12.5	14.0	24.5	34.7	45.2	54.7	59.2	56.5	49.6	38.1	30.1	19.3	36.53
	Normal	20.6	22.8	33.8	45.8	57.8	67.2	71.4	68.8	62.0	49.7	38.7	26.9	47.11
	Precip	1.63	1.44	2.78	3.33	3.28	3.54	3.41	3.16	2.86	2.15	2.76	2.54	35.65
56. Napoleon	Max	29.6	32.1	43.9	57.6	71.3	80.8	84.5	81.5	75.0	62.1	48.3	35.5	58.52
	Min	14.0	15.4	25.5	35.6	47.3	57.1	61.6	58.6	52.2	40.4	31.4	20.9	38.33
	Normal	21.8	23.8	34.7	46.6	59.3	68.9	73.1	70.1	63.6	51.3	39.8	28.2	48.43
	Precip	1.55	1.40	2.46	3.27	3.44	2.97	3.75	2.83	2.53	2.10	2.53	2.48	35.38

STATION		JAN.	FEB.	MAR.	APR.	MAY	JUN.	JUL.	AUG.	SEPT.	OCT.	NOV.	DEC.	ANNUAL
57. Newark	Max	36.2	40.3	52.5	64.0	74.4	82.4	85.4	83.9	77.5	66.1	53.2	40.7	63.05
	Min	17.5	20.2	30.5	40.4	48.3	56.6	61.0	59.2	52.6	40.9	32.8	23.3	40.28
	Normal	26.9	30.3	41.5	52.2	61.4	69.5	73.2	71.6	65.1	53.5	43.0	32.0	51.66
	Precip	2.16	2.53	3.20	3.83	4.52	3.89	4.37	2.98	2.67	2.34	3.16	2.97	41.43
58. New Lexington	Max	34.4	38.3	50.0	61.5	73.6	81.2	84.6	82.4	76.5	64.6	51.8	39.8	61.56
	Min	14.2	16.0	25.7	34.9	46.0	54.6	59.5	57.5	50.5	37.7	29.5	21.1	37.27
	Normal	24.3	27.2	37.9	48.2	59.8	67.9	72.1	70.0	63.5	51.2	40.7	30.5	49.41
	Precip	2.44	2.50	3.39	3.70	3.90	3.79	4.32	3.26	2.34	2.08	2.95	3.23	41.24
59. New Philadelphia	Max	33.1	35.7	47.4	59.4	72.1	80.6	84.6	82.4	75.9	62.8	50.2	38.1	60.19
	Min	16.1	16.7	26.4	35.1	45.3	54.8	59.3	57.6	50.7	38.8	31.7	22.7	37.93
	Normal	24.6	26.2	36.9	47.3	58.7	67.7	72.0	70.0	63.3	50.8	41.0	30.4	49.06
	Precip	2.01	2.47	3.37	3.38	4.15	4.11	4.00	3.39	3.13	2.18	2.88	2.68	39.65
60. Norwalk	Max	30.8	33.7	44.3	57.7	70.1	79.4	83.2	80.9	74.9	62.3	49.5	36.4	58.60
	Min	15.2	16.8	26.6	36.2	46.7	56.4	60.7	58.8	52.2	40.9	33.0	21.8	38.78
	Normal	23.0	25.3	35.5	47.0	58.4	67.9	72.0	69.9	63.6	51.6	41.3	29.1	48.69
	Precip	1.46	1.83	2.69	3.28	3.76	3.84	3.37	3.25	2.90	1.83	2.56	2.77	35.53
61. Oberlin	Max	31.6	35.5	46.1	59.1	71.1	80.1	84.2	81.9	75.5	63.7	50.5	36.8	59.67
	Min	13.7	15.6	25.0	34.9	45.1	54.3	58.8	56.9	50.5	39.4	31.3	20.1	37.13
	Normal	22.7	25.6	35.6	47.0	58.1	67.2	71.5	69.4	63.0	51.6	40.9	28.5	48.40
	Precip	1.75	1.95	2.68	3.12	3.78	3.49	3.78	3.08	2.65	2.18	2.93	2.63	35.98
62. Ottawa Nat'l Wildlife Refuge	Max	33.2	36.7	47.9	60.6	71.8	81.7	84.7	82.3	77.4	66.0	51.8	38.0	61.01
	Min	18.5	20.6	30.1	41.1	51.2	60.4	63.9	61.6	56.0	45.2	35.3	24.4	42.36
	Normal	25.9	28.7	39.0	50.9	61.5	71.1	74.3	72.0	66.7	55.6	43.6	31.2	51.68
	Precip	1.54	1.16	2.29	2.55	2.84	3.20	3.34	3.07	2.99	2.08	2.49	2.57	34.03
63. Painesville	Max	35.1	37.0	46.8	57.4	68.5	77.7	81.7	80.7	75.3	64.7	52.9	40.4	59.85
	Min	21.0	21.5	30.2	40.7	50.9	59.9	63.8	63.4	57.6	47.5	38.2	27.3	43.50
	Normal	28.1	29.3	38.5	49.1	59.7	68.8	72.8	72.1	66.5	56.1	45.6	33.9	51.68
	Precip	1.60	1.60	2.55	2.41	2.90	3.68	3.19	2.99	3.82	3.22	3.29	2.60	36.59
64. Pandora	Max	31.4	34.7	46.9	59.8	71.5	80.9	83.9	81.7	75.6	63.4	49.4	36.3	59.63
	Min	15.5	18.0	28.1	37.9	48.7	58.0	61.5	59.0	52.6	41.6	33.0	21.7	39.63
	Normal	23.5	26.4	37.5	48.9	60.1	69.5	72.7	70.4	64.1	52.5	41.2	29.0	49.63
	Precip	1.36	1.75	2.56	3.07	3.29	3.58	3.30	2.41	2.88	1.86	2.48	2.78	35.08

STATION		JAN.	FEB.	MAR.	APR.	MAY	JUN.	JUL.	AUG.	SEPT.	OCT.	NOV.	DEC.	ANNUAL
65. Paulding	Max	29.7	32.3	45.1	59.3	71.8	81.2	84.8	82.5	76.2	62.9	49.2	35.4	59.20
	Min	12.7	14.6	25.3	35.6	46.3	55.8	59.8	57.1	50.5	38.4	30.3	19.3	37.14
	Normal	21.2	23.5	35.2	47.5	59.1	68.5	72.3	69.8	63.4	50.7	39.8	27.4	48.17
	Precip	1.40	1.57	2.27	2.89	3.49	3.37	3.23	2.38	2.59	2.28	2.73	2.53	33.15
66. Peebles	Max	40.9	45.4	57.1	67.5	76.2	83.0	86.0	85.1	79.5	68.9	56.7	45.1	65.95
	Min	21.9	24.2	34.4	42.6	51.2	59.6	63.8	62.3	55.8	44.0	36.1	26.9	43.57
	Normal	31.4	34.8	45.8	55.1	63.7	71.3	74.9	73.7	67.7	56.5	46.4	36.0	54.76
	Precip	2.20	2.35	3.90	3.93	4.15	3.25	4.21	3.88	2.73	2.27	3.03	3.23	41.70
67. Philo	Max	36.7	40.9	53.2	64.0	73.4	80.6	83.5	82.5	75.5	66.3	53.5	41.3	62.62
	Min	20.5	22.7	32.9	42.0	50.8	58.5	62.3	61.0	54.7	44.1	35.7	25.7	42.58
	Normal	28.6	31.8	43.1	53.0	62.1	69.6	72.9	71.8	65.1	55.2	44.6	33.5	52.60
	Precip	1.67	1.89	2.65	2.59	3.87	3.79	4.13	3.04	2.58	2.14	2.53	2.38	36.83
68. Portsmouth	Max	40.0	44.1	56.0	67.0	76.4	83.6	86.8	85.8	79.8	69.0	57.1	44.9	65.88
	Min	20.8	23.8	33.5	42.7	51.8	59.8	64.0	62.4	55.8	43.9	35.7	26.3	43.38
	Normal	30.4	34.0	44.8	54.9	64.1	71.7	75.4	74.1	67.8	56.5	46.4	35.6	54.63
	Precip	2.50	2.40	3.13	3.20	3.98	3.61	3.83	4.03	2.51	2.26	2.81	3.03	39.89
69. Put-in-Bay	Max	29.1	31.7	40.9	54.1	67.0	77.1	81.9	79.9	73.7	60.5	48.1	35.3	56.61
	Min	16.2	17.2	26.4	37.9	50.5	60.3	66.0	64.9	58.7	46.3	35.7	23.9	42.00
	Normal	22.7	24.5	33.7	46.0	58.8	68.7	74.0	72.4	66.2	53.4	41.9	29.6	49.30
	Precip	1.23	1.21	2.06	2.62	3.23	3.11	2.85	3.43	2.45	2.24	2.26	2.43	31.52
70. Ripley	Max	35.6	40.5	51.5	63.3	73.6	81.6	84.8	83.3	77.8	65.7	53.2	41.4	62.69
	Min	18.4	21.0	31.1	41.0	50.6	59.0	63.2	61.5	54.9	42.4	34.1	24.3	41.80
	Normal	27.0	30.8	41.3	52.2	62.1	70.3	74.0	72.4	66.4	54.1	43.7	32.9	52.24
	Precip	2.57	2.19	4.06	3.91	4.79	3.60	4.69	3.87	2.86	2.45	3.36	3.21	43.62
71. Sandusky	Max	31.2	32.6	42.5	55.3	68.1	78.0	82.5	80.0	73.6	61.2	48.9	36.7	57.55
	Min	17.4	18.8	28.5	38.9	50.2	59.9	64.8	62.9	56.2	44.5	35.3	23.7	41.76
	Normal	24.3	25.7	35.5	47.1	59.2	69.0	73.7	71.5	64.9	52.9	42.1	30.2	49.65
	Precip	1.29	1.71	2.18	2.80	3.68	3.26	3.27	3.17	2.53	2.01	2.50	2.82	34.53
72. Springfield	Max	32.2	36.6	48.3	59.8	71.0	80.0	83.7	82.3	76.2	64.0	50.8	38.6	60.29
	Min	15.2	16.6	27.2	36.1	47.1	56.2	60.7	57.9	49.6	38.8	31.4	22.1	38.24
	Normal	23.7	26.6	37.8	48.0	59.1	68.1	72.2	70.1	62.9	51.4	41.1	30.4	49.27
	Precip	1.60	1.83	2.53	3.21	4.02	3.68	3.92	3.28	3.01	2.41	2.88	2.96	38.23

STATION		JAN.	FEB.	MAR.	APR.	MAY	JUN.	JUL.	AUG.	SEPT.	OCT.	NOV.	DEC.	ANNUAL
73. Steubenville	Max	34.8	39.2	50.6	62.1	72.5	80.6	83.8	76.5	65.4	52.7	41.0	40.3	58.29
	Min	17.4	20.4	29.3	38.4	49.1	57.9	62.6	61.4	55.2	43.1	34.7	24.2	41.14
	Normal	26.1	29.8	40.0	50.3	60.8	69.3	73.2	69.0	60.3	47.9	37.9	32.3	49.72
	Precip	2.21	2.16	3.64	3.13	3.49	3.44	3.93	2.70	2.93	2.58	2.74	2.68	37.18
74. Tiffin	Max	30.2	32.9	44.1	57.5	70.7	79.8	83.7	80.6	74.3	61.8	48.2	35.8	58.30
	Min	15.4	17.0	26.7	36.7	48.3	57.7	62.2	59.5	53.0	41.2	32.7	22.0	39.37
	Normal	22.8	25.0	35.4	47.1	59.5	68.8	73.0	70.1	63.7	51.5	40.5	28.9	48.83
	Precip	1.67	1.93	2.80	3.38	4.06	3.40	3.44	3.55	2.70	2.08	2.73	2.98	37.37
75. Toledo Airport	Max	30.2	33.4	45.5	58.8	70.5	79.8	83.4	81.3	74.4	62.4	48.5	35.2	58.62
	Min	14.9	17.0	26.8	36.4	46.7	56.0	60.6	58.4	51.5	40.0	31.5	20.5	38.36
	Normal	22.6	25.2	36.2	47.6	58.6	67.9	72.0	69.9	63.0	51.2	40.0	27.9	48.49
	Precip	1.53	1.31	2.33	2.81	2.68	3.45	3.27	3.16	2.42	1.90	2.53	3.13	32.37
76. Upper Sandusky	Max	30.7	33.9	45.2	58.4	71.3	80.4	84.4	82.8	75.7	62.7	48.9	36.4	59.23
	Min	15.0	16.8	26.6	36.5	47.8	57.2	61.5	58.8	52.4	40.9	32.2	21.8	38.96
	Normal	22.9	25.4	35.9	47.5	59.6	68.8	73.0	70.8	64.1	51.8	40.6	29.1	49.10
	Precip	1.54	1.81	2.51	2.95	4.22	3.16	3.81	2.90	2.93	1.91	2.60	2.66	35.07
77. Urbana	Max	31.7	34.6	46.1	58.9	71.3	80.2	84.1	81.9	76.0	62.9	49.7	37.3	59.56
	Min	14.5	16.1	27.0	36.3	47.3	56.5	60.5	57.2	50.2	39.2	31.0	21.2	38.08
	Normal	23.1	25.4	36.6	47.6	59.3	68.4	72.3	69.6	63.1	51.1	40.4	29.3	48.82
	Precip	1.67	2.00	2.86	3.05	3.91	3.54	4.14	3.45	2.91	2.23	3.04	2.74	38.32
78. Van Wert	Max	30.7	34.0	46.4	60.8	73.3	82.3	85.6	83.3	77.2	64.0	50.0	36.1	60.31
	Min	14.2	16.1	26.7	37.4	48.5	58.0	62.2	59.5	52.8	40.9	32.3	21.0	39.13
	Normal	22.5	25.1	36.6	49.1	60.9	70.2	73.9	71.4	65.0	52.5	41.2	28.6	49.72
	Precip	1.68	1.79	2.74	3.18	3.98	3.89	3.08	2.70	2.43	2.28	2.76	2.89	36.88
79. Warren	Max	33.4	36.7	48.0	59.9	70.9	79.3	83.2	81.4	74.7	63.1	50.5	38.3	59.95
	Min	15.3	16.8	26.2	34.5	44.6	53.6	57.8	56.5	50.2	39.3	31.7	22.1	37.38
	Normal	24.4	26.8	37.1	47.2	57.8	66.5	70.5	69.0	62.5	51.2	41.1	30.2	48.67
	Precip	1.72	1.53	2.84	2.71	3.50	3.89	3.26	2.91	3.18	2.55	2.64	2.45	36.63
80. Washington Court House	Max	36.4	40.4	52.5	64.0	73.2	80.6	83.4	82.3	77.1	66.9	53.6	41.0	62.62
	Min	19.9	22.5	32.5	41.5	51.7	60.4	64.4	62.7	56.1	44.6	35.1	25.3	43.06
	Normal	28.2	31.5	42.5	52.8	62.4	70.5	73.9	72.5	66.6	55.8	44.4	33.2	52.84
	Precip	2.00	2.08	3.43	3.20	3.93	3.75	3.62	3.64	2.73	2.25	2.89	2.95	39.68

STATION		JAN.	FEB.	MAR.	APR.	MAY	JUN.	JUL.	AUG.	SEPT.	OCT.	NOV.	DEC.	ANNUAL
81. Wauseon	Max	32.5	36.5	48.2	62.2	73.5	82.7	85.3	83.4	77.3	65.6	51.1	37.1	61.28
	Min	16.3	19.2	29.1	39.4	49.3	58.4	61.3	59.5	53.2	42.4	33.5	22.0	40.30
	Normal	24.4	27.9	38.7	50.8	61.4	70.6	73.3	71.5	65.3	54.0	42.3	29.6	50.79
	Precip	1.54	1.35	2.38	3.15	3.10	3.28	3.36	2.68	3.14	2.13	2.69	2.68	35.57
82. Waverly	Max	40.4	44.4	56.4	67.2	76.0	83.3	86.3	85.1	79.4	69.2	57.2	44.7	65.80
	Min	19.8	22.0	32.4	41.0	49.9	58.5	63.0	61.5	54.6	42.1	33.6	24.7	41.93
	Normal	30.1	33.2	44.4	54.1	63.0	70.9	74.7	73.3	67.0	55.7	45.4	34.7	53.86
	Precip	2.20	2.24	3.55	3.55	3.68	3.00	3.71	3.85	2.60	2.07	3.10	2.85	39.63
83. Westerville	Max	36.5	40.9	53.3	64.8	75.3	83.2	86.0	84.6	78.8	67.7	54.1	39.1	63.69
	Min	18.4	20.7	31.8	40.8	50.0	58.3	62.1	53.8	42.3	34.7	24.6	24.7	38.52
	Normal	27.5	30.8	42.6	52.8	62.7	70.8	74.1	69.2	60.6	51.2	39.4	31.9	51.10
	Precip	1.98	2.09	2.75	3.24	3.84	4.43	4.07	3.33	3.22	1.92	3.34	2.74	38.53
84. Wilmington	Max	33.4	36.6	48.3	60.3	72.2	80.8	84.1	82.2	76.2	63.9	50.6	38.8	60.62
	Min	16.4	18.2	28.5	38.0	48.5	57.2	61.2	58.8	52.1	40.7	32.3	22.7	39.55
	Normal	24.9	27.4	38.4	49.2	60.4	69.0	72.7	70.5	64.2	52.3	41.5	30.8	50.08
	Precip	2.33	2.64	3.78	3.50	4.01	3.46	4.32	3.26	2.79	2.39	3.15	3.06	41.43
85. Wooster	Max	31.9	35.3	47.0	58.6	69.2	77.9	81.6	79.7	73.2	61.7	49.2	36.7	58.50
	Min	16.5	18.5	28.4	37.0	47.0	55.7	59.7	58.1	51.6	40.7	33.0	22.6	39.07
	Normal	24.2	26.9	37.7	47.8	58.1	66.8	70.7	68.9	62.4	51.2	41.1	29.7	48.78
	Precip	1.60	2.01	2.60	3.00	3.73	3.37	3.47	3.58	2.78	1.78	2.72	2.50	36.03
86. Xenia	Max	36.8	41.1	53.2	64.7	74.1	81.3	82.7	77.1	66.4	53.6	41.7	41.5	59.52
	Min	19.6	22.1	33.2	42.1	51.2	59.4	62.8	60.6	54.3	43.0	34.5	24.7	42.29
	Normal	28.2	31.6	43.2	53.4	62.7	70.4	72.8	68.9	60.4	48.3	38.1	33.1	50.90
	Precip	1.94	2.10	3.39	3.78	4.13	3.33	3.91	3.00	2.98	2.71	3.27	2.80	38.45
87. Youngstown Airport	Max	30.7	33.9	45.3	57.7	68.7	77.4	81.3	79.6	72.6	60.9	48.4	36.0	57.71
	Min	16.4	17.9	27.3	36.8	46.2	54.9	59.2	57.9	51.6	41.5	33.6	22.9	38.85
	Normal	23.6	25.9	36.3	47.3	57.5	66.2	70.3	68.8	62.1	51.2	41.0	29.5	48.28
	Precip	1.93	1.93	3.23	2.88	3.30	3.53	3.45	2.98	3.43	2.60	2.93	2.90	37.66
88. Zanesville	Max	35.3	39.2	51.2	62.1	72.3	80.4	83.5	82.0	75.8	64.5	52.0	40.1	61.53
	Min	18.3	20.5	30.5	39.0	48.9	57.4	61.8	60.3	53.5	41.6	33.6	24.1	40.79
	Normal	26.8	29.9	40.9	50.6	60.6	68.9	72.7	71.2	64.7	53.1	42.8	32.1	51.16
	Precip	1.99	2.29	3.15	3.14	3.88	3.71	4.31	3.48	2.91	2.05	2.74	2.69	39.08

APPENDIX TWO

Ohio's Records and Extremes

EXTREMES OF TEMPERATURE, precipitation, snowfall, wind, and pressure are given in Appendix 2. Primary sources for this information were Alexander (1924), Ludlum (1982), National Weather Service offices in Ohio, and the government publications *Monthly Weather Review* and *Climatological Data—Ohio*. Records are limited to those measured at official government weather stations in most cases. More extreme values may have occurred at other locations. Methods of measuring these weather elements at official government weather stations have varied over time. Some nineteenth-century records are incomplete in the archives. A number and letter after a community name indicates the distance, in miles, and compass direction of the weather station from the post office, i.e., Danville 2W is two miles west of the Danville Post Office.

Temperatures

Cold
Monthly Cold Records

MONTH	TEMPERATURE	LOCATION	DATE
January	-37°	Milligan	13 January 1912
		Logan	19 January 1994
February	-39°	Milligan	10 February 1899
March	-21°	Fredericktown 4S	9 March 1984
April	-1°	Mansfield 5W	1 April 1964
May	17°	Jackson	10 May 1966
June	27°	Danville 2W	11 June 1972
July	34°	Norwalk	4 July 1895
		Auburn	9 July 1895
		Caldwell 6NW	1 July 1988
August	27°	Canfield	29 August 1982
		Millport	29 August 1982
September	23°	Norwalk	23 September 1896
		Orangeville	22 September 1904
October	7°	Hedges	30 October 1895
November	-17°	Mansfield 6W	30 November 1958
December	-32°	Wauseon	19 December 1884

Coldest Monthly Average

January 1977	6.8°	Eaton

Coldest Annual Average

1843	42.2°	East Cleveland

Heat
Monthly Heat Records

MONTH	TEMPERATURE	LOCATION	DATE
January	81°	Ironton	unknown
February	84°	Portsmouth	February 1883
March	96°	Portsmouth	23 March 1907
April	97°	Portsmouth	30 April 1894
		Portsmouth	24 April 1925
May	103°	Wauseon	May 1874
June	108°	Germantown	29 June 1934
July	113°	Gallipolis 5NW	21 July 1934
August	111°	Napoleon	6 August 1947
September	107°	Logan	5 September 1899
		Philo	4 September 1953
October	99°	Ironton	October 1884
November	89°	Gallipolis 5NW	7 November 1938
December	80°	Athens	1 December 1982
		Gallipolis	1 December 1982
		Ironton	1 December 1982

Warmest Monthly Average

July 1881	86.4°	Hamilton

Warmest Annual Average

1854	59.3°	Portsmouth

Precipitation
Rain
GREATEST RAINFALL IN ONE HOUR

3.58"	Toledo	16 August 1920

GREATEST RAINFALL IN TWENTY-FOUR HOURS

10.51"	Sandusky	12 July 1966

Greatest rainfall in one month

17.33"	Carthagenia	June 1887

Least rainfall in one month

0.00"	New Alexandria	October 1897
0.00"	Three stations	September 1963
0.00"	Thirty stations	October 1963
0.00"	Five stations	February 1987

Greatest rainfall in one year

70.82"	Little Mountain (Geauga County)	1870
70.48"	Kings Mills	1926

Least rainfall in one year

16.96"	Elyria 3E	1963

Snow

Most snow in twenty-four hours

20.7"	Youngstown	24–25 November 1950

Most snow in one storm

42"	Canton	19-22 April 1901
	Gratiot	19-22 April 1901

Most snow in one month

69.5"	Chardon	December 1962

Most snow in one winter

161.5"	Chardon	1959-60

Maximum depth

45"	Ashtabula County	11 December 1962

Wind

Fastest recorded

87 mph	Toledo	19 March 1948

Tornadoes

Deadliest

85 killed	Sandusky-Lorain	28 June 1924

Most in one day

28	12 July 1992

Most in one month

44	July 1992

Most in one year

61	1992

Freezes

Latest spring freeze

32°	Dorset	22 June 1992

Earliest autumn freeze

32°	Youngstown Oberlin	29 August 1982
30°	Dorset Warren 3S	29 August 1982
27°	Canfield 1S Millport 2NW	29 August 1982

Atmospheric Pressure

Highest

31.04"	Toledo	26 January 1927

Lowest

28.28"	Cleveland	26 January 1978

Bibliography

Abbey, R. F., and T. T. Fujita. 1981. "Tornadoes as Represented by the Tornado Outbreak of 3–4 April 1974." In *Thunderstorms: A Social, Scientific, and Technological Documentary.* Vol. 1, *The Thunderstorm in Human Affairs.* Washington, D.C.: U.S. Department of Commerce, National Oceanic and Atmospheric Administration.

Alexander, W. H. 1913. "Storm of November 7–10: At Cleveland, Ohio." *Monthly Weather Review* 41:1680.

———. 1918. "The Cold Wave of January 11–12, 1918." *Climatological Data— Ohio Section* 23 (1): 4. Washington, D.C.: Weather Bureau, U.S. Department of Agriculture.

———. 1924. *A Climatological History of Ohio.* Ohio State University Engineering Experiment Station Bulletin 26. Columbus.

Alexander, W. H., and C. A. Patton. 1929. *The Climate of Ohio.* Ohio Agricultural Experiment Station Bulletin 445. Wooster.

Alley, W. M. 1984. "The Palmer Drought Severity Index: Limitations and Assumptions." *Journal of Climate and Applied Meteorology* 23:1100–1109.

American National Standards Institute (ANSI). 1982. *Minimum Design Loads for Buildings and Other Structures.* ANSI A58.1-1982. New York: ANSI.

American Red Cross. 1938. *Spring Flood and Tornadoes—1936.* Washington, D.C.: American Red Cross.

———. 1939. *The Ohio-Mississippi Valley Flood Disaster of 1937.* Washington, D.C.: American Red Cross.

Appleby, A. B. 1980. "Epidemics and Famine in the Little Ice Age." *Journal of Interdisciplinary History* 10:643–63.

Archer, R. J. 1960. *Sediment Discharges of Ohio Streams during Floods of January– February 1959.* Columbus: U.S. Geological Survey, Ohio Department of Natural Resources, Division of Water.

Assel, R. A., F. H. Quinn, G. A. Leshkevich, and S. J. Bolsenga. 1983. *Great Lakes Ice Atlas.* Ann Arbor, Mich.: U.S. Department of Commerce, Great Lakes Environmental Research Laboratory.

Atwater, C. 1838. *A History of the State of Ohio, Natural and Civil.* 2d ed. Cincinnati: Glezen and Shepard.

Baldwin, J. L. 1943. "Preliminary Report on Tornadoes in the United States during 1943 and Totals and Averages, 1916–42, by States." *Monthly Weather Review* 71:195–97.

———. 1973. *Climates of the States.* Washington, D.C.: U.S. Department of Commerce, National Oceanic and Atmospheric Administration.

Becker, C. M., and P. B. Nolan. 1988. *Keeping the Promise: A Pictorial History of the Miami Conservancy District.* Dayton, Ohio: Landfall Press.

———. 1989. "They Gathered at the River." *Timeline* 6 (5): 34–47.

Bilello, M. A. 1971. "Frozen Precipitation—Its Frequency and Associated Temperatures." In *Proceedings of the 28th Eastern Snow Conference,* 68–80. Fredericton, Canada: Eastern Snow Conference.

Blackburn, T. 1978. "The Phenomenal Storm of January 25–26, 1978." *National Weather Digest* 3 (2): 20–25.

Bluestein, H. B., and J. H. Golden. 1993. "A Review of Tornado Observations." In *The Tornado: Its Structure, Dynamics, Prediction, and Hazards,* edited by C. Church, D. Burgess, C. Doswell, and R. Davies-Jones, 319–52. American Geophysical Union Geophysical Monograph Series 79. Washington, D.C.

Bock, C. A. 1918. *History of the Miami Flood Control Project.* Miami Conservancy District Technical Reports, part 2. Dayton, Ohio.

Boyce, D. 1978. "Great Lakes Ice Season, 1977–78." *Mariners Weather Log* 22:401–9.

Brazel, A. J., and D. W. Phillips. 1974. "November 1972 Floods on the Lower Great Lakes." *Weatherwise* 27:56–62.

Brooks, C. F. 1918a. "The 'Old-Fashioned' Winter of 1917–18." *Geographical Review* 5:405–14.

———. 1918b. "The 'Old-Fashioned' Winter of 1917–18." *Science* 47:565–66.

Brooks, C. F., and A. H. Thiessen. 1937. "The Meteorology of Great Floods in the Eastern United States." *Geographical Review* 27:269–90.

Buckley, W. T. 1935. "The Ohio River Flood of March 1933." *Ohio Journal of Science* 35:67–77.

Burgess, D. W., R. J. Donaldson Jr., and P. R. Desrochers. 1993. "Tornado Detection and Warning by Radar." In *The Tornado: Its Structure, Dynamics, Prediction, and Hazards,* edited by C. Church, D. Burgess, C. Doswell, and R. Davies-Jones, 203–21. American Geophysical Union Geophysical Monograph Series 79. Washington, D.C.

Byers, H. R. 1974. *General Meteorology.* 4th ed. New York: McGraw-Hill.

Calderazzo, J. 1983. "Come Spring and High Water." *Ohio Magazine* 5 (12): 30–37.

Catton, B. 1985. "The Ultimate Storm: The Great Lakes Hurricane of 1913." *Weatherwise* 38:248–53.

Changnon, S. A., and W. E. Easterling. 1989. "Measuring Drought Impacts: The Illinois Case." *Water Resources Bulletin* 25:27–42.

Churchill, D. D., S. H. Houston, and N. A. Bond. 1995. "The Daytona Beach Wave of 3–4 July 1992: A Shallow-Water Gravity Wave Forced by a Propagating Squall Line." *Bulletin of the American Meteorological Society* 76:21–32.

Clarke, J. F. 1969. "Nocturnal Urban Boundary Layer over Cincinnati, Ohio." *Monthly Weather Review* 97:582–89.

Clatworthy, L. M. 1913. "Ohio Libraries in the Flood." *Library Journal* 38 (11): 602–7.

Clem, J. C. 1978. *After Action Report (RCS ARNGB-98), Blizzard of '78, 9 January to 5 February 1978.* Worthington: Ohio Adjutant General's Department.

Conover, C. R. 1917. *The Story of Dayton.* Dayton, Ohio: Otterbein Press.

Cross, W. P. 1947. *The Flood of June 1946 in Wayne and Holmes Counties, Ohio.* U.S. Geological Survey, Ohio Water Resources Board Bulletin 9. Columbus.

———. 1948. *Local Floods in Ohio during 1947.* U.S. Geological Survey, Ohio Water Resources Board Bulletin 14. Columbus.

———. 1949. *Local Floods in Ohio during 1948.* U.S. Geological Survey, Ohio Water Resources Board Bulletin 18. Columbus.

———. 1950. *The Crooksville Area Flood of June 16–17, 1950: A Preliminary Report.* Columbus: U.S. Geological Survey, Ohio Department of Natural Resources.

———. 1961. *Floods of January–February 1959 in Ohio: Summary of Flood Stages and Discharges.* U.S. Geological Survey, Ohio Department of Natural Resources Bulletin 35. Columbus.

———. 1964a. *Floods of March 1963 in Ohio and the Flash Flood of June 1963 in the Vicinity of Cambridge.* U.S. Geological Survey, Ohio Department of Natural Resources Bulletin 38. Columbus.

———. 1964b. *Floods of March 1964 in Ohio.* U.S. Geological Survey, Ohio Department of Natural Resources Bulletin 39. Columbus.

———. 1966. *Flood of July 23, 1965 in the Vicinity of Hillsboro.* U.S. Geological Survey, Ohio Department of Natural Resources Miscellaneous Report 16. Columbus.

———. 1967. "Floods of July 12, in the Vicinity of Sandusky, Ohio." In *Summary of Floods in the United States during 1966,* D36-D38. U.S. Geological Survey Water Supply Paper 1870-D. Washington, D.C.

Cross, W. P., and R. I. Mayo. 1969. *Floods in Ohio, Magnitude and Frequency: A Supplement to Bulletin 32.* Ohio Department of Natural Resources, Division of Water Bulletin 43. Columbus.

Cross, W. P., and E. E. Webber. 1959. *Floods in Ohio, Magnitude and Frequency Based on Records through 1956.* Ohio Department of Natural Resources, Division of Water Bulletin 32. Columbus.

Crowther, H. G. 1993. "Tornadoes Hit New Heights." *Weatherwise* 46:29–37.

Dare, P. M. 1981. "A Study of the Severity of Midwestern Winters of 1977 and 1978 Using Heating Degree Days Determined from Both Measured and Wind Chill Values." *Bulletin of the American Meteorological Society* 62:974–82.

Davis, J. M. 1973. *Probabilities of Thunderstorm and Hail Days in Ohio.* Department of Geography, Ohio State University, Discussion Paper 34. Columbus.

Day, P. C. 1918. "The Cold Winter of 1917–18." *Monthly Weather Review* 46:570–79.

Devereaux, W. C. 1917. "Tornado at Cincinnati, Ohio, March 11, 1917." *Monthly Weather Review* 45:115–17.

———. 1919. "Weather in Cincinnati, Ohio, for 130 Years." *Monthly Weather Review* 47:480–86.

———. 1930. "Drought in Ohio Valley and Water Supply." *Monthly Weather Review* 58:401.

DeWeese, T. 1924. *Lorain Tornado: Souvenir and Memorial Book.* Lorain, Ohio: R. Moc and T. DeWeese.

Diaz, H. F. 1979. "The Extreme Temperature Anomalies of March 1843 and February 1936." *Monthly Weather Review* 107:1688–94.

Diaz, H. F., and R. G. Quayle. 1980. "An Analysis of the Recent Extreme Winters in the Contiguous United States." *Monthly Weather Review* 108:687–99.

Dickerson, W. H., and B. E. Dethier. 1970. *Drought Frequency in the Northeastern United States.* West Virginia University Agricultural Experiment Station Bulletin 595. Morgantown.

Dickson, R. R. 1978. "Weather and Circulation of February 1978—Record or Near-Record Cold East of the Continental Divide with a Major Blizzard in the Northeast." *Monthly Weather Review* 106:746–51.

Dingle, A. N. 1954. "Ohio's Contributions to Meteorology, a Brief Historical Resume." *Ohio Journal of Science* 54:378–79.

Doswell, C. A., and D. W. Burgess. 1993. "Tornadoes and Tornadic Storms: A Review of Conceptual Models." In *The Tornado: Its Structure, Dynamics, Prediction, and Hazards,* edited by C. Church, D. Burgess, C. Doswell, and R. Davies-Jones, 161–72. American Geophysical Union Geophysical Monograph Series 79. Washington, D.C.

Edgell, D. J. 1988. "An Analysis of the Snow Water Equivalent Measurement in Ohio with Applications for Snowmelt Climatology." Master's thesis, Kent State University, Kent, Ohio.

———. 1992. "The Climatology of the Extreme Minimum Winter Temperature in Ohio." Ph.D. diss., Kent State University, Kent, Ohio.

Ewing, M., F. Press, and W. L. Donn. 1954. "An Explanation of the Lake Michigan Wave of 26 June 1954." *Science* 120:684–86.

Feyerherm, A. M., L. D. Bark, and W. C. Burrows. 1966. *Probabilities of Wet and Dry Days in Ohio.* Kansas Agricultural Experiment Station Technical Bulletin 1391. Manhattan.

Finley, J. P. 1889. "State Tornado Charts—Ohio." *American Meteorological Journal* 6:205–10.

Forbes, G. S., R. M. Blackall, and P. L. Taylor. 1993. "'Blizzard of the Century'—The Storm of 12–14 March 1993 over the Eastern United States." *Meteorological Magazine* 122:153–62.

Fujita, T. T., D. L. Bradbury, and C. F. van Thullenar. 1970. "Palm Sunday Tornadoes of April 11, 1965." *Monthly Weather Review* 98:29–69.

Fujita, T. T., and H. R. Byers. 1977. "Spearhead Echo and Downburst in the Crash of an Airliner." *Monthly Weather Review* 105:129–46.

Fujita, T. T., and F. Caracena. 1977. "An Analysis of Three Weather-Related Aircraft Accidents." *Bulletin of the American Meteorological Society* 58:1164–81.

Fujita, T. T., and B. E. Smith. 1993. "Aerial Survey and Photography of Tornado and Microburst Damage." In *The Tornado: Its Structure, Dynamics, Prediction, and Hazards,* edited by C. Church, D. Burgess, C. Doswell, and R. Davies-Jones, 479–93. American Geophysical Union Geophysical Monograph Series 79. Washington, D.C.

Galbreath, C. B. 1925. *History of Ohio,* vol. 2. Chicago: American Historical Society.

Glatfelter, D. R., and E. H. Chin. 1988. *Floods of March 1982 in Indiana, Ohio, Michigan, and Illinois.* U.S. Geological Survey Professional Paper 1467. Washington, D.C.

Goldthwait, R. P. 1959. "Scenes in Ohio during the Last Ice Age." *Ohio Journal of Science* 59:193–216.

Grazulis, T. P. 1990. *Significant Tornadoes, 1880–1989.* Vol. 2, *A Chronology of Events.* St. Johnsbury, Vt.: Environmental Films.

———. 1991. *Significant Tornadoes, 1880–1989.* Vol. 1, *Discussion and Analysis.* St. Johnsbury, Vt.: Environmental Films.

————. 1993. *Significant Tornadoes 1680–1879, 1990–1991*. St. Johnsbury, Vt.: Environmental Films.

Groneweg, L. 1856. *Meteorological observations made in Montgomery County, southern Ohio, and a condensed treatise on meteorology in general*. Germantown, Ohio: L. Groneweg.

Heim, R. R. 1988. "About that Drought . . ." *Weatherwise* 40:266–71.

Henry, A. J. 1913. "The Precipitation and Floods in the Ohio Basin, March 23 to 27, 1913." *Monthly Weather Review* 41:485–92.

Hickcox, D. H. 1984. "The Winter of 1982–83 in Ohio." *Ohio Journal of Science* 84:236–41.

Hildreth, S. P. 1832. "Seasons, productions & etc. in the state of Ohio." *New England Farmer* 10, no. 43 (May 9, 1832): 337–38.

Hill, N. N. 1881. *History of Licking County, Ohio: Its Past and Present*. Newark: A. A. Graham.

Hiscock, B. 1993. *The Big Storm*. New York: Atheneum.

Horstmeyer, S. L. 1989. "In Search of Cincinnati's Weather." *Weatherwise* 42:320–27.

Horton, A. H., and H. J. Jackson. 1913. *The Ohio Valley Flood of March–April, 1913*. U.S. Department of the Interior, Geological Survey Water Supply Paper 334. Washington, D.C.

Howe, H. 1847. *Historical Collections of the State of Ohio,* vol. 2. Cincinnati: Cincinnati, Derby, Bradley.

Hughes, P., and R. Wood. 1993. "Hail: The White Plague." *Weatherwise* 45:16–21.

Hunter, H. C. 1924. "The Lorain, Ohio, Tornado, June 28, 1924." *Monthly Weather Review* 52:309–10.

Hutter, H. K. 1952. "Eighty Years of Weather and Climate at Toledo, Ohio." *Ohio Journal of Science* 52:62–75.

Hyde, J. A. 1905. "Fifty Years' Weather at Cleveland." *Journal of the Association of Engineering Societies* 35:171–90.

Irish, S. M., and G. W. Platzman. 1962. "An Investigation of the Meteorological Conditions Associated with Extreme Wind Tides on Lake Erie." *Monthly Weather Review* 90:39–48.

Kalkstein, L. S., and R. E. Davis. 1989. "Weather and Human Mortality: An Evaluation of Demographic and Interregional Responses in the United States." *Annals of the Association of American Geographers* 79:44–64.

Kalkstein, L. S., and K. M. Valimont. 1987. "An Evaluation of Winter Weather Severity in the United States Using the Weather Stress Index." *Bulletin of the American Meteorological Society* 68:1535–40.

Karl, T. R. 1983. "Some Spatial Characteristics of Drought Duration in the United States." *Journal of Climate and Applied Meteorology* 22:1356–66.

Karl, T. R., and R. W. Knight. 1985a. *Atlas of Monthly Palmer Drought Severity Indices (1895–1930) for the Contiguous United States*. National Climatic Data Center Historical Climatology Series 3-10. Asheville, N.C.

————. 1985b. *Atlas of Monthly Palmer Drought Severity Indices (1931–1983) for the Contiguous United States*. National Climatic Data Center Historical Climatology Series 3-11. Asheville, N.C.

Karl, T. R., L. K. Metcalf, M. L. Nicodemus, and R. G. Quayle. 1983. *Statewide Average Climatic History: Ohio, 1883–1982*. National Climatic Data Center Historical Climatology Series 6-1. Asheville, N.C.

Kaser, P. 1959. *Meteorology of Floods in Ohio, January 1959, February 1959*. Columbus: Ohio Department of Natural Resources, Division of Water.

Kenealy, J. 1909. "Severe Local Storm at Cleveland, Ohio." *Monthly Weather Review* 37:153–54.

Killits, J. M. 1923. *Toledo and Lucas County, Ohio 1623–1923,* vol. 1. Chicago: S. J. Clarke Publishing.

Kirk, J. M. 1913. "Destructive Storms of July 13–14 in Ohio." *Monthly Weather Review* 41:996–97.

Knepper, G. W. 1989. *Ohio and Its People.* Kent, Ohio: Kent State University Press.

Kochar, N., and T. W. Schmidlin. 1989. "Heat Island of the Akron-Canton Regional Airport." *Geographical Bulletin* 32:46–55.

Kocin, P. J., and L. W. Uccellini. 1990. *Snowstorms along the Northeastern Coast of the United States: 1955–1985.* American Meteorological Society Meteorological Monographs Vol. 22, No. 44. Boston.

Konrad, C. E., and S. J. Colucci. 1989. "An Examination of Extreme Cold Air Outbreaks over Eastern North America." *Monthly Weather Review* 117:2687–2700.

Landsberg, H. E. 1985. "The Value of Weather Chronicles." *Weatherwise* 38:322–23.

Lewis, T. W. 1913. *Zanesville in the Flood of 1913.* Zanesville, Ohio: A. E. Starr.

Ludlum, D. M. 1966. *Early American Winters 1604–1820.* Boston: American Meteorological Society.

———. 1968. *Early American Winters 1821–1870.* Boston: American Meteorological Society.

———. 1971. *Weather Record Book: The Outstanding Events 1871–1970.* Princeton, N.J.: Weatherwise.

———. 1976. *The Country Journal New England Weather Book.* Boston: Houghton Mifflin.

———. 1982. *The American Weather Book.* Boston: Houghton Mifflin.

———. 1993. "Weatherwatch—March 1993." *Weatherwise* 46 (3): 43–51.

Mark, E. H. 1884. "The Jamestown Tornado." *Report of the Ohio Meteorological Bureau for the Month of April 1884,* 6–23. Columbus: G. J. Brand.

Martin, M. J. 1992. "The Big Blow." *Timeline* 9 (3): 30–43.

Miller, A., and D. H. Gould. 1951. "The Extensive Cold Air Outbreak of January 24–31, 1951." *Monthly Weather Review* 79:20–26.

Miller, M. E. 1969a. "Bucket Survey Data of July 4–5, 1969, Storm." *Climatological Data—Ohio* 74 (12): 185–92.

———. 1969b. *Climatic Guide for Selected Locations in Ohio.* Ohio Department of Natural Resources, Division of Water Miscellaneous Report 17. Columbus.

———. 1969c. "Summary of Ohio Tornadoes." *Ohio Journal of Science* 69:343–46.

———. 1973. *Frequency and Intensity of Freezing Rain/Drizzle in Ohio.* U.S. Department of Commerce, National Oceanic and Atmospheric Administration Technical Memorandum NWS ER-51. Washington, D.C.

Miller, M. E., and R. E. Hamilton. 1969. "A Holiday Weekend Holocaust in Ohio." *Weatherwise* 22:190–94.

Miller, M. E., and V. L. Seidel. 1969. *Climatic Studies for Ohio: An Annotated Bibliography.* Ohio Agricultural Research and Development Center Research Circular 163. Wooster.

Miller, M. E., and C. R. Weaver. 1968. *Monthly and Annual Precipitation Probabilities for Climatic Divisions in Ohio.* Ohio Agricultural Research and Development Center Research Bulletin 1005. Wooster.

————. 1969. *Monthly and Annual Precipitation Probabilities for Selected Locations in Ohio.* Ohio Agricultural Research and Development Center Research Bulletin 1017. Wooster.

————. 1970a. *Extreme Monthly and Annual Temperatures in Ohio.* Ohio Agricultural Research and Development Center Research Bulletin 1041. Wooster.

————. 1970b. *Mean Recurrence Tables of Daily Precipitation Amounts for Selected Locations in Ohio.* Ohio Agricultural Research and Development Center Research Bulletin 1034. Wooster.

————. 1971. *Snow in Ohio.* Ohio Agricultural Research and Development Center Research Bulletin 1044. Wooster.

Mindling, G. W. 1944. *Weather Headlines in Ohio.* Ohio State University Engineering Experiment Station Bulletin 120. Columbus.

Minor, J. E., J. R. McDonald, and R. E. Peterson. 1982. "Analysis of Near-Ground Windfields." In *Preprints of the 12th Conference on Severe Local Storms,* 289–92. Boston: American Meteorological Society.

Mitchell, C. L. 1920. "The Thirteen Tornadoes of March 28, 1920." *Monthly Weather Review* 48:191–98.

Mogil, H. M., A. Stern, and R. Hagan. 1984. "The Great Freeze of '83: Analyzing the Causes." *Weatherwise* 37:304–8.

Morgan, A. E. 1917. *The Miami Valley and the 1913 Flood.* Miami Conservancy District Technical Report, part 1. Dayton, Ohio.

————. 1951. *The Miami Conservancy District.* New York: McGraw-Hill.

Namias, J. 1983. "Some Causes of United States Drought." *Journal of Climate and Applied Meteorology* 22:30–39.

National Oceanic and Atmospheric Administration (NOAA). 1974. *Natural Disaster Survey Report 74-1: The Widespread Tornado Outbreak of April 3–4, 1974.* Rockville, Md.: U.S. Department of Commerce, National Weather Service.

————. 1985. *Natural Disaster Survey Report: The Ohio-Pennsylvania Tornadoes of May 31, 1985.* Silver Spring, Md.: U.S. Department of Commerce, National Weather Service.

————. 1991. *Natural Disaster Survey Report: Shadyside, Ohio, Flash Floods June 14, 1990.* Silver Spring, Md.: U.S. Department of Commerce, National Weather Service.

Ohio Almanac. 1980. *The Ohio Almanac 1980.* Dayton, Ohio: Kids Come in Special Flavors.

Ohio Department of Agriculture. 1993. *1992 Annual Report & Statistics.* Columbus: Ohio Agricultural Statistics Service, Ohio Department of Agriculture.

Ohio Historical Society. 1993. "Fearsome Flood." *Echoes* 32 (3): 4.

Owenby, J. R., and D. S. Ezell. 1992. *Monthly Station Normals of Temperature, Precipitation, and Heating and Cooling Degree Days 1961–90, Ohio.* Climatography of the United States No. 81. Asheville, N.C.: U.S. Department of Commerce National Climatic Data Center.

Palmer, W. C. 1965. *Meteorological Drought.* U.S. Department of Commerce Weather Bureau Research Paper 45. Washington, D.C.

Paris, J. 1984. "Tall Winters." *Ohio Magazine* 7 (11): 40–51.

Perry, J. B., R. Hawkins, and D. M. Neal. 1988. "The Blizzard of 1978 in Wood County, Ohio." *Northwest Ohio Quarterly* 60:3–16.

Pierce, L. T. 1959. *The Occurrence of Freezing Temperatures in Late Spring and Early Fall.* Ohio Agricultural Experiment Station Special Circular 94. Wooster.

Quayle, R. G., D. R. Easterling, T. R. Karl, and P. Y. Hughes. 1991. "Effects of Recent Thermometer Changes in the Cooperative Station Network." *Bulletin of the American Meteorological Society* 72:1718–23.

Riedel, B. L. 1974. *Tornado at Xenia April 3, 1974.* Cleveland: Carpenter Printing.

Riordan, P., and P. G. Bourget. 1985. *World Weather Extremes.* Ft. Belvoir, Va.: U.S. Army Corps of Engineers, Engineering Topographic Laboratories ETL-0416.

Robinson, D. A., and D. M. Ludlum. 1989. "The Weather Where You Live." *Weatherwise* 42:328–30.

Rogers, J. C. 1993. "Climatological Aspects of Drought in Ohio." *Ohio Journal of Science* 93:51–59.

Rogers, J. C., and A. Yersavich. 1988. "Daily Air Temperature Variability Associated with Climatic Variability at Columbus, Ohio." *Physical Geography* 9:120–38.

Rogot, E., P. D. Sorlie, and E. Backlund. 1992. "Air-Conditioning and Mortality in Hot Weather." *American Journal of Epidemiology* 136:106–16.

Sanderson, E. E. 1950. *The Climatic Factors of Ohio's Water Resources: Precipitation, Temperature, Evaporation, Trends and Cycles, Excessive Rainfall.* U.S. Geological Survey, Ohio Department of Natural Resources Bulletin 15. Columbus.

Schmidlin, T. W. 1988. "Ohio Tornado Climatology, 1950–85." In *Preprints of the 15th Conference on Severe Local Storms,* 523–24. Boston: American Meteorological Society.

———. 1989a. "Climatic Summary of Snowfall and Snow Depth in the Ohio Snowbelt at Chardon." *Ohio Journal of Science* 89:101–8.

———. 1989b. "A Climatology of Shallow Winter Temperature Inversions in Lake Erie Vineyards." In *Preprints of the 19th Conference on Agriculture and Forest Meteorology,* 6–9. Boston: American Meteorological Society.

———. 1989c. "The Urban Heat Island at Toledo, Ohio." *Ohio Journal of Science* 89:38–41.

———. 1990. "The Climate of Ohio." In *The Changing American Heartland: A Geography of Ohio,* edited by L. Peacefull, 17–32. Needham, Mass.: Ginn Press.

———. 1992. "The Midwest and Appalachian Cold Wave of July 1988." *American Weather Observer,* July, 5.

———. 1993a. "Impacts of Heavy Snowfall during December 1989 in the Lake Erie Snowbelt." *Journal of Climate* 6:759–67.

———. 1993b. "Tornado Fatalities in Ohio, 1950–1989." In *The Tornado: Its Structure, Dynamics, Prediction, and Hazards,* edited by C. Church, D. Burgess, C. Doswell, R. Davies-Jones, 529–34. American Geophysical Union Geophysical Monograph 79. Washington, D.C.

Schmidlin, T. W., D. J. Edgell, and M. A. Delaney. 1992. "Design Ground Snow Loads for Ohio." *Journal of Applied Meteorology* 31:622–27.

Schott, C. A. 1868. *Results of Meteorological Observations Made at Marietta, Ohio, Between 1826 and 1859, Inclusive by S.P. Hildreth, M.D.* Smithsonian Institution Contributions to Knowledge 120. Washington, D.C.

Shane, L. C. K. 1987. "Late-Glacial Vegetational and Climatic History of the Allegheny Plateau and the Till Plains of Ohio and Indiana, U.S.A." *Boreas* 16:1–20.

Smith, C. D. 1950. "The Destructive Storm of November 25–27, 1950." *Monthly Weather Review* 78:204–9.

Smith, G. H. 1933. "Weather Conditions during Washington's Western Journey of 1770." *Ohio Journal of Science* 33:37–47.

Smith, H. E. 1982. *Killer Weather: Stories of Great Disasters.* New York: Dodd, Mead.

Smith, J. W. 1907. "Flood of March 12 to 20, 1907." *Climatological Report: Ohio Section, March 1907.* Washington, D.C.: U.S. Department of Agriculture, Weather Bureau.

———. 1908. "Severe Windstorms in Ohio, June 19, 1908." *Monthly Weather Review* 36:165–66.

———. 1912a. *The Climate of Ohio.* Ohio Agricultural Experiment Station Bulletin 235. Wooster.

———. 1912b. "Winter Damage to Peaches." *Monthly Weather Review* 40:29–30.

———. 1914. "Possibility of Recurrence of the Floods of March 1913." *Monthly Weather Review* 42:176–78.

———. 1917. "Thomas Mikesell, 1845–1917." *Monthly Weather Review* 45:368–69.

Stoddard, O. N. 1854. "The Brandon Tornado of January 20th, 1854." *American Journal of Science and Arts,* 2d ser. (July 1854).

Swayze, D. 1992a. "The Great Spring Gale of 1894." *Inland Seas* 48:99–112.

———. 1992b. *Shipwreck!* Boyne City, Mich.: Harbor House Publishers.

Thurber, J. 1983. "The Day the Dam Broke." *Ohio Magazine* 5 (12): 38–39.

Trenberth, K. E., G. W. Branstator, and P. A. Arkin. 1988. "Origins of the 1988 North American Drought." Abstract in *EOS* 69 (44): 1067.

U.S. Environmental Science Services Administration (ESSA). 1969. *Report of Weather Bureau Survey Team, Storm of July 4–5, 1969 Northern Ohio.* Garden City, N.J.: ESSA, Weather Bureau Eastern Region.

U.S. Weather Bureau (USWB). 1965. *Weather Bureau Survey Team Report of Palm Sunday Tornadoes of 1965.* Washington, D.C.: U.S. Department of Commerce Weather Bureau.

Verber, J. L. 1955. "The Climates of South Bass Island, Western Lake Erie." *Ecology* 36:388–99.

Wagner, A. J. 1977. "Weather and Circulation of January 1977." *Monthly Weather Review* 105:553–60.

Webber, E. E., and W. P. Bartlett. 1977. *Floods in Ohio: Magnitude and Frequency.* Ohio Department of Natural Resources, Division of Water Bulletin 45. Columbus.

Whittier, B. B. 1923. "Snowstorm of May 8–9, 1923, in Michigan." *Monthly Weather Review* 51:200–201.

Witten, D. E. 1985. "May 31, 1985: A Deadly Tornado Outbreak." *Weatherwise* 38:193–98.

Wolfson, M. M. 1988. "Characteristics of Microbursts Observed in the Continental U.S." In *Preprints of the 15th Conference on Severe Local Storms,* 372–79. Boston: American Meteorological Society.

Woodward, S. M. 1920. *Hydraulics of the Miami Flood Control Project.* Miami Conservancy District Technical Reports, part 7. Dayton, Ohio.

Young, R. F. 1917. "Tornadoes of March 11, 1917, in Montgomery County, Ohio." *Monthly Weather Review* 45:117–18.

Newspapers Used as Sources

Akron American Balance, 26 October 1837
Akron Beacon Journal, 10 April 1890–21 January 1994
Alliance Review, 3 May 1972
Ashland Times-Gazette, 5–11 July 1969
Athens Journal, 21 March 1907
Athens Messenger, 20 May 1886–3 June 1990
Batavia Clermont Courier, 7 June 1916
Bellefontaine Republican, 14 June 1872
Bryan Press, 24 May 1894
Bryan Times, 5 July 1957–29 September 1967
Cambridge Daily Jeffersonian, 17 July 1914–20 July 1961
Canfield Republican Sentinel, 9–21 June 1859
Canton Reporter, 4–6 May 1972
Canton Repository, 25 June 1884–10 August 1992
Celina Daily Standard, 2–5 November 1966
Chardon Geauga Record, 4 November 1954
Chillicothe Ohio Centinel, 1 July 1812
Cincinnati Enquirer, 22 May 1860–9 February 1994
Cincinnati Post, 20 August 1983–9 February 1994
Cincinnati Republican, 9 February 1835
Cincinnati Times Star, 25 March 1913–25 January 1937
Cleveland Plain Dealer, 6 June 1859–24 April 1996
Cleveland Record, 26 January 1963
Cleveland Suburban Sun, 11–13 December 1962
Cleveland Sun-Press, 24–25 January 1963
Columbus Dispatch, 5 February 1884–21 January 1994
Columbus Ohio State Journal, 8 January 1856–15 January 1912
Conneaut News-Herald, 3 November 1967–18 December 1972
Coshocton Tribune, 3–14 August 1935
Dayton Daily News, 29 March 1920–24 November 1992
Dayton Journal (Herald), 26 January 1884–21 January 1985
Defiance Crescent-News, 30 March 1928–15 July 1936
Delaware Gazette, 3 October–31 December 1963
Eaton Register Herald, 26 April–3 May 1961
Elyria Democrat, 12 July 1900
Elyria Republican, 12–19 July 1900
Findlay Hancock Courier, 20 May 1886
Findlay Morning Republican, 27 March–3 April 1928
Findlay Republican Courier, 14 May 1947–15 July 1959
Findlay Republican Jeffersonian, 18 February 1909
Fremont Messenger, 6–27 July 1934
Gallipolis Tribune, 9 July 1897–23 July 1934
Greenville Daily Advocate, 26–28 May 1962
Hamilton Butler County Democrat, 24 May 1883–5 September 1895
Hamilton Evening Journal, 26 February 1929–15 July 1966
Hillsboro News Herald, 12 February 1959
Ironton Tribune, 5–26 December 1982

Jefferson Gazette, 5 December 1944–18 December 1962
Kenton News Republican, 16–20 July 1915
Lancaster Eagle-Gazette, 2 October 1953–3 March 1954
Lima News, 10 January 1930–22 January 1985
Lima Times Democrat, 15 June 1895–17 July 1915
Lisbon Buckeye State, 15–22 August 1861
Mansfield News Journal, 16 June 1899–4 July 1987
Marietta Daily Times, 15 February 1899–27 November 1950
Marietta Register, 12 February 1884–30 June 1902
Martins Ferry Daily Times, 16 August 1926–7 June 1933
Mount Gilead Morrow County Sentinel, 18 June 1981
Mount Vernon News, 9 March 1984
Napoleon Northwest Signal, 20 December 1917–24 March 1982
Newark Advocate, 26 May 1825–26 April 1989
Norwalk Reflector-Herald, 11 May–31 July 1934
Paulding Progress, 24 October 1963
Portsmouth Times, 26 May 1860–21 January 1994
Ravenna Record Courier, 3 October 1968
St. Clairsville Belmont Chronicle, 21 April 1887
Sandusky Register, 22 February 1912–1 July 1977
Sandusky Star Journal, 30 June 1924–25 September 1926
Sidney Daily News, 12 April 1965–21 October 1974
Sidney Journal, 25 May 1883–25 January 1884
Springfield Daily News, 11–12 April 1922
Springfield Weekly Republican, 14–21 July 1892
Steubenville Daily Gazette, 6–12 February 1884
Steubenville Herald-Star, 16 April 1887–14 January 1964
Tiffin Advertiser Tribune, 12 April 1965
Toledo Blade, 2 January 1864–21 January 1994
Urbana Mad River Courant, 27 March–3 April 1830
Van Wert Times (Bulletin), 5 January 1904–30 January 1967
Washington Court House Fayette Republican, 9–16 September 1885
Wauseon Democratic Expositor, 24 May 1894
Wauseon Republican, 7 May 1887
Wilmington News-Journal, 9 May 1923–2 March 1962
Wooster Daily Record, 9 May 1923–20 June 1946
Wooster Republican, 9–23 June 1859
Xenia Gazette, 29 April 1884–13 May 1933
Xenia Herald, 8 June 1916
Youngstown Vindicator, 8 June 1912–3 June 1985
Zanesville Courier, 9 February 1899–20 June 1912
Zanesville News, 17–20 June 1950
Zanesville Signal, 9 February 1899–19 June 1928
Zanesville Times Recorder, 14 January 1968–7 April 1987

Index

Names of towns and cities mentioned in the text are indexed. Counties are generally not indexed at each reference in the text unless the weather event was specific to that county and other towns or cities in the county are not indexed. Bridges and buildings are not indexed unless they were the focus of a major event. Water vessels are indexed under "Boats." References to figures are in **boldface.**

Feb. 1929, 186; Jan. 1959, 204; Mar. 1964, 209;
Dec. 1990, 226
Miami University: Jan. 1978 blizzard, 65
Miamisburg: Mar. 1907 flood, 171
Middle Bass Island: Feb. 1940 snowstorm, 32
Middlefield: Dec. 1993 snow, 75
Middletown:
—drought: 1895, 148
—flood: Mar. 1913, 179; Feb. 1929, 186; Jan. 1959,
204
Mikesell, Thomas, 93, 240
Milan: July 1969 flood, 215
Milford:
—cold: Jan. 1977, 111
—flood: Mar. 1964, 209; May 1968, 212
—heat: Sept. 1953, 141
—tornado: Aug. 1969, 279
Milk production: effects of 1930 drought, 149
Mill Creek: Mar. 1913 flood, 184
Millersburg:
—cold: Feb. 1951, 101; Dec. 1989, 124; Jan. 1994, 126
—flood: Aug. 1935, 188; Sept. 1979, 219
—snow: Feb. 1971, 55
Milligan, and cold temperatures: coldest temperature recorded in Ohio (Feb. 1899), **89**, 90; Jan.
1904, 92; January state cold record (1912), 93, **94**,
126
Millport, and cold weather: May 1947, 107; Dec.
1958, 102; June 1972 (freeze), 108; Aug. 1982
(freeze), 116; June 1992, 124; Jan. 1994, 126
Mingo Junction, and flooding: Mar. 1936, 189; July
1943, 196
Mogadore: Apr. 1943 tornado, 259
Monroe Center: May 1985 tornado, 293
Monroe County: May 1969 tornado, 278
Montgomery County:
—flood: July 1915, 249
—hail: Nov. 1992, 302
—tornado: Apr. 1884, 235; Mar. 1917, 250; June 1981,
290
Montpelier:
—heat: July 1934, 135
—snow: Apr. 1957, 43
Mooresville: May 1968 flood, 212
Morrow: May 1968 flood, 212
Morrow County: Apr. 1965 tornado, 275
Moulton: Mar. 1920 tornado, 253
Mt. Vernon:
—cold: July 1930, 99; Mar. 1984, 120

—drought: 1953–54, 151
—flood: Mar. 1913, 182; Feb. 1929, 186; Jan. 1959,
203
Moxahala Creek: June 1950 flood, 199
Murray City: May 1968 flood, 212
Muskingum College: Mar. 1986 tornado, 296
Muskingum County: June 1981 tornado, 290
Muskingum River, and flooding: Feb. 1884, 163;
Mar. 1913, 173, 182; Jan. 1937, 195; Jan. 1959, **204**;
Mar. 1964, 209

Namias, Jerome, 268
Napoleon:
—cold: Jan. 1918, 97
—flood: Feb. 1883, 160; Mar. 1913, 182
—heat: July 1934, 135; July 1936, 138; Aug. 1947, 137,
140; Sept. 1953, 141; June 1988, 145
—ice storm: New Year's 1948, 34
—tornado: Sept. 1885, 239; July 1992, 300
—wind: Mar. 1913, 247; Apr. 1957, 269
Nashville: Mar. 1920 tornado, 253
National Guard. *See* Ohio National Guard
Navarre: May 1894 hail, 306
Nelsonville, and flooding: Mar. 1907, 172; May 1968,
212
Neptune: Jan. 1936 snow, 31
Nettle Lake: Mar. 1991 tornado, 297
New Albany: Apr. 1974 tornado, 287
New Bremen: Jan. 1904 cold, 92
New Concord: Mar. 1986 tornado, 296
New Lexington:
—cold: Jan. 1948, 35; Feb. 1951, 101; Jan. 1963, 103;
Jan. 1984, 120; Dec. 1989, 124; Jan. 1994, 126
—snow: Jan. 1968, **52**, 53
New Lisbon. *See* Lisbon
New London: July 1992 tornado, 301
New Miami: Feb. 1929 flood, 186
New Philadelphia: Jan. 1937 flood, 195
New Vienna: Apr. 1961 tornado, 269
New Waterford: Jan. 1912 cold, 93
New Weston: Mar. 1920 tornado, 253
New Year's Day: 1864 blizzard, 86; 1948 ice storm, 34
New York Central Railroad: damage from Mar. 1928
ice storm, 28
Newark:
—cold: Jan. 1936, 100; Feb. 1951, 101
—flood: Mar. 1913, 182; Jan. 1937, 195; Jan. 1959,
202; June 1990, 221
—ice storm: Feb. 1962, 44

Siberian Express, 119
Siberian Winter, 83
Sidney:
—cold: Jan. 1884, 87; Jan. 1977, 111; Jan. 1985, 121
—drought: 1963, 152
—flood: Mar. 1907, 171
—snow: May 1883, 9
Silverton: Aug. 1969 tornado, 279
Sleet, 7
Snow loads, 15
Snowbelt. *See* Lake Erie snowbelt
Snowfall: annual average, 4, **5**; latest, 9; deepest
    (Apr. 1901), 13
Soldiers and Sailors Orphan Home: and Apr. 1884
    tornado, 235
Solon: May 1983 tornado, 292
South Bass Island:
—cold: Jan. 1994, 127
—flood: Nov. 1972, 217; Apr. 1973, 218
South Lebanon: Mar. 1964 flood, 209
South Logan: Mar. 1964 flood, 208
Sowash, Dr. H. L., 98
Soybeans: damage from 1988 drought, 153
Spring: general weather patterns, 2
Springfield:
—cold: Jan. 1856, 84; Jan. 1884, 87; Feb. 1899, 90;
    Jan. 1912, 95; Christmas 1983, 117
—flood: Mar. 1907, 171; Feb. 1929, 187; Jan. 1959, 204
—heat: summer 1934, 136
—tornado: Jan. 1947, 34; May 1973, 281
Standard Oil Works: during Feb. 1883 flood and fire,
    162
Stark County:
—flood: June 1884, 164
—tornado: May 1969, 278; May 1985, 295
Steubenville:
—flood: Feb. 1883, 162; Feb. 1884, 163; Mar. 1907,
    171; Mar. 1936, 189; Jan. 1937, 191, 194; July 1943,
    195
—heat: Aug. 1930, 149
—snow: Jan. 1936, 30; Feb. 1940, 32; Nov. 1950, 36;
    Jan. 1964, 46; Mar. 1993, 75; Jan. 1994, 76
Stoddard, Orange N., 231
Stow: July 1992 tornado, 301
Strongsville: Apr. 1965 tornado, 272
Stryker: Mar. 1982 flood, 220
Sugar beets: and damage from 1930 drought, 149
Summer, general weather patterns, 2; hottest (1934),
    133

Summerfield: Jan. 1918 cold, 96
Sunday Creek: Mar. 1907 flood, 171
Swan Creek, and flooding: Mar. 1913, 183; Feb. 1959,
    206
Swanton:
—flood: Feb. 1959, 206
—tornado: Mar. 1920, 253
Sweet corn: and damage from 1930 drought, 149
Sylvania: Mar. 1920 tornado, 253

Tappan Lake: May 1969 tornado, 278
Ten Mile Creek: Mar. 1913 flood, 183
Terrace Park: July 1915 wind, 249
Texas: Mar. 1913 flood, 183
Thanksgiving, and snowfall: 1950, 36; 1974, 55
Thermometer exposure, 126
Thornville: June 1950 flood, 199
Thurman: dubious heat record (July 1897), 130
Tiffin:
—flood: Mar. 1913, 183; Jan. 1959, 203; Dec. 1990,
    226
—heat: June 1988, 145
—ice storm: Mar. 1928, 27
—snow: Apr. 1957, 43; Dec. 1974, 55
—wind: Mar. 1913, 247
Tiffin River: Mar. 1982 flood, 220
Tipp City: Feb. 1990 snow, 73
Tobacco: and effect of 1930 drought, 150
Toledo:
—atmospheric pressure: Jan. 1978 (lowest), 61; Jan.
    1927 (state record high), 309
—cold: New Year's 1864, 86; Jan. 1884, 87; Feb. 1899,
    89; Jan. 1912, 95; Jan. 1918, 96; Christmas 1924,
    98; Jan. 1936, 100; Nov. 1950, 38; Jan. 1963, 103,
    120; Apr. 1964, 105; Jan. 1972, 120; June 1972,
    108; Jan. 1982, 115, 120; Apr. 1982, 67; Christmas
    1983, 117; Jan. 1984 (coldest temperature), 103,
    119; Jan. 1985, 122; Dec. 1989, 124; Jan. 1994, 127
—flood: Feb. 1867, 157; Feb. 1881, 158; Feb. 1883, 160,
    161; Jan. 1904, 169; Mar. 1913, 183; Aug. 1920,
    185; Feb. 1959, 206; Apr. 1966, 210; July 1969,
    214; Nov. 1972, 216; Apr. 1973, 218
—hail: Apr. 1912, 307
—heat: Aug. 1918, 132; July 1934, 135; July 1936
    (hottest temperature), 138, 139; Aug. 1947, 141;
    Christmas 1982, 144; June 1988, **145**, 146
—ice storm: Mar. 1928, 27; 3 Jan. 1947, 33; 29 Jan.
    1947, 34; New Year's 1948, 34
—snow: greatest snowfall (Mar. 1900), 11; Feb. 1894

Youngstown *(cont.)*
   (coldest temperature), 126
—flood: Feb. 1884, 163; Jan. 1904, 169; Mar. 1913,
   184; Jan. 1937, 195; Jan. 1959, 202
—snow: Nov. 1913 (blizzard), 21; Jan. 1948, 35;
   Thanksgiving 1950, 36; Jan. 1964, 46; May 1966,
   48; Feb. 1971, 55; Oct. 1989, 71

Zanesville:
—cold: Feb. 1899, 91

—flood: Feb. 1884, 163; Mar. 1907, 171; Mar. 1913,
   174, 182; Jan. 1937, 195; Jan. 1959, 203, **204**; Mar.
   1964, 207
—snow: Feb. 1910, 17; Oct. 1917, 25; Feb. 1940, 32;
   Jan. 1968, 53; Apr. 1987, 71
—tornado: June 1912, 245
Zimmerman. *See* Beavercreek

THUNDER IN THE HEARTLAND

was composed in 11/14 Adobe Garamond
on Power Macintosh 7100/80 using PageMaker 6.0
at The Kent State University Press;
printed by sheet-fed offset
on 60# Domtar White
notch case bound over binder's boards
in Roxite natural cloth
and wrapped with dust jackets printed in four colors
on 100# enamel stock finished with film lamination
by Braun-Brumfield, Inc.
designed by Diana Gordy
and published by

THE KENT STATE UNIVERSITY PRESS
Kent, Ohio, 44242